A GUIDE TO MARKETS: PARTICIPANTS, INSTRUMENTS AND COMPLIANCE

Abe Mastbaum CPA, MST, Esq.

2012

To the Stolers — Good friends + soul mates

WEST.

A Thomson Reuters business

For Customer Assistance Call 1-800-328-4880

Mat #41243689

ISBN 978-0-314-60917-5

Dedication

For my sons, Matthew and Jason

and

My long-suffering wife, Celia

About the Author

Abe Mastbaum CPA, MST, Esq.

Abe Mastbaum is Tax & Capital Markets Counsel at New York based law firm Barton LLP. His practice areas include hedge funds, private equity, broker dealer regulation and tax. He is also a certified public accountant and has a master's degree in taxation. He was recently a partner, chief financial officer and chief compliance officer for a New York based money manager with $ 3 billion AUM. Previously, Abe was a capital markets specialist at The First Boston Corporation. He began his career at Oppenheim, Appel, Dixon & Co, a CPA firm specializing in the broker-dealer and money management industries.

Abe has designed, developed and delivered over 1,500 live lectures during his career. He has extensive experience teaching classes in securities analysis, accounting, capital markets, finance and securities regulation. He has presented domestically and internationally for large investment banks, hedge funds and money managers, ratings agencies and industry regulators.

Abe earned his Bachelor of Business Administration from Baruch College (Accounting and Finance), his Master of Science (Taxation) from Pace University and his Juris Doctor from the Benjamin N. Cardozo School of Law. He and his wife Celia have two adult sons, Jason and Matthew.

Contributors

Richard Bloom CPA, PFS, MST

Richard Bloom joined Rothstein Kass in July, 2009 and is based in the Firm's Roseland (NJ) office. Richard specializes in personal tax and financial planning matters affecting high net worth individuals, such as closely held business owners, executives, and hedge fund managers. He provides tax consulting; income and estate tax planning; federal, state and local tax compliance services; and representation before federal and state tax authorities for such individuals. He also works with clients on multi-generational tax planning, philanthropic planning, wealth preservation strategies, and risk management.

Prior to joining Rothstein Kass, Richard honed his wealth planning expertise through his senior executive positions at two prominent family office advisory firms. He also has over 17 years of Big Four experience at KPMG, LLP where he served in the Personal Financial Planning division and select subgroups.

Richard received a Bachelor of Science degree in Accounting from the University of Delaware and a Master of Science degree in Taxation from Seton Hall University. He is a certified public accountant in New Jersey and a personal financial specialist. Richard is a member of the New York Jersey Society of Certified Public Accountants and the American Institute of Certified Public Accountants (AICPA) including the personal financial planning section of the AICPA.

Richard is the proud father of two daughters and is an active supporter of the Memorial Sloan Kettering Cancer Center.

Joseph Pacello CPA

Joseph Pacello is a tax principal in Rothstein Kass' Roseland, New Jersey office. Joe specializes in advising hedge funds, fund of funds, private equity funds and other types of alternative investment entities on matters related to taxation and organizational structure. He also advises clients on various regulatory issues impacting the industry. In addition, Joe serves as the head of Rothstein Kass University, where he leads the Firm's efforts in continuing professional education, staff training and curriculum development.

Joe started his career as an auditor in the financial services practice of a national accounting firm. He also has Big Four experience and was formerly Senior Vice President and head of Tax at a prominent fund administrator.

Joe earned his Bachelor of Science degree in accounting from Seton Hall University and his Juris Doctor degree from New York Law School. Additionally, Joe earned a Master of Laws degree (LL.M.) in taxation from Temple University School of Law. He is a member of the American Institute of Certified Public Accountants (AICPA), the New York State Society of Certified Public Accountants (NYSSCPA) and the Wall Street Tax Association (WSTA). Joe has authored numerous articles regarding tax issues, taught as an adjunct professor at St. John's University and has taught a graduate course at Fairleigh Dickinson University on the taxation of financial products.

Foreword and Acknowledgments

I now know how much work it takes to produce a book, but the effort was worth it. This volume is intended to provide a non-technical overview of capital markets, financial instruments, pricing relationships and market operations. I hope that university students at all levels, newly hired finance professionals and general interest readers will find this book demystifies the jargon that often makes this subject sound harder than it really is.

This book is really a compilation of a series of lectures I regularly deliver at investment banks and institutional investors. I've been teaching for about thirty years. I realized I was getting good at it when schools that wouldn't admit me as a student began asking me to teach at their institutions. I believe the order of the materials provides a logical progression through the topical matter. These chapters can be read sequentially or piecemeal. Chapter 15, *Tax Consequences of Investment Decisions*, was contributed Joseph Pacello. Chapter 16, *Tax Issues Related to Wealth Transfers*, was contributed by Richard Bloom. Both of these fine gentlemen are tax professionals at Rothstein Kass & Co, a large CPA firm with a large financial services practice. I thank them for their thoughtful and valuable contributions.

A very special thanks goes to my production assistant, Jonathan Hale. Jon is currently a college student at Washington and Lee University in Virginia pursuing a degree in Politics and Business Administration. Jon was an intern at my law firm during the summer of 2011. He was a valued assistant in preparing the manuscript that became this book, particularly in creating the graphics. A British native, he was raised in London and attended the International School of Cobham. He hopes to pursue a career in finance and will be a valuable addition to any organization he ultimately joins.

Lastly, I got hooked on finance and capital markets after taking my first finance class at Baruch College in New York City. The class was taught by a great professor, Dr. Howard Ross. I learned that Dr. Ross recently passed away. He really made a big difference in my career. I regret having not told him how much.

Abe Mastbaum, New York City, March 2012

CONTENTS

Chapter
1

Capital Markets Instruments & Participants

What are capital markets and what purpose do they serve? Finding the answers to this question is the purpose of this book. Capital markets are the environments in which financial instruments are traded between buyers and sellers. Some of these participants have an opinion regarding the price direction of markets or specific securities. Others have points of view regarding the degree of volatility without regard to the direction. Still others have a view regarding a combination of the two. Collectively these groups can be referred to as **speculators**. They seek and take risks. Is a speculator the same thing as an investor? A gambler? It depends on your point of view. We'll examine the way these participants use capital markets to exploit their market expectations.

Not all market participants take risks. Some look to dispose of risks. Much in the same way that a homeowner buys home insurance to protect against risk of fire or flood, many market participants look to dispose of financial market risk. These participants are referred to as **hedgers**. A word about capital markets jargon before we move on. It is often needlessly complex. It is the great obstacle in terms of market understanding. Don't get intimidated; the concepts are not nearly as difficult as the terminology. Think of it as shop talk. They same way auto mechanics use incomprehensible language to discuss amongst themselves the inner workings of automobiles, so too, do capital markets professionals have a tribal language that enable coded signals to be passed among members of the tribe. Hedgers are doing nothing more than buying insurance.

But wait; there is a master class of capital markets professionals. These nice people usually have advanced degrees in mathematics or physics and decided they did not want to pass their professional time designing missile systems. Financial instruments trading in the capital markets do not trade at random prices; they must trade to a mathematical parity or else this master class will be able to exploit the pricing discrepancy in a process known as **arbitrage**. As a group they are known as arbitragers. They also perform an important function in that they ensure a degree of pricing integrity. Aside from being humanitarians, they often make a lot of money. Arbitrage can be described two ways:

1. arbitrage is the simultaneous purchase and sale of different financial instrument in the same market (e.g. corn) for the purpose of exploiting a temporary pricing discrepancy, or

2. two things that are functionally equivalent to each other are trading at different prices. Buy the one that is cheap. Sell the one that it is expensive. Do it at the same time. The difference between the purchase price and the selling price is your profit. You've just earned an arbitrage profit. **Arbitrage = buy low + sell high, same time.** Six words to remember.

Financial Instruments

Now that we have met *who* uses the capital markets (speculators, hedgers and arbitragers) we need to look at *what* they trade. Financial instruments are the things that trade in capital markets. They include stocks, bonds, commodities, and other things. If something has a price that goes up and down, someone will be willing to trade it. If they consume it, like a corn flake manufacturer consuming raw corn in its manufacturing process, they may want to lock in a purchase price rather than take a chance that the price of corn will increase. A farmer may want to lock in a selling price rather than risk falling prices while the corn is in the fields. The universe of financial instruments can be illustrated as follows:

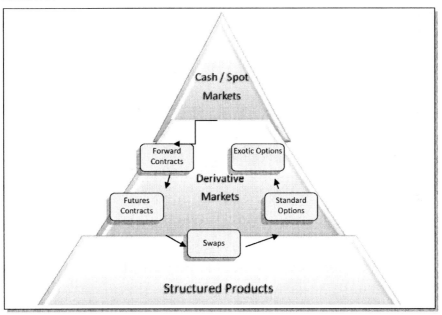

Believe it or not, this diagram explains most of what you need to know to understand capital markets. Let's take a close look at each market segment and put it in its proper context.

Cash Markets

Cash markets are the markets in which payment for the purchase is due upon (or shortly after) execution of the transaction. Sometimes these markets are called **spot markets** (typical in foreign currency) or **physical markets** (typical in commodity markets). Whether you call the market cash, spot, or physical (which are in fact used interchangeably) this is the market where you need cash now. That can be a problem.

Let's use a continuing example to make a series of points. Let's assume that I am in the business of manufacturing corn flakes. I use a lot of corn. Corn prices go up and down. If corn gets cheaper I benefit; my raw materials cost less and presumably my profits increase. Conversely, if prices go up my costs increase and my profit margins suffer. If I do nothing and simply buy corn at the prevailing prices as I consume it, I have become a **speculator**. If I do that deliberately, I must have a view as to the likely direct of corn prices (down).

An effective way of conceptualizing financial risks is to view them visually on a diagram called a **payoff graph**. The vertical axis of the graph represents profit and loss. The horizontal axis represents price movements. Moving to the right horizontally represents increasing prices, to the left decreasing prices. Let's assume today's corn price is $5.00 per bushel. My payoff graph as a consumer of corn would look as follows;

Figure 1.2 - Payoff Graph Showing a Consumer's Risk -- "Short"

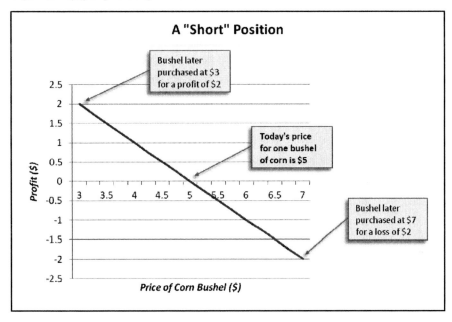

Notice as corn prices fall I benefit (profit); conversely rising prices are to my detriment (loss). This risk is generic to *anyone* who is a consumer of *anything* they do not currently own. The standard term for this risk is "**short**." More jargon. Short means I win when prices go down, and I lose when prices go up. The term is derived from a common speculative activity known as **short selling**. In a short sale a speculator believes a security will fall in price. To profit from this expectation, the short seller does the following:

1. borrows securities (from someone willing to lend them) with an obligation to return the securities at a later date, then

2. sells the borrowed securities into the open market at today's prevailing market price, then

3. waits, then

4. re-enters the market and buys back the securities, then

5. returns the securities to the party who lent them in step #1 above.

We will be exploring short selling in great depth later. At this point it is important to note the following:

- the short seller is "short." If the short seller borrows the securities today (step 1 above) when each share is worth $60 and sells them at that price (step 2), after waiting (step 3) if the shares are bought back (step 4) at $45 and returned to the lender (step 5), the short seller, made $15 per share. If they are purchased back at $75 the short seller loses $15 per share. If prices go down he wins; if they go up he loses. He is short.

- The corn flake manufacturer is also short (corn) and didn't have to borrow anything to establish the short position.

- **Observation:** risks don't differ; the mechanics of establishing them do.

Returning to the corn flake manufacturing example, remember I am short corn. At this point I am a speculator. Is this what I want? Maybe not. Here is a glimpse at the human condition. Possibility 1: I don't want this risk, and I want to hedge it. Possibility 2: I really want the risk (I think corn prices will decline,) but there is an institutional reason I can't maintain the risk. Maybe I work for a publicly traded company that manufactures corn flakes. The shareholders bought the shares of the company because I generate manufacturing profits. They don't need to own shares in a manufacturer of breakfast cereals to speculate corn prices; they can do that on their own in the commodity markets. Possibility 3: I'm not conscious of the fact I have the risk, or I am complacent and ignore it. I'll either be very lucky or bankrupt.

What can I do if I want to hedge the short corn risk?

Hedging in Cash Markets

One way to dispose of the short corn risk is to purchase corn in the cash markets and store it until needed. Buying the corn solves one problem but creates another. By purchasing the corn, I have locked in my purchase price (assume at $5 per bushel). My ownership of the corn can be viewed on the following payoff graph:

Figure 1.3 - Payoff Graph Showing an Owner's Risk -- "Long"

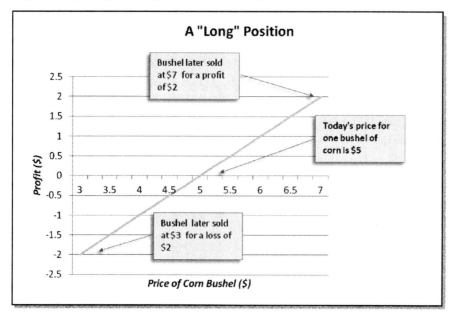

As an owner of corn (ignoring for the moment that I am also a consumer of the corn in my manufacturing process), I benefit (profit) when prices go up and suffer a loss when prices decline. This is the opposite of what a consumer of the commodity faces. This combination of results is referred to as a **"long"** position. In a long position (or long risk) you win when prices go up and lose when prices go down. Notice that that the corn flake manufacturer/consumer is now both long (by owning the corn) and short (otherwise being a consumer of the corn). **When you are both long and short, you are hedged.** The hedge may be perfect (where the risks are completely neutralized) or partial (in which there is a residual risk position). We'll look at how to measure the effectiveness of your hedging strategy later on.

Note the characteristics of my hedge. Had I done nothing, I would have suffered a detriment if corn prices increased (by having to buy more expensive corn) and benefitted if prices declined (because my raw materials cost less). By buying the corn I have a corresponding gain if prices increase above $5 (my purchase price) and a loss if prices decline. This combination of offsetting gains and losses on the separate positions (sometimes called "legs") is the essence of hedging.

Figure 1.4 - Combining Long and Short Positions to Create Hedges

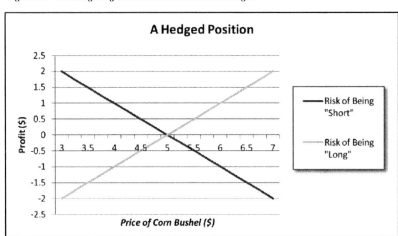

9

Payoff Vectors

A useful way to keep track of your net risk positions is through the use of **payoff vectors**. A payoff vector is a two-row algebraic expression that answers a straightforward question: what happens if prices go up (the top number in the vector), and what happens if prices go down (the bottom number of the vector)? Note the vector for a long position compared to the vector for a short position.

Figure 1.5 - Payoff Vectors and Graphs Comparing a "Long" Position to a "Short" Position

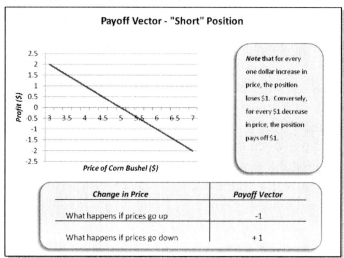

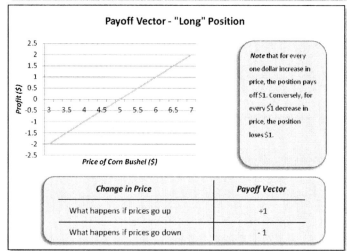

Combining long and short positions to create hedges; combining vectors			
	Original Risk: Short Corn +	Corn Purchased =	Hedged Position
Price goes up	-1	+1	0
Price goes down	+1	-1	0

Note in this example that the risk profiles (and associated vectors) perfectly negate each other to create the perfect hedge. Thus, the corn flake manufacturer has locked in a $5 purchase price to the extent of the quantity of corn purchased. This example assumes the following relationships between the risk (the corn price to the manufacturer) and the hedge (the purchased corn):

- The pricing relationships are linear.

- The risk and the hedge have payoff graphs that are exactly opposite and perfectly negatively correlated to each other. In other words, by being a corn consumer, I would suffer a $1 dollar detriment if corn prices went from $5 to $6; however, if I simultaneously owned corn I would have a $1 profit to offset this loss. Life is rarely this simple. What if the risk and the hedge are not perfectly negatively correlated in that one is more volatile than the other? Worse, what if they are not negatively correlated (meaning the payoff graphs turn out not to be opposite but the same)? Now instead of hedging, you have amplified your risk.

Limitations of hedging with cash instruments

Although we have used the cash markets to successfully eliminate the corn price risk to the corn flake manufacturer, a new problem arises. Where is the manufacturer to get the funds to pay for the corn? Either the manufacturer will need to use idle cash balances (which an operating company is unlikely to have) or, more likely, it will have to borrow. This is the seminal problem associated with hedging in cash markets. Our manufacturer needs to **borrow money now to buy (and store) corn it needs over a period of time.** This problem is sometimes referred to as **premature balance sheet expansion.** Borrowing now to fund future needs increases the size of balance sheets (assets increase because of the purchase of the corn, liabilities increase because of the borrowing). This larger balance sheet will make potential lenders more nervous. Eventually lenders will price the perception of heightened borrower risk into the interest rate they demand. **Larger balance sheets cause credit quality perceptions to suffer which drives up incremental borrowing costs.** Once a particular party is significantly leveraged (dependent on borrowed funds) the market may ultimately cut off credit. **Leverage constraints** are always a problem in cash markets. These constraints can be practical (as in this corn manufacturer example) or, as in the case of trading financial instruments by traders and investors, regulatory in nature. Many countries (the United States included) have significant regulatory structures which are supposed to limit the amount that can be borrowed to purchase or carry securities positions. We'll look at these when we look at trading in so-called **margin accounts**. Suffice it to say it this point that **using leverage is limited by either practical or regulatory constraints.** To address these constraints, the capital markets developed a series of financial instruments referred to as **derivatives**.

Introduction to Derivatives

Chapter 13 provides an in-depth analysis of many derivatives instruments. As an introduction, derivatives are *contract-like* interests which are meant to replicate positions that can be taken in securities or other markets. As the name indicates, derivatives **derive their value** by comparing the contract right embedded within the derivative with the current price of the underlying asset. For example, if you are holding a derivative which obligates you to purchase a commodity at $5 per unit and the current price of that commodity is $6, the derivative instrument has a current value of $1 (the derived value of $6−$5).

Derivatives are often used to establish a vehicle to speculate in markets, hedge away risks that already exist, or to take advantage of market errors in pricing through a process called arbitrage (discussed earlier). The drivers behind the use of derivatives are often:

- Limitations on the use of leverage in cash markets
- Structural impediments in establishing positions in the cash markets.

Derivatives can be structured in almost any market, including weather, agricultural, energy, financial assets, and real assets.

Introduction to Forward Contracts

Also called forward delivery markets, **these contracts call for a purchase or sale of the underlying item at a future date at a price determined at the inception of the contract.** The key to understanding these contracts is that they are non-exchange traded so that each party to the contract (called **"counterparties"**) is exposed to nonperformance risk of the other party. This is referred to as **credit risk**. As we will see, the winning party in a forward always has the credit risk.

How Forward Contracts Work

Forward contracts/forward delivery contracts are direct agreements between two counterparties. In this agreement, one party agrees to buy, and the other agrees to sell something at a future date at a price which is agreed to at the inception of the contract. By doing so, the buyer has locked in a purchase price. Conversely, the seller has locked in a sales price. The purchase/sales price doesn't change hands until the delivery date of the contract. This would appear to solve the problem for our corn flake manufacturer who is adverse to borrowing money today to purchase corn in the cash markets for use at a later date. To dispose of the short risk associated with being a consumer of the corn, the manufacturer simply enters into a forward delivery contract obligating him to take delivery of corn at a known date in the future.

Being the buyer in a corn forward is just another way of establishing a long position.

Pricing of Forward Contracts

If cash and forward markets are available to establish long positions, a pricing parity relationship will evolve between the two markets. If our corn flake manufacturer decides to hedge in the cash market, its total cost is the purchase price of the corn plus carrying costs while held in storage. These carrying costs would include interest on funds borrowed to purchase the corn and storage related costs. If purchased with available idle funds, the opportunity cost of that money must be considered.

The key to understanding capital markets relationships is the principle of **arbitrage**.

Spot, forward, and options markets (which are discussed later) must price to a mathematical parity, otherwise **arbitrage opportunities** will result. Arbitrage is generally defined as the process through which different financial instruments trading on the same underlying asset can be simultaneously purchased and sold for the purpose of exploiting a temporary pricing discrepancy. As market participants execute this trade, the pricing disparity will disappear. The parity price of a corn forward can be illustrated as follows:

Figure 1.6 - Parity Pricing of Forward Contracts - Corn

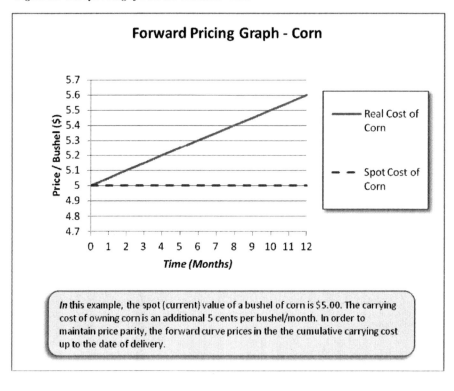

Forward Pricing Graph - Corn

In this example, the spot (current) value of a bushel of corn is $5.00. The carrying cost of owning corn is an additional 5 cents per bushel/month. In order to maintain price parity, the forward curve prices in the the cumulative carrying cost up to the date of delivery.

This gives you a pretty good idea of the gravitational force of arbitrage. If you recall, earlier we described arbitrage as follows:

1. arbitrage is the simultaneous purchase and sale of different financial instruments in the same market (e.g. corn) for the purpose of exploiting a temporary pricing discrepancy, or

2. two things that are functionally equivalent to each other are trading at different prices. Buy the one that is cheap. Sell the one that it is expensive. Do it at the same time.

If carrying costs of corn are 5 cents per bushel/month, the parity price for a one-month forward delivery contract has to be $5.05. If not, someone will arbitrage it and force parity back into the market, eventually eliminating the opportunity. Let's assume spot corn is trading at $5.00 and carrying costs are $.05 cents per bushel per month, yet the one-month forward delivery contract is trading at $5.08. Something isn't right; the forward looks expensive relative to the spot market and the associated carrying costs. **Remember: buy what's cheap. Sell what's expensive. Do it at the same time.** Buy the spot corn at $5.00. Sell the forward at $ 5.08. Carry the corn for a month, incur the $.05 cents of carrying costs, deliver the corn (that now has a cost to you of $5.05), and collect the $5.08 on the delivery under the forward contract. You just made a risk-free $.03 cents. Why risk free? Let's look at the vectors:

Combining Long and Short Positions to create hedges; Combining Vectors

Sell Expensive Forward +	Buy Cheap Spot Corn =	Hedged Position
-1	+1	0
+1	-1	0

Risk-free profits don't last for long. All the other prospective arbitragers are going to see the same thing. What are they going to do? Buying what's cheap. Selling what's expensive. Doing it at the same time. Result: the thing that's cheap is going to rise in price; the thing that's expensive is going to fall. Parity! Gravity! Why then is arbitrage possible? Because markets are sometimes inefficient (information moves at unequal speeds to market participants), and markets are sometimes illiquid.

Uses and limitations of forward contracts

Forward contracts solve a very important limitation associated with cash markets. We are able to acquire corn at a known price at a future date without having to borrow money currently. Therefore, we do not degrade our credit rating and increase our borrowing costs. Forwards are therefore very useful in limiting our needs for current liquidity. There are challenges with the use of forward contracts, however.

As discussed, a forward contract is a bilateral obligation between buyer and seller. These parties are generically referred to as **counterparties**. Each counterparty to any contract takes the risk that the other counterparty will default and fail to honor his end of the bargain. Being a lawyer, I'm less offended by this possibility than many of the students that attend my lectures. The practical implications of counterparty credit risk are significant. Intelligent market participants will always perform pre-transaction credit reviews to determine if they want to take the other side of a given trade. Even if willing to take the trade, no market participant is going to be willing to take unlimited risk to any counterparty. Therefore, a time-consuming credit review will need to be done, and each participant will need to establish **credit limits**. My experience with credit people is they portray their craft as a black art only understood by others who can communicate in Sanskrit. At its core, credit exposure analysis is common sense. Let's take another look at the human condition.

Our cornflake manufacturer wants to buy corn for delivery one month hence at $5.05 (remember parity pricing). The other counterparty (a farmer looking to hedge or a speculator betting on falling corn prices) wants the other side of the trade. Let's call this side of the trade "seller." Buyer wants to buy and seller wants to sell corn for one month delivery at $5.05. What's the credit risk? One of these characters may not show up. Who? Let's see; I'm obligated to buy at $5.05. If the corn is worth $6 at maturity, will I show up? Absolutely, it is in my economic interest to show up with my $5.05 and take delivery of the corn that now is worth $ 6. Will the seller show up? Maybe, maybe not. The seller may default. Why? Well, if the seller is a speculator and doesn't own the corn, he will now need to buy corn at $6 and deliver it at $5.05. This is clearly not in his best economic interest. Fulfilling the obligation will result in a loss. In the parlance of our trade, our seller may now "blow up." Not literally, but figuratively. Does that make the defaulting seller a bad person? No; at least not for this reason. Many of my students find this disturbing, that no moral stigma attaches to defaulting counterparties. That went away at the end of the nineteenth century when bankruptcy in general was de-criminalized and became an issue for the civil judicial system. There isn't even a social stigma. What is the buyer to do? Sue!

What if, instead of going up to $6.00, corn declined to $4.00 at the end of the contract. Who will show now? Certainly the seller who stands to collect $5.05 for corn that is now worth $4.00. How about the buyer? Maybe not. **How do you generalize credit risk and who has it?** The buyer? The seller? The correct answer: **the winner.** Either the buyer or seller can be exposed in a contract depending upon who made the winning trade. The winner is going to show up. The loser may not. The winner always has the credit risk.

How do you protect yourself? Know your counterparty, establish **credit limits,** and provide for **collateral** postings by the loser over the life of the trade.

Credit Limits and Collateral Management

We've established that forward contracts (and as we shall see, all over-the-counter derivatives) generate credit risk. To manage counterparty credit risk, it is imperative to conduct pre-transaction credit reviews and establish prudent credit limits. The simplest credit limit is the amount you are willing to be exposed to by a counterparty before you stop doing new business with it. The credit limit is the net mark-to-market ("MTM") gain you have with the other side. Assume our buyer has a forward contract in place to purchase 1,000,000 bushels of corn at $5.05/bushel and the corn is now worth $6.55/bushel. The MTM is a $1,500,000 gain and also represents the credit exposure if the seller doesn't perform at maturity. Let's say the buyer does lots of other business with the seller. The buyer may want to limit his exposure to the seller to $10,000,000 at which point it wants to cut off any new business with the seller until they have performed on their open obligations. **The $10,000,000 represents the credit limit.** Another limit which may be imposed is a **size limit.** This is a way of providing a frame of reference for the credit limit. If the buyer wishes to have a maximum $10,000,000 credit exposure to the seller, it may also impose a size limit of $100,000,000. In this way, to reach the credit limit of $10,000,000 a 10% market move must occur ($10,000,000/$100,000,000). If the buyer did $1,000,000,000 of contracts with the seller, the $10,000,000 credit limit could be breached with as little as a 1% move in the underlying market.

To further provide protection against counterparty credit risk, market participants may impose collateral requirements upon their counterparty. This is done contractually. Most modern OTC derivatives are governed by contracts

21

developed by the International Swaps and Derivatives Association ("ISDA"). ISDA is a trade group, consisting of large derivatives dealers. (The group began its existence as the International Swap Dealers Association.) The contracts were standardized in the 1980s to facilitate trading without the need to separately negotiate each contract. To that end, "Master Agreements" have evolved to provide a fill-in-the-blanks approach to contract negotiations. The document that normally governs collateral management issues is called a "Credit Support Annex" or "CSA."

The operation of contractual collateral provisions is straight forward enough. Generally, the loser in a contract is required to post acceptable collateral at regular intervals with the winner (or more likely the winner's agent) over the life of the contract. In the real world, things aren't so simple. First, the party with the superior credit (usually the dealer) will generally be unwilling to post collateral at all. Either party can negotiate for an unsecured exposure ceiling (no collateral posting necessary until the credit exposure exceeds the ceiling, and then only for the excess). Each party will be wary of allowing the other party to hold its assets, which then requires the services of a third party collateral agent. These agreements are heavily negotiated (more lawyers). If you manage to get this far, what you've got is a labor intensive, credit dependent contract which can't easily be unwound. Suppose the buyer of the corn forward illustrated earlier got in at a price of $5.05 for one million bushels for delivery one month out. One week in, floods wipe out the corn crop. Corn is trading at $6.05, and the market is panicking. Our buyer wants to take his profit off the table. Can the buyer sell his contract to someone else? Not easily. If the buyer attempts to sell his contract to another party, the seller should object. Why? Because the seller went through all of the effort of analyzing the buyer's credit quality, establishing credit limits, naming collateral agents, etc. The buyer can't just sell and walk away. If the buyer really wants out, he is going to have to ask for seller's permission. What's the seller likely to say? Pay me! For what? To do a credit review of the replacement counterparty. What if the replacement counterparty is known to the seller and is otherwise an acceptable counterparty? What will the seller say then? Pay me! Why? Because the seller probably isn't a communist and is in a position to demand payment, so he or she will. All of this takes time, too. What is the buyer (who is after all just a corn flake manufacturer) to do? He could neutralize his position by contracting to sell one million bushels of corn at the same delivery date as the purchase contract. This is known as a **reversal.** However, now our buyer needs to manage two credit risks with two different parties

Introduction to Futures Contracts

As can be seen, forward contracts solve the problems initially identified with cash market hedging strategies. Our corn flake manufacturer is able to lock in a known purchase price for corn ($5.05 in one month) without the need to currently borrow money and store the corn. Although this is a great step forward, our discussion of forward contracts illustrates the credit related problems that forward contracts create. Futures contracts were created to provide the same benefits as forward contracts without the embedded credit risks that forwards contain.

Like forward contracts, buyers establish long positions, and sellers establish short positions. Like forward contracts, the buyer is obligated to buy, and the seller is obligated to sell some underlying commodity or financial instrument at some point in the future at a price that is agreed upon today; many futures contracts, however, now provide for *cash settlements* at expiration without a physical delivery. The crucial difference between forward contracts and futures contracts is the fact that forward contracts trade over-the-counter ("OTC") and futures contracts are exchange traded. OTC contracts are by their nature non-exchange traded; it is this feature that results in each of the counterparties accepting the credit risk of the other. Forwards can be tailored to the needs of the counterparties; they can negotiate terms such as acceptable grades of the underlying commodity at delivery, the place where delivery takes place, and the date thereof. Futures contracts eliminate the personalized nature of the credit risk. This occurs because the exchange on which the futures contract trades (or more correctly, the clearing house which facilitates settlements) guarantees the performance of both contract counterparties. For example, agricultural futures trading on the CME (Chicago Mercantile Exchange, now part of the CME Group) are cleared through CME Clearing. In doing so, CME Group is the counterparty to every contract: it buys from sellers and sells to buyers. In providing this protection, both counterparties to a futures contract are not subject to the failure and non-performance of the other but are instead exposed to CME Clearing. The efficiency this provides cannot be overstated. To provide these guarantees, CME never initially takes a speculative position in a contract. Rather, when buyers and sellers enter the market and execute trades, they do so with the understanding that the legal counterparty that buyer and seller each take is CME. To provide the guarantee, CME (and other future exchanges) take over the collateral management function. This is done through a process known as **margining.** Each day the contract is open, CME will **mark to market** "MTM" the contract and require the daily fluctuation in value to be posted between the parties. Let's examine this process through the following example:

A GUIDE TO CAPITAL MARKETS

Figure 1.7 – Initial and Variation Futures Margining Example

Day	At initial trade	Day 1 settle	Day 2 settle	Day 3 settle	Result
Initial and Variation Futures Margining					
Settlement Price	Price at entry $5.05	$5.25	$5.00	$5.30	$5.30
Buyer (Long) Margin Account	Initial Deposit $1.00 *	$1.20	$0.95	$1.25	+ 25 c
Buyer "MTM" (Profit/Loss)	-	$0.20	$0.25	$0.30	-
Clearing House	Takes Initial Margins (Deposits) as Collateral	⬆	⬇	⬆	Arranges Cash Settlement or Delivery
Seller "MTM" (Profit / Loss)	-	$0.20	$0.25	$0.30	-
Seller (Short) Margin Account	Initial Deposit $1.00 *	$0.80	$1.05	$0.75	- 25 c

* Assumed initial deposit

25

This entire process is called **variation margining.** Thus, losers are required to post their losses daily, and such amounts are given to the winners in the contract. The purchase and sale price changing hands at the termination of the contract is adjusted accordingly to reflect the variation margin payments. Because market participants don't necessarily need the commodity delivered at maturity, but seek protection against price volatility on goods they can otherwise purchase in the open market, an increasing number of futures contracts are **"cash settled."** Cash settled futures contracts call for variation margin payments over the life of the contract but simply expire on the close of the last trading day without an actual delivery being made. All futures contracts are otherwise standardized; the exchange determines in advance the deliverable quality of the commodity as well as the date and place of the delivery. Most futures markets make contracts available with monthly or quarterly expirations.

The Capital Market Evolution

Because of the role the clearing houses play in futures contracts, the personalized credit reviews and credit limit processes which are crucial with forwards become unnecessary. Thus future contracts address and solve a number of serious deficiencies in forward contracts. What you will see as you progress through this book is that there is a creeping incrementalism in capital markets; a problem presents itself, an imperfect solution is developed, and then attempts are made to improve the solution. In this chapter you see the beginning of this trend. Cash market hedging creates liquidity/borrowing issues. OTC forward contracts provide an imperfect solution; you solve the liquidity issue but exacerbate credit risks. Forward contracts were then refined into exchange traded futures contracts to address these shortcomings. As explained, this mitigates the credit risk, but other issues remain. One such issue is the need for hedgers to match the life of the hedging instrument with the life of the risk. A critical problem presented itself in the interest rate markets in the 1970s and 1980s. Throughout the 1970s interest rates were on the rise. Corporate treasurers needed to make a decision, borrow longer-term money at fixed rates of interest (and thus lock in borrowing costs), or borrow shorter term and take the risk that rates would later rise on the date funds needed to be borrowed again. A stubborn inflation had taken hold in the United States in the 1970s. Many treasurers decided to borrow long term and lock in their borrowing costs only to come to regret that decision when interest rates began a steady descent in the 1980s. Like agricultural products, futures contracts are available on interest rates and interest-bearing securities. What if our treasurer borrowed fixed rate money with a maturity of 10 years on July 1, 1979? Three years later interest rates are falling, there are seven years remaining on the original loan and our treasurer looks like he has walked into a trap. Unless the original loan/debt agreement has a mechanism for early payoff, the treasurer is stuck with high cost funding for seven more years. Unless futures contracts are available with seven year maturities (which they weren't) the treasurer will need to use a futures contract with a shorter life and roll it over at maturity. This can get expensive (transaction costs) and dangerous; if you have to close hedge number one at its expiration date and replace it with hedge number two, unless both transactions are done simultaneously you run the risk the two trades won't be executed at the same price. This risk is further exacerbated by the fact that liquidity in futures markets is usually limited beyond the near term delivery months. As we'll explore in great detail in chapter 13, this problem ultimately was solved by the development of **interest rate swaps**. Interest rate swaps are essentially a series of individual forward contracts executed as one trade. Swaps solve the problems associated with the limited liquidity in futures markets. Swap techniques are now available in nearly all markets. We'll cover all of these products as we proceed. The point here is this: capital markets are a study in evolution, not revolution. Take one more look at our capital markets triangle.

Figure 1.8 - The Capital Markets Product Triangle - Evolution

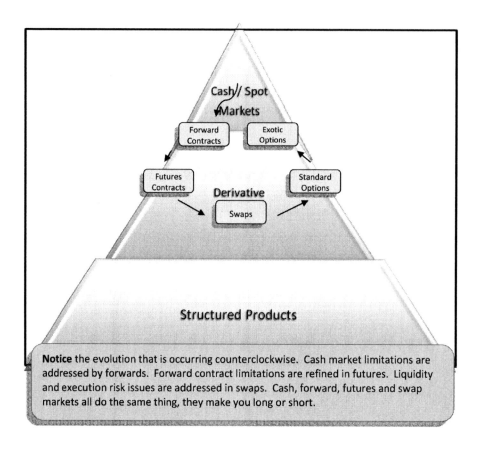

Notice the evolution that is occurring counterclockwise. Cash market limitations are addressed by forwards. Forward contract limitations are refined in futures. Liquidity and execution risk issues are addressed in swaps. Cash, forward, futures and swap markets all do the same thing, they make you long or short.

Options

The last of the markets represented on the *Capital Markets Triangle* is the options market. Options give the buyer/holder the right (but not the obligation) to either buy or sell a certain quantity of a stock, stock index, bond, bond index, commodity, currency, or futures contract ("the underlying" security or instrument) at a certain price (the strike price) up to, or at, a specified point in time (expiration date). The price is the **premium.** A seller/writer/grantor has the corresponding obligation. The types of options and their corresponding vectors are shown on Figure 1.9.

Figure 1.9 – Summary of Option Positions

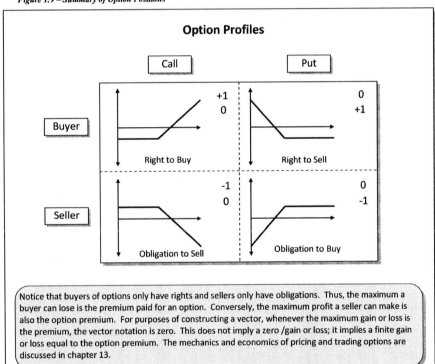

Notice that buyers of options only have rights and sellers only have obligations. Thus, the maximum a buyer can lose is the premium paid for an option. Conversely, the maximum profit a seller can make is also the option premium. For purposes of constructing a vector, whenever the maximum gain or loss is the premium, the vector notation is zero. This does not imply a zero /gain or loss; it implies a finite gain or loss equal to the option premium. The mechanics and economics of pricing and trading options are discussed in chapter 13.

Chapter
2

Defining Investment Objectives Interpreting Macro-Economic Data in Arriving at Investment Decisions

The Investment Process

What is it that people mean when they speak about "investing?" Surprisingly, different people have different ideas about what investing means. Some people pick stocks; others allocate assets. Entire divisions of modern money management institutions are devoted to "private wealth management." The truth is, investing means different things to different people. The meaning varies in terms of what is being invested in and for what period of time. Something most participants agree upon, however, is that investment results should be related to the amount of risk that one is willing to bear. This relationship between risk and return is the foundation of modern finance. A rational investor will demand higher returns for riskier assets. But what does "risk" mean? And how does one measure it?

The examination of risk is by its nature a two-fold process. First, what does risk mean to me? This is personal. Some things may scare me that don't faze other people. Some people are absolutely fearless; others abhor all risk.

The second part of the risk assessment process is somewhat more quantitative. If risk can be measured, then all market participants enter the game equally equipped if they have the proper ruler. In this chapter we will examine many of the personal risk assessments investors make as well as describe some common analytical tools for measuring risk more objectively.

Personal Risk Assessment, Investment Goals & Investor Suitability

This is the personal part of the story. I will be using *suitability* in the general sense, not the legal one (the standard of suitability deals with the standard of business conduct imposed upon broker-dealers when dealing with their customers—this is covered in detail in Chapter 11, *Regulation of Broker Dealers*). Here are some of the things an investor (or his adviser) must consider:

- How much money will be needed by the investor? And when?

- Liquidity needs: how much cash do I need on an ongoing basis or at specific point in time?

- What are the current and future funds available for investment? What future commitments are being made as part of an investment decision?

- What are my unique tax considerations, goals, or preferences? This is the issue that will heavily influence investment decisions. Taxes are both needlessly complicated and incredibly personal. The typical investor will confront two major tax considerations.

  1. ***Income Taxes*** Different categories of income are often taxed at different rates. These rate differentials distort investment decisions. All tax rate differentials reflect policy decisions and compromises embedded within the tax code. Market returns are

thus distorted by these often artificial distinctions. For example, long-term capital gain income (gains on sales of assets held for more than one year) and dividends may be taxed at rates substantially below interest income. Interest paid on many obligations of states and local municipalities are often tax-free. Policy preferences also effect the tax treatment of certain expenses. Adding further complexity is the alternative minimum tax ("AMT"), a feature of the tax code that was originally enacted to assure that very affluent taxpayers did not escape taxation through the use of tax shelters and other deductions. The AMT is a shadow tax. After determining your tax liability under the general rules of the tax code, the AMT requires a second tax computation by each taxpayer under rules that differ from the regular tax regime (the AMT eliminates certain deductions and otherwise realigns the tax preferences bestowed on different categories of income). The taxpayer must pay the higher of the two taxes. Municipal bond interest may be tax free under the general rules but taxable under the AMT. Because of the importance of income taxes in investment decisions, a separate chapter is devoted to this subject. Please see chapter 15, *Tax Consequences of Investment Decisions*.

2. ***Estate of Gift Taxes*** Lifetime and post death wealth transfers present serious tax issues. Generally, wealth transfers are either intergenerational in nature or are driven by philanthropic considerations. Federal (and many state) statutes provide for wealth transfer taxes. The federal estate tax on accumulated wealth is 35% on the taxable estate. The taxable estate is generally the value of property held at date of death, net of certain expenses and transfers to spouses and not for profit entities. The net amount in excess of $5,000,000 is subject to a federal estate

32

tax of 35%. States often impose their own estate tax. A resident of a high tax state often confronts a combined estate tax burden in excess of 40%. Because of these transfer tax burdens, individuals will put estate plans in place to provide for the transfer of wealth in a manner that minimizes the taxes.

The tax code also has substantial benefits for transfers to charities and educational and other non-profit institutions. Transfers of these types at death reduce the taxable estate; lifetime transfers can also provide tax benefits in the way of income tax savings (gifts to charity reduce your taxable income for income tax purposes). Accordingly, estate and gift taxation is a prominent consideration in an investors mind. For a complete discussion regarding these issues, see chapter 16, *Tax Issues Related to Wealth Transfers.*

In order to plan for and address personal risk issues, draw a timeline. Plot your investing life over the line. Typically (but not always), a younger person is willing to take greater risks when investing. The reason is simple enough; if mistakes are made there will be time to make it (the losses) back. Life's needs address portfolio construction. Typically, as one gets older, risk reduction occurs in portfolios as emphasis shifts away from capital growth towards income needs. The usual progression in portfolio emphasis is growth, then balance (growth and income), and then income, as shown on the timeline.

Figure 2.1 - Timeline of Shifting Investor Focus

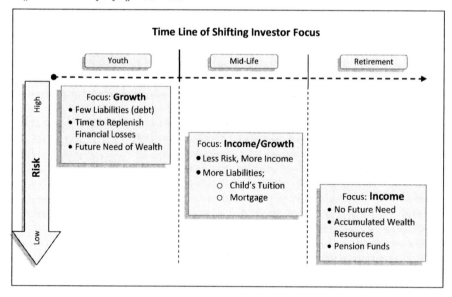

At any point on the timeline, the investor will be viewing the same personal concerns. What is the tolerance the individual has for volatility? For an annual loss? What is the size of an annual loss that will be disastrous on either a financial or personal/emotional basis? People should worry about these issues, and do. The typical investor has become more educated and more cautious in the post-2008 era, although it remains to be seen if this newly found rationality will persevere. 2008 will go down as the year in which all that was impossible actually happened. Bear Stearns, Fannie Mae, Freddie Mac, Merrill Lynch, AIG, Lehman Brothers and a variety of Ponzi scheme scandals. Quite a year. A number of people saw their retirement portfolios vaporize. This brings us to another, but related, issue. How important is long -term capital preservation to an investor. In the post-2008 world a new portfolio category has evolved. It's called the "sleep well" portion of the portfolio.

Risk Assessment: Quantitative Evaluation

Standardized risk definitions and measurements have evolved along with the capital markets. This section will illustrate several of these.

Risk: Definitions

- Systematic risk: This is commonly defined as the component of an asset's risk caused by exposure to sources of risk that are common to all financial assets, such as sensitivity to interest rates or energy prices. Modern portfolio theory suggests that systematic risks cannot be diversified away, although it can be eliminated through hedging or reduced by employing market neutral trading/investment strategies.

- Unsystematic (sometimes called specific) risk: This is the component of risk that can be diversified away by holding a sufficiently large and well diversified portfolio. The methods of diversification are discussed

35

in the section of this chapter that is devoted to the *Capital Asset Pricing Model*.

Risk: Measurements

The following are common risk measures.

- **Standard Deviation:** This is a measurement of return dispersions. Risk measurements generally fall into two broad categories, dispersive and correlative (associative). Dispersive statistics measures the bumpiness of an asset's returns over time, the roller coaster effect. Correlative/associative statistics measure the degree that an asset or portfolio moves together with the larger market. Distinguishing these two types of risk is important in determining how efficiently a portfolio of investments is being managed. The overall concept of risk dictates that investors should be compensated for increases in risk; in other words, investors should expect a higher return on an investment when that investment carries a higher level of risk.

- *Calculating the standard deviation*: Start by calculating the average return (or arithmetic mean) of an asset over a given number of periods. This will give you a sense of the expected return on the asset. Examining how an asset performed in each period versus the expected rate of return gives you some sense of return dispersion, or bumpiness. For each period, subtract the expected return from the actual return. The difference is called the ***variance***. In some periods the asset will do better than the average, in some periods it will do worse. To be able to measure the dispersion of the returns around the average, square the variance. This will give you a better measure of the overall risk of the asset. The larger the variance in a period, the greater risk. The average of the squared variances results in the measurement of overall units of risk associated with the asset, and is called the *standard deviation* of the investment. Using this measurement together with average returns for assets (or asset classes) provides a better method of comparing investment opportunities.

- **Beta:** A measure of an asset's degree of movement with an underlying index or other benchmark. For example, an asset with a beta of 1.2 would be expected to return 12% if the market returned 10 percent and decline by 12% if the market declined by 10%. Beta is a correlative/associative statistic and measures the degree of broad market-related risk generated by a portfolio (or specific asset). It suggests that an asset's return can be measured as an index times the ratio of the assets standard deviation to the index's standard deviation. Portfolios (or assets) with betas in excess of 1 are more volatile than the overall market and are usually selected by aggressive investors. Conversely, portfolios (or assets) that have betas of less than 1 are less volatile than the overall market and are suitable for conservative investors looking to construct a more defensive portfolio.

- **Coefficient of Variation**
  The coefficient of variation represents the ratio of the standard deviation to the mean (average return). It is useful in scaling the standard deviation and for comparing how much volatility (risk) you are assuming in comparison to the amount of return you can expect from your investment. The lower the ratio of standard deviation to mean return, the better your risk-return tradeoff.

- **Sharpe Ratio**
  The Sharpe ratio attempts to distinguish the amount of return attributable to superior investment management skill rather than excessive risk taking. It is calculated by subtracting the risk-free rate from the rate of return for a portfolio and dividing the result by

the standard deviation of the portfolio returns. The higher a portfolio's Sharpe ratio, the better its risk-adjusted performance.

Modeling Risk and Developing Asset Allocation Models

As risk measurements became standardized, various efforts were made to model risk and return as a means of providing discipline to portfolio construction processes. This developed into a method of portfolio construction known as **top-down** investing. Under this method of investing, the following steps are generally followed:

1. An assessment is made of an investor's investment goals and risk tolerances. This is done subjectively, considering those issues which are important to specific investors, and objectively, which attempts to measure risk quantitatively.

2. A forecast of anticipated economic activity is made.

3. The construction and implementation of an asset allocation framework, differentiating the investment objectives and deployments of investors whose risk tolerances differ. The baseline model discussed in the chapter is the **Capital Asset Pricing Model.**

4. With respect to equity market and riskier asset allocations, an allocation of assets to industry sectors anticipated to perform well in the forecasted market environment.

5. Selection of individual stocks and other issuer sensitive securities.

The Capital Asset Pricing Model

Portfolio theorists began to develop models which integrated risk measurement applications with risk reduction objectives. The Capital Asset Pricing Model ("CAPM") is the result of such an effort. Recognizing that risk can be characterized as either systematic (broad market based) or unsystematic (specific), CAPM is a model which first attempts to separate these risks and eliminate the unsystematic/specific risk through a process of **diversification**. Think of diversification as **risk spreading** as opposed to risk elimination. By holding a sufficiently diversified portfolio, specific risks can be reduced or eliminated leaving only systematic risk. Remember, unsystematic risks are specific to an individual asset and therefore can be reduced or eliminated through the diversification process. The market rewards holders of market risk, but not specific risk. The metric used to measure systematic risk is the **beta**, previously discussed. Although a theoretical analysis of CAPM is beyond the scope of this book, a broad conceptual framework would be helpful. Think of the marketplace of a universe of assets, each containing different levels of risk. Some assets contain virtually no risk. The market proxy for so-called "risk free assets" is the short term United States treasury obligation. (Recent events involving the threatened default of the United States debt during the summer months of 2011, coupled with Standard & Poor's downgrade of long term debt of the United States, have thrown a harsh spotlight on the validity of this assumption.) Portfolios containing assets other than treasury bills must compensate the investor for the market (systematic) risk being taken. The excess return therefore is paying the investor a risk premium. If a portfolio is constructed representing the broad market, it will pay a risk premium compensating the investor for the systematic risk being accepted. The risk premium for the systematic risk must in turn be related to the beta of the portfolio. Therefore, CAPM generalizes expected market returns as:

Expected return = Risk free rate + beta (systematic risk premium in excess of risk free rate).

Accordingly, the CAPM assumes that the expected risk premium for an asset (expected return less the return on some riskless asset) is proportional to its systematic risk (beta).

Graphically, the CAPM can be conceptualized as:

Figure 2.2 - The Capital Asset Pricing Model

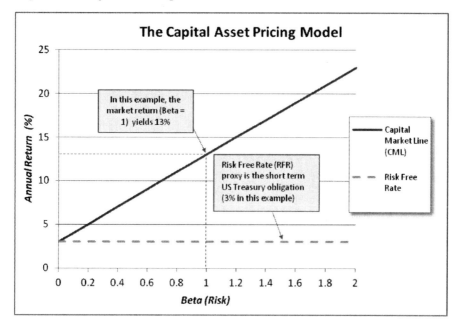

40

In portfolio theory, the beta adjusted return line is referred to as either the Capital Market Line ("CML" in the case of portfolios) or the Security Market Line ("SML" in the case of specific assets). Of the infinite number of potential portfolios available to investors, those portfolios which properly balance the risk and returns of the portfolio are those which are depicted on the CML.

There are many variations of CAPM. The usual critique of CAPM is that it tends to be backward looking in that portfolio construction is too often dictated by historical returns. The modification that is normally made to address this shortcoming is the derivation of returns from expected, as opposed to historical, equilibrium conditions. This involves extensive macroeconomic forecasting and assumptions concerning yields on asset classes and the correlation (and inter-correlation) of these assets in the forecasted environment. Some of these models are single factor models; others are multi-factor. While models of these types are improvements, the assumptions fed into them are subjective and are of course subject to error.

Once unsystematic/specific risk has been removed from a portfolio via diversification, additional return can presumably be generated through superior investment management skills, as opposed to increased risk taking. The metric which measures this skill driven yield increment is referred to as **Alpha**. Alpha can be generated through active allocations to certain investment styles or through tactical (near term) over-allocations.

Alpha is generally measured as:

- (Portfolio return—risk free rate), less beta × (market return-risk free rate).

Figure 2.3 - The Capital Asset Pricing Model Depicting Alpha

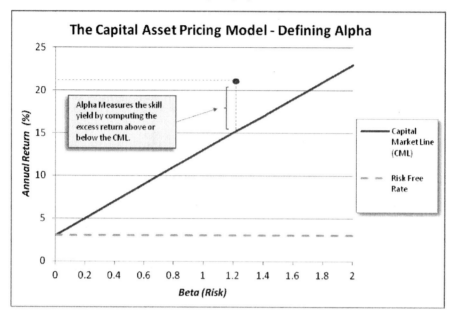

To generate alpha, portfolio managers attempt to identify and implement **market neutral trading strategies**. Market neutral strategies are trading strategies which involve being simultaneously long and short, the effect of which is to insulate the portfolio from beta driven market returns. The key to executing market neutral strategies is identifying mispriced asset categories so that a profit can be made by buying the perceived cheap asset while at the same time selling the overpriced asset. Each market neutral strategy is based on this type of relative value assumption. The ability to generate the alpha is therefore based on the correctness of the underlying assumption. All of these strategies share a common trait: a portfolio of long and short positions is maintained to be beta neutral. Long and short positions are also managed to eliminate net industry, market capitalization, and regional or other exposures.

A simple example of a market neutral equity trade is referred to as **pairs trading**. In this strategy, pairs of stocks whose prices tend to move together are identified. The underlying relative value assumption driving this trade is that although the stocks move together, one of the companies is "strong" and the other is "weak" relative to each other. If you go long the stronger stock and short the weaker, you will have insulated yourself from beta driven market risk and still make a profit regardless of the direction of market movements. For example, assume that you are tracking the trading relationships of Company A and Company B. Both companies operate in the same industry and are highly correlated to each other. You believe that A is the stronger of the two companies. Accordingly, you go long Company A and short a comparable dollar amount of Company B. If your assumption is correct and the market increases, you should make a larger profit on your long position in A than you lose in your short position in B, as A is stronger than B and should increase by a larger amount in an upward moving market. Conversely, if the market falls, your profit on the Company B short sale should be greater than your loss on the Company A long position as the weaker company should fall by more in a declining market. Thus, regardless of marker direction (the beta effect) you are generating profits (the alpha) on this market neutral strategy. Of course, your results will only be as good as the validity of your assumption; if B is stronger than A, you will lock in corresponding losses. Pairs trading also can be executed in individual securities or inter-related indices.

Fixed income market neutral strategies involve identifying and exploiting inconsistencies in the numerous term structure trades, liquidity spreads, and credit spreads found in fixed income markets. These may involve term structure trades, capital structure mispricings, and cross market trades. Fixed income arbitragers try to identify deviations from historical patterns for spreads or term structure relationships and put on a long-short position in anticipation of the historical relationship being reestablished. They also look for situations where credit risk or liquidity risk is being over compensated and will then put on a long-short position hoping to exploit the deviation. The methods for implementing these market neutral strategies will be developed in chapters 3, 4 and 5.

Using Economic Analysis in Constructing Client Portfolios

An important step in the investment process involves making broad macroeconomic forecasts about the direction of the domestic and world economy. The investment world is awash in statistics. We must begin by considering monetary and fiscal conditions on a global context. The most significant force in driving economics is normally central bank activity in various countries. In the United States this is the Federal Reserve Bank/System. Governments and central banks try and manage economies so that they achieve these basic objectives:

- **The first objective is to target growth in gross domestic product (GDP).** The long-term goal is to direct the economy through business cycles. If GDP stops growing it means that companies producing things build up inventories and productive capacity needs to be shed (capacity includes manufacturing capability, labor, etc.). This will normally bring on recessionary environments and cause the labor force to grow more slowly than central planners want or to shrink. **A related objective is therefore to achieve an economic environment that provides low unemployment.**

- If GDP grows too quickly inflation ignites. Inflation causes many difficulties and is hard to get out of the economy once it establishes itself. **The second objective is therefore to control inflation.**

  - Inflation is measured using a price index, such as the Consumer Price Index (CPI).

Governments and central banks have two main controls over an economy:

1. **Monetary policy** is the raising and cutting of interest rates, which changes the money supply. This is normally the responsibility of the Fed (or any other economy's central bank), and

2. **Fiscal policy** is the use of government spending and tax policy.

Looking at interest rate policy, let's consider the United States market and the activities of the Federal Reserve Bank. The Fed is the U.S. central bank. Unlike other central banks, it is a network of 12 District Federal Reserve Banks

45

Figure 2.4 - The Federal Reserve - Structure and Functions

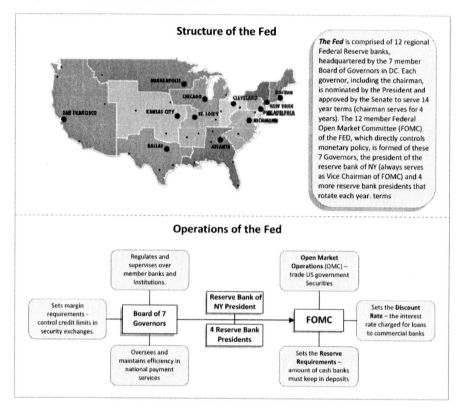

Source: www.federalreserveonline.org

To understand the market dynamics of interest rate policy, let's consider a **yield curve**. A yield curve is a graphical depiction of interest rates, the vertical axis showing rate levels and the horizontal axis showing time to maturity. There are many yield curves as not all borrowers are equally credit worthy. To focus on central bank activities, let's examine the yield curve for obligations of the United States.

Figure 2.5 - Yield Curve for Obligations of the US

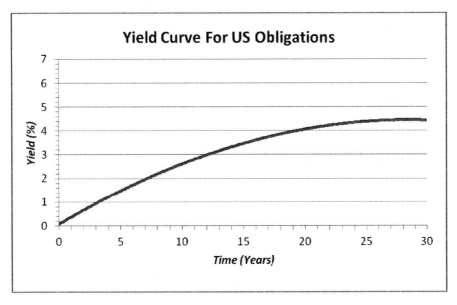

In order to effect the direction of the economy, the Federal Reserve will set short-term interest rates through the FOMC. This is done by setting the target federal funds rate, which is the rate of interest paid on interbank loans made through the Federal Reserve System. This activity will have the most significant impact on short-term obligations. The Fed will use interest rate policy to direct the future course of the economy. The Fed has significant influence on the direction of markets. If the Fed wants to stimulate markets, it may choose to lower interest rates to encourage borrowing and consumption. If the Fed decreases rates too aggressively, the economy will run out of capacity to produce the goods and services now in demand. Accordingly, prices of available goods and services will rise and inflation risks will increase. In reaction to this inflation, long- term investors will demand higher interest rates to compensate them for the loss of purchasing power. These long- term investors include insurance companies, pension funds, foreign central banks, and increasingly, sovereign investment funds. Sovereign investment funds are government-sponsored entities which act as government-owned private investment vehicles performing duties outside the traditional scope of central banks. Collectively, this group of investors is often referred to as **institutional investors**. In an over-stimulated economy interest rates at the shor- term end of the yield curve are falling and rising rates at the long term end. Thus, the yield curve is said to be **steepening**. A steepening yield curve is a sign of building inflation pressures in the fixed income markets. A commonly watched inflation gauge is the differential (or spread) between two year and ten year treasury securities. This is referred to as the 2/10 spread.

Figure 2.6 - The 2/10 Treasury Spread

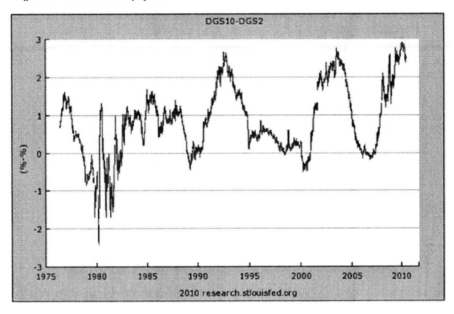

Source: http://pulse.zecco.com/2010/06/low-2-year-yield-high-treasury-spread/

When inflation risks increase, the Fed will reverse policy course and raise interest rates in the short-term market. As money becomes more expensive, demand for goods and services will fall, and a recession may begin if the drop in demand begins to idle productive capacity. Long -term investors will expect the Fed to reverse course and begin lowering rates to stimulate the now recessionary economy. Thus, yield curve shapes are somewhat predictive of future economic environments. Normally, the steeper the yield curve, the more the market is indicating an expectation of inflation. Conversely, an inverted yield curve (one in which short term interest rates are higher than long term interest rates) is suggestive of a recession and the increasing anticipation of a rate cut by the Fed. Flat yield curves (a curve in which short term and long term interest rates are about the same) can be indicative of relative market indecision of future economic direction, or, more likely, may represent a transition point. If the yield curve preceding a flat yield curve was steep, the economy may be heading into (or already be in) a recession. If the curve which preceded the flat curve was inverted, economic activity may be picking up and inflationary pressures may be building up in the economy.

The different yield curve shapes appear below.

Figure 2.7 - 4 Examples of Yield Curves

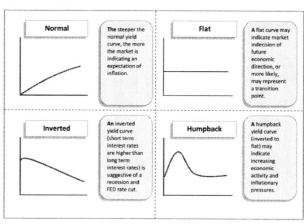

50

Available Economic Statistics

There are multitudes of economic statistics which are helpful in predicting future economic activity. Statistics in the following areas receive widespread attention

Figure 2.8 - Table Showing Economic Indicators and their Sources

Consumer Spending	Retail Sales Data	Census Bureau
	Consumer Confidence Index	Consumer Confidence Bureau
Housing markets		
Prices	House Price Index	Federal Housing Finance Agency
Sales Activity	Housing Starts	Department of Commerce
Business Activity	Philadelphia Fed Index	Federal Reserve Bank of Philadelphia
	Purchasing Managers Index	Association of Purchasing Managers
Government Spending	Gross Domestic Product (GDP)	Commerce Department
Inflation	Consumer Price Index	Bureau of Labor and Statistics
	Producer Price Index	Bureau of Labor and Statistics
Labor Market and Monetary Policy	Beige Book	Federal Reserve Board
	Employment Situation Report	Bureau of Labor and Statistics
	Employee Cost Index	Bureau of Labor and Statistics

Figure 2.9 - Example Graphic Indicators of Economic Conditions

The census department of the Bureau of Labor and Statistics undertakes monthly household surveys to investigate personal earnings and the labor force. The resulting data forms the Current Population Survey, from which the national unemployment rate (*right*), can be accurately estimated and graphically presented.

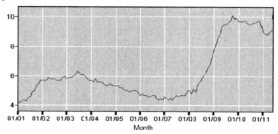

Bureau of Labor and Statistics: http://data.bls.gov/timeseries/LNS14000000

GDP is the primary and broadest measure of the national economy. It provides detailed information on consumption, government spending, trade and income. The Bureau of Economic Analysis releases GDP figures on a quarterly basis, but records GDP growth as an annualized rate.

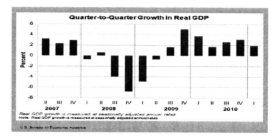

Bureau of Economic Analysis:www.bea.gov/newsreleases/national/gdp/gdp_glance.htm

Chapter
3

Debt Markets-Core Relationships and Motivations

We now turn to specific markets where investors deploy their capital. The first will be **debt markets**, which are essentially markets for borrowings made by governments (including their subdivisions) and corporations. When borrowings are made in publicly traded form, the debt instruments are issued in the form of securities which are called **bonds or notes.** Direct lending by banks and other financial institutions are referred to as **loans.** Loans are generally not securities but are direct obligations of the borrower to the lender that provided the funds. The bond and loan markets are channels through which governments and corporations that need to borrow money are matched with investors who have funds to lend.

In this chapter we will identify those risks which are faced by debt market investors as a group, and then in the following chapters look at debt obligations of specific issuers.

When an investor buys a debt instrument, he takes a number of risks. These risks include:

- Interest rate risk
  This is generally the price risk associated with changes

in interest rate levels after the date a debt instrument is purchased. For **fixed income** securities, prices will fall as interest rates rise (as the bond coupon becomes unattractive to current market opportunities) and vice-versa.

- Credit risk

  This is the risk that a borrower will be unable to honor his obligation to pay interest during the life of the obligation or repay principal at maturity. This risk is placed in the frame of reference of the bankruptcy system in which the issuer resides.

- Reinvestment risk

  The risk associated with the need to reinvest cash flows generated by a bond at a rate different than what was anticipated on the date the bond was purchased.

Pricing and Valuing Debt Instruments

The price (or value) of a debt instrument is the present value of the instrument's future cash flows. The value of a debt instrument may be expressed as:

Figure 3.1 – Calculating the Price of a Bond

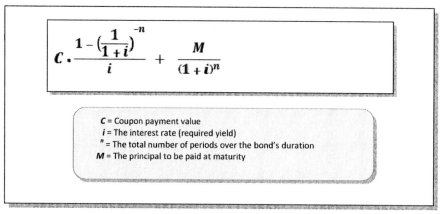

$$C \cdot \frac{1 - \left(\frac{1}{1+i}\right)^{-n}}{i} + \frac{M}{(1+i)^n}$$

C = Coupon payment value
i = The interest rate (required yield)
n = The total number of periods over the bond's duration
M = The principal to be paid at maturity

The interest rate, or required yield, is selected from the yield curve of the market in which the instrument is issued (e.g. government or corporate). Selecting the appropriate yield curve is crucial. The appropriate discount rate will be determined by the type of issuer/borrower, the maturity of the obligation, and the credit worthiness of the issuer/borrower. At this point we should recognize that different investors have different motivations when they invest in debt obligations. Some are traders, looking to profit by buying or selling debt obligations as interest rates change. Others will buy debt obligations and hold them until their maturity dates and collect the principal amount at that point in time. A market participant looking to speculate the direction of interest rates will either buy or sell debt obligations based upon these expectations. As discussed in chapter two, the shape of the yield curve will tell you what the market as a whole expects. We saw that steepening yield curves normally express market expectations of inflationary pressures and resultant increases in interest rates. Inverted curves are predictive of recessionary expectations and falling interest rates. The future level of interest rates can be derived through a process of computing **implied forward rates.** Assume you observe a market that has the following interest rate characteristics:

- One year rates 4%
- Two year rates 5%
- Five year rates 6%

The resulting yield curve is illustrated in Figure 3.2.

Figure 3.2 - Yield Curve - Term Structure

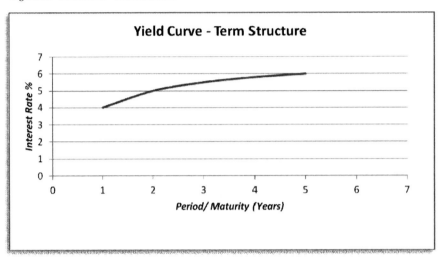

Example: In figure 3.2, the two- year interest rate is 5% while the one- year interest rate is 4%. Thus an investor has a choice, invest in the two-year obligation paying 5% or invest for one year at 4% and then reinvest in the second year at whatever the prevailing rate is then. Because arbitragers would eliminate structural inefficiencies, these two investment opportunities must be equivalent. Therefore, the one-year interest rate which is forecasted one year hence (the implied forward rate) is 6.01%;

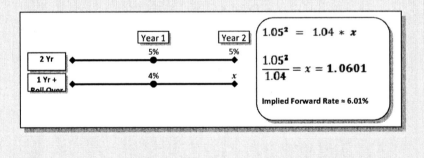

Debt Market Math Fundamentals

Present value
Single cash flows: The value of a single cash flow to be received in the future is that cash flow discounted back to today using a rate of interest indicative of the opportunity cost of money over that period.
Multiple even cash flows (annuities): The arithmetic sum of the present value of each of the single cash flows in the annuity.

Returning to our yield curve, we can use these present value techniques to determine future expectations of interest rates.

Bond Metrics: Measuring Price Sensitivity

If our expectations differ from the market, we can position ourselves to profit from this difference in expectations. If we believe that interest rates will be lower than market expectations, we would buy fixed rate debt obligations because we would expect debt instruments to increase in value if interest rates fall. Our exposure to interest rate movements could be described as benefiting from falling interest rates and suffering from higher interest rates. Using our graphing technique developed in chapter one, we would profit if we owned (or were long) bonds and interest rates fell. If we expected interest rates to rise, we could borrow bonds from an owner of them and sell them at today's price, hoping to repurchase them at a lower price in the future to return them to the lender. In this situation we would be short. Thus, we can say we are **long interest rates** when we benefit from lower interest rates and suffer from higher interest rates without regard to actually owning debt instruments. Conversely, we are **short interest rates** when we profit from higher interest rates and suffer from lower interest rates without regard to actually selling debt securities short. Thus, we can conceptualize these risks as shown on the following payoff graphs:

Figure 3.3 - Long Position vs. Short Position - Bonds

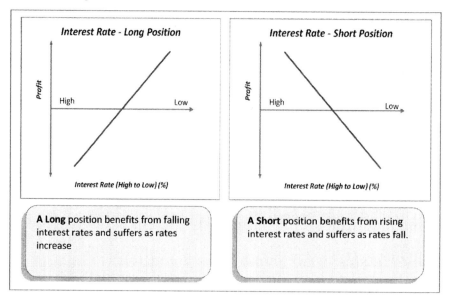

Note that in Figure 3.4 that the horizontal axis depicts interest rates, not prices. Because fixed income prices and interest rate movements are inversely related, the movement of interest rates is inverted. Lower interest rates are to the right, higher interest rates are to the left.

Although this is a useful conceptualization, the price yield relationships for debt securities are not linear. To accurately depict the price yield relationship, we must turn to the concept of **bond price convexity.** Convexity is a measure of the curvature in the relationship between bond prices and bond yields. Graphically it would look as follows

Figure 3.4 - Convexity Curve

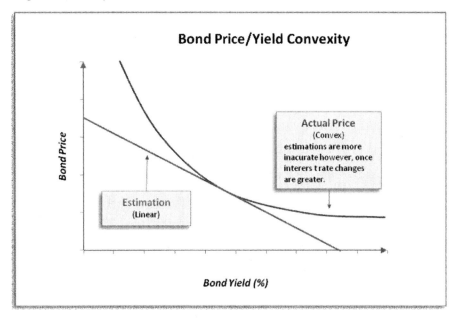

Mathematically, convexity is the second derivative of the price of the bond with respect to changes in interest rate. **Duration**, a closely related metric, measures how a bond's price changes as interest rate changes and also measure sensitivity to reinvestment risk. The relationship is non-linear since duration changes as interest rates change.

Not all debt instruments will change by the same amount as interest rates change. Bonds and other debt instruments will be more or less sensitive to changes in interest rates depending upon the maturity of the debt and its coupon rate. Debt traders will want to select those debt instruments that will appreciate most as interest rates decline and own those that will depreciate the least if the fear is that interest rates may increase. In order to be able to compare price sensitivity of different debt instruments in the face of interest rate changes, we must select a formula which measures the gain or loss in percentage terms rather than in absolute dollar amounts. We will use the following formula:

$$\frac{\textit{New Price After Interest Rate Change} - \textit{Old Price, Prior to Interest Rate Change}}{\textit{Old Price, Prior to Interest Rate Change}} =$$

$$\% \text{ change}$$

There are generally three characteristics that will determine relative sensitivity to interest rate movements. These are:

1. the **maturity** of the debt instrument;

2. the **coupon rate**; and

3. the **direction** of interest rates.

Preliminary Observations Concerning Sensitivity of Bond Prices to Interest Rate Changes

1. *Observation: Longer Maturity Debt Instruments are More Sensitive to Interest Changes Than Shorter Maturities*

   Let's consider two bonds with a 5% coupon rate, one maturing in two years, the other maturing in 20 years. Let's assume that the yield curve on which these bonds are price currently looks as follows:

Figure 3.5 - Yield Curve Example 1 - 2Yr @ 5%, 20 Yr @7%

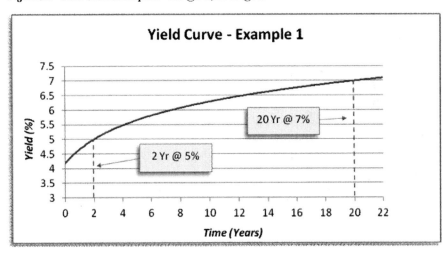

The price of each $1,000,000 face value bond would be:

2 year bond: **$ 1,000,000**   20 year bond: **$786,449.28**

Payment Period (1/2 Yr)	Coupon Payment ($)	PV of Interest Payment ($)
1	25,000	24,390.24
2	25,000	23,795.36
3	25,000	23,214.99
4	25,000	22,648.77
+ PV of Principal	-	+ 905,950.64
= Price of Bond	-	= $1,000,000

Payment Period (1/2 Yr)	Coupon Payment ($)	PV of Interest Payment ($)
1	25,000	24,154.59
2	25,000	23,337.77
3...	25,000	22,548.57
...40	25,000	6,314.31
+ PV of Principal	-	+ 252,572.47
= Price of Bond	-	= $786,449.28

Let's now assume that interest rates decline by 100 basis points (bps). The yield curve would now look as follows:

Figure 3.6 - Yield Curve - Example 1 - Change in Interest Rates

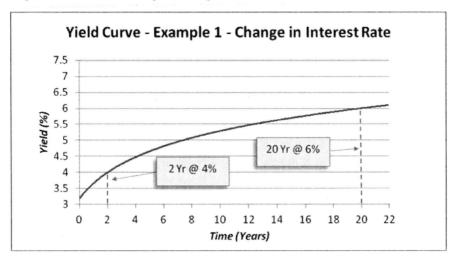

The price of each $1,000,000 face value bond would be:

2 year bond: **$1,019,038.64**   20 year bond: **$884,426.14**

Payment Period (1/2 Yr)	Coupon Payment ($)	PV of Interest Payment ($)
1	25,000	24,509.80
2	25,000	24,029.22
3	25,000	23,558.06
4	25,000	23,096.14
+ PV of Principal	-	+ 923,845.43
= Price of Bond	-	= $1,019,038.64

Payment Period (1/2 Yr)	Coupon Payment ($)	PV of Interest Payment ($)
1	25,000	24,271.84
2	25,000	23,564.90
3...	25,000...	22,878.54...
...40	...25,000	...7,663.92
+ PV of Principal	-	+ 306,556.84
= Price of Bond	-	= $884,426.14

Percentage increase: **1.90** %   Percentage increase: **12.46** %

Notice that the 20-year bond increased by a larger percentage than the two-year bond. Why? The answer lies in the cumulative nature of the compounding process. Both bonds have a principal amount of $1,000,000. The 100 bp decline has a much more pronounced effect on the principal in the 20-year bond as compared to the two- year bond. Secondly, although both bonds have a 5% coupon (2½% semi-annually), the 20-year bond has 40 coupons stretched out over the 20 years whereas the two- year has only four such coupons over its lifespan. The cumulative effect of the 100bp decline on the 20-year bond is much more significant that the effect on the two-year bond. Thus, **longer maturity bonds are more sensitive to interest rate changes than shorter maturity bonds.**

2.   *Observation: Lower coupon bonds are more sensitive to interest rate changes than are higher coupon bond where both bonds mature on the same date.*

Let's now consider two $1,000,000 face value bonds that mature on the same date but have different coupon rates. Let's look at two bonds maturing in five years: one carries a 6% coupon (Bond A); the second carries a 3% coupon (Bond B). The yield on comparable obligations is 6%. Intuitively the Bond A is worth more

64

than Bond B. In fact the 6% obligation is worth its face value and the 3% obligation is worth $872,046.96. The price of each $1,000,000 face value bond would be:

Bond A

5 year/6% bond: **$1,000,000**

Payment Period (1/2 Yr)	Coupon Payment ($)	PV of Interest Payment ($)
1	30,000	29,126.21
2	30,000	28,277.87
3...	30,000...	27,454.25...
...10	...30,000	...22,322.82
+ PV of Principal	-	+ 744,093.91
= Price of Bond	-	= $1,000,000

Bond B

5 year/3% bond: **$872,046.96**

Payment Period (1/2 Yr)	Coupon Payment ($)	PV of Interest Payment ($)
1	15,000	14,563.12
2	15,000	14,138.94
3...	15,000...	13,727.12...
...10	...15,000	...11,161.41
+ PV of Principal	-	+ 744,093.91
= Price of Bond	-	= $872,046.96

Notice that while Bond A is worth more than Bond B, the present value of the principal payment in each bond is the same. Let's look at the same two bonds if the yield in the market in which it trades now drops 100bps to 5% (from 6%).

Bond A

5 year/6% bond: **$1,043,760.32**

Payment Period (1/2 Yr)	Coupon Payment ($)	PV of Interest Payment ($)
1	30,000	29,268.29
2	30,000	28,554.43
3...	30,000...	27,857.98...
...10	...30,000	...23,435.95
+ PV of Principal	-	+ 781,198.40
= Price of Bond	-	= $1,043,760.32

Percentage increase: **4.38**%

Bond B

5 year/3% bond: **$912,479.36**

Payment Period (1/2 Yr)	Coupon Payment ($)	PV of Interest Payment ($)
1	15,000	14,634.14
2	15,000	14,277.22
3...	15,000...	13,928.99...
...10	...15,000	...11,717.98
+ PV of Principal	-	+ 781,198.40
= Price of Bond	-	= $912,479.36

Percentage increase: **4.64**%

Notice that both bonds increase in price, but Bond B increases in price by a larger percentage than Bond A. Why? The reason can be explained in relatively non-mathematical terms. Let's see in which bond the principal amount (which is the last and most distant cash flow) accounts for a larger proportion of the bond's total value. If we look at the prices when the market yield was 6%, we find:

Bond A

5 year/6% bond: **$1,000,000**

Payment Period (1/2 Yr)	Coupon Payment ($)	PV of Interest Payment ($)
1	30,000	29,126.21
2	30,000	28,277.87
3...	30,000...	27,454.25...
...10	...30,000	...22,322.82
+ PV of Principal	-	+ 744,093.91
= Price of Bond	-	= $1,000,000

Portion of total value

represented by principal: **$744,093.91**

= __74.41__%

Bond B

5 year/3% bond: **$872,046.92**

Payment Period (1/2 Yr)	Coupon Payment ($)	PV of Interest Payment ($)
1	15,000	14,563.12
2	15,000	14,138.94
3...	15,000...	13,727.12...
...10	...15,000	...11,161.41
+ PV of Principal	-	+ 744,093.91
= Price of Bond	-	= $872,046.96

Portion of total value

represented by principal: **$744,093.91**

= __85.33__%

Notice that Bond B has a larger portion of its total value represented by its principal payment than does Bond A. The same cumulative effects of compounding of interest that we discussed in the maturity section are at work here. A bond which has more of its value represented by the more distant cash flow will be more sensitive than bonds which have more of its value represented by nearer term cash flows. The most interest-sensitive bond of all therefore is a zero coupon bond, which is a bond that has a single cash flow paid at its maturity. **In bullet structure bonds, bonds with lower coupons will be more sensitive to interest rate changes than higher coupon bonds to the same maturity.** A bullet structure is a debt instrument which provides for payment of all of the principal at maturity.

3. *Observation: Interest rate movements do not cause symmetrical price sensitivities; bonds are more sensitive to falling interest rates than to rising interest rates.*

   This one is a little tough to get at first. Let's look at a convexity curve and make a couple of visual observations.

Figure 3.7 - Convexity Curve Revisited

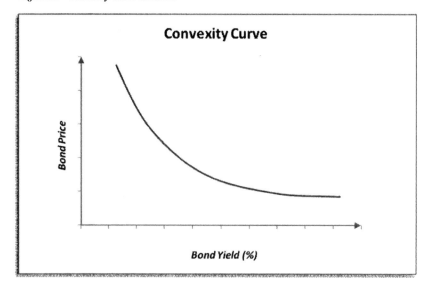

4. *Observation: Looking at the curve, one sees the general price/yield relationship; as rates decline bond prices increase, as rates increase, bond prices decline.* As a curve, something else is true by definition; the price yield relationship is not linear. As rates decline, prices increase at an *increasing* rate. As rates increase, bond prices decline at a *decreasing* rate. This is explained by the reinvestment effect at point of sale. If rates decline, you will sell your bond at a gain. Ignoring income taxes, if you take the sales proceeds and reinvest them after the bonds are sold, you will receive both a lower coupon and less reinvestment income. To compensate the seller for these adverse effects, the bond price increases geometrically. Likewise, if rates increase, the bond price will fall, but at a decreasing speed. This is because the combined effects of being able to invest at a higher coupon and higher reinvestment rate will cause the rate of devaluation to slow. Thus, **interest rate movements do not cause symmetrical price sensitivities; bonds are more sensitive to falling interest rates than to rising interest rates.**

Applications and critiques of these bond metrics

The discussion in the previous sections would lead debt traders to adjust their portfolios to reflect their expectations regarding interest rates. If I'm trading bonds in search of making trading profits and if my expectation were falling interest rates, I would want the maximum possible gain. To do this, I would likely lengthen the maturity profiles in my portfolio while simultaneously seeking relatively lower coupon bonds. These types of bonds, long term/low coupon bonds, will have those characteristics which are most sensitive to interest rates. I want the maximum convexity and will position myself to profit from my expectations. Conversely, if my expectations were in the direction of rising interest rates, I would want to avoid losses through holding bonds. To the extent I owned bonds at all, I would buy shorter maturity/high coupon bonds which are the least sensitive to interest rate movements. The price yield relationship of these bond types are the least convex. The process of adding or shedding convexity (price sensitivity to interest rate changes) in a portfolio is sometimes referred to as a **bond rotation**.

An astute reader might see a problem with this approach. In chapter two we discussed Fed policy actions in the short term interest market sometimes leading to interest rates moving in opposite directions in the longer term markets. If yield curve shifts are not parallel, these techniques may have more limited utility. Adjustments need to be made to address which points of the curve I expect to move.

Another issue relates to the phenomenon is known as **negative convexity.** Positive convexity describes an inverse price yield relationship. Negative convexity describes a price yield relationship that does not. A debt instrument or portfolio that exhibits negative convexity is acting counter-intuitively. The negative convexity relationship is exhibited as follows:

Figure 3.8 - Negative Convexity

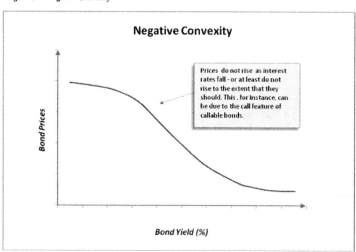

70

Notice in this situation, as interest rates fall, prices don't rise, or don't rise as fast as they should. This can occur because the issuer/borrower may have the ability to refinance the debt if interest rates decline. This is a relatively common feature in corporate obligations and is referred to as a **call feature**. Callable bonds therefore display negative convexity. Negative convexity characteristics may also be present when yields are rising and the debt obligation does not lose value. This may be because the owner of the bond may have the right to cause the issuer to retire the bond as interest rates increase. These types of bonds are referred to as **putable bonds**.

Bond Metrics: measuring sensitivity to reinvestment risk

Debt market speculators seeking to profit by trading bonds as interest move are only one part of the debt market universe. Some market participants buy the bonds with the explicit intention of holding them to maturity, using the intervening cash flows to pay liabilities as they come due. These parties are often referred to as **buy and hold investors**. These types of buyers often include pension funds, insurance companies, and others that use the cash flows from their bond portfolio to pay bills as they come due. This is sometimes referred to as **liability immunization**. These types of investors are acutely exposed to **reinvestment risk**. As we have seen, traditional bond pricing employs present value mathematics to calculate the present value of a future cash flow stream. The sum of these present values is the price, or market value of the bond. When a bond is valued, the present value process may be viewed as follows:

Figure 3.9 - Diagram Illustrating the Compound Nature of Present Valuing Multiple Cash Flow Periods

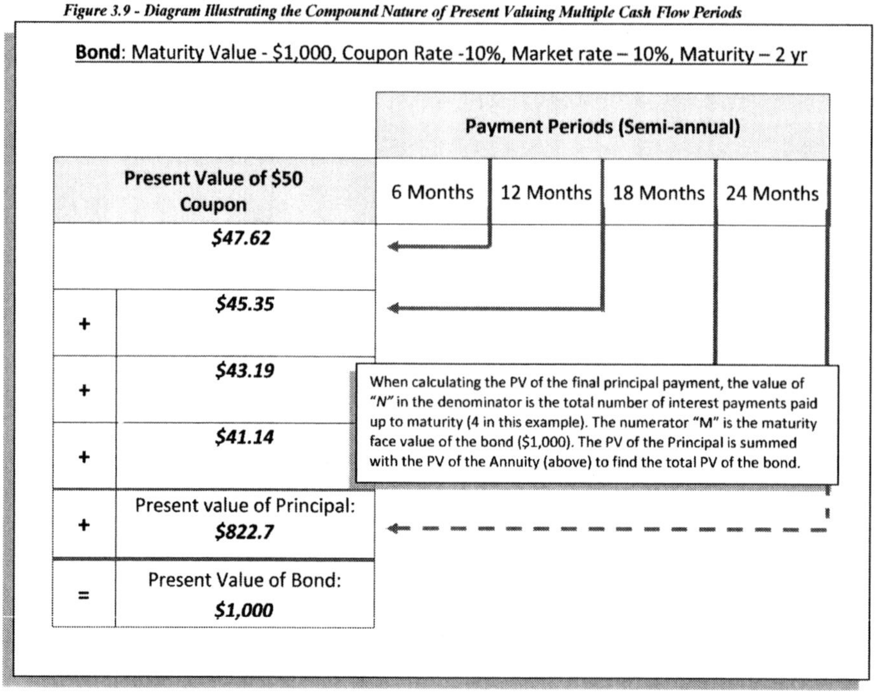

Bond: Maturity Value - $1,000, Coupon Rate -10%, Market rate – 10%, Maturity – 2 yr

	Present Value of $50 Coupon	Payment Periods (Semi-annual)			
		6 Months	12 Months	18 Months	24 Months
	$47.62				
+	$45.35				
+	$43.19	When calculating the PV of the final principal payment, the value of "N" in the denominator is the total number of interest payments paid up to maturity (4 in this example). The numerator "M" is the maturity face value of the bond ($1,000). The PV of the Principal is summed with the PV of the Annuity (above) to find the total PV of the bond.			
+	$41.14				
+	Present value of Principal: $822.7				
=	Present Value of Bond: $1,000				

Calculating the Present Value of each Coupon Payment (C = $50 – 5%, twice a year);

$$\frac{C}{(1+i)^n} = \frac{50}{1.05^n}$$

Thus, due to the compound effect of money investing and the increasing power of n (payment period), the PV of coupon payments decrease as the payment periods (n) chronologically increase. The sum of the coupon present values paid up to maturity is referred to as the Present Value of the Annuity.

Calculating the Present Value of the Principal Paid at Maturity (M = $1,000);

$$\frac{M}{(1+i)^N} = \frac{1,000}{1.05^4}$$

72

By applying the present value mathematics in this manner, an implicit assumption is being made; all cash flows generated by the bond are deemed to be reinvested at the same rate the cash flows are being discounted by. This <u>never</u> happens. Thus, a buy and hold investor is taking the risk cash flows generated by the investment in excess of the amount needed to pay the liability will ultimately be reinvested at a rate lower than the assumed purchase date discounting rate. This risk is very significant because portfolio managers at pension funds, insurance companies, etc will be unable to pay their bills as they come due and may therefore seek to increase risk elsewhere in their portfolio to make up the difference. Thus, a buy and hold investor is keenly interested how long it takes to earn the yield to maturity (which is the purchase date discount rate). If rates decline, the period of time it takes to earn the anticipated yield to maturity extends as the investor is earning less reinvestment income than anticipated. Conversely, if rates increase, it takes less time to earn the anticipated yield to maturity as the investor is earning reinvestment income in excess of original expectations. A popular bond metric, called **duration**, attempts to measure this risk.

Duration is a measure of the average (cash-weighted) term-to-maturity of a bond. There are two types of duration:

1. **Macaulay duration** is the weighted-average term to maturity of the cash flows from a bond. The weight of each cash flow is determined by dividing the present value of the cash flow by the price. It measures the time taken to recover the full cost of the bond.

2. **Modified duration**, an extension of Macaulay duration, is a formula that expresses the measurable change in the value of a security in response to a change in interest rates. It is a measure of price sensitivity.

73

DEBT MARKETS-CORE RELATIONSHIPS AND MOTIVATIONS

Bond: Maturity Value - $1,000, Coupon Rate -10%, Market rate – 10%, Maturity – 2 yr

Macaulay Duration;

$$\sum_{y=1}^{n} \frac{(PV\ of\ cash\ flow)\,X\,(year)}{Market\ Price} = \frac{(90.91\,X\,1) + (909.10\,X\,2)}{1000} = 1.91\ Years$$

In this 2 year bond, the Macaulay duration measure indicates that it will take 1.91 years until the full cost of the bond is repaid and recovered. All income generated after 1.91 years is profit ("y" = years commencing at 1, "n" = Number of years to maturity and in year 2, the coupon PV is combined with the principal payment PV)

Modified Duration;

$$\frac{Macaulay\ Duration}{1 + \frac{YTM}{f}} = \frac{1.91\ Years}{1.0s} = 1.82$$

In this calculation, "YTM" refers to the coupon rate generated by the bond (in this case 10%) and "f" refers to the frequency of payments per year (in this case 2). The Modified Duration result of 1.82 indicates that for every 100bp (1%) change in interest rates, the bond's market price inversely shifts by 1.82%.

An Introduction to Credit Risk in Fixed Income Markets

Much of what has been discussed thus far relates to understanding and quantifying interest rate risk. When loans are made to municipal entities, corporations, and other borrowers, the investor/lender runs the risk that the interest or principal on the loan will not be paid. This nonpayment is a breach of the agreement between the parties and is referred to as either **default** or **credit** risk. The investor will need to pursue the enforcement of their rights against the borrower. This may lead the borrower to seek protection of the bankruptcy courts within their jurisdiction. Modern bankruptcy systems have de-stigmatized debt repudiation, a concept which often troubles the newcomer to this subject. In the 19th century, nonpayment of a debt could actually lead to imprisonment in many countries. Modern legal processes have transferred these disputes to the civil (as opposed to criminal) court systems. In the United States there are separate bankruptcy courts which adjudicate debtor/creditor relations. In the United States, the law is written to encourage financial reorganization as opposed to liquidation. It is important to note that investors in debt securities containing credit risk will demand higher yield to compensate them for the credit risk. In the United States, debt of the United States government has historically been viewed as containing no or little credit risk. During the summer months of 2011, the United States Congress and President Barack Obama engaged in a protracted budget battle ostensibly linked to raising the federal debt ceiling, the statutory limit for indebtedness taken in the name of the United States. Under the threat of a default on the United States debt, the two sides engaged in a battle of brinksmanship with a deal being struck at the very last minute. The issue of real structural budgetary reform was left unaddressed and Standard & Poor's Ratings Services downgraded the debt of the United States from AAA to AA+ on August 5, 2011. The implications of this downgrade are not yet fully understood.

Historically, the additional compensation for accepting credit risk is linked to yields of US Treasury securities to comparable maturities. This additional compensation is referred to as the **credit spread** and represents the investors' risk premium. The amount of the credit spread will depend on the market's perception of the likelihood of default by the issuer. Large rating agencies quantify the default likelihoods of issuers and stratify issuers into comparable categories. Although the credit spread is issuer dependent, similarly situated corporations will pay roughly the same credit spread. The more likely the default, the higher the yield demanded by investors will be.

Figure 3.10 - Credit Spread of US Corporate Bonds and US Treasuries

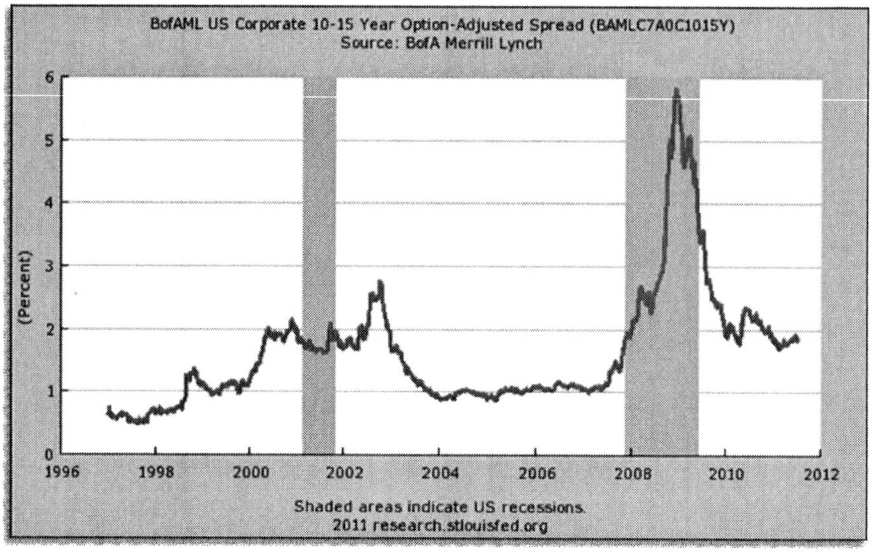

Source: Federal Reserve of St. Louis Database

Over time credit spreads change with market conditions. The three major variables that determine the size of the credit spread at any point in time are:

1. The **maturity** of a debt obligation. As a general matter longer-term obligations will have larger credit spreads than short term obligations. The reason for this is that there is a larger likelihood of default over a longer period of time as opposed to a shorter period of time. As the default risk is cumulative, it stands to reason that investors in longer-term debt obligations will demand higher credit spreads than shorter term investors.

2. **The direction of interest rates**. We discussed earlier in chapter two that the direction of the economy will drive the direction of interest rates (and vice versa). If interest rates in general are declining, perceptions of credit risk change along with them. In most situations the market will conclude that lower interest rate environments are conducive to more favorable conditions for borrowers to meet their debt obligations (if rates are lower, so are interest charges on the borrowed money). As this perception becomes more widespread, fears concerning credit will wane, and credit spreads in general will narrow as investors will demand less compensation for accepting a risk they now view as more remote. Conversely, rising interest rates will cause concerns about credit risks to increase and credit spreads will widen.

3. **Flights to quality**. Flights to quality occur during periods of extreme market stress. For example, during 2008 a number of financial firms either failed or were in the imminent danger of doing so. Government intervention was necessary on a global scale to prevent a collapse of the financial system. Panicked investors sold off their riskier assets, including credit risk bear-

ing debt securities. As prices fell, yields rose. Having sold their riskier assets, these investors put their money into the perceived safety of government securities. As a result, these prices rose and yields fell. The credit spread, which is the difference between the yields on government securities and the yields on credit risk bearing assets, expanded dramatically. This expansion is typical; in market panics, credit spreads will expand beyond normal market conditions. As markets calm, the process reverses and the safer assets are sold with proceeds redeployed into riskier investments and the credit spread narrows.

Figure 3.11 - Credit Spread of US Corporate Bonds and US Treasuries – Examined During Times of Economic Stress

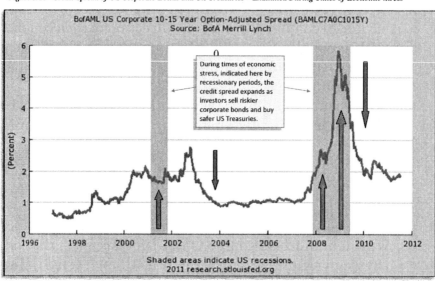

Source: Federal Reserve of St. Louis Database

Chapter
4

U.S. Treasury Securities & Markets

United States Treasury securities are debt instruments issued by the United States Department of Treasury. They are direct obligations of the Federal Government. In an era in which the federal government is running annual budget deficits in excess of $1.5 trillion and the accumulated national debt now exceeds $14 trillion ($14,103,090,580.84 as of 07/15/2011), the smooth operation of these markets has become increasingly critical to global economic stability. Historically, debt of the U.S. Government has been viewed as free of credit risk because the federal government has the power to tax and, through monetary policy, to effectively print money. Because of the effects of the growth in the deficits and national debt, one of the major rating agencies (Standard & Poor's Rating Service) recently downgraded long-term debt of the United states to AA+ from AAA.

Due to the principles of federalism embedded in the United States Constitution, income on debt obligations of the U.S. Government (and many political subdivisions) is taxed by the Federal Government but not by state or local governments. Due to their liquidity and favorable credit characteristics, United States government debt pays interest at rates below other issuers of debt. Municipal securities (obligations of states and local governments) actually pay lower *nominal* rates of interest, but this is due to differences in taxability. Municipal securities are discussed in detail in chapter 5.

With a national debt the size of the United States, the U.S. Treasury Department must regularly refinance parts of the debt as it comes due. You may recall that earlier we discussed how the market reacts to central bank activities in steering the course of the economy. This market is a prime example of how this happens.

To refinance maturing portions of the debt as they come due, the Treasury Department conducts regular auctions. Due to the size of the sums involved, these auctions can only be conducted with very large financial institutions. The institutions that can deal directly with the U.S. Treasury Department are called **primary dealers**. Primary dealers are generally large commercial and investment banks that perform traditional dealer functions; they buy securities at one price hoping to sell them at a higher price.

List of the Primary Government Securities Dealers Reporting to the Government Securities Dealers Statistics Unit of the Federal Reserve Bank of New York

Bank of Nova Scotia, New York Agency

BMO Capital Markets Corp.

BNP Paribas Securities Corp.

Barclays Capital Inc.

Cantor Fitzgerald & Co.

Citigroup Global Markets Inc.

Credit Suisse Securities (USA) LLC

Daiwa Capital Markets America Inc.

Deutsche Bank Securities Inc.

Goldman, Sachs & Co.

HSBC Securities (USA) Inc.

Jefferies & Company, Inc.

J.P. Morgan Securities LLC

MF Global Inc.

Merrill Lynch, Pierce, Fenner & Smith Incorporated

Mizuho Securities USA Inc.

Morgan Stanley & Co. LLC

Nomura Securities International, Inc.

RBC Capital Markets, LLC

RBS Securities Inc.

SG Americas Securities, LLC

UBS Securities LLC.

Source: Federal Reserve Bank of New York, October 4, 2011

The government auctions securities with a wide variety of maturities. The types of securities include:

1. Treasury bills, which are discount instruments (non-coupon bearing) with initial maturities of up to a year.

2. Treasury notes, which pay semiannual coupons and have initial maturities of more than one year and up to 10 years.

3. Treasury bonds, which pay semiannual coupons and have initial maturities greater than 10 years.

4. Treasury Inflation-Protected Securities (TIPS), which are coupon paying instruments with a principal amount that is adjusted over time for inflation.

The Treasury Department conducts almost 200 auctions a year. The Treasury publishes a schedule for auctions that is modified as the federal government's funding needs change.

U.S. Treasury Securities & Markets

Treasury Auction Schedule: 05/04/11 – 05/12/11

Security Type			Announcement Date	Auction Date	Settlement Date
3-Year NOTE			Wednesday	May 04	2011 Tuesday
10-Year NOTE			Wednesday	May 04	2011 Wednesday
30-Year BOND			Wednesday	May 04	2011 Thursday
13-Week BILL			Thursday	May 05	2011 Monday
26-Week BILL			Thursday	May 05	2011 Monday
4-Week BILL			Monday	May 09	2011 Tuesday
13-Week BILL			Thursday	May 12	2011 Monday
26-Week BILL			Thursday	May 12	2011 Monday
10-Year TIPS	R	T	Thursday	May 12	2011 Thursday

82

Each auction is announced in advance, and the dollar amount that the government is seeking to raise is made publicly available. These securities settle on a so-called "when-issued" basis; that is deliveries and payments are made when the securities are issued by the government. Regular trading in the secondary market for treasury securities settles in one business day (one day after the trade is executed, or "T+1," where T is the trade date). The "when-issued" trading in the primary dealer market can be thought of as a type of forward market. The "regular-way" treasury markets can settle quickly because these markets are now paperless. This occurred during the modernization of securities settlement procedures that occurred in the early 1980s. Ownership of these (and many other types of securities) is now tracked electronically. This is called "book entry" and helped facilitate a trading revolution as the inefficient and time-consuming process of physically settling securities transactions was eliminated.

Treasury securities trade in an over-the-counter market facilitated by large financial institutions acting as dealers, buying from or selling to their clients. As we previously discussed, those dealers that deal directly with the New York Federal Reserve in its open market operations are called primary government securities dealers (or primary dealers). Primary dealers serve as trading counterparties of the New York Fed in its implementation of monetary policy. This role includes the obligations to: (i) participate consistently in open market operations to carry out U.S. monetary policy pursuant to the direction of the Federal Open Market Committee (FOMC); and (ii) provide the New York Fed's trading desk with market information and analysis helpful in the formulation and implementation of monetary policy. Dealers trade with one another through interdealer brokers.

The treasury securities with the greatest amount of activity are those which were issued at the most recent auctions.

These are referred to as **on-the-run** securities. In a typical auction, the details of the securities issuance are announced by the Fed, and secondary market participants begin to trade on a when-issued basis through the primary dealers and with each other. Although the amount any particular dealer is limited to (to prevent market manipulation) dealers typically acquire large holdings in any auction in order to settle with clients. Previously issued securities are referred to as **off-the-run**. These securities have less trading liquidity and trade with higher yields.

Treasury Bills, Quotations and Trading Conventions

Treasury bills (T-bills) are issued with original maturities of one year or less. These obligations are issued without coupons. The purchaser acquires the obligation at a discount to its maturity (or face) value. The Treasury issues T-bills in denominations of $1,000. The difference between what the Treasury bill is purchased for and the amount it pays at maturity represents the amount earned by the holder if held to maturity. T-bills are quoted on a discounted basis. Thus, if a one-year t-bill is quoted at a discount of 1%, the purchaser pays $ 990,000 now for a maturity payment of $1,000,000 in one year. The difference of $10,000 represents the investor's earnings. Notice that the investor's actual yield is greater than 1% as the $10,000 was earned on an investment of only $ 990,000. The actual yield, referred to as the **bond equivalent yield** is $10,000/$990,000 or 1.01%. T-bills may also be bought and sold in the secondary market before their maturity date. All bond markets, including treasury markets, have trading conventions. One such convention involves day counting. When computing the discount and bond equivalent yield, the treasury market operates on the basis of an *"actual"* day month and a *365*-day year. Each market (treasury, corporate, municipal, etc) has their own conventions. The following table summarizes the day counting conventions applicable to each market.

Figure 4.1 - Table Summarizing the Day Counting Conventions and their Markets

Day Count Convention		Respective Markets
Days Per Month *Actual refers to standard Calendar Days	Days Per Year *Actual refers to standard Calendar Days	
30	360	- Corporate, Agency and Municipal Bonds - All Eurocurrency Bonds except Sterling
Actual	360	- Commercial Paper - T-Bills and other short-term (S-T) debt - Money Markets and S-T loan of currency
Actual	365 *fixed*	- Canadian, NZ and Australian money markets - All Sterling interest rates
Actual	365	- US Gov. Treasury Bills - Eurodenominated Bonds - Some USD interest rate swaps
Actual	Actual	- Some USD interest rate swaps

The non-coupon bearing nature of T-bills is an attractive feature to duration sensitive (reinvestment risk averse) investors. The investment matures at a sum certain without the need to reinvest intervening cash flows. In chapter three we discussed the challenge that buy-and-hold (investors such as pension funds) face when seeking to fund future liabilities. The type of cash flow structure in a T-bill is perfectly suited to eliminate this problem. The only problem is that T-bills are only issued with maturities of one year or less. As an insatiable borrower of funds, the Government quickly adapts to the needs of lenders.

Treasury Notes and Bonds

Treasury notes and treasury bonds are coupon bearing debt instruments issued with maturities of between two and 30 years. These obligations are quoted in terms of a percentage of their par value. Thus, a price of 100 denotes 100% of the bond or note's par value. These securities have a couple of quirks, however. Fractional prices are quoted in 32nds, not decimals. Thus, a quote of 97'03 means 97 and 3/32% of par or a percentage of 97.09375% of par value. Further, the coupons on these obligations are normally paid semi-annually. The holder of record on the coupon payment date gets the entire coupon regardless of how long it was held by that party. As a result, a trading convention evolved to settle up interest payments by intervening holders between coupon payment dates. This is called **accrued interest**. If bonds/notes trade between coupon dates, the purchaser pays not only the purchase price but also the amount of interest that was earned on the bond/note since the last payment date. In this way, everyone is made whole on the interest they are due up to the date a bond/note is sold. Once again there are day counting conventions that are unique to specific markets.

Treasury Inflation-Protected Securities (TIPS)

These securities are relative newcomers to the Treasury Market, having been initially introduced in 1997. TIPS are structured to address investor inflation concerns. The Treasury auctions TIPS intermittently with maturities up to 30 years. TIPS are coupon bearing, which are paid semiannually. Their maturity/principal value is indexed to inflation, and this is how TIPS are different from conventional Treasury securities. A TIPS coupon is fixed at the time of issuance, but it is applied to the inflation-adjusted principal, so coupon payments will fluctuate as the underlying principal value is adjusted for inflation. At maturity, investors receive the final interest payment and the inflation-adjusted principal (or the original principal, if that amount is higher).

U.S. Treasury Strips and a Brief History of Interest Rates in the United States

As I have pointed out earlier, the best way to understand market innovation is to examine the actual markets that the innovations took place in. The U.S. Treasury market is a case in point.

Beginning in 1971, interest rates began to rise dramatically in the United States. A perfect storm had gathered:

- 1971: the Vietnam War was winding down and the bills associated with it were all coming due. The "crowding out" effect, that is the government competing for capital, drove up interest rates.

- 1971: the Nixon administration took the dollar off of the gold standard. This led to a period of cheap money fueling inflation.

- 1973: oil and other energy related prices began to rise in 1973 as Middle Eastern oil exporting nations instituted an embargo in response to the 1973 Middle East War.

- 1974: political instability resulting from the Nixon resignation.

- 1976–1978: Carter era inflation.

- 1979: the Iranian Revolution delivers a second oil shock, sending oil prices (and related inflation) soaring.

- 1980: Ronald Reagan elected US president.

- 1981–1982: Interest rates peak, Fed Chairman Paul Volcker increases interest rates to combat inflation and a severe recession takes hold.

Figure 4.2 - Graph Presenting the Federal Funds Rate from 1971 - 1982

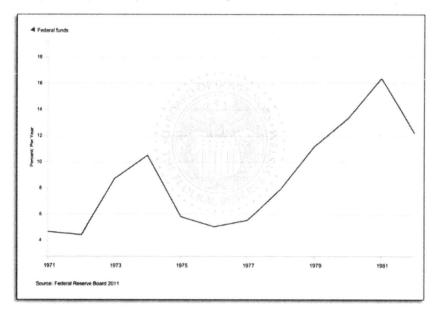

Source: Federal Reserve Economic Research and Data

During this 1971–1982 era, the winners and losers in the fixed income markets are fairly easy to identify; bond traders were getting battered in the face of rising interest rates while buy and hold investors are reaping a duration (excess reinvestment income) windfall. What happened next defined the marketplace. Ronald Reagan ran on and delivered upon election significant income tax cuts. When Congress failed to curtail spending, budget deficits of then unprecedented amounts appeared. Volcker was succeeding in taming inflation, the economy was in a severe recession, and interest rates fell dramatically.

Figure 4.3 Graph Presenting the Federal Funds Rate from 1982 - 1985

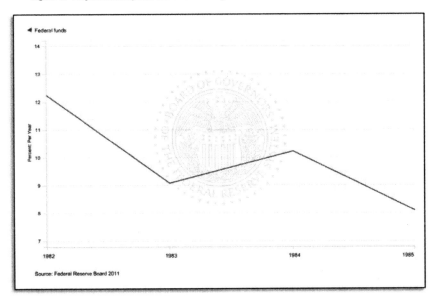

Source: Federal Reserve Economic Research and Data

Now the fortunes of bond market participants reversed. The great bond-trading era of the 1980s began as rates continued to fall. The impact of these falling rates was widespread and profound as we will continue to see in chapter five. The impact of falling interest rates on pension funds and other buy and hold investors was devastating. Falling interest rates ate into anticipated reinvestment income, and durations (the measure of reinvestment risk discussed in chapter three) began to extend. What the buy and hold investor crowd needed were long term bonds modeled after T-bills. In that way exposure to reinvestment income isn't a problem; simply buy T-bill like securities that mature at the same time liabilities must be paid. The perfect duration matching strategy.

This confluence of events corresponded with the modernization of settlement procedures in the securities markets. With government deficits exploding, the Fed was in a very accommodating mood, particularly to its traditional lender base, the pension fund and insurance company community. With the advent of paperless/book-entry treasury security trading, de-facto long term T-bills could be created by allowing the separate payments contained in treasury note/bond to be stripped off of the host obligation and traded independently. And that is exactly what happened.

Thus came into existence the **STRIPS program**, which the Treasury launched in 1985. STRIPS is an acronym which stands for Separate Trading of Registered Interest and Principal of Securities.

STRIPS are created through the disaggregation of regular treasury notes and treasury bonds. For example, a newly issued 10-year note could be stripped into 21 separate securities—20 representing the note's semiannual coupon payments and one representing its final principal payment. The new securities representing the now disaggregated coupon payments are called **coupon strips.** The security evidencing the right to the final principal payment is called a **principal strip.**

To an investor, STRIPS are really nothing more than long term T-bills. Each STRIP is issued its own CUSIP number. A CUSIP number is a type of serial number which uniquely identifies a security and allows for efficient settlement. CUSIP stands for Committee on Uniform Securities Identification Procedures. Coupon strips maturing on the same date, regardless of whether they were detached from the same host obligation or different host obligations, are given the same CUSIP. The principal strips are each given a unique CUSIP identifying it with the original host obligation from which it was separated.

Chapter
5

United States Agency Securities, Mortgage Backed Securities and the Beginning of Securitizations

Federal borrowing takes many shapes. In chapter four, we examined the manner in which the federal government finances its operations and accumulated deficits. As we saw, this is done with **direct** issuances of debt by the government facilitated by the operations of the primary dealer marker. The government also borrows money **indirectly**. These borrowings take the following forms:

1. Certain subdivisions of the government, called **federal agencies,** are authorized by Congress to borrow in their own name. Some of these agencies have the backing of the federal government in the form of guarantees. **Guarantees** can be **explicit**, in which case the full faith and credit of the U.S. government stands behind the debt. From a credit point of view, these are as safe as debt obligations issued directly by the U.S. government. In some instances the guarantee on agency obligations is **implicit**. These types of

guarantees are trickier since, as the name indicates, the guarantee is not absolute but rather assumed. These types of guarantees are rather controversial, particularly in the aftermath of the credit market collapse of 2008. Investors want to know how strong the credit quality of debt instruments they hold actually is without having to guess. Congress, and to a growing degree the general public, has become weary of guarantees as they represent a potential drain on dwindling public resources. The following is a representative list of federal agencies:

2. **Government sponsored enterprises** (GSE) are private corporations empowered by Congress to pursue a specific public purpose. Accordingly, GSEs are empowered by their Federal Government charter to achieve that mandated purpose. This often results in market -based advantages, such as being able to access public securities markets without the need to register securities with the Securities and Exchange Commission.

Figure 5.1 – GSE and Agency Securities

Bond Issuer	Full Name	GSE or Agency	Guarantee Implicit or Explicit
FFCB	*Federal Farm Credit Banks*	GSE	Implicit
FNMA	*Federal National Mortgage Association "Fannie Mae"*	GSE	Implicit
FHLMC	*Federal Home Loan Mortgage Corporation "Freddie Mac"*	GSE	Implicit
SLMA	*Student Loan Marketing Administration "Sallie Mae"*	GSE	Implicit
FHLB	*Federal Home Loan bank*	GSE	Implicit
PEFCO	*Private Export Funding Corporation*	Agency	Explicit
GNMA	*Government National Mortgage Association "Ginnie Mae"*	Agency	Explicit
SBA	*Small Business Administration*	Agency	Explicit
FHA	*Federal Housing Administration*	Agency	Explicit
VA	*Department of Veterans Affairs*	Agency	Explicit

Debt obligations of both of these types of entities are collectively called **agency securities.** The largest of the agency markets involves the financing of home mortgages. A brief history of mortgage finance will be helpful in understanding these markets.

1970s Era Home Mortgage Markets

The 1970s was a period in which the United States experienced a prolonged and profound period of inflation. The implications of this inflationary period became obvious in two interconnected markets, residential real estate and mortgage finance. As inflation began to accelerate, real asset prices climbed, particularly precious metals and real estate. The allure of owning financial assets was fading as inflation eroded the purchasing power of money. The action moved to real estate.

Figure 5.2 - Graph of Historical Home Values

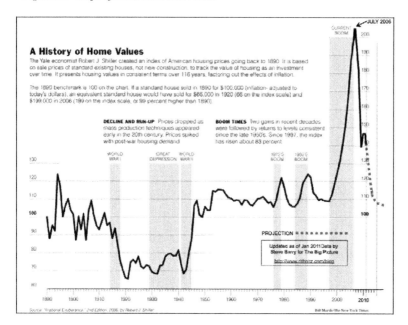

Source: http://www.ritholtz.com/blog/wp-content/uploads/2011/04/2011-Case-SHiller-updated.png

Figure 5.3 - Graph of Historical Gold Prices - Indicating Rise in the 1970's

Source: http://www.goldprice.org/spot-gold.html

Buying and financing homes was a relatively straightforward affair during this era. Virtually all home mortgages
were originated by local savings and loan institutions (S&Ls)
that held, rather than sold, the mortgages they originated.
The S&Ls took in deposits on which they paid interest at
prevailing market rates, subject however to statutory interest rate caps (more on the implications of this shortly). A
couple of observations:

1. The S&L had good reason to demand that borrowers
    meet stringent credit standards; the loan remained on
    the S&L's books and ultimate losses were incurred by
    the S&L directly.

2. Most mortgages originated during this era carried
    fixed rates. The S&L had to manage an important (but
    heretofore non-apparent) risk: funding gaps. Here the
    gap has two edges. First, the mortgage carried a fixed
    rate, but the deposits taken to fund them had to be
    paid competitive market rates of interest (again,
    subject to a soon to be discussed cap). Second, the
    mortgage had a lifespan of up to 30 years, but the
    deposits could be withdrawn at any time. This combi-
    nation of gaps creates a trap, and the S&Ls were
    ultimately consumed by it.

Let's work with an example. Let's assume its 1970. S&Ls are
paying 5% on deposits and making home mortgage loans at
7%. Until 1970, interest rates had been relatively stable.
With very little effort the S&L is earning a 200 basis point
spread (remember that 1 basis point equals 1/100th of 1%,
thus 200 basis points is 2%). If interest rates stay where they
are, the S&L continues to pocket this spread. What if interest rates fall? We are in an era where homeowner refinancing is not yet common; in fact, homeowners had to pay penalties for mortgage prepayments resulting from events other
than sales of the underlying homes. Thus, if interest rates
fall, the spread the institution earns increases as deposits

now command lower payment rates than the original 5%, yet the mortgage is still yielding 7%. Further, the value of the 7% mortgage is higher (as 7% is now above the now prevailing market and thus are attractive and more valuable asset in the hands of the S&L).

If interest rates rise, life at the S&L becomes decidedly unpleasant. The S&L is stuck with the 7% mortgage in a market environment in which new origination is at a higher rate. Worse yet, the costs of the deposits are increasing as rates go up. The spread earned by the S&L is shrinking. If deposit rates go above 7%, the S&L is now in a *negative* spread situation. If the cap the S&L can legally pay depositors is breached, the depositors will withdraw their money leaving the S&L unable to fund itself and continue to finance its mortgage portfolio. The risks and profits of these activities in fact fit nicely into the graphing technique we have already developed. **Both the funding activities and the portfolio ownership expose the S&L to a long risk to interest rates** (remember that being long interest rates means benefiting from lower rates and suffering when rates are higher).

Figure 5.4 - Payoff Graph for Funding and Portfolio Holdings

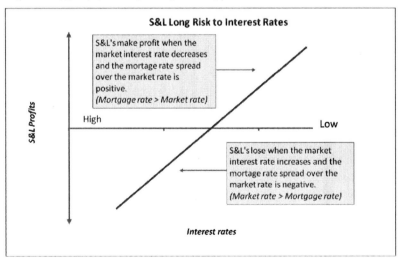

This parade of horribles is exactly what transpired as interest rates started to increase in the early 1970s. As rates
increased, S&Ls began to fail. When the statutory deposit
interest cap was breached, depositors began to pull money
out of the banking system in search of higher yielding
investments. Because of this, modern money market mutual
funds were developed. This flight of funds from the banking
system is called **disintermediation**. The American dream
was slipping away. Qualified homebuyers (meaning homebuyers with solid credit) were unable to find financing for
homes. Many of these homebuyers were returning Vietnam
War era veterans. The public demanded, and ultimately
received, a solution to this problem.

The funding gap issue on the S&L's books was the obvious
problem that needed fixing. What was needed was a mechanism to fund the origination of mortgages in a manner other
than the quirky deposit markets. The maturity of the funding had to match the maturity of the mortgage and the fixed-
rate mortgage/short-term deposit rate mismatch had to be
eliminated. In response, the U.S. government created the
securitization market, although it wasn't thought of in
those terms at the time.

The Government National Mortgage Association—
Securitizations 1.0

To eliminate the positioning and funding risk in the mortgage
origination process, the government looked to innovations
that were becoming available in the mortgage backed security market. The solution that presented itself follows.

1. Rather than have S&Ls borrow in the deposit market
    to fund/originate new mortgage loans, **mortgage
    backed securities (MBS)** were created. Investors
    purchase the MBS and the proceeds are used to pur-
    chase qualifying origination (more on this concept
    shortly) from participating financial institutions.

98

Thus, securities are sold to investors and the proceeds are used to purchase mortgages. This creates a new problem; if the underlying homeowner defaults on the mortgage, the security holder is left with the messy prospect of having to foreclose on the property.

2. To eliminate the need to foreclose, the mortgages are only made to borrowers who meet predetermined credit criteria and these mortgages are assembled as **pools**, or bundles of mortgages. These pools act as the payment source for the MBS. As interest and principal are collected on the mortgages contained within the pools, these amounts (net of certain expenses) are paid through to the MBS investors. This type of MBS is referred to as a **pass-through**. The interest rate paid on the security is lower than the interest rate of the underlying mortgages to allow for payment of servicing and guarantee fees. Note the elegance of the security in terms of solving the gap problem for S&Ls. S&Ls no longer borrow and carry the mortgages; rather they originate and sell them. The S&L earns compensation for originating the mortgage, typically in the form of an upfront fee. Each month they collect the mortgage payment from the homeowner and pass through the amounts to the MBS investors, net of a so-called **servicing fee**. Thus, the investor in the MBS provides funds which match the life of the mortgage. The credit risk of a default is eliminated by obtaining a timely payment guarantee from the **Government National Mortgage Association (GNMA).** The Government National Mortgage Association (GNMA) was created in 1968 to serve a relatively simple purpose: to provide a guarantee to investors for the timely payment of principal and interest on MBS backed by federally insured or guaranteed loans— mainly loans insured by the Federal Housing Adminis-

tration (FHA) or guaranteed by the Department of Veterans Affairs (VA).

Thus, a financing star was born. GNMA securities are the only MBS to carry the full faith and credit guaranty of the United States government.

Government Sponsored Entities and Mortgage Finance-The Federal National Mortgage Association and the Federal Home Loan Mortgage Corporation-The Early Years

Because of the importance home ownership has played in American policy decisions, Congress has periodically created institutions to facilitate that goal. The first such effort occurred in 1937, during the Great Depression, when the Federal National Mortgage Association (FNMA) was founded. Established as a GSE, FNMA became a publicly traded corporation in 1968 with a continuing federal mandate of providing liquidity into the home mortgage market. It now accomplishes this goal by purchasing mortgages originated consistent with its standards, bundling these mortgages into MBS, and selling these securities (with a FNMA guarantee) to investors. The funds generated are then used to originate more home mortgages. In 1970, Congress created the Federal Home Loan Mortgage Corporation (FHLMC), also a publicly traded corporation, to compete with FNMA. Thus, two mortgage behemoths came into existence to pursue an odd dual mandate: serve a **public purpose** of providing liquidity to residential mortgage markets while at the same time earning profits for its shareholders. This, as we shall see, is a difficult balancing act to accomplish.

The Mortgage Finance Triumvirate, GNMA, FNMA and FHLMC-The 1980s

As the inflation fueled 1970s came to a close, GNMA, FNMA, and FHLMC came to dominate the mortgage finance marketplace. The constituency that each served and the features of the securities that each entity issued or guaranteed are summarized as follows:

Figure 5.5 - Mortgage Finance Institutions-A Summary

Institution	Inception	Agenda	MBS Products	Agency security Type	Guarantee Type
GNMA	1968	To provide liquidity in the housing market and facilitate stable and accessible mortgage lending. They act as intermediaries between issuers and investors of mortgage backed securities.	Does NOT issue MBS's, *only* provides guarantee.	Federal Agency	Explicit (Backed by full faith of US Government)
FNMA	1937		DOES issue original MBS's *and* provides guarantee.	Government Sponsored Enterprise	Implicit (Backed by full faith of FNMA only)
FHLMC	1970		DOES issue original MBS's *and* provides guarantee.	Government Sponsored Enterprise	Implicit (Backed by full faith of FHLMC only)

Investment Performance of MBS and Participation Certificates in the Face of Falling Interest Rates

MBS are securitized interests in a pool of mortgages. It is a type of debt instrument. Holders of the MBS receive the cash flows from the pool of mortgages that are bundled to create the MBS. MBS come in a number of different forms. The simplest form of MBS are pass-through or participation certificates. With these structures, all principal and interest payments (less a servicing fee) from the pool of mortgages are passed directly to investors each month.

In a typical 30-year fixed-rate residential mortgage of this era, homeowners make a fixed payment each month until its maturity. These mortgages are said to be self-amortizing; each payment represents a partial repayment of principal along with interest on the outstanding principal. Over time, as more of the principal is paid off, the size of the interest payment declines. Accordingly, the portion of each payment representing principal repayment increases over the life of the mortgage. This is illustrated as follows:

Figure 5.6 - Scheduled Cash Flows for a 30-Year Self Amortizing Fixed-Rate Mortgage

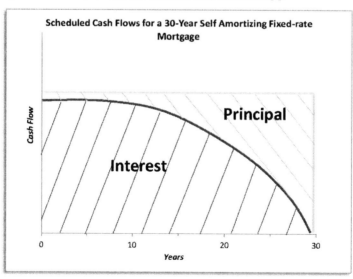

Each mortgage contained in the pool is subject to its own amortization schedule. There is a significant variation of actual payments from this schedule, however. This is because homeowners have the right to refinance or otherwise prepay their mortgages. When a homeowner prepays, the principal prepayment is paid to investors in the pass-through. This changes the expected cash flows to the investors in the MBS, who receive the principal payments earlier than originally anticipated. As the principal balances of the mortgages included in the pool decline, so do the future interest payments that would have been made on that principal. Investors in MBS will need to forecast the levels of these prepayments in order to be able to accurately compute the yields they will earn on these investments and to otherwise properly plan to use the cash that is being generated from their investment portfolios. As we discussed earlier, the population of investors in debt instruments is not monolithic; some are in the market to speculate on the direction of interest rates to earn trading profits; others hold the investments to match the cash flows with known liabilities. Thus the homeowner's right to refinance or otherwise prepay their mortgages presents a serious quantitative dilemma to the MBS investor.

Prepayments introduce uncertainty into the cash flows of a mortgage pass-through. In the 1970s/early 1980s time period, the vast majority of home mortgages were standard, 30-year fixed-rate loans. The rate at which homeowners with these types of loans prepay is influenced by a number of factors. By far the most significant factor is the level of interest rates. Homeowners with fixed rate mortgages will refinance when mortgage rates fall. When they do so, a new mortgage is taken out on the house, and the proceeds are used to retire (prepay) the original, higher interest rate loan. By doing so, <u>both</u> constituencies of bond investors are adversely affected. A bond owner who bought the MBS as a trading vehicle to speculate interest rates will not enjoy price appreciation as interest rates fall. **This is an example of negative convexity** that was discussed in chapter three. Separately, the investor that purchased the MBS to provide cash flows to pay off liabilities (pension funds, insurance companies, etc) will also have a problem. Although they had no intention of trading the MBS, the prepayments return funds to the investor that must now be reinvested at a lower interest rate than anticipated. Worse yet, not only are interest coupon payments being reinvested at lower than expected interest rates but the MBS is returning principal quicker than expected, and those must be reinvested as well. This exacerbates the duration risk problem we also discussed in chapter three. This is exactly what happened in the early 1980s as interest rates began to fall.

Analyzing Prepayments

The *right* to refinance or prepay is just that; it's a right, not an obligation. In this regard, this privilege can be conceptualized as an option. Let's look at the respective positions of the homeowner and the MBS investor in the following payoff graphs:

Figure 5.7 - Payoff Graphs Comparing the Synthetic Put Option Positions a MBS Creates

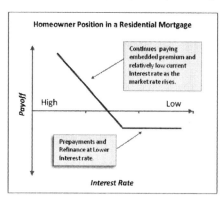
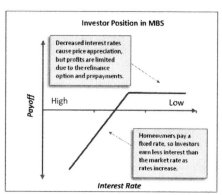

The graphs that emerge resemble put options. In fact, **synthetic** puts are created by combining the original mortgage with the embedded right to prepay/refinance. Absent the refinancing privilege, the homeowner would be short interest rates and the investor would be long interest rates. Remember that being long interest rates is accomplished when one benefits from lower rates and suffers from higher rates. A short position to interest rates results when you benefit from higher rates and suffer from lower rates. This is analogized from owning or selling short fixed-interest bearing obligations, whose prices would move inversely to interest rates.

Figure 5.8 – Homeowner and Investor Positions without Refinancing Option

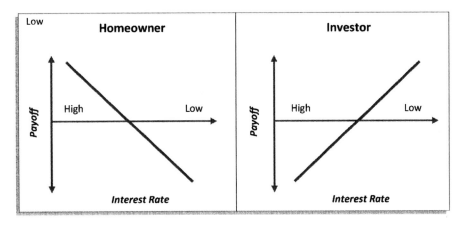

The homeowner's refinancing/prepayment right resembles
an option we recognize as a call option. Extending the fixed
income security analogy, the refinancing/prepayment right
would be exercised when rates are falling, but not (normally)
when rates are rising. If rates rise, the rational homeowner
will remain with the original mortgage and continue to pay
the embedded premium for the future right to refinance. The
homeowner doesn't acquire this option for free; he pays for it
in his mortgage rate.

Figure 5.9 – The Embedded Refinancing Privilege

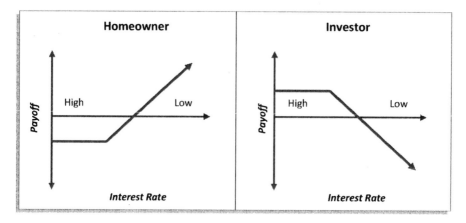

The synthetic put option that emerged in Figure 5.7 is the combination of the mortgage position illustrated in Figure 5.8 and the embedded call option illustrated in Figure 5.9.

An interesting observation now comes into focus. We've discussed three different types of MBS: GNMAs, FNMAS and FHLMCs. As we have discussed, GNMA is directly guaranteed by the US Government; FNMA and FHLMC are guaranteed by the GSE entities. It stands to reason that yields on FNMA/FHLMC MBS will be above GNMA as more credit risk is being absorbed by the investor. Why then do GNMAs yield more than treasuries? The answer lies in the prepayment risk. **The incremental yield that GNMAs pay above Treasuries is the amount the homeowner is paying for the embedded prepayment option**. The amount by which yields on FNMA/FHLMC exceed GNMAs is attributable to the difference in credit quality. Thus, to compensate investors for taking prepayment risk, MBS offer higher yields than comparable fixed income instruments without embedded options.

The Development of MBS Metrics

The key to understanding MBS lies in the ability to predict the manner in which the embedded option is likely to behave. This is not as straight forward as it may appear at first blush. Although interest rates decline, homeowners may not all refinance. Here is a partial list of things that might influence the decision:

- Refinancing is not cost free; significant legal and other costs must be borne by the homeowner. Thus not only must interest rates fall, they must fall by enough to compensate for the costs associated with refinancing.

- There is no "bright line" drop in rates in which homeowners will jump at the refinancing opportunity. Some will refinance in the face of modest drops; others may

want to take the risk of interest rates falling still
further.

- Some homeowners may be considering moving and
  won't refinance regardless of the size of the drop in
  rates.

- Some homeowners may no longer be credit worthy or
  may not have equity in the home to support a newly
  originated mortgage. This phenomenon is now more
  significant in the face of the credit crisis of 2008/2009
  and the associated collapse in housing prices in many
  regions of the United States.

- Through ignorance, laziness, or worse, homeowners
  don't act in their best interests when the opportunity
  presents itself.

Further, prepayments may occur when you don't expect
them. Homeowners could prepay as interest rates are rising.
These are almost certainly not refinancing but sales or voluntary prepayments being made by homeowners seeking to
extinguish their loans early. In short, this option has **ir-
rational features.** Homeowners may not refinance at times
when they should and may also prepay when it appears that
they shouldn't. In the late 1970s and early 1980s the manner
in which prepayments were estimated and quoted were ad-
hoc and subjective. Because of the pervasive influence of
prepayments on valuing and evaluating risks associated
MBS, the industry needed to develop standardized metrics
for prepayment. This occurred in the early 1980s through a
study conducted through the Federal Home Loan Bank
System, another GSE with lending mandates in the United
States.

The key to the exercise lies in the practical inability to
interview actual homeowners whose mortgages found themselves in MBS pools. Statistics needed to be developed that
could answer two simple questions concerning any particu-

lar MBS: how has it prepaid in the past and how was it projected to prepay in the future? The answer to the first question is a matter of verifiable historical fact; the second requires critical analysis to determine its relative correctness. What emerged was an attempt to quantify prepayment propensity without regard to underlying cause, rather what was measured is the estimated amount of prepayment from all sources. To that end the most basic metric, which still serves as the key building block for the standardized models is called **single monthly mortality** (SMM). It indicates, for any given month, the fraction of mortgages principal that had not prepaid by the beginning of the month but does prepay during the month. For computational purposes, if a mortgage does prepay in a given month, its scheduled principal payment for that month is not considered part of the prepayment.

SMM is then used to build what has come to be known as the **Constant Prepayment Rate Model** (CPR), which is an annualized SMM metric. Specifically, CPR indicates, for any given year, the fraction of mortgages principal that had not prepaid at the beginning of the **year** that does prepay during the year.

Thus, a standard means of communication to express the potential for a pool of mortgages to prepay over its lifetime developed. The shortcoming of this approach, of course, is that a constant CPR projection is not realistic. However, it can be useful for communicating the potential for a given pool to prepay. Further, this methodology fosters comparisons between pools. Another thing that this method ignores is the delicate state of the human condition. Prepayment behavior will differ depending in part on which segment of the lifespan of the mortgage you are examining. People are less likely to refinance early in the mortgage (because they are now broke, they just bought the house). The dealer group encouraging the development of these statistics, the Public Securities Association introduced a metric for projecting prepayments over the life of a pool. This was coined the **Prepayment Speed Assumption**. The metric is called **PSA**. A pool is said to have 100% PSA if its CPR starts at 0 and increases by 0.2% each month until it reaches 6% in month 30 (the likely time it would take a homeowner to rebuild their savings and make the refinancing decision solely on the merits). It is a constant 6% after that. A PSA of 50% indicates CPRs that are half those of 100% PSA. A PSA of 150% indicates CPRs that are one-and-a-half those of 100% PSA. This is illustrated as follows:

Figure 5.10 - Prepayment Speed Assumption Illustrated

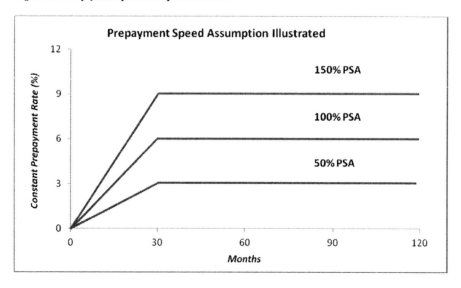

Note that PSA indicates prepayment *rates*. It assumes a constant rate after 30 months, but actual *cash flows* due to prepayment decline over time as outstanding principal is reduced. This is illustrated as follows:

Figure 5.11 – Cash Flow Differences Arising from Varying PSA's

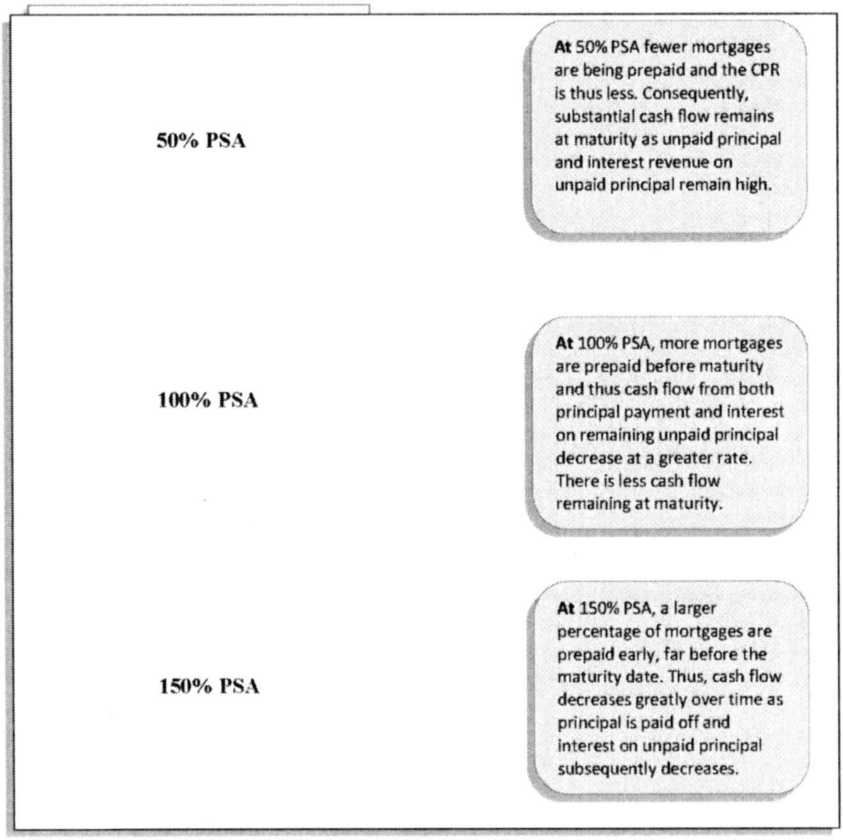

50% PSA	At 50% PSA fewer mortgages are being prepaid and the CPR is thus less. Consequently, substantial cash flow remains at maturity as unpaid principal and interest revenue on unpaid principal remain high.
100% PSA	At 100% PSA, more mortgages are prepaid before maturity and thus cash flow from both principal payment and interest on remaining unpaid principal decrease at a greater rate. There is less cash flow remaining at maturity.
150% PSA	At 150% PSA, a larger percentage of mortgages are prepaid early, far before the maturity date. Thus, cash flow decreases greatly over time as principal is paid off and interest on unpaid principal subsequently decreases.

With the development of these statistics, standardized
methodologies of communication and valuation became
available. Now all market participants speak the same
language and are able to use the same valuation methods.
The following box illustrates how PSA models are used to
value MBS.

Figure 5.12 – PSA and MBS Value

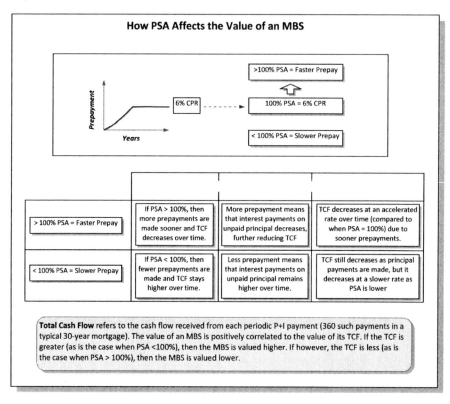

By 1983, with interest rates dropping, the embedded option made MBS unattractive as a stand-alone investment. The dilemma: separating the embedded option (the prepayment right) from the mortgage. Once separated, the option could be sold to one group of investors and the debt instrument to another. The collateralized mortgage obligation provided the mean of accomplishing this.

Collateralized Mortgage Obligations and the Genesis of Securitizations

It is hard to overstate the importance, and impact, that the development of the **collateralized mortgage obligation** (CMO) had on a variety of debt markets. It was originally developed to address the dearth of investors willing to take the duration-based optionality risk associated with holding MBS. To achieve this goal, rather than have investors purchase the MBS directly, the investors purchased debt instruments issued by an intervening entity (called a special purpose entity, or SPE) which in turn held the MBS. The SPE was precluded from engaging in any other business activity; thus, owners of SPE-issued debt securities took only the credit risk associated with the SPE's ownership of the MBS. The MBS, remember, has guarantees of either the U,S. Government (GNMA) or of the issuing GSEs (FNMA/ FHLMC). Thus, the debt issued by the SPEs had significant credit enhancement in the form of these guarantees.

U.S. Agency Securities, Mortgage Backed Securities, Beginning of Securitizations

Figure 5.13 – Diagram Showing CMO Security and Origin

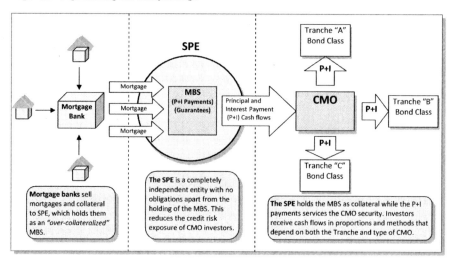

Mortgage banks sell mortgages and collateral to SPE, which holds them as an *"over-collateralized"* MBS.

The SPE is a completely independent entity with no obligations apart from the holding of the MBS. This reduces the credit risk exposure of CMO investors.

The SPE holds the MBS as collateral while the P+I payments services the CMO security. Investors receive cash flows in proportions and methods that depend on both the Tranche and type of CMO.

114

CMOs are actually a type of MBS derivative. Unlike a MBS, in which all investors participate proportionately in the net cash flows from the mortgage (and thus share in the embedded option risk), in a CMO issuance through a SPE, as illustrated above, different bond classes are issued. These bonds, called tranches (tranche means "slice" in French) participate in different components of the net cash flows. A CMO is any one of those bonds, so called because the obligation issued by the SPE is collateralized by the MBS the SPE holds. The tranches are structured to allocate cash flows from the underlying MBS on a predetermined basis. In this way, investors can select a bond offering the characteristics which most closely meet their needs.

The manner in which CMOs are structured is limited only by the imagination and investor appetite. One of the earliest structures, meant to address the problem of the embedded option in a MBS, is a **sequential pay** structure. This usually involves three (or more) tranches that mature sequentially. All tranches participate in interest payments from the mortgage collateral, but initially, only the first tranche receives principal payments. It receives all principal payments until it is retired. Once the first tranche has been retired, all principal payments are paid to the second tranche until it is retired, and the process is continued until the entire series is paid down. By allocating prepayments from the MBS to retire earlier tranches first, the SPE/CMO structure has the effect of partitioning the embedded option in a way that gives a greater share of the option to tranche one holders and less to later tranches.

Chapter
6

Municipal Securities

General Considerations

Municipal securities are issued by state and local governments and their political subdivisions. They include securities issued by agencies or authorities established by those governments. These entities administer toll roads, utility associations, and other comparable revenue generating municipal and state services. Most of these obligations are issued to finance traditional government operations and infrastructure, although they may also be issued to facilitate economic development within the state by providing debt subsidies to corporations. The latter type is referred to as private activity bonds.

Interest on most municipal obligations is exempt from federal income tax. There is elaborate constitutional history surrounding this issue, specifically pitting the rights of the several states against the power of the federal government. Under current judicial interpretations, congress has a right to tax interest income from municipal securities, but it chooses not to where the bonds are used to finance traditional governmental services. In certain circumstances, interest on bonds used to pursue activities related to economic development outside of traditional state functions (such as subsidizing the construction of a factory for a private corporation) are subject to tax. These bonds are called **private activity bonds**. Further, most states also exempt interest on securities issued by in-state issuers from their own taxes, which makes those securities particularly attractive investments

116

for their own residents. Gains and losses from selling the obligations are not afforded these tax exemptions and are fully taxable as capital gains or losses.

Because of their tax-exempt status, municipal obligations pay interest at a rate below obligations of the United States or corporations. In order to compare the yields on municipal obligations with their fully taxable counterparts, one can either:

1. compare what is left on two (or more) investment opportunities <u>after</u> taxes are paid, or

2. compute the fully **taxable equivalent yield** which would be required to keep the yield generated by a municipal obligation not subject to income taxes.

The market convention is to compute taxable equivalent yields. Keep in mind that tax positions are highly personal and will differ from person to person. Also keep in mind that municipal obligations can, and do, default. Therefore, to be comparable, the credit quality of the municipal obligation and the taxable alternative must also be comparable. That having been said, the standard formula for computing taxable equivalent yields is:

$$Taxable\ Equivalent\ Yield = \frac{Municipal\ Yield}{1 - Marginal\ Tax\ Rate}$$

This indicates the yield a comparable taxable bond would have to earn in order to be equivalent, after taxes, to the yield available on the untaxed municipal obligation. Note that to complete this computation we consider the **marginal tax rate** of the investor. This is the rate of tax that would be paid on the next dollar of income. For many reasons, using average tax rates is distortive. Remember, the taxable equivalent yield depends on the specific investor's marginal tax rate. Further, interest on municipal obligations is not always tax exempt.

General Issues Concerning Income Taxation

In the United States, individuals and other investors need to file annual tax returns. Income from all sources must be declared on these forms. Certain expenses and exemptions are deductible from income. The amount by which income exceeds these deductions is referred to as **taxable income**. The taxpayer then is required to apply a tax rate schedule to this taxable income to determine the amount of tax due the government. The rate schedule which is used is dependent upon the marital status of the taxpayer and the components of the income being declared (certain categories of income are taxed at lower tax rates). This is referred to as the **regular tax system**.

Because of the perception that the nation's wealthiest taxpayers were able to avoid the payment of taxes through the use of available deductions, Congress enacted the **Alternative Minimum Tax (AMT)**. Under the AMT, the taxpayer is required to compute their tax obligation a second time, this time with far fewer deductions and exemptions allowed. The amount of tax the taxpayer is obligated to pay is the higher of the regular tax or the AMT. A given taxpayer's marginal tax rate will be dependent upon whether or not the AMT applies. Chapter 15 contains a complete discussion on the tax consequences of investment decisions.

118

Interest on some municipal obligations is taxed under the AMT. These obligations are called **AMT bonds**. If a state/municipality issues debt to fund a commercial enterprise, such as a factory, warehouse, or entertainment facility, the securities are called **private activity bonds**. Congress decided that extending a full tax exemption to obligations issued for these purposes was not consistent with the policy objectives favoring tax-exempt status. Because these bonds may be taxed, AMT bonds pay interest rates above normal tax-exempt obligations. Note, however, that AMT bonds are only taxable if one is in the AMT, not if they are subject to the regular tax system. Thus, an investor not in the AMT reaps a windfall on these bonds. If a taxpayer is in the AMT, the additional yield is usually insufficient to pay the AMT tax.

Issuer and Dealer Restrictions

To prevent municipalities from issuing debt at tax-free yields and reinvesting the proceeds at higher rates, the tax code can revoke the tax exemption on otherwise qualifying municipal obligations rendering the interest taxable to investors. Also, to prevent tax arbitrage by securities dealers, any interest paid to finance a position in municipal obligations is not deductible by the dealer in computing their income tax liability.

Credit Risk in Municipal Obligations

Unlike direct debt of the Federal government, municipal obligations entail credit risk. There have been several municipal bankruptcies, with a growing perception that more are likely, so the risk of default is real. (On October 12, 2011, the city of Harrisburg, Pennsylvania announced its intention to file for bankruptcy protection under Chapter 9 of the US Bankruptcy Code.) Municipal obligations are rated by the nation's credit rating agencies (the roles of which are described in detail in chapter seven) in a manner similar to corporate obligations. Some municipal obligations are issued with insurance against default and nonpayment by third-party insurers. This may include an actual insurance policy, a surety bond, or other payment guarantee.

Municipal Bonds

Similar to U.S. Treasury obligations, these typically pay semiannual coupons with a bullet maturity payment. Some issues provide for periodic payments of principal (sinking funds) or can have other payment features, such as long-term zero coupon structures. The payment sources for municipal obligations generally fall into broad categories:

1. Tax-backed bonds and general obligation bonds are backed by tax revenues or user fees. Some are backed by general tax revenue, others from taxes or user fees from specific sources (sales taxes or other fees).

2. Revenue bonds are issued to finance specific projects, the revenue on which is used to pay the debt service required by the indebtedness. These can include toll roads, university tuitions, or facility user fees. It is important to note that these types of obligations <u>do not</u> carry the backing of the broader taxing power of the state or municipality. The bonds are usually labeled in a way that identifies the underlying project.

Just as the U.S. Government needs to periodically refinance its debt, so do state and local governments. This is done through a process called **refunding**. Refunded bonds are tax-backed (or revenue bonds), the proceeds of which the issuer has earmarked to retire other outstanding bonds. The issuer hasn't retired the original debt at the point of the new issuance, possibly because the original debt obligations can't be retired until a specific date (referred to as non-callable bonds). In a related transaction, sometimes called a defeasance, the issuer may choose to issue debt to purchase a portfolio of other issuer's bonds, which are placed in escrow or a trust for the benefit of the existing bondholders.

Shorter Term Municipal Obligations

Municipal notes have maturities from three months to three years. These can be either issued as discount instruments or can be coupon bearing. Often, notes are issued to address mismatches in the timing of operating expenses and anticipated revenues.

Tax and Revenue Anticipation Notes

State, cities, and municipal subdivisions often borrow in anticipation of receiving funds from tax collections or other revenue producing sources. These can include tax anticipation notes (TANs) which are issued in anticipation of tax revenues or revenue anticipation notes (RANs) which are issued in anticipation of other revenues, such as federal aid or other specific sources.

Chapter 7

Corporate Capital Structures Corporate Bonds and Loans

Corporate Funding Alternatives

Corporations may enter the capital markets in a number of ways to fund their activities. They can access the public capital markets and borrow money and issue corporate IOUs called **bonds**. Bonds are securities which entitle the holder to the payment of interest and the repayment of principal. As such, holders of bonds and other debt instruments have legal **claims** on a corporation's assets. Bonds are securities. Accordingly, the issuance of bonds must comply with various provisions of the securities laws. Once issued, the bonds are normally traded in the secondary markets.

Corporations may also take on indebtedness in the form of a direct loan from a bank or another lender. These obligations also call for the payment of interest and the repayment of principal. Loans also represent a claim on a corporation's assets. Unlike bonds, **loans are not securities** but represent a private contractual relationship between borrower and lender. Although loans (and loan participations) do change hands in a secondary market, they are not publicly traded, and the market for these instruments has significantly less liquidity than bond markets.

Corporations may alternatively choose to issue securities evidencing ownership in the entity; these securities are referred to as **equities** or **stock**. The corporation can issue either **common stock** or **preferred stock**. The holders of these instruments do not have a claim on the corporation's assets; they have what is referred to as an **interest**.

A share of common stock is the basic ownership unit in a corporation. Common stock has the last right to be paid in the event the corporation is liquidated. Owners of common stock participate in the success of the enterprise through periodic distributions of income, called dividends, or through the reinvestment of profits in the company. Dividends only become legally payable upon declaration by the corporation's board of directors, who are normally elected through a vote of the common stockholders. Dividends may only be paid from current or accumulated earnings and profits, after required dividends on preferred stock (discussed below) are paid. Owners of common stock are said to take on the enterprise risk of the entity.

The corporation may also issue preferred stock. The preference relates to two separate potential payments. First, preferred stockholders have payment priority upon liquidation of the corporation. The liquidation preference is in the amount of the **par** (or **stated**) value of the shares. The par or stated value is established at the time of issuance. Preferred stockholders are also paid periodic dividends before dividends may be paid to common stockholders. The dividends may be fixed or variable, but must also be declared by the board of directors before they become legally payable. As dividends are only payable from current or accumulated earnings and profits, there may be periods in which there are insufficient amounts available to declare and pay dividends. Generally, each year stands on its own; if in any given year there are insufficient current or accumulated earnings to declare dividends, no amounts are paid on account of that year. Thus, any claim to the dividend for that year is lost unless the preferred stock has a **cumulative dividend preference**. With a cumulative feature, any dividends on the preferred stock which have not been paid in prior years must be caught up before any dividends may be paid on common shares. Generally, preferred shares do not share in the profits of the corporation beyond any rights the holder has to dividend distributions. In many ways preferred stocks have characteristics of debt instruments, but have fewer protections and normally earn a higher rate of return. Preferred stocks are sometimes referred to as hybrid securities. Collectively, claims and interests comprise what is called a corporation's **capital structure**. In this chapter we will examine debt obligations representing claims on corporate assets, bonds and loans. In chapter eight we shall examine corporate equity interests.

Corporate Bond Markets, Credit Risks and the Bankruptcy Process

We briefly examined credit risk in chapter three. In order to understand corporate bonds and loans and their place in the corporate capital structure, we must first have a basic understanding of the bankruptcy system.

A bankruptcy proceeding normally commences when a corporation has fewer assets than are necessary to meet all of the claims against it. A bankruptcy proceeding can be initiated by the corporation or by its creditors. When initiated by the corporation, the proceeding is called a **voluntary bankruptcy**. When initiated by the corporation's creditors, it is referred to as an **involuntary proceeding.** Many people are surprised to learn that the law discourages involuntary proceedings. A sense of fairness suggests that parties due payment should be able to enforce their claims if payment is not made. The overwhelming majority of bankruptcy cases in the United States are voluntary filings.

First, the basic ground rules. Filing for bankruptcy is not a criminal offense or evidence of a moral deficit. In the nineteenth century, there were in fact criminal implications associated with certain bankruptcies. Debtor prisons existed to house those unable or unwilling to make good on their debts. In 1898, the first of the major bankruptcy reforms moved the proceedings into a civil forum. The bankruptcy code in the United States (Title 11 of the U.S. Code) now has a clear policy dictate; it is much more desirable to reorganize bankrupt debtors than to liquidate them. The policy statements embedded within the Code clearly encourage that a debtor seek the refuge of the court system to enable continuation of an enterprise in a reorganized form. This is often called the "fresh start" approach to bankruptcy.

Voluntary Bankruptcies-The Basic Steps

The bankruptcy process normally begins with the filing of a bankruptcy **petition** in federal bankruptcy court by the debtor seeking protection from creditors. Absent a successful allegation of fraud, the debtor will continue to control the process until creditor approval of a reorganization plan is sought, which occurs later. A petition is a request for relief of the court. By filing the petition, the debtor is requesting the court issue what is referred to as a "**stay**" order, which precludes creditors from enforcing their claims while the bankruptcy proceeding is in progress. Enforcement of claims by creditors during the bankruptcy process generally requires approval of the bankruptcy judge. The bankruptcy court is a special part of the federal judiciary with its own rules and procedures. Decisions of the bankruptcy court may be appealed to the federal district court in the district where the bankruptcy court sits. District court decisions may be appealed to the appropriate federal circuit court of appeals. These appeals are as a matter of right. Decisions of the circuit court of appeals may be appealed to the Supreme Court, but the Supreme Court may decide not to hear the case. In limited situations, decisions of the bankruptcy court may be appealed directly to the Court of Appeals, thus bypassing the district court.

The issuance of the stay order gets the ball rolling. Upon issuance of the stay order, the debtor is generally not required to make any interest or principal payments on pre-petition claims. Every bankruptcy case implicates four chapters of the bankruptcy code. Chapters 1, 3, and 5 are common to all proceedings. These are sometimes collectively referred to as the "administrative" chapters. Chapter 1 contains general provisions, chapter 3 deals with case administration, and chapter 5 deals with the bankruptcy "estate." When a bankruptcy filing is made, by definition there are insufficient assets to meet all claims against the corporation. Thus, a bankruptcy estate comes into existence into which assets are gathered for ultimate distribution to creditors. The objective is to sort the creditors into groups that will share in the assets that are ultimately marshaled. Some classes of creditors stand earlier in line than others.

The fourth chapter which comes into play in a bankruptcy is the so-called "operative" chapter. In the context of a corporate bankruptcy, chapter 7 deals with liquidations, and chapter 11 deals with reorganizations. (Chapter 9 deals with certain municipal bankruptcies, chapter 12 with family farms, chapter 13 with individuals, and chapter 15 with international cases.

Upon the issuance of the stay order, the corporate case will either be a chapter 7 or chapter 11. In a chapter 7 filing, the assets of the bankrupt estate are distributed to creditors depending upon their relative priority. Assets are distributed first to favored classes and then to other, less favored classes, based on availability of assets. Similarly situated creditors share equally in assets available to satisfy the claims of their class. This is referred to as "equitable distribution." This process normally occurs under the direction of a Trustee who is named by the court for the purpose of marshaling the assets and overseeing the liquidation.

In a chapter 11 case, the assets are also marshaled, but the entity is not liquidated. Rather, holders of prepetition claims and interests surrender those instruments and receive new claims and interests in the post bankruptcy entity. Normally claims holders will surrender their existing claims and receive debt and equity securities in the post-bankruptcy entity. As there are typically insufficient assets to satisfy the claim holders, equity interests in the pre-petition bankrupt debtor become worthless. The terms of this reorganization exchange are determined by the contents of the **reorganization plan**. In a chapter 11 case, there is normally no trustee; the bankrupt debtor operates the business subject to court oversight and approval. The bankrupt debtor is referred to as a **debtor-in-possession**, or **DIP**. The DIP has the exclusive right to offer the reorganization plan for the first 18 months following the filing of the bankruptcy petition, subject to court sanctioned extensions. Once filed, the reorganization plan is subject to approval by the creditor groups. If approval cannot be obtained, the creditors then have the right to offer competing plans. The ultimate approval by the creditors creates an opportunistic market for debtor debt securities after the original filing of the bankruptcy petition. Creditors may not want to ride out the bankruptcy proceeding and may choose instead to sell their claims.

Priority of Claims and Capital Structure of a Corporation

As can be seen, not all claims on a corporation have equal standing to its assets in the event of a bankruptcy. The priority of the claim depends upon where the claim stands in a company's capital structure and whether the claim arose before of after the bankruptcy petition was filed.

Only pre-petition debts are affected by the stay order. Debts incurred after the stay order has been filed are subject to special rules. Consistent with the objectives of the bankruptcy code, reorganizations are encouraged to provide the bankrupt debtor with a fresh start. Accordingly, special incentives are provided to allow bankrupt debtors access to fresh capital. The most common of these types of financings are referred to as **debtor-in-possession, or DIP, financing.** These claims have higher priority than pre-petition debt. Other claims incurred during the administration of the bankruptcy, referred to collectively as administrative claims, also have priority to pre-petitions debts of the corporation. These include fees of bankruptcy professionals and other select service providers to the now bankrupt debtor. Most tax obligations of the debtor, whether incurred before or after the filing, also enjoy priority standing.

Pre-Petition Claims and Interests, Standing in Bankruptcy

Think of the pre-petition claims and interests as a line forming at the door of the bankruptcy court. The order of the line will generally be as follows:

1. **Secured claims** These types of debt claims have specific collateral pledged as security for the loan. The collateral interest is called a **lien.** This is a publicly filed attachment providing the lien holder with the highest form of credit protection. Although a stay order will generally delay a lien holder from immediately enforcing their claim, the asset acting as collateral can only be used to satisfy the secured party. The secured party's claim, however, is only protected up to the fair market value of the collateral. If the assets which act as collateral are worth less than the claim, the party is only secured to the extent of the fair value of the collateral. The remaining portion is unsecured and falls further back in the line. This is called a **cram down.** In this situation, the creditor's pre-petition claim is only partially secured.

2. **Senior claims** These are claims in which there is no specific collateral but other forms of claim protection exist, usually in the form of **covenants**. Covenants are contractual protections embedded in the bond or loan. These covenants typically provide for acceleration clauses (the right for the creditor to accelerate demand for repayment in the event a covenant is breached). The terms of the covenant may provide for mandatory debtor profitability levels, working capital, or other financial terms. Senior claims normally are the party first in line after secured claimholders.

3. **Unsecured claims** These are the general debts of the corporation. They include amounts due suppliers, service providers, and other general creditors. These are normally the last claims to be paid in a bankruptcy proceeding, and because of their junior status, the class of creditor that gets paid the least in the event of liquidation. It is also the class being paid less than their entire pre-petition claim that normally receives equity securities in the post bankruptcy company in reorganization.

4. **Preferred stocks (interest)** This is the equity security described earlier in this chapter that stands after all debt claims but before the common stockholders. Now that we have described the claims, let's review the terms of the preference. The preference relates to two separate issues. First, preferred stockholders are paid first upon liquidation of the corporation. The liquidation preference is in the amount of the **par** (or **stated**) value of the shares. The par or stated value is established at the time of issuance. Preferred stockholders are also paid periodic dividends before dividends may be paid to common stockholders. The dividends may be fixed or variable, but to be legally payable must first be declared by the board of direc-

tors before they become legally payable. As dividends are only payable from current or accumulated earnings and profits, there may be periods in which there are insufficient amounts available to declare and pay dividends. Generally each year stands on its own; if there are insufficient earnings to declare dividends, no amounts are paid on account of that year. Thus, any claim to the dividend for that year is lost unless the preferred stock has a cumulative dividend feature. With a cumulative feature, any dividends on the preferred stock which have not been paid in prior years must be caught up before any new dividends may be paid. Generally, preferred shares do not share in the profits of the corporation beyond any rights the holder has to dividend distributions.

5. **Common stocks (interest)** This is the end of the bankruptcy ordered payment line. As previously stated, a share of common stock is the basic ownership unit in a corporation. Common stock has the last right to be paid in the event the corporation is liquidated. Owners of common stock participate in the success of the enterprise through periodic distributions of dividends or through the reinvestment of profits in the company. Owners of common stock are said to take on the enterprise risk of the entity.

Capital Structures, Credit Ratings and the Cost of Borrowed Money

Now that we can see the different positions that various creditors find themselves in the event of a corporate failure, it stands to reason that not all debt issued by the same corporation will have the same credit rating or bear the same level of borrowing costs. In the risk-reward world of investing, the higher the risk an investor takes on, the higher the level of compensation they expect. Thus, in a given corporation's capital structure one would expect that claims with lower risks (secured claims) would be rated higher and thus pay less of an interest rate than riskier debt classes such as unsecured debt. Many credit analysts will study the relative position of one class to another in a corporation's capital structure to determine if the market is accurately pricing these risks. If they determine that one class of bonds is selling at too high a price (and therefore paying too little in the way of interest) and another class is trading too cheaply, this belief can be exploited in a trade known as **capital structure arbitrage**. In this trade, you buy the cheap security and sell the expensive one, waiting for the market to properly value the separate instruments. Despite its name, the trade isn't riskless, and your view can be wrong.

Using Securitizations to Separate Originator Credit Risk from the Credit Risk of the Assets Originated

Whole Loan Securitizations

In chapter five we examined the beginnings of the securitization market as it was used to deal with the prepayment option embedded within home mortgages. That early era of securitization really had to focus only on interest rate risk, the risk that rates would fall and homeowners would refinance. We identified this as an embedded interest rate option. The purpose of early era securitizations was to deal with the unpredictability of that option and sell it to those investors most willing to own it. You may recall this was a duration based (reinvestment risk) problem, predominantly in the hands of long-term pension fund investors and the like.

The credit risk didn't enter into the early analysis as the securitizations were only being done with debt of federal agencies and GSEs. Early on, it became apparent that this was only a partial solution to mortgage market liquidity constraints because only about one-third of all mortgages were included in agency securities. This occurred for several reasons. The agencies and GSEs had strict underwriting criteria; unless a mortgage lender adhered to these criteria, the agencies/GSEs would not purchase the originated mortgage. There were also size limits on the mortgages that would be purchased; any mortgage above this limit was considered a *Jumbo* and did not qualify for purchase by the agencies/GSEs. Further, most mortgages which could have been sold to the agencies/GSEs weren't; they were held out voluntarily by the originators to be held in their portfolios or otherwise sold in nonpooled form. Mortgages of this type are called **whole loans** because the owner of the mortgage owns the whole loan and not a pooled interest in a group of mortgages. Being outside of pools, these mortgages lacked the guarantees associated with those bundled into pools and MBS. If whole loans are securitized, the buyer of the securitization tranches takes the risk of loss on the underlying default of the home mortgages. The ability to securitize whole loans therefore depended upon the ability to mitigate this risk. The manner in which this is accomplished is called **credit enhancement**.

Credit Enhancement Essentials

The whole loan market was the first to deal with credit enhancement, and its successful development revolutionized the credit markets, ultimately scandalizing them as well. In a whole loan securitization, a special purpose entity (SPE) is formed to purchase mortgages from an originator. The originator can be a bank or mortgage finance company. The SPE issues debt of its own and uses the funds to purchase the mortgages issued by the originator. The process looks like this:

Figure 7.1 – Diagram Showing CMO Credit Enhancement in the Mortgage Market

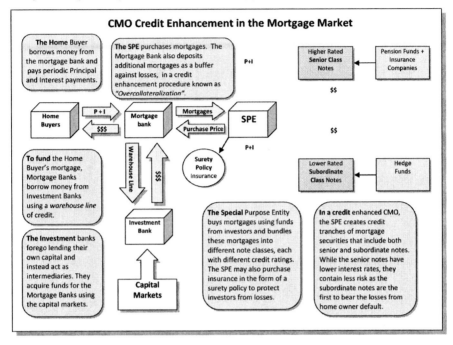

CMO Credit Enhancement in the Mortgage Market

The ability to have the debt rated on the basis of the quality of the assets held by the SPE is dependent upon the SPE being viewed as the legal owner of the assets. This is a subtle but crucial point. After the mortgages have been sold by the originator to the SPE, the SPE must be immune from credit events affecting the originator. In the absence of this protection, lenders to the originator would, in the event of a subsequent originator bankruptcy, assert that the "sale" of the mortgages to the SPE wasn't a sale at all but rather a loan by the SPE with the mortgages being held as collateral. If this argument prevailed, the creditors of the SPE would not have sole access to the collateral they thought was supporting the claim. Instead, the SPE creditors would be viewed as creditors of the originator and would have to share in available assets with the originator's other creditors. It is therefore critical for the transfer of the mortgages to the SPE to be respected as a **"true sale."**

Generally, for a true sale to occur all risks and benefits of ownership must pass to the SPE. In the event the mortgages appreciate after transfer, the originator cannot affect a repurchase at a lower prearranged price. Likewise, the SPE cannot compel the originator to buy back mortgages in the event of post transfer devaluation. Virtually all securitization transactions will include a legal letter from appropriate counsel opining on the validity of the true sale. These are called **true sale opinions**. To further insulate against the risk that an originator bankruptcy will not impact the SPE's ownership status in the mortgages, the originator will normally utilize a subsidiary which has an independent board of directors and other governance features as the seller of the mortgages. This is done because "independent" subsidiaries are not compelled to join in their parent organization's bankruptcy filings. The legal opinion that accompanies the transaction assuring this result is called a **nonconsolidation opinion** (meaning the subsidiary acting as the seller of the mortgages will not be consolidated in its parent's bankruptcy filing).

Now that the SPE's ownership of the assets is established, the debt issued by the SPE can be rated based on the quality of the mortgage portfolio. Note the entity is referred to as a "special purpose entity" because the only purposes it can exist for is issuing debt for the purpose of purchasing the mortgages. There is no unrelated business activity, and care is taken to assure that the SPE has no other creditors (who could otherwise force an involuntary bankruptcy). The SPE has no employees, and all services (loan serviceing, accounting, administration, etc) are done via contracts that are funded from mortgage cash flows. Because there are no government or GSE guarantees, the ratings process involves a projection of losses over the lifetime of the mortgages. These forecasts are referred to as **ratings criteria**. The level of losses assumed increases with the ratings sought on the SPE debt. Thus, the ratings process is reverse engineered and is somewhat outcome driven. We'll examine later the criticisms these processes came in for in the aftermath of the 2008-09 credit panic. At this point let's focus on the purpose of the exercise; if losses are projected to be incurred on the mortgages held by the SPE, who will absorb the loss?

Allocating these losses is what credit enhancement is all about. If there are multiple tranches of SPE debt, those tranches being allocated the losses first will need to pay a higher interest rate as compensation for that risk to investors. This is called **credit tranching**. To insulate the tranches from credit losses, the originator may cause a transfer of excess assets to the SPE to act as first loss provider. This is referred to as **over-collateralization**. To further provide protection to investors, the SPE may acquire a type of insurance policy on the losses incurred on its mortgages. This type of thirdparty insurance is called a **monoline** policy. In the typical credit enhancement configuration, losses on the mortgages held by the SPE are allocated as follows:

1. Over-collateralization

2. Junior debt tranche issued by the SPE (often called the subordinate tranche, or "sub")

3. Monoline insurance/surety policy

4. Senior debt tranche issued by the SPE.

Note that the senior debt tranche only incurs losses after the stated dollar amount of credit enhancement has been exhausted. Thus, senior debt tranches are structured to carry less risk (and thus pay a lower interest rate) than junior debt. The relative size of each of these credit enhancement slices in a given transaction will depend upon pricing considerations at point of issue and the speed at which the transaction is targeted to close.

Observations

With the successful development of credit enhancement, the market for debt instruments was revolutionized. Corporations (in this case mortgage originators) are now able to access the credit markets based on the credit quality of the assets they originate, as opposed to the strength of their own balance sheet. In doing so they are able to grow their businesses "off balance sheet," meaning that originated financial assets are sold off rather than held for the corporation's own account. Thus, corporations are spared the need to raise equity capital to support the level of debt that would otherwise appear on their books. Further, the originating entity (the mortgage finance company) acts as a servicing agent for the originated assets, earning a processing fee referred to as a **servicing fee**.

Figure 7.2 – Securitized Origination and "Off-Balance Sheet" Financing

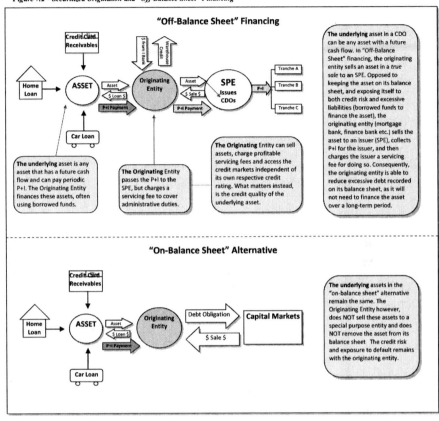

"Off-Balance Sheet" Financing

Credit Card Receivables

Home Loan

ASSET

$ Loan $

Asset

$ from I Bank

Warehouse Credit

Originating Entity

Asset

$ Sale $

P+I Payment

SPE Issues CDOs

P+I

Tranche A

Tranche B

Tranche C

P+I Payment

Car Loan

The underlying asset in a CDO can be any asset with a future cash flow. In "Off-Balance Sheet" financing, the originating entity sells an asset in a *true sale* to an SPE. Opposed to keeping the asset on its balance sheet, and exposing itself to both credit risk and excessive liabilities (borrowed funds to finance the asset), the originating entity (mortgage bank, finance bank etc.) sells the asset to an issuer (SPE), collects P+I for the issuer, and then charges the issuer a servicing fee for doing so. Consequently, the originating entity is able to reduce excessive debt recorded on its balance sheet, as it will not need to finance the asset over a long-term period.

The underlying asset is any asset that has a future cash flow and can pay periodic P+I. The Originating Entity finances these assets, often using borrowed funds.

The Originating Entity passes the P+I to the SPE, but charges a servicing fee to cover administrative duties.

The Originating Entity can sell assets, charge profitable servicing fees and access the credit markets independent of its own respective credit rating. What matters instead, is the credit quality of the underlying asset.

"On-Balance Sheet" Alternative

Credit Card Receivables

Home Loan

ASSET

$ Loan $

Asset

P+I Payment

Originating Entity

Debt Obligation

$ Sale $

Capital Markets

Car Loan

The underlying assets in the "on-balance sheet" alternative remain the same. The Originating Entity however, does NOT sell these assets to a special purpose entity and does NOT remove the asset from its balance sheet The credit risk and exposure to default remains with the originating entity.

137

With the advent of credit enhancements, a multitude of assets began to be securitized, including car loans and leases, credit card receivables, trade receivables, and virtually anything else with a future cash flow stream. One of the less desirable side effects of these developments became apparent during the highly stressful days of 2008–09. Entities originating assets without the intent of holding them become less selective about whom they do business with. This became abundantly clear in the aftermath of the real estate bubble and the lending practices which surrounded it.

Chapter
8

Public Equity Markets

Overview of Public Market Regulation

In response to the 1929 stock market crash and the depression that followed, the United States enacted a series of securities laws which fundamentally changed the way that markets are regulated. With the collapse of the market, there was widespread recognition that a public marketplace could not exist without the confidence of the public. The first of these statutes, **The 1933 Securities Act,** provides that securities (including equities, debt securities and others) are subject to registration with the federal government prior to their offer and sale. The agency with which securities must be registered is the **United States Securities and Exchange Commission**. Certain issuances, made to private groups of sophisticated investors, may qualify for exemptions from the registration process. The first part of this chapter will examine the registration process and the exemptions that currently exist. The second part of this chapter will examine secondary market trading and the regulation of those trading environments.

The Securities Issuance Process

When a business seeks to raise capital, several choices are available. They can examine their capital structure and determine whether they choose to incur liabilities (claims), or issue equity securities (interests). If the company decides to go the debt route, they may choose to take a conventional loan from a bank or other licensed lender. Strictly speaking, a direct loan from a bank is not a *securities* transaction. As such, these types of transactions do not implicate the public interest and are generally exempt from securities laws and regulations. If the borrowing is sought in the form of a debt security which will be sold to the public, the public securities laws are implicated. The same is true if the company chooses to sell either preferred or common stock to the public.

Once a decision is made to issue securities, the operative provisions of the 1933 Securities Act become relevant. Section 5 of the Act requires that securities offerings not otherwise qualifying for an exemption to be registered through a registration statement process. The SEC reviews the registration statement, which becomes "effective" after the review and a mandatory waiting period. Only then can "offers" for the securities be legally solicited and accepted.

Participants in the Process

Let's first consider the example of a privately owned corporation seeking to access the public securities markets for the first time. Let's further assume that the decision has been made to sell common stock in the company, rather than incur indebtedness. The corporation and its ownership and governance structure may look something like this:

Figure 8.1 – Corporate structure: Public Corporation

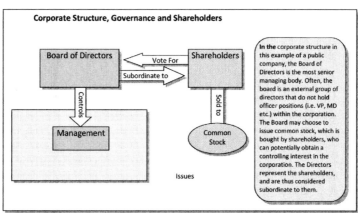

140

The shares of the corporation will be sold to the "public" as part of this transaction. Here are some questions to be considered:

1. Where are the proceeds of the sale going? Are the proceeds going to the company to be used for general corporate purposes? Is the money going to the existing shareholders who may be looking to cash out? Both?

2. How was the price of the shares arrived at?

3. Will the management team that has been running the company be staying in place after the share sale? Are there restrictions on the amount of shares that they can sell at any time? Will this team be subject to employment agreements after the share sale?

4. If the pre-transaction owners and managers are also shareholders, are they holding shares with the same or enhanced features as the ones being sold?

Don't necessarily assume that the corporate ownership structure is a democratic organization; every shareholder is not necessarily treated equally. The purpose of a public registration statement is to assure that all members of the potential investing public are equally informed to make the decision as to whether or not to invest in the security. The vehicles through which information is conveyed to members of the public is generally either SEC Registration Form S-1 or Form S-3. A Form S-1 is used when a company is accessing the public markets for the first time; a Form S-3 is used when a company that already has publicly traded securities is returning to the market. A Form S-3 is an abbreviated version of the S-1; because the issuer using the S-3 already has publicly traded securities, the issuer is already filing periodic information statements on Forms 10Q and 10K with the SEC (more on this later). The company whose securities are being sold into the marketplace is called the **registrant.** The registration statement will contain extensive information re-

141

lating to the registrant. This information will normally include:

1. Information concerning the distribution and its proceeds, including the use of the proceeds of the particular securities sale in question. This will highlight whether the securities are being sold by the company or the existing group of company insiders who may be seeking to cash out. It will also disclose the existence of so-called "lock-up" agreements which preclude insiders from selling their shares until predetermined lockup dates have passed. Normally, the selling shareholders will cash out, at least in part, on these dates causing downward price pressure as those dates approach.

2. A detailed description of the securities of the registrant. This includes an in-depth discussion of the rights, privileges, and preferences of the securities being offered. Differences between the securities being offered and those held by company insiders are disclosed here. A common type of preference is the existence of "supervoting" provisions in the shares retained by the insiders. Remember, the corporation's governing body, the board of directors, is selected by a vote of the shareholders.

3. Detailed exhibits are included in the registration statement. These include;

    a. The registrants articles of incorporation,

    b. Corporate bylaws,

    c. Legal opinions regarding the legality of the securities being sold,

    d. In the case of an S-3 registration, various financial filings required to have previously been submitted to the SEC. These include quarterly (Form 10Q) and annual (Form 10K) financial filings.

Underwriters

An underwriter is a broker-dealer selected by the registrant (or its shareholders) for the purpose of assisting in the sale and distribution of the securities of the registrant. The role of the underwriter is significant, but as a technical matter not mandatory. A company can legally sell its shares without the assistance of an underwriter. A short digression is necessary to illuminate this point.

Parties who sell securities to the public are generally required to register as broker-dealers under the 1934 Securities Exchange Act (which is described in detail later in this chapter). A broker-dealer is really engaging in two different roles; one is arranging securities transactions for the accounts of others for compensation. (This is what a broker does; a brokerage relationship is an agency role.) The second function, a dealer, differs in that the party is in the business of acting as principal (buying or selling for its own account). An important exemption to broker-dealer registration is the "issuer's exemption." The SEC, in its guide to broker-dealer registration, exempts issuers from broker dealer registration because . . .

> issuers generally are not "brokers" because they sell securities for their own accounts and not for the accounts of others. Moreover, issuers generally are not "dealers" because they do not buy and sell their securities for their own accounts as part of a regular business.

Thus, as a technical matter, issuers could sell their own shares without the participation of an underwriter. If instead the issuer hires a third party to assist it in the sale and distribution of its securities, the third party must be a broker-dealer. This relationship is referred to as underwriting.

Let's take a look at the typical timeline of a corporate secu-

143

rity underwriting.

Figure 8.2 – Corporate Security Underwriting Process

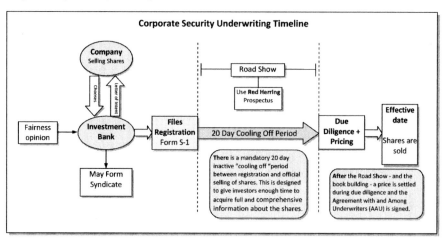

Underwriters are often selected to assist in the sale and distribution of securities because of their presumed expertise in completing the process. They assist in the preparation of the registration statement and otherwise assist the issuer in distributing the securities. There are generally two types of underwritings: a **firm commitment** and **best efforts**.

In a firm commitment underwriting, the underwriter purchases the securities from the issuer with the purpose of reselling them. Any unsold shares are owned by the underwriter. This exposes the underwriter to the risk that that the shares will not be able to be sold. To protect themselves, the underwriter may form an underwriting group to share that underwriting risk. This group is called a **syndicate**. A syndicate is a partnership of underwriters sharing in the risk of the transaction. The party that won the initial assignment is called the lead **underwriter** or **bookrunner**. There are important competitive motivations to be recognized as the lead underwriter, not the least of which is to attract future business by projecting the aura of market leadership. Periodic standings, called league tables, are published by Investment Dealers' Digest showing who won the most assignments for the previous, month, quarter, or year.

There are a number of important observations that come from understanding firm commitment underwritings. First, the interests of the issuer and the underwriter(s) are not necessarily aligned. Because the underwriter is obligated to purchase any unsold securities, the underwriter may be more inclined to under price the offering so that it can be sold, which is contrary to the issuer's presumed interest in getting the highest possible price for the security. To alleviate this concern, the issuer will normally contract for and obtain a "fairness opinion" from a valuation firm (or another broker-dealer) unaffiliated with the syndicate or the underwriters. The provider of the fairness opinion will value the company as it will appear after the capital is raised. Normally a minority stake is sold in the initial public offering, typically around 15–20% of the company. The provider of the fairness opinion will establish a range which constitutes a fair price for the entire concern after the capital is raised. If the range is established as $800 million to $1 billion, a 20% stake in the company will be valued at $160–$200 million. Next the syndicate and the issuer will need to decide how many shares the ownership of the company will be evidenced by. If the company is worth $1 billion and the ownership is evidenced by 100 million shares, each share is worth $10. Alternatively, if the ownership is evidenced by 10 million shares, each share is worth $100. Think of this as cutting a pie into many or few pieces. The pie is only so big, the fewer slices it is cut into, the larger each piece shall be. Conversely, if the pie is cut into many pieces, each slice will be smaller. Thus, the number of shares evidencing ownership is really a decision as to whom the issuer wants owning the shares. If a retail investor base is sought (because of the lower likelihood of investor factions meddling in management affairs), there will be a larger number of shares authorized and issued by the company, each of which would have a lower share price. If institutional ownership is sought, the opposite would be true.

After the selection of the underwriter, the forming of the syndicate and the receipt of the fairness opinion, the registration statement is filed with the SEC. This is an important mark in time because offers of the securities can only legally be binding on the effective date of the registration statement. The issuer is also required to file a prospectus which acts as a selling document for the issue and is really a summary of the registration statement. The 1933 Securities Act is based on the assumption that a fair and even dissemination of information to prospective investors can only take place through these documents. Accordingly, the SEC will take a dim view of pre-filing statements concerning the offering as the Commission is concerned that the issuer and its designees may be "puffing" the securities by cherry picking favorable information to disclose. Thus, issuers should be exceedingly careful not to prematurely discuss the impending offering with anyone, especially the press. The same admonition is directed to the syndicate members. There are several unfortunate incidents that have occurred that have led to unnecessary difficulties and embarrassment concerning these issues.

Upon the filing of the registration statement, a preliminary prospectus is prepared to assist in gauging investor interest in the securities. There is a minimum 20-day waiting period that commences upon the filing of the registration statement until the date it becomes effective. The syndicate uses the preliminary prospectus, referred to as a "red herring," to make presentations to potential investors during a so-called "road show." The preliminary prospectus is called a red herring because of the precautionary legend printed on the spine of the document in red letters. The potential investors are put on notice that the document is incomplete on a number of terms, especially the ultimate price. Further, binding offers cannot be made during this period. The presentation process is called a "road show" for the reasons you would expect.

During the road show process, the syndicate members and management present to potential investors and obtain nonbinding indications of interest. This process is known as book-building and can be conceptualized as follows:

Figure 8.3 - Graph Comparing Price to Demand in an IPO Underwriting

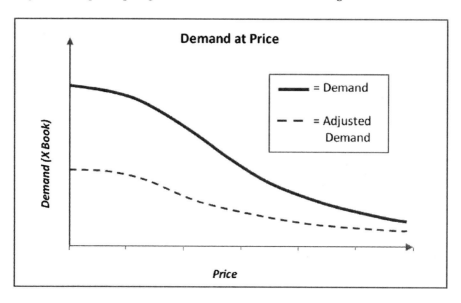

The underwriters' challenge is determining the real strength of the demand for the issue.

- Is all the demand real? IPOs are often oversubscribed which means they will receive less than the number of shares they are seeking.

- Syndicate's expertise: Where is the real demand? Which investors should be scaled back more than others?

The last part of the underwriting process is the final due diligence and pricing. The agreement the issuer entered into with the underwriter and syndicate will govern what happens here. This agreement is called the Agreement with and Among Underwriters (AAU). If the issue is over-subscribed, the AAU will normally have a clause which allows the syndicate to exercise an over-allotment option called a "Green Shoe" option. This odd name is for the issuer that first had this feature, the Green Shoe Manufacturing Corporation which is today known as Stride Rite. This feature will allow the syndicate to sell an additional stake, typically equal to 10-15% of the original issue size (if 20% was originally planned, the over-allotment option would allow the syndicate to sell 23%, which is 115% of 20%). When an over-allotment option is exercised by the syndicate, the issue will likely be priced at the top of the range established by the fairness opinion. When new issues are well received, but not oversubscribed, the over-allotment option is not exercised, and the issue will typically price to the middle of the fairness range. In certain cases, the issue is poorly received. Although a firm commitment, underwriting, in theory, requires the syndicate to take the issue for its risk, the AAU will contain clauses that protect the syndicate in the event of poor investor response. One such clause is referred to as a "material adverse change" (MAC) clause. In the event that the fortunes of the company deteriorated (within proscribed ranges) from the date the underwriting agreement was struck, or some other unforeseen event occurs, the syndicate may cancel the underwriting. Another protective clause may condition the firm commitment upon receiving investor interest for a predetermined percentage of the issue. In this event the issuer may have to reduce the size of the offering, lower the price, or both. In the event the market is unreceptive, the issuer and the syndicate may choose to cancel the issue.

Upon final pricing of the issue, a final prospectus is prepared and distributed which completes the information missing from the red herring. Final orders are accepted, and the shares are prepared for delivery.

The Conclusion of the Offering Process

When the offering process reaches its conclusion, the syndicate takes delivery of the shares from the issuer and makes delivery to the parties who purchased from the syndicate. Each individual purchaser is said to have received an "allotment." Remember that in a firm commitment underwriting the issuer isn't selling to the public; the issuer sells to the syndicate, which in turn resells to the parties receiving allotments. Thus, each party receiving an allotment pays the same price. Let's assume that an issue was finally priced at $100 per share. The public group purchasing allotments from the syndicate members pays $100 per share. From the $100, the syndicate group takes its fee, usually in the range of 4–6%. This is called the "underwriting discount." The underwriting discount is divided among the syndicate members in a manner which is determined by the role each member played (lead underwriter, book runner, etc) and the number of shares the syndicate member was responsible for. The syndicate's books are closed by the lead underwriter(s), giving credit for earned underwriting discounts and charges for allocable syndicate expenses (lawyers, printers, road show and others). A final distribution is normally made within 30 days of the termination of the syndicate. If all the shares are not sold, the unwanted securities are distributed to the syndicate members. If the total underwriters discount was $5 per share, the issuer receives $95.

As you might expect, oversubscribed public offerings are often coveted by investors and sell at an immediate premium in the secondary market. An issuer will assess the underwriting experience by the price the shares sell in the secondary market. If the securities immediately sell at a very high premium, the issuer will feel that the offering price was set too low. If they trade down, the customers of the syndicate who received allotments will be unhappy. This is the Goldilocks effect, not too high, not too low but just right to make everyone happy. A new issue trading in the secondary market 10-20% above its issue price will generally meet this Goldilocks standard.

Regulations Concerning Public Offerings

The public offering process is subject to extensive regulation. Two of these rules are discussed here in summary form because of the frequency with which questions arise in this area.

1. **Withholding and Free-riding Rules** These rules place restrictions on how new issues are distributed. The rules are designed to protect the integrity of the public offering process by attempting to insure that members do not hold securities for their own benefit over the benefit of others, and that individuals connected to the firm do not take advantage of their relationship with the firm to purchase new issues at the expense of the public. Imagine a highly anticipated new issue; absent restrictions to the contrary, syndicate members would be tempted to hold back securities of the issuer for their own account to be sold in the secondary market at a premium. This is an example of an impermissible **withholding** of shares from the public marketplace. Likewise, broker-dealers and their

employees are precluded from buying shares in new issues from syndicate members, without regard to
whether the employer firm is a member of the
syndicate. Absent rules of this type, broker-dealers
would be able to enrich other industry members, who
then would be able to reciprocate the favor. **Free-
riding** occurs when a customer is able to sell an allotment on the same date of its purchase without ever
having to independently settle the purchase
transaction. For example, if a customer is allotted
shares at a price of $100 and immediately sells the
shares for $125 without first paying for the purchase,
the customer has made a $25 profit without having
any money at risk.

2. **Regulation M** This series of rules prohibits the cover-
ing of short sales made within five days of a public offering to be covered with shares acquired in the public
offering.

*Secondary Markets for Equity Securities, Listing
Alternatives and Trading Environments*

Once public shares are issued by a company, a decision must
be made as to where to list the issue. The issue can trade in
the over-the-counter market (generally the NASDAQ marketplace), the New York Stock Exchange, or possibly on
foreign exchanges. The decision on where to list is made by
the issuing company, which must pay the listing fees and ad-
here to listing requirements. Where a company *lists* is not
necessarily where the shares will *trade*.

The NASDAQ in its current incarnation is a national exchange consisting of three tiers. The first tier is called the
NASDAQ Global Select Market. This is the NASDAQ's
premier tier and has the most stringent listing standards.
There are approximately 1,200 companies that are listed in
this tier. The second tier is called the NASDAQ Global Mar-

ket (formerly the NASDAQ National Market). This consists of large companies not in the Global Select Market. There are approximately 1,400 companies listed on the NASDAQ Global Market. The remaining 550 or so companies list on the NASDAQ Capital Market (formerly known as the NAS-DAQ SmallCap Market). A number of financial criteria are used to determine in which tier a company can list. A smaller but noteworthy segment of the OTC market is the OTC Bulletin Board, which is an inter-dealer quotation system run by the NASD for securities not quoted on NASDAQ. These are often smaller companies subject to special rules for "penny stocks."

NASDAQ securities trade on a computerized trading platform run by **market makers**. A market maker is a broker-dealer that registers with the NASDAQ for the purpose of displaying quotations in the securities that they are registered for. Like any dealer market, a market maker will display a **bid** and **ask** price, as well as the number of shares that the market maker is willing to trade at those prices. The bid is the price at which the market maker is willing to buy from a seller; the ask (sometimes called the offer) is the price that the market maker is willing to sell to buyers. The difference between the bid and ask is the market maker's spread, or compensation for making the market. Let's look at an example:

Figure 8.4 – Market Maker Bid/Ask Example

Market Maker Bid/Ask Prices for Share XYZ

Market Makers	Bid (Buy)	Ask (Sell)	Spread
A Price # of Shares	59.98 10,000	60.05 10,000	0.07
B Price # of Shares	60.00 40,000	60.02 40,000	0.02
C Price # of Shares	60.01 15,000	60.06 15,000	0.05

The OTC marketplace is an environment in which market makers compete against one another. Thus market participants are motivated to deal with:

- The market maker displaying the highest bid, if the participant is a seller of the stock, or

- The market maker displaying the lowest ask, if the market participant is a buyer of the stock.

The best publicly displayed price is that combination consisting of the highest bid and the lowest ask. This often is referred to as the **inside market**. Notice in the example that appears above, the highest bid is displayed by Market Maker C who is willing to pay $60.01 per share for as many as 15,000 shares. Further note that the lowest asking price is displayed by Market Maker B, who is willing to sell as many as 40,000 shares at $60.02. Thus, the inside market for this security is $60.01/$60.02, but only up to the size displayed by the market makers. If you wanted to buy more than 40,000 shares, B would likely increase the asking price. If you choose not to deal with B, the next most attractive ask is $60.05 displayed by A. The number of shares the market makers are willing to transact is a reflection of what they may be holding in their own positions (called inventory), the number of customer orders the market maker is holding, or a combination of the two. Market prices are all about supply and demand; large buy orders will push market prices up; large sell orders will push market prices down. The more market makers there are, the more competitive the market will be. The spread on the inside market will be a good gauge as to how much liquidity there is in a particular security; the tighter the spread, the more liquid the security and vice-versa. The advent of competitive market maker trading environments, together with technology advances, has significantly decreased bid/ask spreads in public securities markets.

Companies may alternatively choose to list their shares on

the New York Stock Exchange Euronext (NYSE). Historically the premier listing environment, the NYSE has come under a series of competitive assaults over the years. The NYSE is the oldest stock exchange in the United States. The original model for the exchange was a **specialist** system. A specialist firm is a broker-dealer that focuses on a physical trading floor market making system. If an issuer lists on the NYSE, it will select specialist to make a market on the floor of the exchange. Orders which reach the floor will be executed by the specialist who displays a two-sided bid/ask market. The display is for the number of shares indicated, just as described for NASDAQ market makers. Prior to the advent of various electronic alternatives, the specialist had an exclusive on the NYSE listed securities that it was selected for. The NYSE is now a hybrid market; the physical trading floor still exists, but most trades are matched electronically and bypass the specialist. The paradigm shifting event that revolutionized the way that stocks trade today was the development of electronic communications networks (ECNs). To understand how ECNs developed, let's consider the general flow of a stock order through a typical brokerage environment.

Figure 8.5 – Example of a Brokerage Transaction

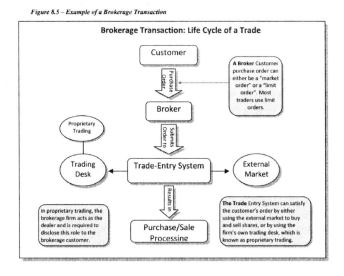

155

When a brokerage customer enters a stock purchase order, it can be done as a **"market order"** or as a **"limit order."** A market order is an order to purchase at whatever the prevailing market price is. As long as there is activity in the stock, these types of orders will normally be filled without problem. The buyer does take a significant risk that the price can run up after the order is entered, but before execution. Professional traders rarely use market orders because of this risk. Further, large orders in excess of displayed sizes (by either market makers or specialists) will have the effect of pushing the price up. Limit orders, by comparison, put a qualification on the order. Usually the qualification is the price.

Assume a customer is interested in buying 100,000 shares of XYZ Corporation which is currently trading at $60 per share. Note that the order is entered into a trade entry system which routes the order for execution. The brokerage firm handling the order for the customer may have a position in the stock and may therefore fill the order from its inventory. This possibility is depicted above as the "trading desk." In most situations there is no reason the broker cannot sell the customer shares owned by it. In this case, the brokerage firm is acting as principal, will add a commission/fee for executing the trade, and disclose its role as a dealer to the customer when the order is confirmed. Confirmations are normally sent one day after the trade execution date (referred to as the trade date). Settlement of the transaction occurs three business days after trade date. If the firm does not own XYZ, or chooses not to sell XYZ shares it does own, the brokerage firm will look outside the firm to an "external market."

Regardless of where XYZ is listed, it may trade in multiple markets. This was part one of the electronic revolution; when NASDAQ market makers were allowed to compete with specialists for NYSE listings, spreads tightened significantly. When NYSE listings are traded away from the NYSE, these are referred to as "third market" trades.

The 100,0000 share market order will get executed as there is sufficient size to absorb the trade (there are enough sellers to satisfy the order). Brokers have the regulatory burden of giving the customer the best available price, known as a **duty of best execution**. Note that this duty must be fulfilled even if the firm is filling the order from inventory. In that case, the sales price the firm will charge will be determined by reference to prices prevailing in the external market.

Orders entered as limits can be more challenging. If the 100,000-share order has a $60 limit, the customer is unwilling to pay more than $60 for the shares. If the external markets are showing asked prices/displays above $60, the order won't be filled. Any order that doesn't get executed on the business day it is entered, expires at the end of that day unless the customer specifies otherwise at point of order entry. Orders that are left open by the customer are referred to as **good until cancelled** (or good until killed) orders. These orders are more problematic. If a $60 limit is entered by a customer and the market is above $60 all day, the order will remain in queue for execution the next training day. This invites the possibility that other, later entered orders can get executed first. Worse, a firm may place its orders ahead of the customer in a way that denies that customer the best possible execution. See if you have a problem with the following sequence of events.

A customer enters a 100,000-share/$60 limit order in XYZ, good until cancelled. XYZ trades above $60 all day, so the trade is not executed. There is bad news on XYZ at the opening of the next trading day (disappointing earnings); as a result XYZ trades at $59 at the opening of trading. The brokerage firm handling the customer limit order immediately buys the stock for its own account and then sells it to the customer at $59.50. This is an example of an illegal practice known as **inter-positioning**. The perception (and reality) of endemic inter-positioning was a key reason ECNs developed.

ECNs and other alternative trading systems (ATS) allow buyers and sellers to display their orders directly, without necessarily having to go through market makers or specialists. Although ECNs and ATS come in different forms, the important characteristics that are common in many are:

1. Buyers and sellers are able to display their orders in an open trading environment. ECNs are subscriber based systems in which the operator can act as principal on both sides of the trade; others are agency-only models which electronically match buy and sell orders.

2. Limit orders are freely displayed. As such, limit orders that are away from the market in terms of price or size can be partially filled or negotiated for a complete fill.

As order details become more transparent, dealer spreads tighten even more. Because of this, market participants began to flock to ECNs as an alternative to the traditional trading platforms. One early ECN, Instinet, began to dominate the volume in NASDAQ listings. Another ECN, initially called the Archipelago Exchange (Arca), began to make significant inroads into NYSE listed securities. Rather than compete with the newer technologies, NASDAQ acquired the Instenet ECN (now called INET), and the NYSE engineered a combination with Arca. Thus, ECNs and ATS have now become part of the conventional trading mediums. The result has been ever tightening dealer spreads and the conversion of the floor-based, specialist-directed NYSE into a hybrid market where a substantial majority of trades are now matched electronically without any specialist intervention.

Settlement Procedures-Generally

Corporate stocks and bonds trading on U.S. exchanges and trading platforms generally settle three business days after the date the trade is executed. The trade execution date is called the **trade date (T)**. The date on which the securities delivery and cash payments are made among all parties to

the transaction is referred to as **settlement date (T+3)**.
This type of trade is called a **regular way cash market**
transaction and can be conceptualized as follows:

Figure 8.6 – Regular Way Cash Market Transaction

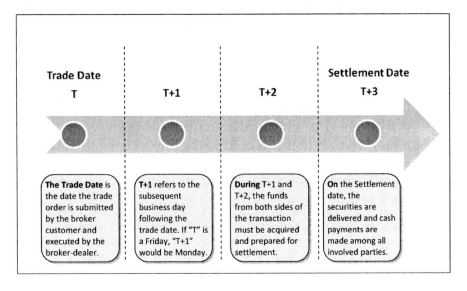

Trade Date — T

T+1

T+2

Settlement Date — T+3

The Trade Date is the date the trade order is submitted by the broker customer and executed by the broker-dealer.

T+1 refers to the subsequent business day following the trade date. If "T" is a Friday, "T+1" would be Monday.

During T+1 and T+2, the funds from both sides of the transaction must be acquired and prepared for settlement.

On the Settlement date, the securities are delivered and cash payments are made among all involved parties.

Several years ago, regular way trades settled on T+5. Keep in mind that all of the contractual terms of the trade are established on trade date, including the number of chares, price, commission per share, etc. Therefore, credit risk exists until the trade is settled and cleared. If the customer purchased 100,000 shares of XYZ Corporation at $60 through its broker dealer, one of these parties is going to be exposed to the non-performance risk of the other when settlement date arrives. If the shares have traded up to $80, the customer will surely be there to take delivery at $60. The broker dealer may fail in the interim and not make the delivery to the customer; conversely if the shares decline in price to $40, the selling broker dealer will insist on settling, but the customer may fail before fulfilling his obligations. The longer the period between trade date and settlement date, the more pronounced these movements might be and the greater the attendant credit risk. The SEC, therefore, has been seeking ways to shorten settlement periods to alleviate systemic credit risk in the financial industry. Broker-dealers are required to maintain sufficient capital to allow them to meet their obligations to counterparties in the event that either trading partners or customers default on their obligations. This capital adequacy requirement is mandated by the **Uniform Net Capital Rule**, which is described in chapter 11.

Once the transaction has settled, the customer will need to instruct the broker as to what to do with the client shares now in their possession. The three alternatives are:

1. The customer can instruct that the securities be physically delivered. This would bring the transactional relationship to its conclusion; the securities transaction has been **cleared,** and the monies due among all the participants have been **settled**. The delivery of the shares to the customer therefore brings the transaction to its ultimate conclusion.

2. The customer can instruct the securities be delivered

160

to a third party that will act as a custodian for the shares.

3.   The broker that executed the transaction may be asked to retain the shares after settlement and act as custodian. This creates a credit risk to the customer; if the broker-dealer fails, its creditors may attempt to seize the client securities in satisfaction against claims against the firm. Accordingly, the broker-dealer is required to segregate these fully paid shares so they are outside the reach of broker-dealer creditors. This requirement, contained in the **Customer Protection Rule** is a central feature of broker-dealer regulation which is described in Chapter 11.

Margin Trading and Broker-Dealer Financing Alternatives

Many securities markets participants seek to borrow money from their broker dealer or a bank to pursue their trading strategies. These are called **margin loans**. Investors use margin loans because they believe that the appreciation and earnings on the portfolio holdings will exceed to cost of the borrowed money. The incremental return accrues to the benefit of the customer and enhances the rate of return earned on the customer's own funds. This is another example of the use of leverage in the financial markets. Leverage, however, is a two-sided knife. If the shares decline in value, the customer is still liable for the loan. If the shares fall to a value less than the loan, the customer will have to come up with other funds to make up the shortfall. If the customer cannot come up with those other funds, the lender, who is now holding collateral of insufficient value to satisfy the claim, will experience a loss.

The use of excessive margin lending was identified as a major contributor to the depth of losses incurred the 1929 stock market crash. The spiral goes like this; the shares fall in value causing brokers to make margin calls, which require customers to post more collateral or pay down the loan. Customers in turn sell shares to raise cash, causing share prices to fall further. Eventually, the shares are worth less than the margin loan; unable to meet their margin requirements, the customer defaults on the loan causing a loss to the lending broker-dealer or bank. When enough customers default, the magnitude of the losses experienced by the lenders erodes their capital bases causing the banks and broker dealers to fail. We now have a systemic breakdown putting the financial system at risk.

To alleviate these risks, all margin lending in the United States is subject to Federal Reserve Board regulation. The primary regulations are **Regulation T** and **Regulation U.** Regulation T governs margin lending to customers by broker dealers. Regulation U governs margin lending to customers by banks. The objective of the regulations is to limit the amount of money a lending institution can lend to a person (or entity) where the purpose of the loan is to **purchase or carry** securities positions. Notice that the regulatory emphasis is on limiting what the lender can lend to the customer, not what the customer can borrow from the lender (this is added as a supplementary safeguard in Regulation X). This distinction, while subtle, is important. It forces the customer to be substantially at risk to the securities position by requiring a partial payment by the customer. Let's look at a sample transaction to get a better feel for the operation of these rules.

Margin Example

Customer Smith directs his broker dealer (BD # 1) to purchase 100,000 shares of XYZ Corporation in a $60 limit order. BD # 1 executes the transaction by purchasing the shares from BD # 2 (BD #1 did not own the shares in inventory). The transactions settle and clear on the third business day following the execution date. BD #1 charges Smith a commission of five cents per share. Therefore, on trade date,

- Smith owes BD #1 $6,005,000 (100,000 shares @ $60 per share plus a commission of $5,000), and

- BD #1 owes BD #2 $6,000,000.

Figure 8.7 – Margin Example at Trade Date

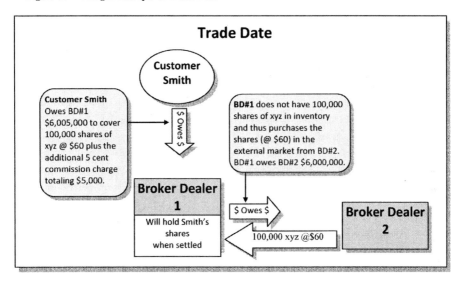

On settlement date,

- Smith pays BD #1 $3,005,000, representing half of the purchase price of XYZ and $5,000 of commission.

- BD #1 lends $3,000,000 to Smith. Under Regulation T, margin financing is limited to 50% of the purchase price.

- BD #1 pays BD #2 $6,000,000 (the full purchase price).

Figure 8.8 – Margin Example at Settlement date

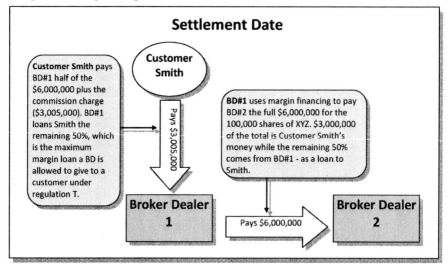

As the client only pays 50%, BD #1 must finance the balance. Of the amount due of $6,005,000, the customer only paid $3,005,000. Therefore the BD #1 must come up with the other $3,000,000. The unpaid customer balance of $3,000,000 ($6,005,000 owed less $3,005,000 paid) is called a **customer debit balance** or a **margin debit**. Notice the term "debit" appears in both descriptions. On BD #1's books, it has an accounts receivable from Smith. The account receivable is an asset of BD #1. In bookkeeping language, assets are debits. Thus, the terms customer debit balance or margin debit.

Let's examine the transactions just described in a diagram.

Customer Perspective

Figure 8.9 – Customer Perspective in Margining Example

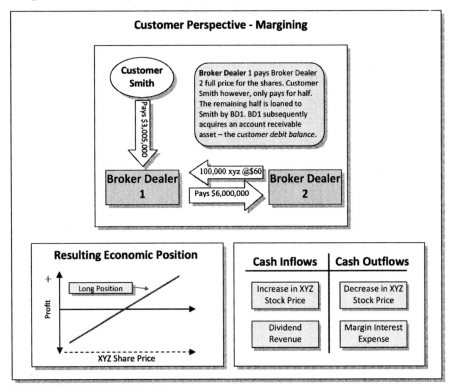

The client's cost of carrying the position is the margin interest paid less dividends received on the stock. Conceptually, the total cost of carrying the position includes the opportunity cost of the customer funds used to make the margin deposit for the purchase.

BD #1's Perspective—Financing Margin Balances

BD #1 must now choose how to finance its customer debits. Generally, there are four available alternatives. The sources of funding are:

1. **Firm capital**; BD #1 may choose to lend Smith some of its own capital.

2. **Customer credit balances**. A customer credit balance is money on deposit with the broker-dealer which is due to a customer. In the United States broker dealers are generally permitted to use these funds to make loans to margin customers.

3. **Bank loans**; these are direct loans made to the broker-dealer by a bank or other lending institution.

4. **Loans from other broker dealers.** These are often referred to as **stock/securities loans and/or repurchase agreements**.

The objective of BD #1 is to earn more interest income from Customer Smith than it is paying for the funds to finance Smith's debit. The resulting difference is the **financing spread** earned by the broker dealer. BD #1's objective is to maximize this spread. This can be done by charging Smith more, which at some point will encourage Smith to take his account to another broker dealer, or to find cheaper money to borrow.

From the list of financing alternatives illustrated above, firm capital (choice 1) is normally the most expensive and otherwise least attractive alternative to a broker-dealer carrying margin debits. Broker-dealers financing customer debits with firm capital usually do so because they were unable to borrow funds from other sources. Thus, BD #1 will seek to borrow from the cheapest available lender listed in alternatives 2, 3, or 4. Alternative 2 (customer credits) is normally very cheap. The rate of interest paid on customer credit balances is substantially lower than any other third party financing and will be utilized by the broker dealer. Earlier in this chapter, I made reference to a Customer Protection Rule which requires broker-dealers to segregate customer securities after they have been fully paid for. How can it be that the broker-dealer is required to segregate customer securities but is allowed to use customer cash balances to finance other customer debit balances?

When customers engage with broker-dealers, a series of credit risks are introduced into the financial system. Policy makers aim to protect brokerage customers so that creditors of the brokerage firm cannot seize customer assets to satisfy claims against the firm. By instituting a 50% lending limit under Regulation T, policy makers concluded that there are sufficient safeguards to protect the customer to allow use of their cash balances to finance customer debits. Assume that in addition to Smith, the broker-dealer in our continuing example (BD #1) also carries the account of customer Jones. Jones has a number of securities positions, all fully paid for, which are properly segregated. Jones also has a $7,000,000 cash balance which is kept in her account. The Customer Protection Rule, as we shall see, will require that these funds be segregated. However, if BD #1 is also carrying Smith's account with the $3,000,000 debit balance, BD #1 is permitted to borrow up to $3,000,000 from Jones and use those funds to finance Smith's debit. The remaining $4,000,000 of Jones' funds will be segregated. The reasoning is that Smith's account contains securities that are worth $6,000,000 which are in BD #1's possession and must be segregated. If BD #1 were to experience financial distress and liquidate its operations, it would still be able to sell Smith's securities at a price that would enable Smith to repay his debit balance ($3,000,000). The repaid $3,000,000 can now be added to the $4,000,000, which has been previously segregated, and Jones can be repaid the $7,000,000 which is owed to her. Potential difficulty arises when the value of the securities in Smith's account falls below the amount of the debit that Smith owes to BD #1. In this case, Jones is potentially exposed, and BD #1 will need to set aside its own capital to cover any shortfall after Smith's securities are sold to liquidate the debit.

Figure 8.10 – Margin Transaction Financed with a Customer Credit Balance

Financed with a Customer Credit Balance

$ 4,000,000 segregated pursuant to customer protection rule.

Margin Customer

$ 3,005,000

Customer Jones
$ 7,000,000 Cash Balance

$ 3,000,000

Broker Dealer #1

100,000 XYZ

$ 6,000,000

Broker Dealer #2

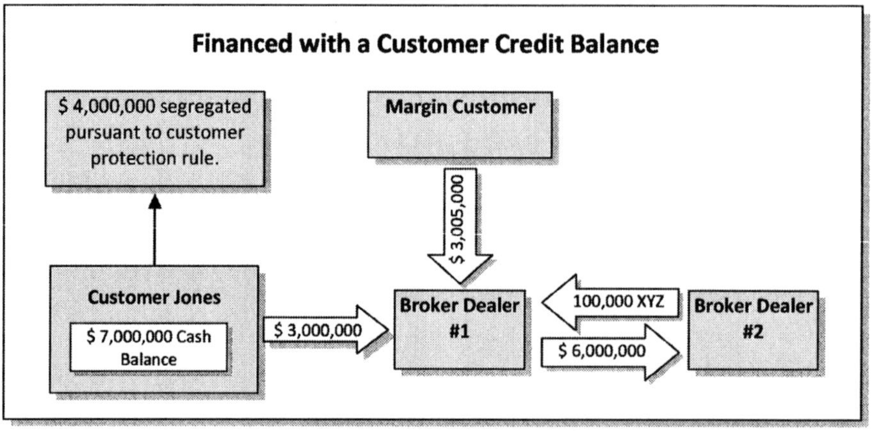

Bank financing, while more expensive, is usually easily available and is regularly used by the broker-dealer community. When broker-dealers borrow from banks, they naturally will be required to pay interest on these borrowed funds. The bank will also require the broker-dealer to post collateral with the bank to support the loan. Because the customer has not fully paid for their securities, the broker-dealer is permitted to use the customer securities as collateral for the loan used to finance the customer debit balance. Because the broker-dealer is using customer securities to collateralize the loan, strict limits are imposed on the broker-dealer through the operation of the customer protection rule. First, the broker-dealer may not borrow more than the customer's debit balance. Our customer, Smith, has a debit balance of $3,000,000 (Smith paid the other $3,000,000 and the $5,000 commission when the securities were purchased). If the broker-dealer were permitted to borrow more than what was owed it by the customer, the broker-dealer would be left in possession of loan proceeds which are collateralized by customer securities, which unfairly places the customer at risk if the broker dealer is unable to repay those funds. The customer's securities should not be at risk to creditors of the broker dealer. A loan in the amount necessary to finance the customer's debit, collateralized by that customer's securities, is deemed to be appropriate, but not more. Further, there are limits on the amount of securities that can be used to finance customer debits and additional restrictions on what needs to be done with securities in the possession of the broker dealer in excess of the amounts necessary to finance the debit.

Banks lending to broker-dealers (or anyone else) will normally ask for collateral in excess of the amount of the loan. Thus if BD #1 wants to borrow $3,000,000 from a bank, the bank will often require more than $3,000,000 of collateral. On its face, giving the bank customer securities with a value in excess of $3,000,000 indirectly puts the customer at risk.

If the bank were to fail and be unable to return the collateral, a simultaneous failure of the broker-dealer could expose the customer to a loss. (These cascading failures, once thought to be highly improbable, became frighteningly real during the tumult of the financial crisis in 2008.) Recognizing that loans would not be made unless a collateral cushion was allowed, brokerage regulators permit the broker- dealer to post collateral in an amount equal to 140% of the customer debit balance. Thus, BD #1 may lawfully post collateral with a value of up to $4,200,000 ($3,000,000 × 140%). Any remaining securities in Smith's account are considered **excess margin securities** (securities in excess of collateral requirements to finance debit balances) and must be segregated by the broker dealer. A broker dealer margin transaction financed with a bank loan appears in the following diagram:

Figure 8.11 – Margin Transaction Financed with a Bank

Financed with a Bank

BD#1 cannot borrow more than the customer debit balance and must post collateral to the bank not to exceed 140% of the debit balance. It is subsequently obliged to pay interest on this bank loan.

Margin Customer

Regulations prevent broker dealers from posting more than 140% of the margin customer's securities as collateral to the banks. Thus BD#1 can post no more than $ 4,200,000.

$ 3,005,000

Bank — Collateral <140% — **Broker Dealer #1** — 100,000 XYZ — **Broker Dealer #2**

$ 3,000,000

$ 6,000,000

Interest Payment

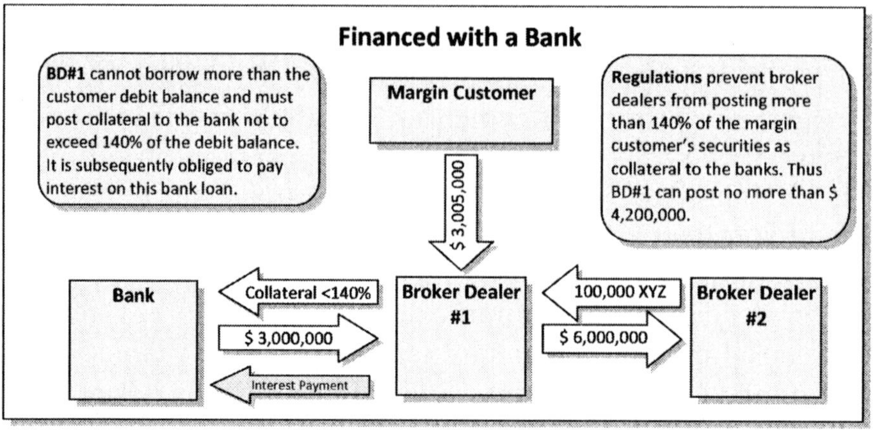

The remaining method of financing margin debits is with other broker-dealers in **stock lending transactions** (and also repurchases agreements). When a broker-dealer lends securities, it takes cash as collateral. On this cash collateral, it must pay interest. The broker-dealer borrowing the security usually needs the specific security for a specific purpose. Therefore, the borrower of the security requesting it will be required to pay a fee to the security lender. This is called a **stock lending fee**. The fee received will lower the cash borrowing costs of the security lender. The difference between the interest on the cash collateral and the stock lending fee is called a **rebate**. A lender of securities is specifically looking to borrow money. That is what is motivating BD #1; it is looking to finance a customer margin debit. Brokerage terminology often confuses the newly initiated. A good way to remember what stock loan means is to focus on the other side of the transaction; **stock (or securities) loaned means money borrowed. Stock borrowed means money loaned.**

Figure 8.12 – Stock Loan/Stock Borrowed Diagram

Stock Loan/Stock Borrowed Diagram

Interest on Cash Collateral

Broker Dealer which is lending Securities

Cash Posted as Collateral

Stock XYZ Loaned

Broker Dealer which is borrowing Securities

Stock Lending Fee

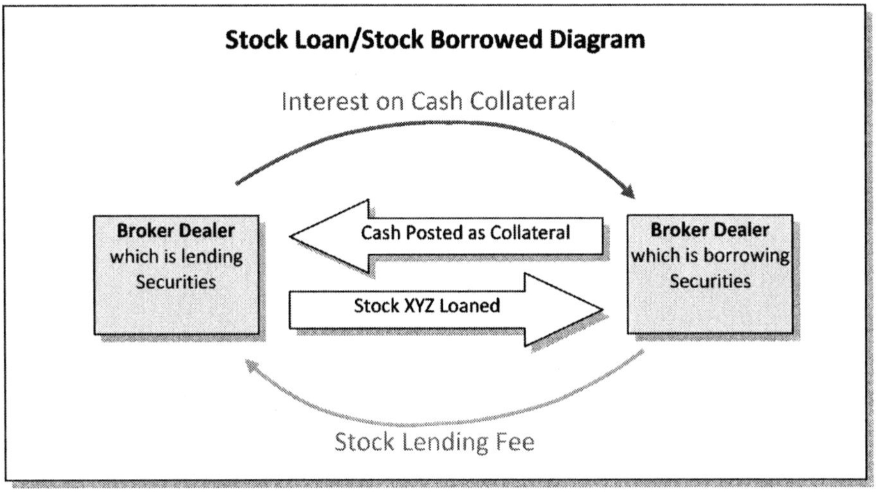

*Controlling Credit Risk When Extending Credit to
Customers—Margin Department Operations*

To control the risk that the value of Smith's securities fall
below the amount of his debit balance, the broker dealer is
required to perform a series of daily computations to assure
that the broker dealer (and by extension its customers and
trading counterparties) does not have credit exposure to its
margin customers. Generally, there are three things the broker dealer is always diligent to assure.

1. That the customer has **equity** in the account. In a long
    account, equity is the difference between the value of
    the qualifying securities owned and the amount of the
    debit. (Similarly, the equity in a short account is the
    difference between the current value of the securities
    sold short and the sum of the original net short sale
    proceeds and qualifying deposits made into the
    account. Short margin will be discussed separately.)

2. That the equity in the account is sufficient to support
    the level of borrowing in the account taking into
    consideration the size of the securities account in
    question. This equity sufficiency computation is re-
    ferred to as **maintenance margin**. As we shall shortly
    see, the 50% Regulation T requirement applies to the
    equity sufficiency at the date of purchase; equity can
    fall below 50% after the purchase date either through
    changes in security market values or through with-
    drawals of cash or securities. After the purchase date,
    the amount of equity can be less than 50% of the value
    of the securities in the account but must be adequately
    above the amount of the debit balance so that a suf-
    ficient safety cushion is afforded the broker dealer car-
    rying the margin debit. Deficiencies below regulatory
    limits (or more stringent broker dealer limits) will
    result in **margin calls**.

3. If the customer is going to be permitted to continue

172

purchasing securities on margin, the customer account must have equity in excess of 50% of the fair market value of the securities held by the account. The difference between the equity in the account (computed as described in #1 above) and 50% of the fair market value of the qualifying securities in the account is referred to as **Regulation T equity (Reg T equity)**. A customer is said to have **buying power** in an amount equal to double their Reg T equity.

Short Selling, Stock Lending and Related Issues

A short sale involves selling stock which the seller does not currently own. The short seller is selling borrowed securities with the expectation that they can be purchased at a later date at a lower price and returned to the securities lender. **This is the predominant reason that securities are borrowed**. Let's look at what is motivating a short seller.

Figure 8.13 – A Short Seller's Short Position

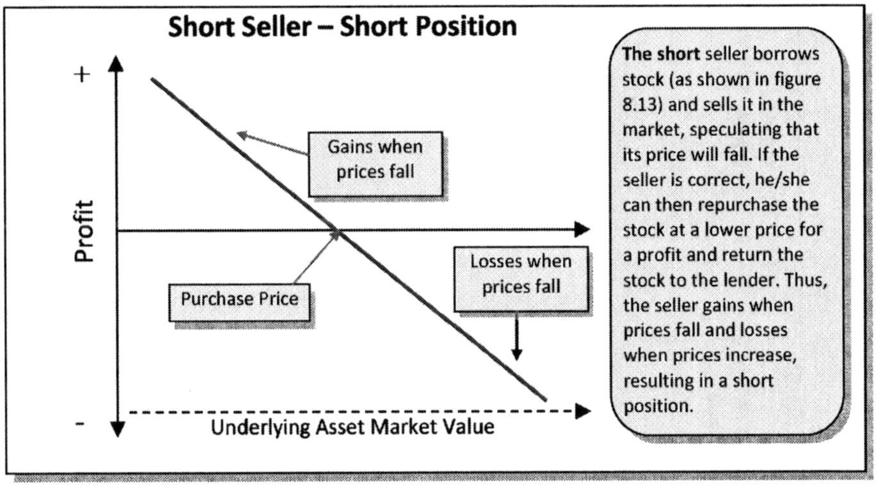

Short Seller – Short Position

Gains when prices fall

Purchase Price

Losses when prices fall

Profit

Underlying Asset Market Value

The short seller borrows stock (as shown in figure 8.13) and sells it in the market, speculating that its price will fall. If the seller is correct, he/she can then repurchase the stock at a lower price for a profit and return the stock to the lender. Thus, the seller gains when prices fall and losses when prices increase, resulting in a short position.

Structural Elements of a Short Sale

1. Before a short sale order can be executed, arrangements must be made to borrow the underlying security to make delivery to the purchaser on settlement date (three business days after the execution of the sale transaction). This is called a "**locate.**"

2. The borrowed stock must be collateralized by a cash deposit with the securities lender (such as the broker dealer, BD #1, financing Smith's margin balance in the continuing example in this chapter).

3. The party borrowing the stock earns interest on the cash balance collateralizing the stock borrowed; this is paid by the stock lender.

4. The party borrowing the stock will pay a fee to the lender of the stock. This fee is based upon the availability of the stock. Stocks in short supply or for which there is a high borrowing demand will command a higher stock lending fee. These types of securities are referred to as **hard to borrow**.

5. As noted earlier, the difference between the interest earned on the cash given as collateral and the stock lending fee is called a rebate. In a normal transaction where the stock is not hard to borrow, the rebate will be paid to the broker dealer executing the short sale (the interest paid on the cash collateral exceeds the stock lending fee).

6. The short seller will share in this rebate. This is done pursuant to a rebate sharing agreement between the short seller and his broker-dealer. The difference between the rebate the broker-dealer receives and the amount shared with the short seller represents a **rebate spread** and is retained by the broker-dealer as additional income for handling the short seller's account. If the stock is hard to borrow, the stock lend-

ing fee may exceed the interest earned on the cash collateral. In this case, there is a **negative rebate** which is paid by the short seller's broker to the stock lender. The broker will charge the negative rebate, plus a spread, to the short seller in this case. Note the enviable position the stock lender is in; through lending the stock they have not only receive funds which are cost free (which can be used to finance customer margin debits or proprietary positions) but also earns the negative rebate. A knowledgeable margin customer of a securities lender would be well advised to negotiate for a reduced margin rate when hard to borrow securities held in their account are used to finance the margin debits.

7. The short seller must deposit 50% of the short sale on the date of the short sale. Short sales are subject to Reg T.

8. Short sellers are responsible for dividends paid on stocks they have borrowed to sell short. This occurs because the dividend paying corporation will only pay holders of the shares of the stock on the record date of the dividend. If the shares have been loaned, the borrower of the shares (who has in a short sale sold them to a party who will be paid by the corporation) will be responsible for the dividend. Thus, this obligation will fall onto the short seller.

Figure 8.14 – Margin Buyers and Short Sellers

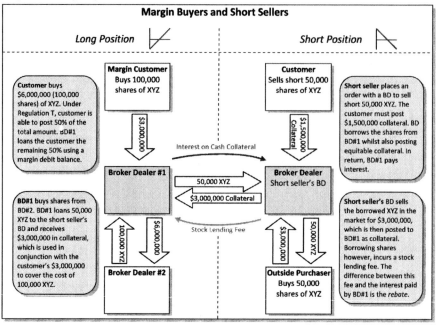

Hard to Borrows and "Squeeze" Risk

The ability to sell short securities is predicated on the ability to borrow the securities. When securities are borrowed, they are subject to recall upon demand unless alternative arrangements are made at the inception of the stock loan. This demand recall provision exists because the lending broker-dealer may be financing a customer margin transaction; in the event that the customer decides to sell the securities or pay off the margin debit, the securities must be obtained to settle the transaction (in the case of a sale) or to satisfy the broker's segregation obligation (in the case of a margin debit being paid off).

Because the stock which is borrowed for short sale purposes can be recalled by the lender at any time, the short seller must assess their ability to re-borrow the stock if it is recalled. If the short seller is unable to re-borrow the stock, it must be repurchased terminating the position. This is referred to as "squeeze risk." Stocks/securities which are in low supply or in high demand are referred to as "hard to borrow" securities and subject the short seller to the highest degree of squeeze risk.

What Makes Stocks Hard to Borrow?

There are certain categories of securities that will present inordinate amounts of squeeze risk. The first group involves participants in merger and acquisition transactions. Assume Bidder Corporation ("Bidder") is interested in taking over Target Corporation ("Target"). Immediately prior to the announcement of the transaction, Target is trading at $70 and Bidder is trading at $120. In order to entice Target shareholders to sell their shares to Bidder, a premium to market prices is normally offered. As a result, Target shares increase in price and Bidder Shares fall. Assume after the announcement, Target is selling at $85 and Bidder is trading at $100 (Bidder falls because it is paying the premium). Let's assume that for each share of Target outstanding, Bidder is willing to issue one new share of Bidder in exchange. Thus, Target is selling at a 15% discount to Bidder despite the fact that they will be equivalent after the merger is approved. The discount exists because of the uncertainty that the transaction will actually close; shareholders, regulators, or market upheavals can scuttle the transaction. If you believe that this transaction will close, you would buy Target shares and sell short an equivalent amount of Bidder. This is called **risk arbitrage**. If the deal closes, you will exchange your Target shares for newly issued Bidder shares and use those shares to close your short sale. If that occurs, you will get to keep the 15% discount. If enough people believe the deal will close, Bidder will become hard to borrow. It's called risk arbitrage because the deal may not close. If that happens, Target will likely fall in price and Bidder will go up, and the risk arbitrager will lose on both legs of the transactions.

Securities also become hard to borrow when companies issue convertible securities (either a convertible bond or a convertible preferred stock). A convertible security is a security which gives the holder the option of converting the security into a predetermined number of shares. In certain circumstances it may be attractive to buy the convertible security and sell short the equivalent number of shares. This is known as **convertible arbitrage** and will also make the common stock harder to borrow.

Lastly, a company may have a relatively small number of shares trading in the marketplace. This often occurs because many of the shares are owned by founders or employees. Because of the low supply of available shares, the shares will be hard to borrow.

Chapter
9

Private Placements
General Securities Law
Considerations

Alternatives to the Public Marketplace—Private Placements

The United States securities laws are structured on a periodic reporting model. The laws' purpose is to protect the public interest by providing uniform disclosures to investors. The 1933 Securities Act requires registration of securities in advance of public offers. The 1934 Securities Exchange Act mandates a continuing flow of information to the investing public through the filing of Forms 10Q, 10K, 8K, and other filings. Recognizing that not all securities issuances implicate the interests of the "public," the 1933 Securities Act and the SEC (through its regulatory rule making authority) provide for a number of exemptions from registration. These are commonly referred to as **private placement exemptions**.

To qualify for the various private placement exemptions, the issuer cannot engage in a general distribution to the public. No advertising can be used, and the issuer (and its agents) must only deal with parties with whom they have substantial pre-existing relationships. To allow advertising or general solicitation of investors in "private placements" would render the registration sections of the 1933 Act meaningless. As private placements are offered without a registration statement, they can only be directed to parties with the financial sophistication to understand and shoulder the risks associated with the investment. The main registration exemptions are contained within **Regulation D**, promulgated by the SEC under the 1933 Securities Act. As used in the securities laws, a regulation is a series of rules. Accordingly, Regulation D consists of Rules 501 through 507. The following table summarizes the exemptions contained within the rules that comprise Regulation D. The rule with the most widespread significance in the financial markets is Rule 506, which will be the focus of our attention in this chapter.

Figure 9.1 – Exemptions in Regulation D; Rules 504, 505 and 506

Regulation D Exemptions	Rule Summaries
Rule 504	Companies are exempt from Regulation D when they offer or sell up to $1,000,000 of securities in a 12 month time period; - Company cannot be a Blank Check Company (microcap) - Must be a company that does not have to file reports under the 1934 SEC act. - Rule 504 generally does not allow the company to solicit or advertise its (generally restricted) securities.
Rule 505	To qualify for an exemption, the company in question may; - Only sell up to $5,000,000 of its securities in a 12 month period. - Sell to an unlimited number of accredited investors, but only 35 other "non-sophisticated" investors. - Must sell *registered* securities that cannot be traded for up to 6 months without registration. - Not solicit or advertise its securities. - Must give financial disclosure documents to non-accredited investors, and must be able to answer purchaser questions - Financial statements must be checked by 3rd party CPA.
Rule 506	Companies can raise an unlimited amount of money if they meet the following standards outlined in rule 506; - Sell to an unlimited number of accredited investors, but only 35 other *sophisticated and wealthy* investors. - Must give financial disclosure documents to non-accredited investors, and must be able to answer purchaser questions - Financial statements must meet same standards in 505 - Must sell *registered* securities that cannot be traded for up to 1 year without registration. - Do not solicit or advertise its securities.

Accredited Investors

To assure that private placements are only sold to parties able to understand and shoulder the risks associated with private placements, Regulation D emphasizes the concept of an **accredited investor**. An accredited investor is a party or institution that is deemed to have the financial sophistication to invest in private placements. These parties include:

1. a bank, insurance company, registered investment company, business development company, or small business investment company;

2. an employee benefit plan, within the meaning of the Employee Retirement Income Security Act, if a bank, insurance company, or registered investment adviser makes the investment decisions, or if the plan has total assets in excess of $5 million;

3. a charitable organization, corporation, or partnership with assets exceeding $5 million;

4. a director, executive officer, or general partner of the company selling the securities;

5. a business in which all the equity owners are accredited investors;

6. a natural person who has individual net worth, or joint net worth with the person's spouse, that exceeds $1 million at the time of the purchase, excluding the value of their primary residence;

7. a natural person with income exceeding $200,000 in each of the two most recent years or joint income with a spouse exceeding $300,000 for those years and a reasonable expectation of the same income level in the current year; or

8. a trust with assets in excess of $5 million, not formed to acquire the securities offered, whose purchases a sophisticated person makes.

In a private placement qualifying under Rule 506 (the most common exemption), the shares may be sold to a group which consists of accredited investors and up to 35 non-accredited investors. If shares are sold to non-accredited investors, those parties must have "purchaser representatives" who will watch out for their interests. The issuer must also provide expanded disclosure to non-accredited investor purchaser representatives which approach the level of disclosure required in a registration statement under the 1933 Act. For this reason, most issuers will choose not to offer their shares to non-accredited investors.

Regulation D Exemptions and the Investment Company Act of 1940 ("ICA")

While an offering may qualify for an exemption under the 1933 Securities Act, a separate limitation applies under the ICA. An "investment company" is essentially a mutual fund, or more formally, a pooled investment vehicle. An entity claiming exemptive relief under Regulation D for purposes of the 1933 Securities Act still faces limits with respect to the number of shareholders the issuer may have under the ICA. Section 3c-1 of the ICA generally limits the number of shareholders to fewer than 100 separate beneficial interests. The ebb and flow of the direction of securities regulation follows the emotions of the markets; during times of rising asset prices and market stability, regulations tend to be liberalized. In periods following market declines (or crashes), the protective and defensive instincts of the regulatory apparatus present themselves.

In the late 1990s there was a general push toward deregulation and liberalization of market regulation. Among the manifestations of this trend was the amendment of the ICA to permit a larger number of investors to own entities qualifying for exemptions under Regulation D without requiring registration as a mutual fund. The result was Section 3c-7 of the ICA. Generally, if the ownership of the entity is limited to those who are "qualified purchasers," the entity can in theory have an unlimited number of owners. In practice, however, when the entity reaches 500 investors it will need to begin filing reports under the 1934 Securities Exchange Act. For this reason, the overwhelming majority of issuers operating under a Section 3c-7 exemption will limit the number of owners it has below that level.

Qualified Purchasers

The definition of qualified purchaser is found in the ICA. The definition includes:

i. any natural person (including any person who holds a joint, community property, or other similar shared ownership interest in an issuer that is excepted under section 3(c)(7) with that person's qualified purchaser spouse) who owns not less than $5,000,000 in investments, as defined below;

ii. any company that owns not less than $ 5,000,000 in investments and that is owned directly or indirectly by or for 2 or more natural persons who are related as siblings or spouse (including former spouses), or direct lineal descendants by birth or adoption, spouses of such persons, the estates of such persons, or foundations, charitable organizations, or trusts established by or for the benefit of such persons;

iii. any trust that is not covered by clause (ii) and that was not formed for the specific purpose of acquiring the securities offered, as to which the trustee or other person authorized to make decisions with respect to the trust, and each settlor or other person who has contributed assets to the trust, is a person described in clause (i), (ii), or (iv); or

iv. any person, acting for its own account or the accounts of other qualified purchasers, who in the aggregate owns and invests on a discretionary basis, not less than $25,000,000 in investments.

v. any qualified institutional buyer as defined in Rule 144A under the Securities Act, acting for its own account, the account of another qualified institutional buyer, or the account of a qualified purchaser, provided that (i) a dealer described in paragraph (a)(1)(ii) of Rule 144A shall own and invest on a discretionary basis at least $25,000,000 in securities of issuers that are not affiliated persons of the dealer; and (ii) a plan referred to in paragraph (a)(1)(D) or (a)(1)(E) of Rule 144A, or a trust fund referred to in paragraph (a)(1)(F) of Rule 144A that holds the assets of such a plan, will not be deemed to be acting for its own account if investment decisions with respect to the plan are made by the beneficiaries of the plan, except with respect to investment decisions made solely by the fiduciary, trustee or sponsor of such plan;

vi. any company that, but for the exceptions provided for in Sections 3(c)(1) or 3(c)(7) under the ICA, would be an investment company (hereafter in this paragraph referred to as an "excepted investment company"), provided that all beneficial owners of its outstanding securities (other than short-term paper), determined in accordance with Section 3(c)(1)(A) thereunder, that acquired such securities on or before April 30, 1996 (hereafter in this paragraph referred to as "pre-amendment beneficial owners"), and all pre-amendment beneficial owners of the outstanding securities (other than short-term paper) or any excepted investment company that, directly or indirectly, owns any outstanding securities of such excepted investment company, have consented to its treatment as a qualified purchaser.

vii. any natural person who is deemed to be a "knowledgeable employee" of the [fund], as such term is defined in Rule 3c-5(4) of the ICA; or

viii. any person ("Transferee") who acquires Interests from a person ("Transferor") that is (or was) a qualified purchaser other than the [fund], provided that the Transferee is: (i) the estate of the Transferor; (ii) a person who acquires the Interests as a gift or bequest pursuant to an agreement relating to a legal separation or divorce; or (iii) a company established by the Transferor exclusively for the benefit of (or owned exclusively by) the Transferor and the persons specified in this paragraph.

ix. any company, if each beneficial owner of the company's securities is a qualified purchaser.

For the purposes of above, the term Investments means:

(1) securities (as defined by section 2(a)(1)of the Securities Act of 1933), other than securities of an issuer that controls, is controlled by, or is under common control with, the prospective qualified purchaser that owns such securities, unless the issuer of such securities is: (i) an investment vehicle; (ii) a public company; or (iii) a company with shareholders' equity of not less than $50 million (determined in accordance with generally accepted accounting principles) as reflected on the company's most recent financial statements, provided that such financial statements present the information as of a date within 16 months preceding the date on which the prospective qualified purchaser acquires the securities of a Section 3(c)(7) Company;

(2) real estate held for investment purposes;

(3) commodity interests held for investment purposes;

(4) physical commodities held for investment purposes;

(5) to the extent not securities, financial contracts (as

such term is defined in section 3(c)(2)(B)(ii) of the ICA entered into for investment purposes;

(6) in the case of a prospective qualified purchaser that is a Section 3(c)(7) Company, a company that would be an investment company but for the exclusion provided by section 3(c)(1) of the ICA, or a commodity pool, any amounts payable to such prospective qualified purchaser pursuant to a firm agreement or similar binding commitment pursuant to which a person has agreed to acquire an interest in, or make capital contributions to, the prospective qualified purchaser upon the demand of the prospective qualified purchaser; and

(7) cash and cash equivalents (including foreign currencies) held for investment purposes. For purposes of this section, cash and cash equivalents include: (i) bank deposits, certificates of deposit, bankers acceptances and similar bank instruments held for investment purposes; and (ii) the net cash surrender value of an insurance policy.

Resale of Securities Purchased in a Private Placement

Because the securities obtained in a private placement are not registered with the SEC, their resale is difficult and time consuming. Great care must be exercised to assure that secondary transfers of the shares do not invalidate the Regulation D exemption the issuer is relying upon. Therefore, the sales process for unregistered securities is slow and cumbersome. For this reason, privately placed securities generally lack a secondary market and are priced at a significant discount to their fully registered counterparts. As a result, the SEC has provided limited, but significant, relief in the form of resale exemptions.

Rule 144A and Qualified Institutional Buyers

Rule 144A is a "safe harbor" provision under the 1933 Securities Act which allows for resale of restricted securities to "qualified institutional buyers" (also referred to as QIBs) by parties other than the issuer of the securities. The major practical importance of Rule 144A is the facilitation of resales of securities originally issued pursuant to a Regulation D exemption. The existence of a liquid secondary market reduces the issue discount when issuers decide to privately place (rather than publicly issue) securities. To avoid creating a side-by-side markets with publicly traded securities of the same issuer, there are restrictions on "fungibility" between privately placed securities with those securities of the issuer which are publicly traded. The purchaser of unregistered securities must make an attestation that they qualify as a QIB (although registries of QIBs now exist to avoid transactional attestations). Following are several important terms under Rule 144A and their definitions.

1. *qualified institutional buyer* shall mean:

   i. Any of the following entities, acting for its own account or the accounts of other qualified institutional buyers, that in the aggregate owns and invests on a discretionary basis at least $100 million in securities of issuers that are not affiliated with the entity:

      A. Any *insurance company* as defined in section 2(a)(13) of the Act;
      Note: A purchase by an insurance company for one or more of its separate accounts, as defined by section 2(a)(37) of the Investment Company Act of 1940 (the "Investment Company Act"), which are neither registered under section 8 of the Investment Company Act nor required to be so registered, shall be deemed to be a purchase for the account of such insurance company.

B. Any *investment company* registered under the Investment Company Act or any *business development company* as defined in section 2(a)(48) of that Act;

C. Any *Small Business Investment Company* licensed by the U.S. Small Business Administration under section 301(c) or (d) of the Small Business Investment Act of 1958;

D. Any *plan* established and maintained by a state, its political subdivisions, or any agency or instrumentality of a state or its political subdivisions, for the benefit of its employees;

E. Any *employee benefit plan* within the meaning of title I of the Employee Retirement Income Security Act of 1974;

F. Any trust fund whose trustee is a bank or trust company and whose participants are exclusively plans of the types identified in paragraph (a)(1)(i)(D) or (E) of this section, except trust funds that include as participants individual retirement accounts or H.R. 10 plans;

G. Any *business development company* as defined in section 202(a)(22) of the Investment Advisers Act of 1940;

H. Any organization described in section 501(c) (3) of the Internal Revenue Code, corporation (other than a bank as defined in section 3(a)(2) of the Act or a savings and loan association or other institution referenced in section 3(a)(5)(A) of the Act or a foreign bank or savings and loan association or equivalent institution), partnership, or Massachusetts or similar business trust; and

188

I.   Any *investment adviser* registered under the Investment Advisers Act.

ii. Any *dealer* registered pursuant to section 15 of the Exchange Act, acting for its own account or the accounts of other qualified institutional buyers, that in the aggregate owns and invests on a discretionary basis at least $10 million of securities of issuers that are not affiliated with the dealer, *Provided,* That securities constituting the whole or a part of an unsold allotment to or subscription by a dealer as a participant in a public offering shall not be deemed to be owned by such dealer;

iii. Any *dealer* registered pursuant to section 15 of the Exchange Act acting in a riskless principal transaction on behalf of a qualified institutional buyer;
     Note: A registered dealer may act as agent, on a non-discretionary basis, in a transaction with a qualified institutional buyer without itself having to be a qualified institutional buyer.

iv. Any investment company registered under the Investment Company Act, acting for its own account or for the accounts of other qualified institutional buyers, that is part of a family of investment companies which own in the aggregate at least $100 million in securities of issuers, other than issuers that are affiliated with the investment company or are part of such family of investment companies. *Family of investment companies* means any two or more investment companies registered under the Investment Company Act, except for a unit investment trust whose assets consist solely of shares of one or more registered investment companies, that have the same investment adviser (or, in the case of unit investment trusts, the same depositor), Provided That, for purposes of this section:

189

    A. Each series of a series company (as defined in Rule 18f-2 under the Investment Company Act) shall be deemed to be a separate investment company; and

    B. Investment companies shall be deemed to have the same adviser (or depositor) if their advisers (or depositors) are majority-owned subsidiaries of the same parent, or if one investment company's adviser (or depositor) is a majority-owned subsidiary of the other investment company's adviser (or depositor);

  v. Any entity, all of the equity owners of which are qualified institutional buyers, acting for its own account or the accounts of other qualified institutional buyers; and

  vi. Any *bank* as defined in section 3(a)(2) of the Act, any savings and loan association or other institution as referenced in section 3(a)(5)(A) of the Act, or any foreign bank or savings and loan association or equivalent institution, acting for its own account or the accounts of other qualified institutional buyers, that in the aggregate owns and invests on a discretionary basis at least $100 million in securities of issuers that are not affiliated with it and that has an audited net worth of at least $25 million as demonstrated in its latest annual financial statements, as of a date not more than 16 months preceding the date of sale under the Rule in the case of a U.S. bank or savings and loan association, and not more than 18 months preceding such date of sale for a foreign bank or savings and loan association or equivalent institution.

2. In determining the aggregate amount of securities owned and invested on a discretionary basis by an entity, the following instruments and interests shall

be excluded: bank deposit notes and certificates of deposit; loan participations; repurchase agreements; securities owned but subject to a repurchase agreement; and currency, interest rate and commodity swaps.

3. The aggregate value of securities owned and invested on a discretionary basis by an entity shall be the cost of such securities, except where the entity reports its securities holdings in its financial statements on the basis of their market value, and no current information with respect to the cost of those securities has been published. In the latter event, the securities may be valued at market for purposes of this section.

4. In determining the aggregate amount of securities owned by an entity and invested on a discretionary basis, securities owned by subsidiaries of the entity that are consolidated with the entity in its financial statements prepared in accordance with generally accepted accounting principles may be included if the investments of such subsidiaries are managed under the direction of the entity, except that, unless the entity is a reporting company under section 13 or 15(d) of the Exchange Act, securities owned by such subsidiaries may not be included if the entity itself is a majority-owned subsidiary that would be included in the consolidated financial statements of another enterprise.

5. For purposes of this section, *riskless principal transaction* means a transaction in which a dealer buys a security from any person and makes a simultaneous offsetting sale of such security to a qualified institutional buyer, including another dealer acting as riskless principal for a qualified institutional buyer.

6. For purposes of this section, *effective conversion premium* means the amount, expressed as a percentage of the security's conversion value, by which the price at

issuance of a convertible security exceeds its conversion value.

7. For purposes of this section, *effective exercise premium* means the amount, expressed as a percentage of the warrant's exercise value, by which the sum of the price at issuance and the exercise price of a warrant exceeds its exercise value.

Regulation S

Regulation S (Rules 901 through 904) is a jurisdictional regulation which allows United States issuers to issue securities which have not been registered in the United States to investors outside of the United States. In certain circumstances these securities may otherwise be fungible to securities which have been issued and outstanding in the United States. In many circumstances, generally after satisfying "aging" requirements, the foreign purchaser of Regulation S exempt securities may resell those securities in the United States and the securities will be considered as registered for securities law purposes.

Chapter
10

Pooled Investment Vehicles Mutual Funds and Exchange Traded Funds Hedge Funds and Private Equity Funds

Introduction

Mutual funds are publicly registered investment vehicles regulated under the Investment Company Act of 1940 ("ICA"). This is the most familiar form of pooled investment vehicle available to investors in the United States. The fund itself is a separate legal entity, typically formed as a corporation or as a business trust. As such, the fund has a board of directors, officers and shareholders. The fund typically itself has no employees; investment and administrative duties are contracted for with outside parties and are provided in exchange for fees. Typically there are separate contracts with the investment manager, a fund custodian, accountants, and administrative agents. The investment manager of a fund marketed in the United States must be a registered as an investment advisor and subject to regulation and oversight as such by the Securities and Exchange Commission. The regulation of investment advisors is discussed separately in chapter 12. The sponsor of the funds arranges for sales of shares through broker-dealers, which may be affiliated with the sponsor.

While the funds are regulated under the ICA, several securities statutes are implicated when mutual fund shares are issued. The investment manager is subject to the Investment Advisers Act of 1940 which imposes a fiduciary obligation on the manager and activates a series of recordkeeping and reporting rules. The ownership interests in the mutual fund are securities subject to the 1933 Securities Act, and therefore the registration obligations inherent with public share issuances are applicable. As a public company, regular reports must be filed with the Securities and Exchange Commission pursuant to the 1934 Securities Exchange Act.

Mutual Fund Capital Structures

There are generally two types of mutual fund structures, open-end and closed-end funds. In an open-end fund structure, shares are sold by the fund to investors on a daily basis at the net asset value (NAV) as established at the end of the trading day. Open-end fund shares do not "trade" in the secondary market. They are issued by the fund upon subscription and redeemed by the fund upon redemption. When an investor in an open- end fund wants to dispose of his holdings, the shares are redeemed directly by the fund (again at the published end of day NAV).

Shares in closed-end funds trade in the secondary market like any other publicly registered securities. Closed-end funds generally do not continuously offer their shares for sale. Rather, they sell a fixed number of shares at one time (in an initial public offering), after which the shares typically trade on a secondary market, such as the New York Stock Exchange, the Nasdaq Stock Market, or another national exchange mechanism. Secondary market prices of closed-end funds are determined by the market and may be greater or less than the shares' net asset value (NAV). Closed-end fund shares generally are not redeemable. That is, a closed-end fund is not required to buy its shares back from investors upon request. Some closed-end funds, commonly referred to as interval or targeted-date funds, offer to repurchase their shares at specified intervals.

Closed-end funds are permitted to invest in a greater amount of "illiquid" securities than are mutual funds. (An "illiquid" security generally is considered to be a security that cannot be sold within seven days at the approximate price used by the fund in determining NAV.) Because of this feature, funds that seek to invest in markets where the securities tend to be more illiquid are typically organized as closed-end funds.

There are anomalies that result from the use of these fund structures. Subscriptions and redemptions of open-end fund shares take place at a NAV which is determined at the end of the trading day. This pricing matter creates investor uncertainty and encourages market gaming strategies. Further, as noted, closed-end funds will trade on a supply and demand basis without regard to the NAV of the underlying fund. Many closed-end funds trade at discounts to their NAV. Absent the ability to liquidate the fund, these discounts cannot easily be captured.

Exchange Traded Funds (ETFs)

The ETF is a hybrid fund type which mitigates the pricing and trading anomalies that effect both open and closed-end funds. Like closed-end funds, ETFs trade in the secondary equity security markets and settle like other shares of stock. The ETF may also continuously issue and redeem shares, like an open-ended fund. These combined features provide arbitrage pricing discipline. Many ETFs are established to fully replicate positions in broader market indices and have become a attractive to fee sensitive, passive investors. ETFs also offer the use of margin and short selling.

195

Alternative Investments

The alternative investment universe consists of **hedge funds, private equity funds,** and other unregistered investment vehicles. Collectively, these funds are referred to as **private funds**. Private funds are pooled investment vehicles which qualify for exemptions under Section 3 of the ICA. The major difference between hedge funds and private equity funds is what they are investing in. Hedge funds tend to invest in marketable securities; private equity fund investments are usually more illiquid. Private equity funds, such as leveraged buyout funds, normally take control positions in their portfolio companies.

Hedge funds and private equity funds also differ in the way that subscriptions are made and capital is deployed. Hedge fund investors typically fund 100% of their investment upon subscription, and the invested amounts are immediately deployed by the manager. In a private equity fund (or other vehicle investing in less liquid markets), it is much more likely for investors to make commitments which are then drawn down as investment opportunities present themselves.

Domestic Funds

Private funds placed with domestic, taxable United States investors are usually structured as limited partnerships (LP) or limited liability companies (LLC). LPs and LLCs are treated as pass-through type entities for income tax purposes; thus the investors in the LP/LLC pay taxes on the fund's income, but the fund is exempt from tax. Further, LPs and LLCs provide limited liability to its investors. The combination of tax efficiency and limited liability makes the LP/LLC an attractive investment vehicle. The interests in the LP or LLC are securities and must be placed with investors in conformity with a private placement exemption to avoid registration under the 1933 Securities Act.

196

Structure of a Typical Hedge Fund Investment

Domestic funds are usually structured as limited partnerships. As such, investors are limited partners, and the limited partnership interests are securities (limited partnership interests are considered securities because they represent a pooled investment in which investment control is delegated to a third party). Because the interests are securities, they must either be registered under the 1933 Securities Act or must be placed pursuant to a valid private placement exemption. See chapter 9 for a discussion of these exemptions.

The investment manager (or a manager affiliate) acts as the general partner (GP). The GP is responsible for all governance matters. Often the investment manager and the general partner are different legal entities. This is done for tax purposes. (The management fee and performance related compensation are often taxed differently; in some jurisdictions the investment manager may be subject to local taxation on the management fee but not on the performance fee.) Use of separate general partners is also advisable when a fund manager brings in investment professionals who share in performance fees in specific, but not all, funds under management.

Fees and Liquidity Terms

The investment may be subject to a **lockup**. A lockup is a period in which investors cannot withdraw or redeem their investment. Managers seek lockups to provide stability to their businesses, but these provisions are usually resisted by investors as the provision restricts liquidity. Managers in high demand can often impose lockups, whereas newer, less proven managers cannot. In some cases a manager will negotiate a lower fee with investors who agree to a lockup.

Management fees are based on capital under management and vary depending upon the investment strategy, the prominence of the manager, and other factors. The management fee is normally 2% of capital committed or invested. In many private equity funds, the management fee is levied on the commitment. An investor in such a fund will actually pay a much higher effective management fee.

Incentive fees/performance fees (sometimes called "carried interests") are a percentage of the profits paid to the manager (or more typically the manager affiliate acting as the general partner). The percentage again varies with the investment style and the prominence of the manager but is typically 20% of net profits, subject to "claw-backs" or "high water marks."

A **claw-back** is a mechanism that requires return of manager performance fees in the case of a fund that later experiences losses. Claw-backs are common in private equity funds but are relatively uncommon with hedge funds.

High water marks require that a manager re-attain a previous peak NAV prior to reinstituting charging performance fees.

Hurdles provide for a minimum performance before performance fees can be charged. The hurdle can be an absolute value or an index to which the manager performance is scaled. When indices are used, the performance fee is sometimes referred to as alpha based.

Investor redemption and liquidity dates are those dates on which investors can redeem their investments. Domestic funds usually provide for quarterly liquidity, subject to investor notice requirements. These notice periods will vary with the liquidity characteristics of the fund. The reason the manager needs the notice is to allow for an orderly period of time to liquidate investments to satisfy investor liquidity requirements. With less liquid investment styles, longer notice periods are required and appropriate.

When large percentages of capital redeem in one period, the

manager often faces the need to liquidate the portfolio in a way that will only exacerbate the decline in the sold assets value. To guard against this potential, many private funds have liquidity restrictions, referred to as **gates**. A gate is a redemption restriction which limits the maximum capital redemption as a percentage of capital on the redemption date, often in the range of 10-25%. Thus a fund with $1 billion at a redemption date may limit the amount that can be redeemed in that quarter at $100 million. Any redemption requests in excess of the gate are transferred to the next liquidity date.

At times markets are severely located, and the manager may believe that it is in the best interest of the fund and its investors to suspend redemptions entirely for some period of time. Suspensions are meant to be temporary and are at the discretion of the governance body of the fund, subject to the contractual agreements that the fund and its managers have entered into.

Side Pockets are used by private funds that have hard to value investments and are still accepting new investors. Because new investors' participation percentages in an existing fund are based upon the market value of the assets held by the fund at the date of entry, the manager of a fund holding a hard to value asset faces a quandary. If the asset in question is marked to market at too low a value, then the incoming investor gets an unintended benefit to the detriment of the existing partner. If the asset is marked at too high a value, the incoming investor has paid too much. Thus, the manager would prefer to isolate the asset in such a way that incoming partners do not participate in either subsequent gains or losses on the asset. This is called a "side pocket." The effect of a side pocket is to freeze the investor group participating in a given asset by a fund that is still open to new investors.

Investor Tax and Performance Reporting

Investors in limited partnerships and LLCs receive a form K-1 reporting the income and its tax character. A form K-1 for the 2010 tax year appears at figure 10.1.

Figure 10.1 – Schedule K-1

651110

☐ Final K-1 ☐ Amended K-1 OMB No. 1545-0099

Schedule K-1 (Form 1065) **2010**

Department of the Treasury
Internal Revenue Service

For calendar year 2010, or tax year beginning ________, 2010 ending ________, 20____

Partner's Share of Income, Deductions, Credits, etc. ▶ See back of form and separate instructions.

Part I

A Partnership's employer identification number

B Partnership's name, address, city, state, and ZIP code

C IRS Center where partnership filed return

D ☐ Check if this is a publicly traded partnership (PTP)

Part II

E Partner's identifying number

F Partner's name, address, city, state, and ZIP code

G ☐ General partner or LLC member-manager ☐ Limited partner or other LLC member

H ☐ Domestic partner ☐ Foreign partner

I What type of entity is this partner? ________

J Partner's share of profit, loss, and capital (see instructions):

	Beginning	Ending
Profit	%	%
Loss	%	%
Capital	%	%

K Partner's share of liabilities at year end:
Nonrecourse . . . . $
Qualified nonrecourse financing . $
Recourse . . . . $

L Partner's capital account analysis:
Beginning capital account . . . $
Capital contributed during the year $
Current year increase (decrease) . $
Withdrawals & distributions . . $ ( )
Ending capital account . . . . $

☐ Tax basis ☐ GAAP ☐ Section 704(b) book
☐ Other (explain)

M Did the partner contribute property with a built-in gain or loss?
☐ Yes ☐ No
If "Yes", attach statement (see instructions)

Part III

1	Ordinary business income (loss)	15	Credits
2	Net rental real estate income (loss)		
3	Other net rental income (loss)	16	Foreign transactions
4	Guaranteed payments		
5	Interest income		
6a	Ordinary dividends		
6b	Qualified dividends		
7	Royalties		
8	Net short-term capital gain (loss)		
9a	Net long-term capital gain (loss)	17	Alternative minimum tax (AMT) items
9b	Collectibles (28%) gain (loss)		
9c	Unrecaptured section 1250 gain		
10	Net section 1231 gain (loss)	18	Tax-exempt income and nondeductible expenses
11	Other income (loss)		
		19	Distributions
12	Section 179 deduction		
13	Other deductions	20	Other information
14	Self-employment earnings (loss)		

*See attached statement for additional information.

For IRS Use Only

For Paperwork Reduction Act Notice, see Instructions for Form 1065. Cat. No. 11394R Schedule K-1 (Form 1065) 2010

As LP/LLCs are pass-through entities for tax purposes, each investor must report his pro rata share of the fund's income and expenses on his own tax returns. This pass-through treatment is unattractive to foreign/non U.S. investors. Accordingly, foreign investors prefer investment vehicles that do not expose the investor to U.S. tax filing requirements.

Offshore Investment Vehicles, General Tax Considerations

The solution for foreign investors investing in United States capital markets is normally the use of a corporate entity incorporated outside of the United States. Certain non-taxable domestic investors (pension funds, endowment accounts, charities, etc) are also permitted to invest in these offshore investment vehicles While corporations are not pass-through entities and normally pay a tax on their own income, the use of corporations established in a country which has a favorable treaty with the U.S. (or in a tax haven such as the Cayman Islands) provides a tax efficient manner for nonU.S. investors to invest in the United States. The United States generally does not require foreign corporations to file U.S. tax returns if the foreign corporation has solely passive portfolio income. Capital gains are normally not taxed, and dividends may be subject to withholding taxes which are withheld at the source (the dividend paying corporation or its agent). In many cases the withholding tax on dividends is eliminated by tax treaty.

Interest income is normally exempt from withholding taxes if it is considered "portfolio interest." Portfolio interest is generally interest paid or accrued on debt obligations issued after July 18, 1984 (the date that Congress enacted this particular provision). To assure that these rules were not being used by United States residents/citizens to evade United States taxes, the tax code and regulations impose a registration requirement on the debt obligations and a certification of foreign status requirement upon the investor. To assure use by only passive investors, interest payments made to

202

certain parties (10% shareholders in the issuer of the debt obligation, foreign banks and certain foreign corporations controlled by US shareholders) do not qualify for the portfolio interest exemption. Newer rules, enacted in 1993, eliminate the portfolio interest exemption for payments of "contingent interest." Contingent interest is a payment that is nominally an interest payment but has the characteristics of equity (usually some type of participation in revenue or profits). These rules were adopted because dividend payments are subject to withholding taxes (unless eliminated by treaty) while portfolio interest is not subject to withholding without regard to treaty protections.

Offshore Vehicles and Effectively Connected Income (ECI)

Withholding tax is not required of United States source income effectively connected with a U.S. trade or business. Rather, a foreign corporation which earns income connected with the conduct of a U.S. trade or business must file a U.S. corporation tax return and pay taxes at the rate of tax generally applicable to U.S. corporations. Most offshore hedge funds take great care to assure they are not engaged in a trade or business. When ECI is earned by a domestic or foreign partnership that is allocable to a foreign (non U.S.) partner, the partnership is required to withhold taxes at the highest rates at which the foreign partner would be taxed.

When assets are acquired by a hedge fund that may trigger the ECI tax, it is common for these assets to be held by a separate corporation formed by the hedge fund for this specific purpose. These separate corporations are referred to as "blockers" and act as a quarantine mechanism to isolate the ECI to a discreet group of assets without infecting the other investments held by the hedge fund. The blocker corporation is normally formed in the United States, files tax returns and pays all relevant taxes, and is ultimately liquidated back into the hedge fund when the underlying assets are disposed of.

Master-Feeder Fund Structures

An investment manager often manages several funds simultaneously. When a common investment objective is being pursued for both domestic and foreign investors, the manager will likely be managing at least two funds, a domestic LP for the United States investors and a foreign corporation for the nonresident investors. This arrangement, known as a "side-by-side" structure, would look this:

Figure 10.2 - Side by Side Hedge Fund Structure

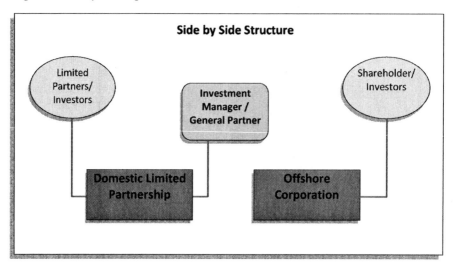

Side-by-side structures create many operational challenges for the manager. Among the more important of these is the inefficiency of having to fill multiple orders when positions are being bought and sold. This can lead to additional costs in the form of duplicative brokerage processing costs (often referred to as "ticket charges"). Further, there may be insufficient market liquidity to entirely fill a buy or sell order leaving the manager with the need to allocate partial fills to the side-by—side funds. Master-feeder structures address and largely solve these problems.

In a master-feeder structure, an additional partnership entity is formed into which the side by side funds invest their assets. The funds into which the investors invest their money are referred to as "feeder funds." The newly formed partnership into which the feeders invest is referred to as the "master fund." The arrangement would look like this:

Figure 10.3 - Master-Feeder Structure

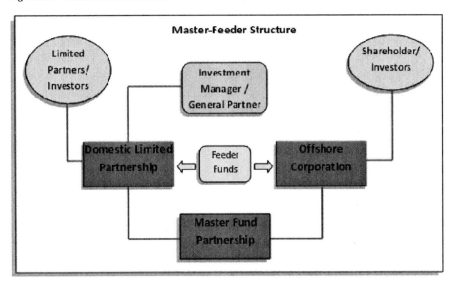

In this way the investment activity takes place at the master fund level, eliminating the duplicative brokerage processing costs and difficulties associated with partial order fills.

Fund of Funds

A fund of funds (sometimes called fund of hedge funds) is an investment vehicle which invests in other hedge funds and private equity funds. This is done to achieve diversification and to provide access to funds in which the individual investor may not be able to invest directly either through lack of access or an inability to meet minimum investment criteria. The fund of funds normally charges a separate set of fees, typically a 1% management fee and a 10% performance fee.

Prime Brokerage Arrangements

Hedge fund managers normally maintain relationships with many broker dealers in the ordinary course of managing their funds. This creates yet another operational challenge; maintaining multiple brokerage accounts requires moving money and securities from account to account as securities are bought and sold at the various brokerages. As the hedge fund industry grew in the early 1990s, the need to create a means of centralizing a hedge fund's operations became apparent. Thus, the prime brokerage arrangement was created.

Think of the prime broker (PB) as a central cashiering and custodial function. The PB will:

- pay for securities that are purchased by the hedge fund at other broker dealers (referred to as executing brokers)and take custody of those securities on settlement date,

- deliver securities sold through an executing broker and receive sales proceeds on settlement date,

- provide margin financing,

206

- facilitate short sales by arranging for securities borrowing, and

- provide trading and risk management analytical support.

Thus, the PB effectively acts as a hedge fund's settlement and clearance department. Because the use of PB arrangements increases industry-wide systemic credit risk, there are several requirements that must be met before a prime brokerage relationship can be initiated. To standardize industry practices, in September 1989 the Securities Industry Association (now called the Securities Industry Financial Markets Association), a brokerage industry trade group, requested no-action guidance from the Securities and Exchange Commission to clarify that emerging industry practices were in conformity with various aspects of federal securities laws (a no-action letter is a letter issued by the Commission stating that enforcement actions will not be taken if the party requesting the letter acts in an agreed upon manner). The SEC issued the no action letter on January 25, 1994, which is reproduced at the end of this chapter. The provisions of this no-action letter continue to guide the operation of prime brokerage relationships.

In order to control concentrations of credit exposure and to maintain confidentiality of trading strategies, many hedge fund managers maintain more than one PB relationship. Although this is understandable, maintaining too large a number of PB relationships ultimately defeats the purpose of centralizing hedge fund operations. Further, if the trading strategy involves short selling, many PBs require that the short sale and the borrowing of the securities both be done within their institution.

Private Equity Funds

Private equity funds are structurally comparable to hedge funds but differ in their investment objective. Hedge funds traditionally invest in publicly traded marketable securities. Private equity funds, by contrast, invest in securities that often have no active trading market. In many private equity transactions, the private equity fund owns all or a controlling interest in the portfolio company, which may have been a publicly traded company prior to its acquisition by the private equity fund.

Other differences relate to the mechanics of fee computations and liquidity availability.

Management fees in hedge funds are computed on investor capital, which is virtually always contributed in full upon subscribing to the hedge fund. In private equity funds, the normal relationship involves the investor making a commitment for a finite investment period which is then drawn upon by the manager as acceptable investment opportunities present themselves. Many private equity funds levy the management fee based on the commitment, which can dramatically increase the effective management fee percentage. Other funds, often with less prominent managers (or those lacking a track record), charge the management fee only on the capital commitment actually drawn.

Performance fees for private equity funds are normally charged only on realized profits subject to claw-backs. In hedge funds, the typical arrangement calls for the payment of performance fees on both realized and unrealized profits, subject to a high water mark (discussed earlier in this chapter). Assets held by hedge funds are marked to market in accordance with Statement of Financial Standards No. 157 of the Financial Accounting Standards Board.

Investor redemption and liquidity provisions for private equity funds are also significantly different than for hedge funds. In private equity funds, money is returned to investors after assets of the fund are sold; there are no redemption rights or other liquidity provisions. Accordingly, the

208

mechanisms that restrict liquidity (gates, suspensions) are not relevant in private equity funds.

Private equity funds have a wide variety of investment objectives. **Leveraged Buy-out (LBO) and Management Buy-out (MBO)** funds buy entire companies, often cashing out public shareholders, and are extremely illiquid. The investment objective is to enhance performance through management improvement, EBITDA (earnings before interest, taxes, depreciation and amortization) and multiple growth, and eventual resale. Typical holding periods within the fund is between three and seven years.

Mezzanine Funds provide the "gap" financing between debt and equity to other private equity funds.

Venture Capital Funds provide seed capital to newer companies with the ultimate objective of going public.

Appendix 10 Prime Broker Committee Request

UNITED STATES
SECURITIES AND EXCHANGE COMMISSION
WASHINGTON, D.C. 20549

DIVISION OF
MARKET REGULATION

January 25, 1994

Mr. Jeffrey C. Bernstein
Prime Broker Committee
c/o Bear, Stearns & Co., Inc.
One Metrotech Center North
Brooklyn, NY 11201

Re: Prime Broker Committee Request

Dear Mr. Bernstein:

This is in response to your letter dated September 13, 1989 on behalf of the Prime Broker Committee[1] in which you requested the views of the Division of Market Regulation of the Securities and Exchange Commission ("Division") and the Division of Banking Supervision and Regulation of the Board of Governors of the Federal Reserve System ("FRS Division") regarding the applicability of Sections 7, 10, 11(d), 15(c)(3) and 17 of the Securities Exchange Act of 1934 ("Exchange Act")[2] and Regulation T[3] thereunder, and Rules 10a-1, 10b-10, 11d1-1, 15c3-1 and 15c3-3 under the Exchange Act[4] to prime broker arrangements.[5]

---

[1]   We understand that the Prime Broker Committee consists of representatives from prime brokers and executing brokers and the Credit Division of the Securities Industry Association. The Committee was organized to review and evaluate the operation of prime broker arrangements and recommend appropriate changes to regulations in order to clarify the responsibilities and obligations of the various parties.

[2]   15 U.S.C. §§ 78g, 78j(b), 78k(d) & 78o(c)(3).

[3]   12 C.F.R. Part 220.

[4]   17 C.F.R. §§ 240.10a-1, .10b-10, .11d1-1, .15c3-1 & .15c3-3.

[5]   This letter discusses some of the most significant provisions applicable to the prime broker arrangement. Nevertheless, it is the responsibility of the parties to a prime broker arrangement to comply with all applicable provisions of the securities laws and regulations.

A GUIDE TO CAPITAL MARKETS

Mr. Jeffrey C. Bernstein
January 25, 1994
Page 2

I. **Background**

On the basis of your letter, and subsequent conversations, we understand the facts to be the following.

Prime brokerage is a system developed by full-service firms to facilitate the clearance and settlement of securities trades for substantial retail and institutional investors who are active market participants. Prime brokerage involves three distinct parties: the prime broker, the executing broker, and the customer. The prime broker is a registered broker-dealer that clears and finances the customer trades executed by one or more other registered broker-dealers ("executing broker") at the behest of the customer. Each of the executing brokers receives a letter from the prime broker agreeing to clear and carry each trade placed by the customer with the executing broker where the customer directs delivery of money or securities to be made to or by the prime broker.

The customer maintains its funds and securities in an account with the prime broker. Orders placed with the executing broker are effected through an account with the executing broker in the name of the prime broker for the benefit of the customer. When a customer places a trade order ("trade date"), the executing broker buys or sells securities in accordance with the customer's instructions. On trade date, the customer notifies the prime broker of the trade performed by the executing broker. The transaction is recorded in the customer's cash or margin account with the prime broker. At the same time, the prime broker records the transaction in a "fail-to-receive/deliver" account with the executing broker.

The prime broker issues a confirmation or notification to the customer and computes all applicable credit and Regulation T amounts. The executing broker confirms the transaction with the prime broker through the Depository Trust Company's Institutional Delivery System. The prime broker then will affirm the trade if its information matches successfully with the information received from the executing broker. The trade may then be submitted to the National Securities Clearing Corporation for clearance and settlement following normal settlement procedures. The prime broker then settles with the customer in the normal way.

The prime broker issues a statement of account to its customer at least on a monthly basis. The statement includes all security transactions during that period and the resultant customer security positions and money balances.

211

Mr. Jeffrey C. Bernstein
January 25, 1994
Page 3

The Prime Broker Committee believes that this arrangement is advantageous to prime brokerage customers because the prime broker acts as a clearing facility and accountant for all of the customer's security transactions wherever executed as well as a central custodian for the customer's securities and funds.

II. Prime Broker Committee Proposal

The Prime Broker Committee has proposed that, for purposes of Regulation T, transactions effected for the customer, between the executing broker and the prime broker, should be deemed broker-to-broker transactions after completion of the affirmation process. The Prime Broker Committee also has proposed that, (*i*) prior to the commencement of any prime brokerage activity, the prime broker send a letter to the executing broker authorizing the executing broker to accept orders from the customer, which will be settled by the prime broker, and (*ii*) the prime broker should have two business days to disaffirm trades before it must accept settlement responsibility for trades executed on behalf of its prime broker clients.

The Prime Broker Committee believes that providing the prime broker with two business days to disaffirm trades before finally accepting settlement responsibility for trades executed on behalf of customers is necessary to allow prime brokers sufficient time to review and ensure, among other things, that the trade is within the credit limits established for the customer's account. In the event the prime broker disaffirms a trade, the executing broker would be precluded from asserting that the prime broker, whose name had been "given up" by the customer, but who had no knowledge of a particular trade at the time it was effected, should be the responsible party for consummating settlement of the transaction. Moreover, disaffirmed trades would be treated as customer transactions on the books of the executing broker, and, therefore, subject to the provisions of Regulation T. Since the trade could be disaffirmed by the prime broker, the Prime Broker Committee believes that the executing broker would be compelled to fulfill its compliance responsibilities with respect to the particular transaction and customer.

III. Discussion

The relationships described in your letter, as outlined above (*i.e.*, "prime brokerage" or "prime broker arrangement"), raise several questions under the Exchange Act. After analyzing current practices, the Division and the FRS Division have determined that there is a need to clarify the obligations and responsibilities under the Exchange Act of each of the parties involved in prime brokerage. The following is a discussion of the application of the margin and credit regulations and the customer

Mr. Jeffrey C. Bernstein
January 25, 1994
Page 4

confirmation, short sale, customer protection, and net capital provisions to prime brokerage.

A.   Regulation T

Regulation T requires a broker or dealer to record all transactions with a single person in a margin account unless specifically authorized for inclusion in another account.[6] Securities transactions effected for a customer of a prime broker should be recorded in a margin account or, where permitted, a cash account. Regulation T currently requires the executing broker to treat the customer as its own customer and record the transaction in a cash or margin account at that firm since it can be said that the executing broker is extending or arranging for the extension of credit to the customer until at least settlement date. The executing broker, however, generally settles prime brokerage transactions following normal settlement procedures through the prime broker's account at the executing broker, which is designated as a broker-dealer credit account. This method appears to regard the customer as an agent of the prime broker for purposes of these transactions, and to disregard the creditor/customer relationship between the executing broker and the customer.

Normally, under Regulation T, if a customer's margin purchase or short sale is involved, the executing broker would have to determine whether a margin deposit is required in a margin account.[7] The required margin amount would have to be deposited in the customer's account at the executing broker within seven business days after the margin deficiency had been created.[8] Regulation T, moreover, would require that the executing broker liquidate securities in a margin account to meet a margin call or to eliminate any margin deficiency exceeding $500, if a margin call is not met in full within the required time.[9]

If the transactions were effected in a cash account, the executing broker would be able to buy from or sell to the customer a security only under certain restrictive

---

[6]   12 C.F.R. § 220.1(b)(1).

[7]   12 C.F.R. §§ 220.4(b), (c) & .5(a), (b) & (c).

[8]   12 C.F.R. § 220.4(c)(3).

[9]   12 C.F.R. § 220.4(d).

Mr. Jeffrey C. Bernstein
January 25, 1994
Page 5

credit conditions.[10] Transactions in the cash account are predicated on the broker accepting in good faith the customer's agreement that all securities sold have already been paid for and all securities bought will be paid for before being sold.[11] In this account, full cash payment for any customer purchases generally must be made within seven business days of trade date.[12]

If the customer has not paid in full for securities before the securities are delivered to the prime broker, the account at the executing broker would be subject to a 90-day freeze.[13] Under prime brokerage as described in your letter, however, the customer never pays the executing broker, but rather the prime broker. If the account at the executing broker were a cash account, it would be "frozen" (i.e., securities purchases could be effected only if cash sufficient to pay for the securities is on hand prior to the execution of the trade) every time a security purchased is sent to the prime broker for payment by the customer.[14]

The 90-day freeze would not apply if the securities are delivered to the prime broker for deposit in a cash account which holds sufficient funds to pay for the delivered securities.[15] For this purpose, the executing broker would need to rely on a written statement from the prime broker specifying that sufficient funds are held in the customer's account at the prime broker to cover that particular trade ("letter of free funds").[16]

B.   Section 11(d)(1)

Section 11(d)(1) of the Exchange Act prohibits a person who is both a broker and a dealer from directly or indirectly extending, maintaining, or arranging for the

---

[10]   See 12 C.F.R. § 220.8(a).

[11]   12 C.F.R. §220.8(a)(1) & (2).

[12]   12 C.F.R. § 220.8(b)(1).

[13]   12 C.F.R. § 220.8(c)(1).

[14]   12 C.F.R. § 220.8(c)(1).

[15]   12 C.F.R. § 220.8(c)(2).

[16]   12 C.F.R. § 220.8(c)(2)(ii).

extension or maintenance of credit on any security "which was part of a new issue in the distribution of which he participated as a member of a selling syndicate or group" within the prior thirty days. Generally, this means that, absent an exemption, a customer of a broker-dealer may not purchase a new issue security from or through that broker-dealer on credit for thirty days after the completion of the broker-dealer's participation in the offering as a member of the selling syndicate or group.

Absent the prime broker relationship, Rule 11d1-1(a) permits the customer's purchase of a security from a selling group member to be financed in a margin account of a second broker (even one involved in the distribution) if the second broker did not arrange the transaction. In a prime broker relationship in which the customer initiates the margin account with the prime broker, the customer generally can be viewed as having arranged for the credit provided through the margin account with the prime broker. Thus, where the prime broker is not a member of a selling group or syndicate, the prime broker's extension of credit for the purchase of the security through an executing broker who is a member of the syndicate is permissible as long as the credit extension was not arranged by the executing broker. Similarly, where the prime broker alone, or both the prime broker and the executing broker are members of the selling group or syndicate, the extension of credit for the purchase of the security from the executing broker is permissible absent an arranging of the credit by either broker.

Whether a financing has been impermissibly arranged is a question of fact. One example of such an "arranging" would be where a salesman of the prime broker that is a selling group member solicited a purchase order from a customer and, after being told by the customer that the customer wished to margin the purchase, the salesperson directed the customer to an executing broker knowing that the transaction would be financed in the customer's prime broker margin account. An impermissible arranging also would be present where an executing broker participating in a distribution arranged for the customer to establish a prime broker account at another broker-dealer to facilitate the financing of the security being distributed.

C.   Customer Confirmations

Rule 10b-10 of the Exchange Act requires a broker or dealer, at or before the completion of a security transaction, to send its customer a confirmation of the trade.[17] The confirmation typically serves as an invoice and gives the customer an

---

[17]   17 C.F.R. § 240.10b-10.

215

opportunity to verify and evaluate the details of the trade. The obligation to send the confirmation normally falls on the broker with whom the customer places the order since that broker generally has most of the information needed to comply with the disclosure requirements of the rule.

In the prime broker arrangement, the executing broker takes the order from the customer, yet the prime broker typically issues the confirmation. Consequently, the prime broker may not have all the information required to be on the confirmation by Rule 10b-10. Moreover, there appears to be uncertainty whether information regarding the executing broker must be included on the confirmation.

We believe that the executing broker is required to send to the customer a confirmation of each trade placed with the executing broker pursuant to the prime broker arrangement and such confirmation must comply with the requirements of Rule 10b-10. You indicate, however, that customers generally do not wish to receive individual confirmations directly from the executing broker, and would prefer to receive notification of transactions solely from the prime broker.

Thus, in lieu of the executing broker sending the confirmation directly to the customer, the executing broker would, based on written instructions from the customer, send such confirmation to the customer in care of its prime broker. Such written instructions to the executing broker would (i) explicitly request that the executing broker send the confirmation to the customer in care of its prime broker, (ii) be a separate instrument from the prime broker agreement, (iii) not be a condition of entering into a prime broker or executing broker arrangement, and (iv) not be induced by differential fees based on whether an instruction is provided. The prime broker would inform the customer in writing that the confirmation sent by the executing broker to the customer in care of the prime broker is available promptly from the prime broker upon request, at no additional charge.

On the day following the trade, the prime broker would send to the customer a notification of each trade placed with the executing broker pursuant to the prime broker arrangement, based on information provided by the customer. The prime broker would request in writing that the customer provide it with all the information required on confirmations by Rule 10b-10; however, the notification from the prime broker to the customer may omit the capacity of the executing broker, a designation of the trade price as an average price, and, in principal trades, the reported trade price and the difference between this price and the net price to the customer, if the customer fails to provide this information. The notification would clearly identify the executing broker and prime broker and their roles in the trade. If the prime broker

216

Mr. Jeffrey C. Bernstein
January 25, 1994
Page 8

charges a transaction-based fee, the notification would indicate the amount of the fee charged in the trade in addition to indicating any commission charged by the executing broker.

We note that, in addition to the specific requirements of Rule 10b-10, the general anti-fraud provisions of the securities laws require broker-dealers to disclose to their customers all facts that are material to the transaction.

D.   Short Sales

Rule 10a-1 under the Exchange Act prohibits any person, for his account or for the account of another, from effecting a short sale of a security covered by the rule under the following conditions: (i) at a price below the price at which the immediately preceding sale was effected ("minus tick"), or (ii) at the last sale price if it was lower than the last preceding different price ("zero-minus tick").[18] Rule 10a-1(c) prohibits broker-dealers from effecting a sell order without marking the order either "long" or "short". The responsibility for compliance with these requirements must obviously rest with the executing broker.

The executing broker has the responsibility of ascertaining, from the prime broker or otherwise, that the shares will be available for borrowing in order to effect a timely delivery. The National Association of Securities Dealers, Inc. ("NASD") and the New York Stock Exchange, Inc. ("NYSE") require a member firm, prior to effecting a customer's short sale, to make an affirmative determination that the security is available or that it can borrow the security on behalf of the customer for delivery by the settlement date.[19] The prime broker also must be aware of the nature of the sale because short sales must be recorded in a margin account and margined in accordance with Regulation T.

IV.   Response

The trading relationship currently in existence between the prime broker, the executing broker and the customer does not fit in any of the account structures of

---

[18]   17 C.F.R. § 240.10a-1(a)(1)(i).

[19]   See Section (b)(2) to the NASD Board of Governors Interpretation on Prompt Receipt and Delivery of Securities; NYSE Rule 440C, "Delivery Against Short Sales," Interpretation of .10/10 "Short Sale."

Mr. Jeffrey C. Bernstein
January 25, 1994
Page 9

Regulation T. The Division's staff believes that under the current terms of Regulation T, the account opened at the executing broker ("the Account") does not appear to be a broker-dealer credit account because there is a client relationship between the executing broker and the customer. However, based on the above discussion, after consultations with the FRS Division, and without necessarily agreeing with the legal conclusions set forth by the Prime Broker Committee in any of the various written and oral communications with the Division, as of six months from the date of this letter, the Division will not recommend that the Commission take enforcement action if, pursuant to a prime broker arrangement as discussed above, the executing broker and the prime broker treat the Account as if it were a broker-dealer credit account pursuant to Section 220.11 of Regulation T,[20] provided that the following conditions set forth below are met.[21]

1. A broker-dealer must notify its Designated Examining Authority ("DEA") that it intends to act as a prime broker.

2. A broker-dealer acting as a prime broker must have net capital[22] of at least $1,500,000. A prime broker that is not in compliance with this provision must notify immediately all parties with whom it engages in prime brokerage activities, either individually or through the facilities of a clearing agency registered under Section 17A of the Exchange Act[23].

3. Broker-dealers acting as executing brokers who clear prime broker transactions or broker-dealers clearing prime broker transactions on behalf of executing brokers must have net capital of at least $1,000,000. An executing broker that is not in compliance with this provision must notify immediately all parties with whom it engages in prime brokerage activities, either individually or through the facilities of a clearing agency registered under Section 17A of the Exchange Act.

---

[20] 12 C.F.R. § 220.11.

[21] Accordingly, if the conditions set forth in this letter are met, a letter of free funds would not be required for transactions in the Account that are paid for through the customer's account at the prime broker.

[22] See 17 C.F.R. § 240.15c3-1.

[23] 15 U.S.C. § 78q-1.

Mr. Jeffrey C. Bernstein
January 25, 1994
Page 10

4.   A prime broker may not settle prime broker trades on behalf of a customer, unless the customer keeps a minimum net equity with the prime broker of at least $500,000 in cash or securities with a ready market.[24] If, as a result of fluctuations in the value of securities kept with the prime broker, the customer's net equity falls below the required minimum amount, the customer shall have until 12:00 noon of the fifth business day after the date when the net equity level fell below the required minimum amount to restore it to the $500,000 level.

If the customer fails to do so, the prime broker settling trades on behalf of such customer will notify, by the close of business of the fifth day, all broker dealers (either individually or through the facilities of a clearing agency registered under Section 17A of the Exchange Act) with whom it has a prime broker contract on behalf of the customer that it is no longer acting as a prime broker for the customer. A prime broker must indicate that it does not know ("DK") any prime brokerage transaction commenced on behalf of the customer on the day after it has sent the notification required by this provision.[25]

A prime broker may settle prime broker trades on behalf of customer accounts managed by an investment adviser registered under Section 203 of the Investment Advisers Act of 1940,[26] if each account has a minimum net equity of at least $100,000 in cash or securities with a ready market.

A prime broker may settle prime broker transactions on behalf of a customer who keeps a minimum net equity with the prime broker of at least $100,000 in cash or securities with a ready market, if said account is subject to a binding, written contract providing for a cross-guarantee by another customer of the prime broker. Pursuant to this provision, a customer may cross-guarantee

---

[24]   17 C.F.R. §240.15c3-1(c)(11) (defining the term "ready market").

[25]   Until January 1, 1995 or such time as The Depository Trust Company's Institutional Delivery System is enhanced to support the possibility of DKs for trades, if later, for purposes of this provision, a prime broker utilizing the facilities of a clearing agency for the issuance of trade confirmations and affirmations may not affirm any prime brokerage transaction commenced on behalf of the customer on the day after it has sent the notification required by this provision.

[26]   15 U.S.C. § 80b-3.

219

Mr. Jeffrey C. Bernstein
January 25, 1994
Page 11

another customer's account only if it keeps net equity with the prime broker of at least $500,000 in cash or securities with a ready market. Cross-guarantees of other customers would require additional net equity of $400,000 for each individual account that is cross-guaranteed. This provision does not affect a prime broker's obligations and responsibilities under Regulation T.[27]

5.   Documentation

A.   Prior to the commencement of any prime brokerage activity, the prime broker and the executing self clearing firm or the clearing firm of an introducing broker acting as an executing broker must execute a contract that specifies the obligations and responsibilities of the parties regarding the prime broker arrangement.

(i)   The obligations and responsibilities set forth in the contract must be consistent with the conditions specified in this letter.

(ii)   The contract must conform to the terms set forth in condition 8 below, and specifically set forth the executing broker's acknowledgement of its responsibility to know its customers, obtain all the proper documentation (including all new account documents), conduct its own credit checks, and determine the availability of shares to cover any short sales and process disaffirmed trades.

(iii)   The contract must specify that, upon termination of the prime broker relationship with respect to a particular customer, the prime broker shall notify the executing brokers, whether individually or through the facilities of a clearing agency registered under Section 17A of the Exchange Act, that it is no longer acting as a prime broker for the customer.

B.   In addition to all written agreements necessary under the Federal securities laws and regulations, the prime broker and the executing broker, individually, must execute contracts with each customer on whose behalf the executing and the prime broker execute or settle prime brokerage transactions. Said contracts must be signed by the customer,

---

[27]   *See* 12 C.F.R. § 220.3(d).

and specify the obligations and responsibilities of the parties regarding the prime broker arrangement. The obligations and responsibilities set forth in these contracts must be consistent with the conditions specified in this letter.

C.   In cases involving introducing broker-dealers who act as executing brokers, the executing broker must inform each broker-dealer clearing its transactions that it intends to act as an executing broker.

   (i)   The executing broker and its clearing firm must execute a contract that specifies the obligations and responsibilities of the parties in the prime broker arrangement.

   (ii)   The obligations and responsibilities set forth in this contract must be consistent with the conditions specified in this letter.

The executing broker and the prime broker must keep in their possession copies of these contracts along with all other written agreements necessary to be able to execute or settle prime brokerage trades on behalf of customers. These documents must be kept in an easily accessible place and be produced upon request by the staff of the Commission or of any self-regulatory organization ("SRO") of which they are members.

6.   The prime broker must keep separate records identifying all customers using the prime broker arrangement, along with the executing brokers employed by such customers. These separate records must be kept in an easily accessible place and be produced upon request by the staff of the Commission or of any SRO of which it is a member.

7.   For all transactions, the customer and the executing broker must inform the prime broker of the contract amount, the security involved, number of shares or number of units, and whether the transaction was a long or short sale or a purchase, by the morning of the next business day after trade date.

Parties to a prime broker arrangement must utilize the facilities of a clearing agency registered under Section 17A of the Exchange Act for the issuance of trade confirmations and affirmations, provided, that such facilities comply with the provisions of this letter and, in particular, that confirmations are issued and received by the morning of the next business day after trade date.

Mr. Jeffrey C. Bernstein
January 25, 1994
Page 13

8.   The prime broker must be responsible to settle each of the customer's transactions placed with the executing broker and timely confirmed to and received by the prime broker in accordance with the provisions of condition 7 above, unless the prime broker disaffirms or DKs a particular transaction by no later than the close of business (as this term is defined by the corresponding clearing agency) of trade date plus one.[28] Accordingly, the executing broker must undertake its own credit review to ensure that it knows the customer as to these transactions.[29]

When utilizing the facilities of a clearing agency registered under Section 17A of the Exchange Act for the issuance of trade confirmations and affirmations, a prime broker may disaffirm or DK[30] a particular transaction before the close of business (as this term is defined by the corresponding clearing agency) of the day following the date when it receives a trade confirmation which was timely entered by the executing broker, if, due to unusual circumstances affecting the operations of the clearing agency (including, but not limited to, technical difficulties, natural disasters or power blackouts), the prime broker receives the trade confirmation for that particular transaction after 12:00 noon (eastern time) of trade date plus one. When necessary, a prime broker must disaffirm

---

[28]   In cases where trade data is corrected in the form of "as of" trades and the corresponding confirmation is received by the prime broker before noon, the prime broker must be responsible to settle such transaction placed with the executing broker, unless the prime broker disaffirms or DKs the trade by no later than the close of business (as this term is defined by the corresponding clearing agency) of the day when the prime broker receives the confirmation. If the confirmation is received after noon the prime broker will have until the close of business of the next business day to disaffirm or DK the trade.

[29]   The ability to disaffirm is otherwise inconsistent with the structure of a broker-dealer credit account under the current language of Regulation T.

[30]   Until January 1, 1995 or such time as The Depository Trust Company's Institutional Delivery System is enhanced to support the possibility of DKs for trades, if later, a prime broker utilizing the facilities of a clearing agency for the issuance of trade confirmations and affirmations will be responsible to settle customers' transactions placed with the executing broker, only when such trades have been affirmed but not disaffirmed in accordance with the time frames set forth in this condition.

222

Mr. Jeffrey C. Bernstein
January 25, 1994
Page 14

or DK a particular transaction through the facilities of the clearing agency that issued the trade confirmation.

In all cases, if the prime broker receives a confirmation on a day when the major securities markets are closed, the prime broker shall have until the close of business (as this term is defined by the corresponding clearing agency) of the next day when the major securities markets are open to DK or disaffirm that trade.

9. The prime broker must keep a record that identifies all trades disaffirmed during the previous three years, specifying the identities of the executing broker and the customer for each trade.

    A. This record kept by the prime broker identifying all trades disaffirmed during the previous three years must be kept in an easily accessible place and be produced upon request by the staff of the Commission or of the SRO of which they are members.

    B. If the prime broker disaffirms or DKs a trade, then the transaction will continue to be treated as a customer transaction on the books of the executing broker. If the disaffirmed or DKed trade is a short sale, the executing broker will treat the transaction as if it had been executed in a customer margin account.

10. The executing broker must comply with all the applicable short sale provisions and, prior to the execution of any short sale, the executing broker must determine that securities can be borrowed to deliver against the short sale.

11. Pursuant to Rule 10b-10 under the Exchange Act, the executing broker must send directly to the customer a confirmation of each trade placed with the executing broker pursuant to the prime broker arrangement. Such confirmation must comply with the specific requirements of Rule 10b-10. Alternatively, the executing broker may send the confirmation to the customer in care of the prime broker if the customer has instructed the executing broker to do so in writing in an instrument separate from the prime broker agreement. Such an instrument must not be a condition for entering into the prime broker arrangement or executing trades through the executing broker, or be induced by differential fees based on whether an instruction is provided. The prime broker must inform the customer in writing that the confirmation sent by the

executing broker to the customer in care of the prime broker is available to the customer without charge promptly on request.

In addition, on the day following the transaction, the prime broker must send to the customer a notification of each trade placed with the executing broker pursuant to the prime broker arrangement, based on information provided by the customer. Such notification must include all the information required for confirmations by Rule 10b-10 except the capacity of the executing broker, an average price designation, and, in principal trades, the reported trade price and the difference between that price and the net price to the customer, if the customer fails to provide this information to the prime broker. Such notification also must disclose any transaction-based charges imposed by the prime broker, in addition to disclosing any commission charged by the executing broker.

12. The executing broker must keep and preserve the records required under subparagraphs (a)(6), (a)(7) and (a)(9) of Rule 17a-3[31] relating to trades placed with the executing broker pursuant to the prime broker arrangement.

13. If the prime broker disaffirms a trade the following steps must be taken:

A. the prime broker must send a cancellation notification to the customer to offset the notification sent on the day following trade date.

B. the executing broker must immediately send a new confirmation of the replacement transaction to the customer.

The replacement confirmation must disclose the information required under Rule 10b-10 under the Exchange Act.

14. Section 11(d)(1) prohibits an executing broker from extending or arranging for a prime broker to extend credit on a security sold by the executing broker to the customer if the executing broker was a member of a selling syndicate or group within the prior thirty days; however, the prime broker may extend credit on such a security in a margin account previously established independently by the customer if this credit was not otherwise arranged by the executing broker. Section 11(d)(1) also prohibits a prime broker from

---

[31]   17 C.F.R. § 240.17a-3(a)(6) & (a)(7).

extending credit on a security that it has sold or arranged for the executing broker to sell to the customer if the prime broker was a member of a selling syndicate or group for the security in the prior thirty days; however, pursuant to Rule 11d1-1(a), a prime broker may extend credit in a prime broker account on a security sold by an executing broker if the prime broker has not otherwise arranged for that sale.

15. The prime broker must treat the customer as its own customer for all purposes including Regulation T and Rules 15c3-1, 15c3-3, 17a-3 and 17a-4 under the Exchange Act, if it does not disaffirm or DK the trade as provided above. For example, if the account at the prime broker is a cash account, the prime broker is responsible for implementing the 90-day freeze under Regulation T if securities are sold before they are fully paid. If the prime broker disaffirms or DKs any trade, the executing broker must treat the customer as its own customer for each transaction which is disaffirmed or DKed.

16. Broker-dealers may not engage in prime brokerage activities with other broker-dealers or with customers if they actually know or have reason to know that such party is not in compliance with the provisions of this letter.

This is a position of the Division's staff concerning enforcement action with regard to certain aspects of Sections 7, 10, 11(d), 15(c)(3) and 17 of the Exchange Act and Regulation T thereunder, and Rules 10a-1, 10b-10, 11d1-1, 15c3-1, 15c3-3, 17a-3 and 17a-4 under the Exchange Act, and does not represent any legal conclusions. This position is based solely on the description and representations made to the Division and the FRS Division, as set forth above. Any factual variations might require a different response. This position may be withdrawn or modified if the Division determines that such action is necessary in the public interest, for the protection of investors, or otherwise, in furtherance of the purposes of the securities laws.

Mr. Jeffrey C. Bernstein
January 25, 1994
Page 17

The staff of the Division believes that the outlined treatment is a reasonable interim approach to the issues associated with prime brokerage. On or before December 31, 1995, the staff of the Division will notify the Prime Broker Committee with respect to extensions, modifications or termination of the no-action position expressed in this letter. During this period we will seek the assistance of the Prime Broker Committee in determining the appropriate course of action.

Sincerely,

Brandon Becker

Brandon Becker
Director

Chapter
11

Regulation of Broker Dealers

The Securities Exchange Act of 1934 ("Exchange Act" or "Act") governs the way in which the nation's securities markets and its brokers and dealers are regulated. The Exchange Act generally imposes registration requirements on "brokers" and "dealers" of securities. In most cases this means registration with the Securities and Exchange Commission (SEC) and oversight by at least one self-regulatory organization (SRO). SROs include the Financial Industry Regulatory Authority (Finra) and exchanges of which the broker dealer is a member. When a party registers as a broker-dealer, the application is made with the SEC on Form BD. The SEC, after examining the Form BD, will normally act on the application within 45 days, although SRO applications take considerably longer, often more than six months. In the day-to-day operations of broker-dealers, the vast majority of a firm's regulatory interaction with regulators will be with the SROs. It is possible for the SEC to do direct audits, which generally fall into three categories: oversight, sweeps, and cause. In most cases, the examinations are left to the SROs to whom the routine business of regulating broker dealers is delegated by the SEC.

The penalties for noncompliance with broker-dealer registration requirements can be extremely severe; accordingly, it is imperative that parties conducting broker-dealer activities properly register under the Act.

Activities Requiring Registration: "Brokers"

Section 3(a)(4)(A) of the Exchange Act defines a broker as any person in the business of effecting transactions in securities for the accounts of others. Sometimes this is an easy call, other times not. Certainly a party executing or directing transactions on a securities exchange must be properly registered. Conversely, if the item being bought or sold isn't a "security," the Exchange Act will not apply as a jurisdictional matter. Among the most contentious questions that arise are the registration requirements applicable to "finders." Finder activities include identifying customers for properly registered broker-dealers on a split fee basis, identifying or soliciting investment banking clients, identifying investors for new business ventures, or assisting in the sale of existing businesses. I can tell you as a practicing lawyer that among the most difficult things I have had to tell clients is they can't take referral fees for this type of activity without registering as a broker-dealer. This usually elicits the "everyone does it" defense. My advice: register. If not, don't take the fee. The SEC will look at several factors to determine if a finder's behavior has crossed the line requiring registration. Several factors are considered by the SEC to determine whether a finder's activities require registration; those usually receiving the greatest scrutiny are:

- the degree of participation the finder had in the transaction, including solicitation, negotiation, and/or execution.

- the manner in which the finder is compensated. The SEC will take a dim view of success-based fees, particularly those which are dependent upon the size of the ultimate transaction.

228

- the degree to which the finder is engaged in facilitating or executing securities transactions.

- the handling of securities or funds of others in connection with the transaction.

Finder issues arise most frequently with raising funds in private placements. Remember that in private placements, the issuer is claiming an exemption from the registration requirements of the 1933 Securities Act. Although the transaction may be exempt under the 1933 Act, if the interests being offered are securities, parties who are compensated for placing these exempt securities must still be registered as broker dealers.

Activities Requiring Registration: "Dealers"

While brokers act in an agency capacity, dealers act in principals. As such, there are far fewer factual disputes regarding the scope of permitted behavior when addressing dealer activity. Section 3(a)(5) of the Exchange Act defines a dealer as any person buying or selling securities for his own account, through a broker or otherwise. Parties who buy and sell for their own account, but are not otherwise engaged in the securities business, are considered "traders" who are exempt from broker dealer registration.

The Regulatory Framework of Coordinating Broker Dealer Registration and Activities of Broker Dealer Personnel

In order to eliminate separate and duplicative broker-dealer registration of securities firms and the personnel that work for them, the regulatory framework for broker-dealer regulation establishes the concept of "associated persons." In this way, the firm registers as a broker-dealer and its personnel register with the firm as being associated with the registered firm. The scope of activities an associated person may conduct is subject to licensing requirements. (There are a series of licensing examinations which enable an associated person to conduct various duties for the firm.) Further, all associated persons are subject to supervision by the broker-dealer with whom they are associated. In the language of the industry, an associated person's licenses are "carried" by the firm with which they are associated. The firm is required to have a documented supervisory procedure guide, and these procedures are subject to audit and examination by the SROs and the SEC.

The Regulatory Framework Protecting the Interests of Customers-What Happens if a Broker Dealer Fails?

When businesses fail, they usually are subject to state law receiver actions or provisions contained in the federal bankruptcy code. Under federal bankruptcy law, the two major mechanisms for dealing with a failed business are Chapter 11 reorganizations or Chapter 7 liquidations. The objective in a court supervised liquidation of an enterprise is to sell or otherwise dispose of the assets of the entity so the proceeds can be distributed to the creditors of the firm. A central premise of bankruptcy law is the fair treatment of all similarly situated creditors of the bankrupt debtor. Obviously, in a bankruptcy there aren't enough assets to satisfy all claims. When there is less money then there are claims, everyone who is owed money should share equally in the available pot of cash. This is called equitable distribution. As a legal matter, broker-dealers cannot be reorganized under Chapter 11 in the event of a bankruptcy filing. Recognizing that general bankruptcy principles may not achieve the overriding policy objective of maintaining the public's confidence in markets, Congress and the SEC have adopted special statutes and regulations for purposes of enhancing the public's confidence.

In order to understand the regulatory framework protecting the interests of customers, it is instructive to examine the historical environment in which the relevant statutes were adopted and the public policy consideration that are embedded in the law.

The period in question was the 1960s and early 1970s. The 1960s witnessed an impressive increase in stock prices. The public naturally wanted in on this action, and stock market speculation became rampant. This wasn't the first time stock market mania took hold in the United States, and obviously, it wasn't the last. At the time, most securities were held in paper or "physical" form; the electronic revolution that transformed securities settlements were still more than a decade away. To facilitate physical settlements and to reduce the time it took physical settlements to occur, it became common to register securities in "street name," that is in the name of the broker- dealer (or a common agent) handling the settlements. This process eliminated the need to deliver settled securities to customers; the street name registered securities were now simply held by the customer's broker-dealer as custodian. This was a long held goal of both industry participants and regulators; eliminating customer-side physical security deliveries and deposits greatly enhance the settlement mechanisms of the securities industry. Further, settlement periods and the attendant systemic credit risk caused by lags between the dates a securities transaction is executed and settled, can be reduced by eliminating the inefficiencies created by physical securities.

One problem not sufficiently addressed during this transformation in the environment of the 1960s was that broker-dealers were now acting as custodians of customer assets, many of which were fully paid for by the customers. If the broker-dealer failed, those very assets, in the possession of the broker-dealer and registered in street name, could potentially be subject to unrelated claims by creditors of the broker-dealers. This is exactly what happened when broker-dealers began to fail in the 1969–1970 timeframe. The risk to customers existed because of the commingling of customer assets with assets belonging to the broker-dealer. Industry participants and regulators were unwilling to return to a system in which physical stock certificates were held directly by customers. Recognizing that customers would be unable to independently perform due diligence on the operations departments of broker-dealers, and in an attempt to restore the public's confidence in the financial system, Congress and the securities industry regulatory apparatus responded.

The Statutory Response: The Securities Investors Protection Act of 1970 (SIPA)

Recognizing the importance of restoring the public's confidence in the operation of the financial services/broker-dealer industry, Congress passed SIPA in 1970. In part, SIPA provided for structural safeguards that would prohibit commingling of customer assets with firm assets and made substantive changes to the US Bankruptcy Code. These changes give brokerage firm customers elevated standing in the event of a broker-dealer failure by giving customer-creditors priority standing. As is common in highly technical areas, Congress delegated its rule make authority to the federal agency expert in the relevant subject matter area, in this case the Securities and Exchange Commission (SEC). The SEC responded by proposing and then adopting a cornerstone regulation called the Customer Protection Rule (Rule 15c3-3 promulgated under the 1934 Securities Exchange Act). The Customer Protection Rule requires broker-dealers to segregate customer securities promptly after settlement to avoid the undesirable commingling previously described. Further, the US Bankruptcy Code was aligned with SIPA and in many meaningful ways is made subordinate to SIPA.

The mandate under the rule is for broker-dealers to "promptly" get customer securities under their "possession and control" after the settlement of the securities transaction. For purposes of the rule, promptly usually means one business day. Possession and control is a term of regulatory art; "possession" needs little in the away of elaboration; "control" alludes for the requirement that the security must be in a location under the physical control of the broker-dealer (or if the broker-dealer has failed, the bankruptcy court). Once reduced to possession and control, the broker-dealer's records must clearly reflect that the securities in question are the property of the customer. This method of reducing customer securities to possession and control (together with timely updating of accounting records) is often referred to as "segregation." By segregating customer assets, they are no longer commingled with firm assets. Thus, the risk that firm creditors will be able to reach customer assets to satisfy claims the creditors have against the firm is eliminated. As a result of a compromise between the industry and the SEC at the time the Customer Protection Rule was proposed, customer money balances generally only need to be segregated weekly. This compromise was struck in an era of physical securities settlements and has not been updated since. Money balances kept at broker-dealers are therefore potentially exposed to commingling risk until the required segregation is completed.

This process, of course, is only effective in the event that the broker-dealer is complying with the rules. In a rapid and unanticipated business failure, a broker-dealer may fail to properly segregate assets. Further, as the recent Bernard Madoff scandal clearly indicates, undetected fraudulent behavior may be taking place inside of the broker-dealer in which case the requisite assets are not segregated at the date of the failure of the broker- dealer. In the event of a broker-dealer bankruptcy, it is quite possible (and common) for there to be insufficient assets segregated to meet customer claims. SIPA therefore constructed a safety net for investors to meet this potentiality.

As part of SIPA, Congress created the Securities Investors

Protection Corporation (SIPC). SIPC is an industry funded entity operating under the authority and direction of the SEC. SIPC receives its operating funds by assessing broker-dealers, who by law must be SIPC members, with annual levies. In the event of a broker-dealer failure, SIPC may be required to advance funds to customers of broker-dealers who are unable to recover their assets from broker-dealers after the bankruptcy. This occurs, among other reasons, if customer assets have not been properly segregated in compliance with the previously described Customer Protection Rule. SIPC is required to advance up to $500,000 per separate customer account for missing customer property, of which $250,000 can be cash. Because of the financial exposure SIPC experiences if a broker dealer fails, if SIPC determines that customers are at financial risk during the liquidation, SIPC may petition the Bankruptcy Court to halt the normal bankruptcy proceeding and convert the case to a SIPA liquidation, overseen by the Bankruptcy Court. SIPC then directs the broker-dealer liquidation by appointing its own trustee. The trustee then acts as the liquidator of the broker-dealer and has all of the powers of a trustee in a standard bankruptcy case, subject to the limitation that he can't do anything inconsistent with SIPA.

Who is considered a "Customer" under SIPA?

In drafting the Customer Protection Rule, the SEC was mindful that the regulatory framework it was constructing was meant to protect the customer public from failures of broker dealers they were dealing with. Under the Rule, the term Customer means ... "any person from whom or on whose behalf a broker or dealer has received or acquired or holds funds or securities for the account of that person . . . ." The SEC then expanded upon the definition in the negative; a certain group is excluded from "customer protection." Most prominent among these are certain parties who are directors and officers of the broker-dealer. The drafters constructed a framework that would deny customer standing to those who have the ability to get an "inside look" or are otherwise involved with the management of the affairs of the failed broker-dealer; all others are afforded the protections of the rule as they lack the access to the operations of broker- dealers to do their own due diligence.

How does SIPC Protect Customers in the Event of a Broker Dealer Bankruptcy?

When customers of failed broker-dealers are found to be at risk, SIPC will take over the liquidation of the broker-dealer. Each separate customer account is covered for $500,000 of losses, of which $250,000 can be cash. (The $250,000 cash limit is meant to coordinate SIPC coverage with FDIC coverage limits for bank accounts.) The amount of the loss is measured as the "net equity" a customer has in the account. Net equity is the sum of the fair market value of securities held in the account (plus cash) less any loans the customer took out against the account through the broker-dealer.

The Regulatory Framework Governing Capital Adequacy of Broker Dealers

Another important feature of broker-dealer regulation is the Uniform Net Capital Rule, Rule 15c3-1. This is a capital adequacy rule that imposes minimum capital requirements and limits overleveraging of broker-dealers. This rule begins by taking a measure of the amount of capital that would survive a hypothetical broker-dealer bankruptcy and liquidation. This is accomplished by converting the broker-dealer's balance sheet from a going-concern to a liquidation basis. Consider the balance sheet of any broker-dealer; it displays the assets, liability, and owner's capital of the enterprise. In liquidation, the assets are sold, and the proceeds are used to pay off claims (liabilities); any remaining funds belong to the owners of the enterprise. The first purpose of the rule is therefore to make sure that there are sufficient post-liquidation funds available to pay off all creditors. The funds remaining after all claims are paid represent the **net capital** of the broker- dealer.

To arrive at net capital resulting from this hypothetical liquidation, it is necessary to assume the selling price of assets. If the assets are sold at less than carrying value, which is likely in a distressed environment, the broker-dealer will incur losses during the course of the liquidation. Collectively, these losses are called **charges**.

Let's take a look at the nature of the various charges a broker-dealer needs to take when computing its net capital. In this presumed distressed environment, some assets may not be able to be sold and are therefore deemed to be completely illiquid and not saleable. These illiquid assets are called **non-allowable assets** and result in a 100% loss, or charge, against capital. Further, the broker-dealer may be owed money for which inadequate collateral is held, or conversely it may be a debtor, and the amount of the collateral given to the lender exceeds the amount of the loan. In these cases, the broker-dealer has **unsecured credit exposures** which are also charged to capital under the rule. The rule also requires charges for certain **unsettled operational items**. Of special interest are charges attributable to valuation adjustments for securities positions owned by the broker- dealer for his own account. As a group, these charges are referred to as **haircuts**. These haircuts are generally product based. (Haircuts for government securities are computed separately from corporate securities with the haircut/charge increasing with the risk profile of the product type.) Certain very large broker-dealers are allowed to elect a portfolio-wide haircut computation with the permission of the SEC.

Lastly, certain liabilities of the broker-dealer may be considered as a capital equivalent for net capital purposes. These liabilities are called **subordinated liabilities,** which are claims subordinated to the claims of general creditors and are subject to agreements which have been approved by the broker-dealer's SRO. Computationally, net capital = capital (as computed under generally accepted accounting principles)—charges + subordinated liabilities. If there is a negative net capital, the broker-dealer must immediately contact the SEC and the appropriate SROs and cease business operations.

Once net capital is computed, the adequacy of this net capital is determined by comparing it to certain components of the broker-dealer's leverage. The rule limits the amount of this leverage to a multiple of net capital. Therefore, net capital is the constraining factor which determines the size of a broker-dealer's business.

Net capital and customer protection computations are regularly reported to the broker-dealer's SROs via the filing of Financial and Operational Combined Uniform Single (FOCUS) reports. A sample FOCUS report is reproduced at the conclusion of this chapter.

Regulating the Conduct of Broker Dealers and Associated Persons

Broker-dealers are subject to extensive regulation with respect to permissible conduct when interacting with customers. The broadest of these are the antifraud provisions of the various securities acts. The purpose of these provisions is to prohibit misstatements or misleading omissions of material facts and fraudulent or manipulative acts and practices in connection with the purchase or sale of securities. The Commission has adopted rules, issued interpretations, and brought enforcement actions that define some of the activities we consider manipulative, deceptive, fraudulent, or otherwise unlawful. Broker-dealers must conduct their activities so as to avoid these kinds of practices.

Suitability Requirements

Broker-dealers generally have an obligation to recommend only those specific investments or overall investment strategies that are suitable for their customers. The concept of suitability appears in specific SRO rules and has been interpreted as an obligation under the antifraud provisions of the federal securities laws. Under suitability requirements, a broker-dealer must have an "adequate and reasonable basis" for any recommendation that it makes. Reasonable basis suitability, or the reasonable basis test, relates to the particular security or strategy recommended. Therefore, the broker-dealer has an obligation to investigate and obtain adequate information about the security it is recommending. A broker-dealer also has an obligation to determine customer-specific suitability. In particular, a broker-dealer must make recommendations based on a customer's financial situation, needs, and other security holdings. The following are representative of the considerations that a broker-dealer must consider:

- the customer's age,
- marital status,
- number of dependents,
- employment,
- net worth,
- income,
- financial needs,
- risk tolerance,
- tax status,
- other security holdings, and
- investment objectives.

This requirement has been construed to impose a duty of inquiry on broker-dealers to obtain relevant information from customers relating to their financial situations and to keep such information current. SROs consider recommendations to be unsuitable when they are inconsistent with the customer's investment objectives.

The recent Dodd-Frank financial services regulation bill has authorized a regulation project which may raise the level of business contact to that of a fiduciary, which is standard required of registered investment advisers. This is a very controversial issue which could increase the potential liability of the industry in the event of customer investment losses. We will examine the fiduciary standard in the context investment advisers in chapter 12.

Duty of Fair Dealing

Another overriding standard of business conduct imposed upon broker-dealers is the duty of fair dealing. This standard is interwoven with general antifraud provisions and is addressed in SEC rules and regulations as well as SRO rules and interpretations. These include the duties to execute orders promptly, disclose certain material information (*i.e.*, information the customer would consider important as an investor), charge prices reasonably related to the prevailing market, and fully disclose any conflict of interest.

Restrictions on Insider Trading

The SEC and the courts interpret Section 10(b) and Rule 10b-5 under the Act to bar the use by any person of material non-public information in the purchase or sale of securities, whenever that use violates a duty of trust and confidence owed to a third party. Section 15(f) of the Act specifically requires broker-dealers to have and enforce written policies and procedures reasonably designed to prevent their employees from misusing material non-public information. Because employees in the investment banking operations of broker-dealers frequently have access to material non-public information, firms need to create procedures designed to limit the flow of this information so that their employees cannot use the information in the trading of securities. Broker-dealers can use these information barriers as a defense to a claim of insider trading. Such procedures typically include:

- training to make employees aware of these restrictions;

- employee trading restrictions;

- physical barriers;

- isolation of certain departments; and

- limitations on investment bank proprietary trading.

Other Customer Relationship Rules

- Disclosure of Credit Terms

- Extending Credit on New Issues

- Restrictions on Private Securities Transactions

- Analysts and Regulation AC

- Penny Stock Rules

- Privacy of Consumer Financial Information (Regulation S-P)

Customer Trading Rules

- Duty of Best Execution

- Customer Confirmation Rule

- Order Execution Obligations

- Restrictions on Short Sales (Regulation SHO)

- Trading During an Offering (Regulation M)

Other Broker Dealer Trading Rules

- Trading by Members of Exchanges, Brokers and Dealers

- Regulation NMS

- Regulation ATS: Broker-Dealer Trading Systems.

Appendix 11 SEC Form x-17A-5

UNITED STATES
SECURITIES AND EXCHANGE COMMISSION
Washington, D.C. 20549

OMB APPROVAL	
OMB Number:	3235-0123
Expires:	April 30, 2013
Estimated average burden hours per response......12.00	

Form
X-17A-5

FOCUS REPORT
(Financial and Operational Combined Uniform Single Report)
PART IIA ⓘ[12]

(Please read instructions before preparing Form.)

This report is being filed pursuant to (Check Applicable Block(s)):
1) Rule 17a-5(a) [16]   2) Rule 17a-5(b) [17]   3) Rule 17a-11 [18]
4) Special request by designated examining authority [19]   5) Other [26]

NAME OF BROKER-DEALER

SEC FILE NO. [14]

FIRM I.D. NO. [15]

[13]

ADDRESS OF PRINCIPAL PLACE OF BUSINESS (Do Not Use P.O. Box No.)

[20]

(No. and Street)

FOR PERIOD BEGINNING (MM/DD/YY) [24]

AND ENDING (MM/DD/YY)

[21]   [22]   [23]

(City)   (State)   (Zip Code)

[25]

NAME AND TELEPHONE NUMBER OF PERSON TO CONTACT IN REGARD TO THIS REPORT

(Area Code) — Telephone No.

[30]

[31]

NAME(S) OF SUBSIDIARIES OR AFFILIATES CONSOLIDATED IN THIS REPORT:

OFFICIAL USE

[32]   [33]

[34]   [35]

[36]   [37]

[38]   [39]

DOES RESPONDENT CARRY ITS OWN CUSTOMER ACCOUNTS?   YES [40] NO [41]

CHECK HERE IF RESPONDENT IS FILING AN AUDITED REPORT   [42]

EXECUTION:
The registrant/broker or dealer submitting this Form and its attachments and the person(s) by whom it is executed represent hereby that all information contained therein is true, correct and complete. It is understood that all required items, statements, and schedules are considered integral parts of this Form and that the submission of any amendment represents that all unamended items, statements and schedules remain true, correct and complete as previously submitted.

Dated the _____ day of _____ 20 ____
Manual signatures of:

1) _____
   Principal Executive Officer or Managing Partner
2) _____
   Principal Financial Officer or Partner
3) _____
   Principal Operations Officer or Partner

ATTENTION — Intentional misstatements or omissions of facts constitute Federal Criminal Violations. (See 18 U.S.C. 1001 and 15 U.S.C. 78:f(a))

Persons who respond to the collection of information contained in this form are not required to respond unless the form displays a currently valid OMB control number.

SEC 1696 (02-03) 1 of 16

242

A GUIDE TO CAPITAL MARKETS

TO BE COMPLETED WITH THE ANNUAL AUDIT REPORT ONLY:

INDEPENDENT PUBLIC ACCOUNTANT whose opinion is contained in this Report

NAME (If individual, state last, first, middle name)

| 70 |

ADDRESS

| 71 | | 72 | | 73 | | 74 |

| Number and Street | City | State | Zip Code |

CHECK ONE

☐ Certified Public Accountant | 75 |

☐ Public Accountant | 76 |

☐ Accountant not resident in United States or any of its possessions | 77 |

FOR SEC USE

DO NOT WRITE UNDER THIS LINE . . . FOR SEC USE ONLY

WORK LOCATION	REPORT DATE MM/DD/YY	DOC. SEQ. NO.	CARD			
	50	51	52	53		

SEC Form x-17A-5

FINANCIAL AND OPERATIONAL COMBINED UNIFORM SINGLE REPORT
PART IIA

BROKER OR DEALER			N3			100

STATEMENT OF FINANCIAL CONDITION FOR NONCARRYING, NONCLEARING AND
CERTAIN OTHER BROKERS OR DEALERS

as of (MM/DD/YY)		99
SEC FILE NO.		98
	Consolidated	198
	Unconsolidated	199

		Allowable	Non-Allowable	Total
1.	Cash .... $	200	$	750
2.	Receivables from brokers or dealers:			
	A. Clearance account .... $	295		
	B. Other	300 $	550	810
3.	Receivable from non-customers	365	600	830
4.	Securities and spot commodities owned at market value:			
	A. Exempted securities	415		
	B. Debt securities	419		
	C. Options	420		
	D. Other securities	424		
	E. Spot commodities	430		850
5.	Securities and/or other investments not readily marketable:			
	A. At cost $ [130]			
	B. At estimated fair value	440	610	880
6.	Securities borrowed under subordination agreements and partners' individual and capital securities accounts, at market value:	460	630	680
	A. Exempted securities $ [150]			
	B. Other securities $ [160]			
7.	Secured demand notes:	470	640	890
	Market value of collateral:			
	A. Exempted securities $ [170]			
	B. Other securities $ [180]			
8.	Memberships in exchanges:			
	A. Owned, at market $ [190]			
	B. Owned, at cost		650	
	C. Contributed for use of the company, at market value		660	900
9.	Investment in and receivables from affiliates, subsidiaries and associated partnerships	480	670	910
10.	Property, furniture, equipment, leasehold improvements and rights under lease agreements, at cost-net of accumulated depreciation and amortization	490	680	920
11.	Other assets	535	735	930
12.	TOTAL ASSETS .... $	540 $	740 $	940

OMIT PENNIES

A GUIDE TO CAPITAL MARKETS

FINANCIAL AND OPERATIONAL COMBINED UNIFORM SINGLE REPORT
PART IIA

BROKER OR DEALER	as of _____

STATEMENT OF FINANCIAL CONDITION FOR NONCARRYING, NONCLEARING AND
CERTAIN OTHER BROKERS OR DEALERS

LIABILITIES AND OWNERSHIP EQUITY

Liabilities	A.I. Liabilities	Non-A.I. Liabilities	Total
13. Bank loans payable	$ _____ 1045	$ _____ 1255	$ _____ 1470
14. Payable to brokers or dealers:			
A. Clearance account	1114	1315	1560
B. Other	1115	1305	1540
15. Payable to non-customers	1155	1355	1610
16. Securities sold not yet purchased, at market value		1360	1620
17. Accounts payable, accrued liabilities, expenses and other	1205	1385	1635
18. Notes and mortgages payable:			
A. Unsecured	1210		1690
B. Secured	1211	1390	1700
19. E. Liabilities subordinated to claims of general creditors:			
A. Cash borrowings: _____ $ ____ 970		1400	1710
1. from outsiders			
2. Includes equity subordination (15c3-1(d)) of . . . $ ____ 980			
B. Securities borrowings, at market value from outsiders $ ____ 990		1410	1720
C. Pursuant to secured demand note collateral agreements		1420	1730
1. from outsiders $ ____ 1000			
2. Includes equity subordination (15c3-1(d)) of . . . $ ____ 1010			
D. Exchange memberships contributed for use of company, at market value		1430	1740
E. Accounts and other borrowings not qualified for net capital purposes	1220	1440	1750
20. TOTAL LIABILITIES	$ ____ 1230	$ ____ 1450	$ ____ 1760

Ownership Equity

		Total
21. Sole Proprietorship		$ ____ 1770
22. Partnership (limited partners) ($ ____ 1020)		1780
23. Corporation:		
A. Preferred stock		1791
B. Common stock		1792
C. Additional paid-in capital		1793
D. Retained earnings		1794
E. Total		1795
F. Less capital stock in treasury	(	1796
24. TOTAL OWNERSHIP EQUITY		$ ____ 1800
25. TOTAL LIABILITIES AND OWNERSHIP EQUITY		$ ____ 1810

OMIT PENNIES

SEC 1696 (02-03) 5 of 16

245

SEC FORM X-17A-5

FINANCIAL AND OPERATIONAL COMBINED UNIFORM SINGLE REPORT
PART IIA

BROKER OR DEALER _____ as of _____

COMPUTATION OF NET CAPITAL

1.	Total ownership equity from Statement of Financial Condition .... $ _____		3480
2.	Deduct ownership equity not allowable for Net Capital .... ¹⁹ (_____		3490)
3.	Total ownership equity qualified for Net Capital .... _____		3500
4.	Add:		
	A. Liabilities subordinated to claims of general creditors allowable in computation of net capital............... _____		3520
	B. Other (deductions) or allowable credits (List) .... _____		3525
5.	Total capital and allowable subordinated liabilities .... $ _____		3530
6.	Deductions and/or charges:		
	A. Total non-allowable assets from		
	Statement of Financial Condition (Notes B and C) .... ¹⁷ $ _____	3540	
	B. Secured demand note delinquency .... _____	3590	
	C. Commodity futures contracts and spot commodities –		
	proprietary capital charges .... _____	3600	
	D. Other deductions and/or charges .... _____	3610	(_____) 3620
7.	Other additions and/or allowable credits (List) .... _____		3630
8.	Net capital before haircuts on securities positions .... ²⁰ $ _____		3640
9.	Haircuts on securities (computed, where applicable, pursuant to 15c3-1(f)):		
	A. Contractual securities commitments .... $ _____	3660	
	B. Subordinated securities borrowings .... _____	3670	
	C. Trading and investment securities:		
	1. Exempted securities .... ¹⁸ _____	3735	
	2. Debt securities .... _____	3733	
	3. Options .... _____	3730	
	4. Other securities .... _____	3734	
	D. Undue Concentration .... _____	3650	
	E. Other (List) .... _____	3736	(_____) 3740
10.	Net Capital .... $ _____		3750

³⁰

OMIT PENNIES

A GUIDE TO CAPITAL MARKETS

FINANCIAL AND OPERATIONAL COMBINED UNIFORM SINGLE REPORT
PART IIA

BROKER OR DEALER	as of _____

COMPUTATION OF NET CAPITAL REQUIREMENT

Part A

11. Minimum net capital required (6⅔% of line 19)	$ _____	3756
12. Minimum dollar net capital requirement of reporting broker or dealer and minimum net capital requirement of subsidiaries computed in accordance with Note (A)	$ _____	3758
13. Net capital requirement (greater of line 11 or 12)	$ _____	3760
14. Excess net capital (line 10 less 13)	$ _____	3770
15. Excess net capital at 1000% (line 10 less 10% of line 19) .... ²² $ _____		3780

COMPUTATION OF AGGREGATE INDEBTEDNESS

16. Total A.I. liabilities from Statement of Financial Condition		$ _____	3790
17. Add:			
A. Drafts for immediate credit .... ²¹ $ _____ 3800			
B. Market value of securities borrowed for which no equivalent value is paid or credited .... $ _____ 3810			
C. Other unrecorded amounts (List) .... $ _____ 3820		$ _____	3830
18. Total aggregate indebtedness		$ _____	3840
19. Percentage of aggregate indebtedness to net capital (line 18 ÷ by line 10)		% _____	3850
20. Percentage of debt to debt-equity total computed in accordance with Rule 15c3-1(d)		% _____	3860

COMPUTATION OF ALTERNATE NET CAPITAL REQUIREMENT

Part B

21. 2% of combined aggregate debit items as shown in Formula for Reserve Requirements pursuant to Rule 15c3-3 prepared as of the date of the net capital computation including both brokers or dealers and consolidated subsidiaries' debits	$ _____	3970
22. Minimum dollar net capital requirement of reporting broker or dealer and minimum net capital requirement of subsidiaries computed in accordance with Note (A) .... ²¹ $ _____		3880
23. Net capital requirement (greater of line 21 or 22)	$ _____	3760
24. Excess net capital (line 10 less 23)	$ _____	3910
25. Net capital in excess of the greater of:		
A. 5% of combined aggregate debit items or $120,000	$ _____	3920

NOTES:

(A) The minimum net capital requirement should be computed by adding the minimum dollar net capital requirement of the reporting broker dealer and, for each subsidiary to be consolidated, the greater of:
    1. Minimum dollar net capital requirement , or
    2. 6⅔% of aggregate indebtedness or 4% of aggregate debits if alternative method is used.

(B) Do not deduct the value of securities borrowed under subordination agreements or secured demand note covered by subordination agreements not in satisfactory form and the market values of memberships in exchanges contributed for use of company (contra to item 1740) and partners' securities which were included in non-allowable assets.

(C) For reports filed pursuant to paragraph (d) of Rule 17a-5, respondent should provide a list of material non-allowable assets.

SEC FORM X-17A-5

FINANCIAL AND OPERATIONAL COMBINED UNIFORM SINGLE REPORT
PART IIA

BROKER OR DEALER

For the period (MMDDYY) from [3932] to [3933]
Number of months included in this statement [3931]

STATEMENT OF INCOME (LOSS)

REVENUE

1. Commissions:
   a. Commissions on transactions in exchange listed equity securities executed on an exchange .... $ _____ [3935]
   b. Commissions on listed option transactions .... ‰25 [3938]
   c. All other securities commissions .... [3939]
   d. Total securities commissions .... [3940]
2. Gains or losses on firm securities trading accounts
   a. From market making in options on a national securities exchange .... [3945]
   b. From all other trading .... [3949]
   c. Total gain (loss) .... [3950]
3. Gains or losses on firm securities investment accounts .... [3952]
4. Profit (loss) from underwriting and selling groups .... ‰26 [3955]
5. Revenue from sale of investment company shares .... [3970]
6. Commodities revenue .... [3990]
7. Fees for account supervision, investment advisory and administrative services .... [3975]
8. Other revenue .... [3995]
9. Total revenue .... $ _____ [4030]

EXPENSES

10. Salaries and other employment costs for general partners and voting stockholder officers .... [4120]
11. Other employee compensation and benefits .... [4115]
12. Commissions paid to other broker-dealers .... [4140]
13. Interest expense .... [4075]
    a. Includes interest on accounts subject to subordination agreements .... [4070]
14. Regulatory fees and expenses .... [4195]
15. Other expenses .... [4100]
16. Total expenses .... $ _____ [4200]

NET INCOME

17. Income (loss) before Federal income taxes and items below (Item 9 less Item 16) .... $ _____ [4210]
18. Provision for Federal income taxes (for parent only) .... ‰28 [4220]
19. Equity in earnings (losses) of unconsolidated subsidiaries not included above .... [4222]
    a. After Federal income taxes of .... [4338]
20. Extraordinary gains (losses) .... [4224]
    a. After Federal income taxes of .... [4239]
21. Cumulative effect of changes in accounting principles .... [4225]
22. Net income (loss) after Federal income taxes and extraordinary items .... $ _____ [4230]

MONTHLY INCOME

23. Income (current month only) before provision for Federal income taxes and extraordinary items .... $ _____ [4211]

FINANCIAL AND OPERATIONAL COMBINED UNIFORM SINGLE REPORT
PART IIA

BROKER OR DEALER

For the period (MMDDYY) from _____ to _____

STATEMENT OF CHANGES IN OWNERSHIP EQUITY
(SOLE PROPRIETORSHIP, PARTNERSHIP OR CORPORATION)

1.	Balance, beginning of period	$_____	4240
	A. Net Income (loss)	_____	4250
	B. Additions (Includes non-conforming capital of .... $ [4262])	_____	4260
	C. Deductions (Includes non-conforming capital of .... $ [4272])	_____	4270
2.	Balance, end of period (From item 1800)	$_____	4290

STATEMENT OF CHANGES IN LIABILITIES SUBORDINATED
TO CLAIMS OF GENERAL CREDITORS

3.	Balance, beginning of period .... $to	$_____	4300
	A. Increases	_____	4310
	B. Decreases	_____	4320
4.	Balance, end of period (From item 3520)	$_____	4330

OMIT PENNIES

SEC 1696 (02-03) 13 of 16

249

SEC FORM x-17A-5

FINANCIAL AND OPERATIONAL COMBINED UNIFORM SINGLE REPORT
PART IIA

BROKER OR DEALER	as of _____

EXEMPTIVE PROVISION UNDER RULE 15c3-3

24. If an exemption from Rule 15c3-1 is claimed, identify below the section upon which such exemption is based (check one only)

A. (k)(1) — $2,500 capital category as per Rule 15c3-1	4550
B. (k)(2)(A) — "Special Account for the Exclusive Benefit of customers" maintained	4560
C. (k)(2)(B) — All customer transactions cleared through another broker-dealer on a fully disclosed basis. Name of clearing firm 30 [4335]	4570
D. (k)(3) — Exempted by order of the Commission (include copy of letter)	4580

Ownership Equity and Subordinated Liabilities maturing or proposed to be withdrawn within the next six months and accruals, (as defined below), which have not been deducted in the computation of Net Capital.

Type of Proposed Withdrawal or Accrual (See below for code)	Name of Lender or Contributor	Insider or Outsider? (In or Out)	Amount to be Withdrawn (cash amount and/or Net Capital Value of Securities)	(MMDDYY) Withdrawal or Maturity Date	Expect to Renew (Yes or No)
31 [4600]	[4501]	[4502]	[4503]	[4504]	[4605]
32 [4610]	[4611]	[4612]	[4613]	[4614]	[4615]
33 [4620]	[4621]	[4622]	[4623]	[4624]	[4625]
34 [4630]	[4631]	[4632]	[4633]	[4634]	[4635]
35 [4640]	[4641]	[4642]	[4643]	[4644]	[4645]

Total $ 36 [4699]

OMIT PENNIES

Instructions: Detail Listing must include the total of items maturing during the six month period following the report date, regardless of whether or not the capital contribution is expected to be renewed. The schedule must also include proposed capital withdrawals scheduled within the six month period following the report date including the proposed redemption of stock and anticipated accruals which would cause a reduction of Net Capital. These anticipated accruals would include amounts of bonuses, partners' drawing accounts, taxes, and interest on capital, voluntary contributions to pension or profit sharing plans, etc., which have not been deducted in the computation of Net Capital, but which you anticipate will be paid within the next six months.

WITHDRAWAL CODE:	DESCRIPTIONS
1.	Equity Capital
2.	Subordinated Liabilities
3.	Accruals

Chapter
12

Investment Adviser Regulation

Individuals or entities providing investment advisory services are subject to both federal and state regulation. The regulatory landscape has changed significantly in this area as the result of the Dodd-Frank financial regulation package enacted in July 2010. The key federal statute is the Investment Advisers Act of 1940 (IAA). Section 202(a)(11) of the IAA defines an investment adviser as follows:

"Investment adviser" means any person who, for compensation, engages in the business of advising others, either directly or through publications or writings, as to the value of securities or as to the advisability of investing in, purchasing, or selling securities, or who, for compensation and as part of a regular business, issues or promulgates analyses or reports concerning securities; but does not include

A. a bank, or any bank holding company as defined in the Bank Holding Company Act of 1956, which is not an investment company, except that the term "investment adviser" includes any bank or bank holding company to the extent that such bank or bank holding company serves or acts as an investment adviser to a registered investment company, but if, in the case of a bank, such services or actions are performed through a separately identifiable department or division, the department or division, and not the bank itself, shall be deemed to be the investment adviser;

B. any lawyer, accountant, engineer, or teacher whose performance of such services is solely incidental to the practice of his profession;

C. any broker or dealer whose performance of such services is solely incidental to the conduct of his business as a broker or dealer and who receives no special compensation therefor;

D. the publisher of any bona fide newspaper, news magazine or business or financial publication of general and regular circulation;

E. any person whose advice, analyses, or reports relate to no securities other than securities which are direct obligations of or obligations guaranteed as to principal or interest by the United States, or securities issued or guaranteed by corporations in which the United States has a direct or indirect interest which shall have been designated by the Secretary of the Treasury, pursuant to section 3(a)(12) of the Securities Exchange Act of 1934, as exempted securities for the purposes of that Act;

F. any nationally recognized statistical rating organization, as that term is defined in section 3(a)(62) of the Securities Exchange Act of 1934, unless such organization engages in issuing recommendations as to purchasing, selling, or holding securities or in managing assets, consisting in whole or in part of securities, on behalf of others; or

G. such other persons not within the intent of this paragraph, as the Commission may designate by rules and regulations or order.

Under law in effect prior to the enactment of Dodd-Frank, significant exemptions from registration were provided by the IAA. Most prominent among these exemptions was the provision contained in Section 203(b)(3) of the IAA, referred to as the "private advisers' " exemption, which read in relevant part as follows:

Investment advisers who need not be registered

. . . . any investment adviser who during the course of the preceding twelve months has had fewer than fifteen clients and who neither holds himself out generally to the public as an investment adviser nor acts as an investment adviser to any investment company registered under title I of this Act . . .

Dodd-Frank generally repealed this exemption. Investment advisers must, depending upon the adviser's assets under management (AUM), now register with either the SEC or a state regulatory body regardless of the number of clients the adviser has. This change, fully effective on March 30, 2012, forced some 4,000 formerly exempt advisers to register with a regulatory body for the first time. Among this group is a significant number of hedge fund and private equity fund managers who were previously able to benefit from the private adviser exemption as "clients" meant the fund, and not the investors therein, to which the adviser provided investment advice. Thus, under the statute in effect prior to the implementation of Dodd-Frank, advisers who had in the aggregate fewer than 15 "clients" were able to claim registration exemptions even if they managed multiple hedge/private equity funds which had hundreds (even thousands) of investors. Now, a manager to hedge funds and private equity funds (collectively "private funds") may only claim a registration exemption based on an AUM test.

Figure 12.1 Summary of Investment Adviser Registration Requirements

Investment Adviser Registration	Pre Dodd-Frank	Post Dodd-Frank
Mandatory	At least $30M in assets under management ("AUM").	At least $100M in AUM; <u>or</u> If at least $25M in AUM, but less than $100M in AUM, IA will be exempt from Federal registration *only if* required to register with their state of primary business and are subject to examination by such state's securities regulator. These advisers are referred to as "mid-sized advisers."
Optional	At least $25M but less than $30M in AUM.	Not applicable.
Exemption	(i) fewer than fifteen (15) clients during the preceding twelve (12) months; (ii) does not advise any registered investment companies or companies electing to be registered as business development companies; and (iii) does not hold itself out generally to the public as an investment adviser.	Solely advises private funds with less than $150M in AUM in the United States.

The SEC Investment Adviser Registration Process

Advisers register with the SEC by filing form ADV through the Investment Adviser Registration Depository (IARD). The system has been developed according to the requirements of its sponsors, the Securities and Exchange Commission (SEC) and the North American Securities Administrators Association (NASAA), along with those of an Industry Advisory Council representing the investment adviser firms. The site itself is operated by the Financial Industry Regulatory Authority (Finra).

Form ADV

The Form ADV consists of two parts. Part 1 contains information which is generally used by regulators. The form contains a series of "items" and a number of required schedules. Following is a summary of the information that must be disclosed on Form ADV, Part I. Form ADV is reproduced at the conclusion of this chapter.

Required Items-Form ADV Part 1 (Regulatory Reporting)

Item 1: Identifying Information

- name
- address
- website information
- regulatory contact information

Item 2: SEC Registration

- category of SEC registration

Item 3: Form of Organization

Item 4: Successions

- information relating to the succession to another adviser's business

Item 5: Information About Your Advisory Business

- Employees; number, functions

- Clients; number, types

- Compensation arrangements

- Regulatory assets under management

- Advisory activities

Item 6: Other Business Activities

Item 7: Financial Industry Affiliations and Private Fund Reporting

Item 8: Participation or Interest in Client Transactions

Item 9: Custody

Item 10: Control Persons

Item 11: Disclosure Information

- Disciplinary history

- Criminal history

- Certain civil litigation disclosures

Item 12: Small Businesses

Schedules (detailed disclosures)-Form ADV Part I

Schedule A: Direct Owners and Executive Officers

Schedule B: Indirect Owners

Schedule C: Amendments to Form ADV

Schedule D: Expanded Disclosures (relating to items 1 through 12)

Criminal Disclosure Reporting

Regulatory Action Disclosure Reporting

Civil Judicial Action Reporting

Required Items-Form ADV Part 2 (Firm Disclosures)

Part 2 of Form ADV is a disclosure document which must be given to each of the adviser's clients. ADV Part 2A is commonly referred to as the "brochure." Part 2B, the Supplement, contains information regarding certain advisory personnel. Appendix 1 contains required disclosures for "wrap fee" programs. (Wrap fee programs are discussed later in this chapter).

The SEC released the current redesigned version of Form ADV Part 2 during July 2010. The current version of the form requires a plain narrative discussion of 18 required items. The manner and the content of these disclosures represent a meaningful expansion of adviser disclosures. The SEC's general instructions and those for completion of Part 2 and specific instructions for the completion of Part 2A appear below.

General Instructions for Part 2 of Form ADV

Under SEC and similar state rules you are required to deliver to *clients* and prospective *clients* a *brochure* disclosing information about your firm. You also may be required to deliver a *brochure supplement* disclosing information about one or more of your *supervised persons*. Part 2 of Form ADV sets out the minimum required disclosure that your *brochure* (Part 2A for a firm *brochure*, or Appendix 1 for a *wrap fee program brochure*) and *brochure supplements* (Part 2B) must contain.

Read all the instructions, including General Instructions for Form ADV, General Instructions for Part 2 of Form ADV, Instructions for Part 2A of Form ADV, Instructions for Part 2B of Form ADV, and (if you are preparing or updating a *wrap fee program brochure*) Instructions for Part 2A Appendix 1 of Form ADV, before preparing or updating your *brochure* or *brochure supplements*.

1. Narrative Format. Part 2 of Form ADV consists of a series of items that contain disclosure requirements for

your firm's *brochure* and any required supplements. The items require narrative responses. You must respond to each item in Part 2. You must include the heading for each item provided by Part 2 immediately preceding your response to that item and provide responses in the same order as the items appear in Part 2. If an item does not apply to your business, you must indicate that item is not applicable. If you have provided information in response to one item that is also responsive to another item, you may cross-reference that information in response to the other item.

2. Plain English. The items in Part 2 of Form ADV are designed to promote effective communication between you and your *clients*. Write your *brochure* and supplements in plain English, taking into consideration your *clients'* level of financial sophistication. Your *brochure* should be concise and direct. In drafting your *brochure* and *brochure supplements*, you should: (i) use short sentences; (ii) use definite, concrete, everyday words; (iii) use active voice; (iv) use tables or bullet lists for complex material, whenever possible; (v) avoid legal jargon or highly technical business terms unless you explain them or you believe that your *clients* will understand them; and (vi) avoid multiple negatives. Consider providing examples to illustrate a description of your practices or policies. The brochure should discuss only conflicts the adviser has or is reasonably likely to have and practices in which it engages or is reasonably likely to engage. If a conflict arises or the adviser decides to engage in a practice that it has not disclosed, supplemental disclosure must be provided to clients to obtain their consent. If you have a conflict or engage in a practice with respect to some (but not all) types or classes of clients, advice, or transactions, indicate as such rather than disclosing that you "may" have the conflict or engage in the practice. **Note:** The SEC's Office of Investor Education

and Advocacy has published A Plain English Handbook. You may find the handbook helpful in writing your *brochure* and supplements. For a copy of this handbook, visit the SEC's web site at www.sec.gov/news/extra/handbook.htm or call 1-800-732-0330.

3. Disclosure Obligations as a Fiduciary. Under federal and state law, you are a fiduciary and must make full disclosure to your *clients* of all material facts relating to the advisory relationship. As a fiduciary, you also must seek to avoid conflicts of interest with your clients and, at a minimum, make full disclosure of all material conflicts of interest between you and your *clients* that could affect the advisory relationship. This obligation requires that you provide the client with sufficiently specific facts so that the client is able to understand the conflicts of interest you have and the business practices in which you engage, and can give informed consent to such conflicts or practices or reject them. To satisfy this obligation, you therefore may have to disclose to *clients* information not specifically required by Part 2 of Form ADV or in more detail than the brochure items might otherwise require. You may disclose this additional information to *clients* in your *brochure* or by some other means.

4. Full and Truthful Disclosure. All information in your *brochure* and *brochure supplements* must be true and may not omit any material facts.

5. Filing. You must file your *brochure(s)* (and amendments) through the IARD system using the text-searchable Adobe Portable Document Format ("PDF"). See SEC rules 203-1 and 204-1 and similar state rules. If you are registered or are registering with the SEC, you are not required to file your *brochure supplements* through the IARD or otherwise. You must, however, preserve a copy of the supplements and make them available to SEC staff upon request. See SEC rule 204-

2(a)(14). If you are registered or are registering with one or more *state securities authorities*, you must file a copy of the *brochure supplement* for each *supervised person* doing business in that state.

Instructions for Part 2A of Form ADV: Preparing Your Firm Brochure

1. To whom must we deliver a firm *brochure*? You must give a firm *brochure* to each *client*. You must deliver the *brochure* even if your advisory agreement with the *client* is oral. See SEC rule 204-3(b) and similar state rules.

If you are registered with the SEC, you are not required to deliver your *brochure* to either (i) *clients* who receive only *impersonal investment advice* from you and who will pay you less than $500 per year or (ii) *clients* that are SEC-registered investment companies or business development companies (the *client* must be registered under the Investment Company Act of 1940 or be a business development company as defined in that Act, and the advisory contract must meet the requirements of section 15(c) of that Act). See SEC rule 204-3(c).

Note: Even if you are not required to give a *brochure* to a *client*, as a fiduciary you may still be required to provide your *clients* with similar information, particularly material information about your conflicts of interest and about your disciplinary information. If you are not required to give a *client* a *brochure*, you may make any required disclosures to that *client* by delivery of your *brochure* or through some other means.

2. When must we deliver a *brochure* to *clients*?

You must give a firm *brochure* to each *client* before or at the time you enter into an advisory agreement with that *client*. See SEC rule 204-3(b) and similar state rules.

Each year you must (i) deliver, within 120 days of the end of your fiscal year, to each *client* a free updated *brochure* that either includes a summary of material changes or is accompanied by a summary of material changes, or (ii) deliver to each *client* a summary of material changes that includes an offer to provide a copy of the updated *brochure* and information on how a *client* may obtain the *brochure*. See SEC rule 204-3(b) and similar state rules.

You do not have to deliver an interim amendment to *clients* unless the amendment includes information in response to Item 9 of Part 2A (disciplinary information). An interim amendment can be in the form of a document describing the material facts relating to the amended disciplinary event. See SEC rule 204-3(b) and similar state rules.

Note: As a fiduciary, you have an ongoing obligation to inform your *clients* of any material information that could affect the advisory relationship. As a result, between *annual updating amendments* you must disclose material changes to such information to *clients* even if those changes do not trigger delivery of an interim amendment. See General Instructions for Part 2 of Form ADV, Instruction 3.

3. May we deliver our *brochure* electronically? Yes. The SEC has published interpretive guidance on delivering documents electronically, which you can find at www.sec.gov/rules/concept/33-7288.txt.

4. When must we update our *brochure*? You must update your *brochure*: (i) each year at the time you file your *annual updating amendment*; and (ii) promptly whenever any information in the *brochure* becomes materially inaccurate. You are not required to update your *brochure* between annual amendments solely because the amount of *client* assets you manage has changed or because your fee schedule has changed. However, if you are updating your *brochure* for a separate reason in between annual amendments, and the amount of *client* assets you manage listed in response to Item 4.E or your fee schedule

listed in response to Item 5.A has become materially inaccurate, you should update that item(s) as part of the interim amendment. All updates to your *brochure* must be filed through the IARD system and maintained in your files. See SEC rules 204-1 and 204-2(a)(14) and similar state rules.

5. We are filing our *annual updating amendment*. The last *brochure*(s) that we filed does not contain any materially inaccurate information. Do we have to prepare a summary of material changes? No, as long as you have not filed any interim amendments making material changes to the *brochure* that you filed with last year's *annual updating amendment*. If you do not have to prepare a summary of material changes, you do not have to deliver a summary of material changes or a *brochure* to your existing *clients* that year. See SEC rule 204-3(b). If you are a state-registered adviser, you should contact the appropriate *state securities authorities* to determine whether you must make an annual offer of the brochure.

6. Do we need to include the summary of material changes that we prepare in response to Item 2 with *our annual updating amendment* filing on IARD? Yes, you need to include the summary in your *annual updating amendment*. Item 2 permits you to include the summary as part of the *brochure* (on the cover page or the page immediately following the cover page) or to create a separate document containing the summary. If you include the summary as part of your *brochure,* the summary will be part of the *annual updating amendment* filing that you submit on IARD. If your summary of material changes is a separate document, you must attach the summary as an exhibit to your *brochure* and upload your *brochure* and the summary together in a single, text-searchable file in Adobe Portable Document Format on IARD for your *annual updating amendment*.

Note: If you include the summary of material changes in your *brochure*, and you revise or update your *brochure* between *annual updating amendments*, you should consider whether you should update the summary as part of that other-than-annual amendment to avoid confusing or misleading *clients* reading the updated *brochure*.

7. We have determined that we have no *clients* to whom we must deliver a *brochure*. Must we prepare one? No, but see note to Instruction 1 above.

8. May we include a summary of the *brochure* at the beginning of our *brochure*? Yes. Although it is not required, you may choose to include a summary of the *brochure* at the beginning of your *brochure*. Such summary, however, may not substitute for the summary of material changes required by Item 2 of Part 2A.

9. We offer several advisory services. May we prepare multiple firm *brochures*? Yes. If you offer substantially different types of advisory services, you may opt to prepare separate *brochures* so long as each *client* receives all applicable information about services and fees. Each *brochure* may omit information that does not apply to the advisory services and fees it describes. For example, your firm *brochure* sent to your *clients* who invest only in the United States can omit information about your advisory services and fees relating to offshore investments. See SEC rule 204-3(e) and similar state rules. If you prepare separate *brochures* you must file each *brochure* (and any amendments) through the IARD system as required in SEC rules 203-1 and 204-1 and similar state rules.

10. We *sponsor* a *wrap fee program*. Is there a different *brochure* that we need to deliver to our wrap fee *clients*? Yes. If you *sponsor* a *wrap fee program*, you must deliver a *wrap fee program brochure* to your wrap fee *clients*. The disclosure requirements for preparing a *wrap fee*

program brochure appear in Part 2A, Appendix 1 of Form ADV. If your entire advisory business is *sponsoring wrap fee programs*, you do not need to prepare a firm *brochure* separate from your *wrap fee program brochure(s)*. See SEC rule 204-3(d) and similar state rules.

11. We provide portfolio management services to *clients* in *wrap fee programs* that we do not *sponsor*. Which *brochure* must we deliver to these *clients*? You must deliver your *brochure* prepared in accordance with Part 2A (not Appendix 1) to your wrap fee *clients*. You also must deliver to these *clients* any *brochure supplements* required by Part 2B of Form ADV.

12. May we include information not required by an item in our *brochure*? Yes. If you include information not required by an item, however, you may not include so much additional information that the required information is obscured.

13. Item 18 requires us to give our *clients* an audited balance sheet. May any public accountant perform the audit? Your auditor must be independent. Article 2 of SEC Regulation S-X sets out the general rules for independence. Please note that these requirements may be different from the rules of professional organizations.

14. We are a new firm. Do we need a *brochure*? Yes. Respond to items in Part 2A of Form ADV based on the advisory services you propose to provide and the practices, policies and procedures you propose to adopt.

15. We are a "separately identifiable department or division" (SID) of a bank. Must our *brochure* discuss our bank's general business practices? No. Information you include in your firm *brochure* (or in *brochure supplements*) should be information about you, the SID, and your business practices, rather than general information about your bank.

Part 2A of Form ADV: Firm Brochure

Item 1 Cover Page

A. The cover page of your *brochure* must state your name, business address, contact information, website address (if you have one), and the date of the *brochure.*

Note: If you primarily conduct advisory business under a name different from your full legal name, and you have disclosed your business name in Item 1.B of Part 1A of Form ADV, then you may use your business name throughout your *brochure.*

B. Display on the cover page of your *brochure* the following statement or other clear and concise language conveying the same information, and identifying the document as a "brochure":

This brochure provides information about the qualifications and business practices of [your name]. If you have any questions about the contents of this brochure, please contact us at [telephone number and/or email address]. The information in this brochure has not been approved or verified by the United States Securities and Exchange Commission or by any state securities authority.

Additional information about [your name] also is available on the SEC's website at www.adviserinfo.sec.gov.

C. If you refer to yourself as a "registered investment adviser" or describe yourself as being "registered," include a statement that registration does not imply a certain level of skill or training.

Item 2 Material Changes

If you are amending your *brochure* for your annual update and it contains material changes from your last annual update, identify and discuss those changes on the cover page of the *brochure* or on the page immediately following the cover page, or as a separate document accompanying the *brochure*. You must state clearly that you are discussing only material changes since the last annual update of your *brochure*, and you must provide the date of the last annual update of your *brochure*.

Note: You do not have to separately provide this information to a *client* or prospective *client* who has not received a previous version of your *brochure*.

Item 3 Table of Contents

Provide a table of contents to your *brochure*.

Note: Your table of contents must be detailed enough so that your *clients* can locate topics easily. Your *brochure* must follow the same order and contain the same headings as the items listed in Part 2A.

Item 4 Advisory Business

A. Describe your advisory firm, including how long you have been in business. Identify your principal owner(s).

Notes: (1) For purposes of this item, your principal owners include the *persons* you list as owning 25% or more of your firm on Schedule A of Part 1A of Form ADV (Ownership Codes C, D or E). (2) If you are a publicly held company without a 25% shareholder, simply disclose that you are publicly held. (3) If an individual or company owns 25% or more of your firm through subsidiaries, you must identify the individual or parent company and intermediate subsidiaries. If you are an SEC-registered adviser, you must identify intermediate subsidiaries that are publicly held, but not other intermediate subsidiaries. If you are a state-registered adviser, you must identify all intermediate subsidiaries.

B. Describe the types of advisory services you offer. If you hold yourself out as specializing in a particular type of advisory service, such as financial planning, quantitative analysis, or market timing, explain the nature of that service in greater detail. If you provide investment advice only with respect to limited types of investments, explain the type of investment advice you offer and disclose that your advice is limited to those types of investments.

C. Explain whether (and, if so, how) you tailor your advisory services to the individual needs of *clients*. Explain whether *clients* may impose restrictions on investing in certain securities or types of securities.

D. If you participate in *wrap fee programs* by providing portfolio management services, (1) describe the differences, if any, between how you manage wrap fee accounts and how you manage other accounts, and (2) explain that you receive a portion of the wrap fee for your services.

E. If you manage *client* assets, disclose the amount of *client* assets you manage on a *discretionary basis* and the amount of *client* assets you manage on a non-*discretionary basis*. Disclose the date "as of" which you calculated the amounts.

Note: Your method for computing the amount of "*client* assets you manage" can be different from the method for computing "regulatory assets under management" required for Item 5.F in Part 1A. However, if you choose to use a different method to compute "*client* assets you manage," you must keep documentation describing the method you use. The amount you disclose may be rounded to the nearest $100,000. Your "as of" date must not be more than 90 days before the date you last updated your *brochure* in response to this Item 4.E.

Item 5 Fees and Compensation

A. Describe how you are compensated for your advisory services. Provide your fee schedule. Disclose whether the fees are negotiable.

Note: If you are an SEC-registered adviser, you do not

need to include this information in a *brochure* that is delivered only to qualified purchasers as defined in section 2(a)(51)(A) of the Investment Company Act of 1940.

B. Describe whether you deduct fees from *clients'* assets or bill *clients* for fees incurred. If *clients* may select either method, disclose this fact. Explain how often you bill *clients* or deduct your fees.

C. Describe any other types of fees or expenses *clients* may pay in connection with your advisory services, such as custodian fees or mutual fund expenses. Disclose that *clients* will incur brokerage and other transaction costs, and direct *clients* to the section(s) of your *brochure* that discuss brokerage.

D. If your *clients* either may or must pay your fees in advance, disclose this fact. Explain how a *client* may obtain a refund of a pre-paid fee if the advisory contract is terminated before the end of the billing period. Explain how you will determine the amount of the refund.

E. If you or any of your *supervised persons* accepts compensation for the sale of securities or other investment products, including asset-based sales charges or service fees from the sale of mutual funds, disclose this fact and respond to Items 5.E.1, 5.E.2, 5.E.3 and 5.E.4.

1. Explain that this practice presents a conflict of interest and gives you or your *supervised persons* an incentive to recommend investment products based on the compensation received, rather than on a *client's* needs. Describe generally how you address conflicts that arise, including your procedures for disclosing the conflicts to *clients*. If you primarily recommend mutual funds, disclose whether you will recommend "no-load" funds.

2. Explain that *clients* have the option to purchase investment products that you recommend through other brokers or agents that are not affiliated with you.

3. If more than 50% of your revenue from advisory *clients* results from commissions and other compensation for

the sale of investment products you recommend to your *clients*, including asset-based distribution fees from the sale of mutual funds, disclose that commissions provide your primary or, if applicable, your exclusive compensation.

4. If you charge advisory fees in addition to commissions or markups, disclose whether you reduce your advisory fees to offset the commissions or markups.

Note: If you receive compensation in connection with the purchase or sale of securities, you should carefully consider the applicability of the broker-dealer registration requirements of the Securities Exchange Act of 1934 and any applicable state securities statutes.

Item 6 *Performance-Based Fees* and Side-By-Side Management

If you or any of your *supervised persons* accepts *performance-based fees*—that is, fees based on a share of capital gains on or capital appreciation of the assets of a *client* (such as a *client* that is a hedge fund or other pooled investment vehicle)—disclose this fact. If you or any of your *supervised persons* manage both accounts that are charged a *performance-based fee* and accounts that are charged another type of fee, such as an hourly or flat fee or an asset-based fee, disclose this fact. Explain the conflicts of interest that you or your *supervised persons* face by managing these accounts at the same time, including that you or your *supervised persons* have an incentive to favor accounts for which you or your *supervised persons* receive a *performance-based fee* and describe generally how you address these conflicts.

Item 7 Types of *Clients*

Describe the types of *clients* to whom you generally provide investment advice, such as individuals, trusts, investment companies, or pension plans. If you have any requirements for opening or maintaining an account, such as a minimum account size, disclose the requirements.

Item 8 Methods of Analysis, Investment Strategies and Risk of Loss

A. Describe the methods of analysis and investment strategies you use in formulating investment advice or managing assets. Explain that investing in securities involves risk of loss that *clients* should be prepared to bear.

B. For each significant investment strategy or method of analysis you use, explain the material risks involved. If the method of analysis or strategy involves significant or unusual risks, discuss these risks in detail. If your primary strategy involves frequent trading of securities, explain how frequent trading can affect investment performance, particularly through increased brokerage and other transaction costs and taxes.

C. If you recommend primarily a particular type of security, explain the material risks involved. If the type of security involves significant or unusual risks, discuss these risks in detail.

Item 9 Disciplinary Information

If there are legal or disciplinary events that are material to a *client's* or prospective *client's* evaluation of your advisory business or the integrity of your management, disclose all material facts regarding those events.

Items 9.A, 9.B, and 9.C list specific legal and disciplinary events presumed to be material for this Item. If your advisory firm or a *management person* has been *involved* in one of these events, you must disclose it under this Item for 10 years following the date of the event, unless (1) the event was resolved in your or the *management person's* favor, or was reversed, suspended or vacated, or (2) you have rebutted the presumption of materiality to determine that the event is not material (see Note

270

below). For purposes of calculating this 10-year period, the "date" of an event is the date that the final *order*, judgment, or decree was entered, or the date that any rights of appeal from preliminary *orders*, judgments or decrees lapsed.

Items 9.A, 9.B, and 9.C do not contain an exclusive list of material disciplinary events. If your advisory firm or a *management person* has been *involved* in a legal or disciplinary event that is not listed in Items 9.A, 9.B, or 9.C, but nonetheless is material to a *client's* or prospective *client's* evaluation of your advisory business or the integrity of its management, you must disclose the event. Similarly, even if more than 10 years have passed since the date of the event, you must disclose the event if it is so serious that it remains material to a *client's* or prospective *client's* evaluation.

A. A criminal or civil action in a domestic, foreign, or military court of competent jurisdiction in which your firm or a *management person*

1. was convicted of, or pled guilty or nolo contendere ("no contest") to (a) any *felony*; (b) a *misdemeanor* that *involved* investments or an *investment-related* business, fraud, false statements or omissions, wrongful taking of property, bribery, perjury, forgery, counterfeiting, or extortion; or (c) a conspiracy to commit any of these offenses;

2. is the named subject of a pending criminal *proceeding* that involves an *investment-related* business, fraud, false statements or omissions, wrongful taking of property, bribery, perjury, forgery, counterfeiting, extortion, or a conspiracy to commit any of these offenses;

3. was *found* to have been *involved* in a violation of an *investment-related* statute or regulation; or

4. was the subject of any *order*, judgment, or decree permanently or temporarily enjoining, or otherwise limiting, your firm or a *management person* from engag-

ing in any *investment-related* activity, or from violating any *investment-related* statute, rule, or *order*.

B. An administrative *proceeding* before the SEC, any other federal regulatory agency, any state regulatory agency, or any *foreign financial regulatory authority* in which your firm or a *management person*

1. was *found* to have caused an *investment-related* business to lose its authorization to do business; or

2. was *found* to have been *involved* in a violation of an *investment-related* statute or regulation and was the subject of an *order* by the agency or authority

(a) denying, suspending, or revoking the authorization of your firm or a *management person* to act in an *investment-related* business;

(b) barring or suspending your firm's or a *management person's* association with an *investment-related* business;

(c) otherwise significantly limiting your firm's or a *management person's investment-related* activities; or

(d) imposing a civil money penalty of more than $2,500 on your firm or a *management person*.

C. A *self-regulatory organization (SRO) proceeding* in which your firm or a *management person*

1. was *found* to have caused an *investment-related* business to lose its authorization to do business; or

2. was *found* to have been *involved* in a violation of the *SRO's* rules and was: (i) barred or suspended from membership or from association with other members, or was expelled from membership; (ii) otherwise significantly limited from *investment-related* activities; or (iii) fined more than $2,500.

Note: You may, under certain circumstances, rebut the presumption that a disciplinary event is material. If an event is immaterial, you are not required to disclose it. When you review a legal or disciplinary event involving your firm or a *management person* to determine whether it is appropriate to rebut the presumption of materiality, you should consider all of the following factors: (1) the proximity of the *person involved* in the disciplinary event to the advisory function; (2) the nature of the infraction that led to the disciplinary event; (3) the severity of the disciplinary sanction; and (4) the time elapsed since the date of the disciplinary event. If you conclude that the materiality presumption has been overcome, you must prepare and maintain a file memorandum of your determination in your records. See SEC rule 204-2(a)(14)(iii).

Item 10 Other Financial Industry Activities and Affiliations

A. If you or any of your *management persons* are registered, or have an application pending to register, as a broker-dealer or a registered representative of a broker-dealer, disclose this fact.

B. If you or any of your *management persons* are registered, or have an application pending to register, as a futures commission merchant, commodity pool operator, a commodity trading advisor, or an associated person of the foregoing entities, disclose this fact.

C. Describe any relationship or arrangement that is material to your advisory business or to your *clients* that you or any of your *management persons* have with any *related person* listed below. Identify the *related person* and if the relationship or arrangement creates a material conflict of interest with *clients*, describe the nature of the conflict and how you address it.

1. broker-dealer, municipal securities dealer, or government securities dealer or broker

2. investment company or other pooled investment vehicle (including a mutual fund, closed-end investment company, unit investment trust, private investment company or "hedge fund," and offshore fund)

3. other investment adviser or financial planner

4. futures commission merchant, commodity pool operator, or commodity trading advisor

5. banking or thrift institution

6. accountant or accounting firm

7. lawyer or law firm

8. insurance company or agency

9. pension consultant

10. real estate broker or dealer

11. sponsor or syndicator of limited partnerships.

D. If you recommend or select other investment advisers for your *clients* and if you receive compensation directly or indirectly from those advisers that creates a material conflict of interest, or if you have other business relationships with those advisers that create a material conflict of interest, describe these practices and discuss the material conflicts of interest these practices create and how you address them.

Item 11 Code of Ethics, Participation, or Interest in *Client* Transactions and Personal Trading

A. If you are an SEC-registered adviser, briefly describe your code of ethics adopted pursuant to SEC rule 204A-1 or similar state rules. Explain that you will provide a copy of your code of ethics to any *client* or prospective *client* upon request.

B. If you or a *related person* recommends to *clients*, or buys or sells for *client* accounts, securities in which you or a *related person* has a material financial interest, describe your practice and discuss the conflicts of interest it presents. Describe generally how you address conflicts that arise.

Examples: (1) You or a *related person*, as principal, buys securities from (or sells securities to) your *clients*; (2) you or a *related person* acts as general partner in a partnership in which you solicit *client* investments; or (3) you or a *related person* acts as an investment adviser to an investment company that you recommend to *clients*.

C. If you or a *related person* invests in the same securities (or related securities, *e.g.*, warrants, options or futures) that you or a *related person* recommends to *clients*, describe your practice and discuss the conflicts of interest this presents and generally how you address the conflicts that arise in connection with personal trading.

D. If you or a *related person* recommends securities to *clients*, or buys or sells securities for *client* accounts, at or about the same time that you or a *related person* buys or sells the same securities for your own (or the *related person's* own) account, describe your practice and discuss the conflicts of interest it presents. Describe generally how you address conflicts that arise.

Note: The description required by Item 11.A may include information responsive to Item 11.B, C or D. If so, it is not necessary to make repeated disclosures of the same information. You do not have to provide disclosure in response to Item 11.B, 11.C, or 11.D with respect to securities that are not "reportable securities" under SEC rule 204A-1(e)(10) and similar state rules.

Item 12 Brokerage Practices

A. Describe the factors that you consider in selecting or recommending broker-dealers for *client* transactions and determining the reasonableness of their compensation (*e.g.*, commissions).

1. Research and Other Soft Dollar Benefits. If you receive research or other products or services other than execution from a broker-dealer or a third party in connection with *client* securities transactions ("soft dollar benefits"), disclose your practices and discuss the conflicts of interest they create.

Note: Your disclosure and discussion must include all soft dollar benefits you receive, including, in the case of research, both proprietary research (created or developed by the broker-dealer) and research created or developed by a third party.

a. Explain that when you use *client* brokerage commissions (or markups or markdowns) to obtain research or other products or services, you receive a benefit because you do not have to produce or pay for the research, products or services.

b. Disclose that you may have an incentive to select or recommend a broker-dealer based on your interest in receiving the research or other products or services, rather than on your *clients'* interest in receiving most favorable execution.

c. If you may cause *clients* to pay commissions (or markups or markdowns) higher than those charged by other broker-dealers in return for soft dollar benefits (known as paying-up), disclose this fact.

d. Disclose whether you use soft dollar benefits to service all of your *clients'* accounts or only those that paid for the benefits. Disclose whether you seek to allocate soft dollar benefits to *client* accounts proportionately to the soft dollar credits the accounts generate.

e. Describe the types of products and services you or any of your *related persons* acquired with *client* brokerage commissions (or markups or markdowns) within your last fiscal year.

Note: This description must be specific enough for your *clients* to understand the types of products or services that you are acquiring and to permit them to evaluate possible conflicts of interest. Your description must be more detailed for products or services that do not qualify for the safe harbor in section 28(e) of the Securities Exchange Act of 1934, such as those services that do not aid in investment decision-making or trade execution. Merely disclosing that you obtain various research reports and products is not specific enough.

f. Explain the procedures you used during your last fiscal year to direct *client* transactions to a particular broker-dealer in return for soft dollar benefits you received.

2. Brokerage for *Client* Referrals. If you consider, in selecting or recommending broker-dealers, whether you or a *related person* receives *client* referrals from a broker-dealer or third party, disclose this practice and discuss the conflicts of interest it creates.

a. Disclose that you may have an incentive to select or recommend a broker-dealer based on your interest in receiving *client* referrals, rather than on your *clients'* interest in receiving most favorable execution.

b. Explain the procedures you used during your last fiscal year to direct *client* transactions to a particular broker-dealer in return for *client* referrals.

3. Directed Brokerage.

a. If you routinely recommend, request, or require that a *client* direct you to execute transactions through a specified broker-dealer, describe your practice or policy. Explain that not all advisers require their *clients* to direct brokerage. If you and the broker-dealer are affiliates or have another economic relationship that creates a material conflict of interest, describe the relationship and discuss the conflicts of interest it presents. Explain that by directing brokerage you may be unable to achieve most favorable execution of *client* transactions, and that this practice may cost *clients* more money.

b. If you permit a *client* to direct brokerage, describe your practice. If applicable, explain that you may be unable to achieve most favorable execution of *client* transactions. Explain that directing brokerage may cost *clients* more money. For example, in a directed brokerage account, the *client* may pay higher brokerage commissions because you may not be able to aggregate orders to reduce transaction costs, or the *client* may receive less favorable prices.

Note: If your *clients* only have directed brokerage arrangements subject to most favorable execution of *client* transactions, you do not need to respond to the last sentence of Item 12.A.3.a. or to the second or third sentences of Item 12.A.3.b.

B. Discuss whether and under what conditions you aggregate the purchase or sale of securities for various *client* accounts. If you do not aggregate orders when you have the opportunity to do so, explain your practice and describe the costs to *clients* of not aggregating.

Item 13 Review of Accounts

A. Indicate whether you periodically review *client* accounts or financial plans. If you do, describe the frequency and nature of the review and the titles of the *supervised persons* who conduct the review.

B. If you review *client* accounts on other than a periodic basis, describe the factors that trigger a review.

C. Describe the content and indicate the frequency of regular reports you provide to *clients* regarding their accounts. State whether these reports are written.

Item 14 *Client* Referrals and Other Compensation

A. If someone who is not a *client* provides an economic benefit to you for providing investment advice or other advisory services to your *clients*, generally describe the arrangement, explain the conflicts of interest, and describe how you address the conflicts of interest. For purposes of this Item, economic benefits include any sales awards or other prizes.

B. If you or a *related person* directly or indirectly compensates any *person* who is not your *supervised person* for *client* referrals, describe the arrangement and the compensation.

Note: If you compensate any *person* for *client* referrals, you should consider whether SEC rule 206(4)-3 or similar state rules regarding solicitation arrangements and/or state rules requiring registration of *investment adviser representatives* apply.

Item 15 *Custody*

If you have *custody* of *client* funds or securities and a qualified custodian sends quarterly, or more frequent, account statements directly to your *clients*, explain that *clients* will receive account statements from the broker-dealer, bank, or other qualified custodian and that *clients* should carefully review those statements. If your *clients* also receive account statements from you, your explanation must include a statement urging *clients* to compare the account statements they receive from the qualified custodian with those they receive from you.

Item 16 Investment Discretion

If you accept *discretionary authority* to manage securities accounts on behalf of *clients*, disclose this fact and describe any limitations *clients* may (or customarily do) place on this authority. Describe the procedures you follow before you assume this authority (*e.g.,* execution of a power of attorney).

Item 17 Voting *Client* Securities

A. If you have, or will accept, authority to vote *client* securities, briefly describe your voting policies and procedures, including those adopted pursuant to SEC rule 206(4)-6. Describe whether (and, if so, how) your *clients* can direct your vote in a particular solicitation. Describe how you address conflicts of interest between you and your *clients* with respect to voting their securities. Describe how *clients* may obtain information from you about how you voted their securities. Explain to *clients* that they may obtain a copy of your proxy voting policies and procedures upon request.

B. If you do not have authority to vote *client* securities, disclose this fact. Explain whether *clients* will receive their proxies or other solicitations directly from their custodian or a transfer agent or from you, and discuss whether (and, if so, how) *clients* can contact you with questions about a particular solicitation.

Item 18 Financial Information

A. If you require or solicit prepayment of more than $1,200 in fees per *client*, six months or more in advance, include a balance sheet for your most recent fiscal year.

1. The balance sheet must be prepared in accordance with generally accepted accounting principles, audited by an independent public accountant, and accompanied by a note stating the principles used to prepare it, the basis of securities included, and any other explanations required for clarity.

2. Show parenthetically the market or fair value of securities included at cost.

3. Qualifications of the independent public accountant and any accompanying independent public accountant's report must conform to Article 2 of SEC Regulation S-X.

Note: If you are a sole proprietor, show investment advisory business assets and liabilities separate from other business and personal assets and liabilities. You may aggregate other business and personal assets unless advisory business liabilities exceed advisory business assets.

Note: If you have not completed your first fiscal year, include a balance sheet dated not more than 90 days prior to the date of your *brochure*.

Exception: You are not required to respond to Item 18.A of Part 2A if you also are: (i) a qualified custodian as defined in SEC rule 206(4)-2 or similar state rules; or (ii) an insurance company.

B. If you have *discretionary authority* or *custody* of *client* funds or securities, or you require or solicit prepayment of more than $1,200 in fees per *client*, six months or more in advance, disclose any financial condition that is reasonably likely to impair your ability to meet contractual commitments to *clients*.

Note: With respect to Items 18.A and 18.B, if you are registered or are registering with one or more of the *state securities authorities*, the dollar amount reporting threshold for including the required balance sheet and for making the required financial condition disclosures is more than $500 in fees per *client*, six months or more in advance.

C. If you have been the subject of a bankruptcy petition at any time during the past 10 years, disclose this fact, the date the petition was first brought, and the current status.

If you are registering or are registered with one or more *state securities authorities*, you must respond to the following additional Item.

Item 19 Requirements for State-Registered Advisers

A. Identify each of your principal executive officers and *management persons*, and describe their formal education and business background. If you have supplied this information elsewhere in your Form ADV, you do not need to repeat it in response to this Item.

B. Describe any business in which you are actively engaged (other than giving investment advice) and the approximate amount of time spent on that business. If you have supplied this information elsewhere in your Form ADV, you do not need to repeat it in response to this Item.

C. In addition to the description of your fees in response to Item 5 of Part 2A, if you or a *supervised person* are compensated for advisory services with *performance-based fees*, explain how these fees will be calculated. Disclose specifically that performance-based compensation

281

may create an incentive for the adviser to recommend an investment that may carry a higher degree of risk to the *client*.

D. If you or a *management person* has been *involved* in one of the events listed below, disclose all material facts regarding the event.

1. An award or otherwise being *found* liable in an arbitration claim alleging damages in excess of $2,500, *involving* any of the following:

(a) an investment or an *investment-related* business or activity;

(b) fraud, false statement(s), or omissions;

(c) theft, embezzlement, or other wrongful taking of property;

(d) bribery, forgery, counterfeiting, or extortion; or

(e) dishonest, unfair, or unethical practices.

2. An award or otherwise being *found* liable in a civil, *self-regulatory organization*, or administrative *proceeding involving* any of the following:

(a) an investment or an *investment-related* business or activity;

(b) fraud, false statement(s), or omissions;

(c) theft, embezzlement, or other wrongful taking of property;

(d) bribery, forgery, counterfeiting, or extortion; or

(e) dishonest, unfair, or unethical practices.

E. In addition to any relationship or arrangement described in response to Item 10.C. of Part 2A, describe any relationship or arrangement that you or any of your *management persons* have with any issuer of securities that is not listed in Item 10.C. of Part 2A.

Issues of Special Interest When Operating as An Investment Adviser Subject to the IAA

Client Solicitation Like any business, investment advisers will seek to grow their businesses by attracting new clients.

Special care must be taken when fees are paid to parties that solicit clients on behalf of the adviser. The SEC has historically taken the view that paid solicitors have a conflict of interest when making investor referrals. Although the practice is not prohibited, it is subject to special rules and scrutiny. The primary thrust of the SEC rules and regulations deal with avoidance of conflicts of interest, registration obligations of the solicitor, and supervision of solicitor activities by the adviser. Extensive disclosure of solicitor activities (and compensation) must be made to investors via Form ADV and a separate solicitor's brochure. Further, the solicitor arrangement must be subject to a written agreement between the adviser and the solicitor.

The solicitor, as a party receiving compensation for investment advice, or arranging securities transaction, may need to register as an adviser under the IAA or as a broker dealer under the 1934 Securities Exchange Act. Further, in many instances the solicitor will be deemed an "associated person" of the investment adviser (or the adviser's broker dealer affiliates) and may be subject to supervision as such by the adviser and/or their affiliate. For specific guidance on these matters, see Rule 206(4)-3 ("Cash Payments for Client Solicitations") under the IAA and IAA Section 202(a)(17).

Advertising Advertising by investment advisers may not be fraudulent, deceptive, or manipulative. This simple dictate in contained in Rule 206(4)-1 ("Advertising by Investment Advisers") under the IAA. Under the rule, advertisements include any notice, circular, letter, or other written communication addressed to more than one person, or any notice or other announcement in any publication or by radio or television, which offers (1) any analysis, report, or publication concerning securities, or which is to be used in making any determination as to when to buy or sell any security, or which security to buy or sell, or (2) any graph, chart, formula, or other device to be used in making any determination as to when to buy or sell any security, or which security to buy or sell, or (3) any other investment advisory service with regard to securities.

Of special interest to the SEC is the use of testimonials, past specific recommendations, graphs, charts, and formulas as well as the furnishing of reports. Each of these areas creates its own challenges and is often the subject of no action letter guidance. In the case of testimonials, the SEC staff has allowed the use of client lists and independent third-party research reports about the adviser. With respect to past recommendations, a limited exception is provided in the rule which makes it permissible to use advertisements which sets out or offers to furnish a list of all recommendations made by such investment adviser within the immediately preceding period of not less than one year if such advertisement, and such list if it is furnished separately: (i) State the name of each such security recommended, the date and nature of each such recommendation (e.g., whether to buy, sell or hold), the market price at that time, the price at which the recommendation was to be acted upon, and the market price of each such security as of the most recent practicable date, and (ii) contain the following cautionary legend on the first page thereof in print or type as large as the largest print or type used in the body or text thereof: "it should not be assumed that recommendations made in the future will be profitable or will equal the performance of the securities in this list."

Performance The most important thing an adviser ultimately has to present to existing and prospective clients is their investment performance. Not surprisingly, this is the area that draws the most concentrated regulatory scrutiny. Rule 206(4)-1(a)(5) aims at preventing false and misleading performance advertising. The major items the SEC will examine in determining whether performance advertising is false or misleading include:

- Failure to disclose the material market or economic

284

conditions and their effects on the advertised performance results,

- Use of actual or model results that do not take into account brokerage or advisory fees,

- Disclosure (or failure to disclose) differences in material characteristics between portfolios and compared indices or benchmarks,

- Failure to disclose the inordinate contribution a particular item contributed to the performance of a portfolio and the ability to replicate that feature,

- Failure to disclose that the results portrayed relate to only a subset of client accounts.

Particular care must be taken when presenting either model or retroactively back-tested results as models are by their nature not based on actual results, and retroactive back-testing has the benefit of hindsight. The SEC has consistently taken the position that advertising deficiencies of this nature cannot be cured by disclosure, performance labeling, or disclaimer.

Another virtual automatic advertising violation is reporting performance without the reduction of fees. Fees include advisory fees, commissions, and other expenses the client would have been required to pay. Thus, the standard for performance advertising is **net-of-fees.**

Finally, when advisers move to a different employer, there is a general prohibition from advertising prior performance with the previous employer unless several conditions are met. Normally, to be "portable" the adviser must have been primarily responsible for achieving the prior results, the clients previously serviced by the adviser must be representative of prospective clients, and the accounts must be managed in a substantially similar manner.

Compensation Fees for services generally fall into two

categories: asset based fees and performance based fees. Asset based fees are fees charged based on the amount of assets the client has under management with the adviser. The fee generally is a reflection of the research and management effort required of the adviser; shorter term money market fund fees are relatively small compared with equity market asset-based fees. Within these categories, smaller capitalization equity markets are more research intensive than larger capitalization funds and thus will command higher fees. The prominence of the manager will, of course, also influence the size of the fees.

The second type of fee is the performance-based fee. Performance fees are allowable only if the client meets certain financial sophistication thresholds. See generally Rule 205-3 under the IAA.

Custody The SEC recently adopted revised rules relating to the custody of client assets. The newly adopted rules require advisers registered with the SEC to undergo surprise annual examinations by an independent accounting firm to independently verify the existence of client assets. Further, unless client assets are maintained by an independent custodian, the adviser must obtain a report on internal controls from an independent CPA firm. These provisions will not apply if the adviser is deemed to have custody solely by reason of being able to deduct advisory fees from client accounts.

Soft Dollars "Soft dollar" arrangements relate to relationships the adviser maintains with broker-dealers in which brokerage commissions, usually at a rate above normal rates, are paid to the broker-dealer for research and other services used by the adviser. (These relationships are sometimes called "directed brokerage.") Because the adviser is receiving goods or services in exchange for client commissions, the SEC understandably views this as an area rife with potential conflict of interests. In short, an adviser may be tempted to violate his fiduciary duty to his client by directing brokerage commissions in a manner which is the interest of the adviser, as opposed to the client. "Hard dollar" arrangements, by contrast, are those in which the research and services are paid for with adviser funds.

The items which normally will draw regulatory scrutiny involve the size of the commission, the quality of trade executions, and the nature of the services received by the adviser in exchange for the client commission flow. The extreme ends of the spectrum are easy to analyze. If an adviser is directing brokerage commissions for research that is for the clear benefit of the client, no problem will normally exist. If however, the adviser is directing brokerage commissions to receive items that should be paid for with hard dollars (adviser accounting software, for example), a violation will be asserted. The harder calls are always in the middle, mixed-use goods and services. Section 28(e) of the 1934 Securities Exchange Act provides "safe harbor" guidance on acceptable arrangements. Goods and services outside the safe harbor may need to be defended if questioned by the SEC.

Compliance Officers Rule 206(4)-7 under the IAA requires the designation of a chief compliance officer of the adviser. That party has the responsibility of administering the written policies and procedures that are designed to prevent violations of the IAA and rules of the SEC. This includes, among other items, the maintenance and administration of business continuity plans, certain anti-money laundering procedures, a code of ethics, personal trading and insider trading procedures, gift and entertainment policies, and the maintenance of the multitude of books and records required of advisers.

Appendix 12 SEC Form ADV

FORM ADV (Paper Version)

- **UNIFORM APPLICATION FOR INVESTMENT ADVISER REGISTRATION AND**
- **REPORT BY EXEMPT REPORTING ADVISERS**

PART 1A

WARNING: Complete this form truthfully. False statements or omissions may result in denial of your application, revocation of your registration, or criminal prosecution. You must keep this form updated by filing periodic amendments. See Form ADV General Instruction 4.

Check the box that indicates what you would like to do (check all that apply):

SEC or State Registration:
- ☐ Submit an initial application to register as an investment adviser with the SEC.
- ☐ Submit an initial application to register as an investment adviser with one or more states.
- ☐ Submit an *annual updating amendment* to your registration for your fiscal year ended _____.
- ☐ Submit an other-than-annual amendment to your registration.

SEC or State Report by *Exempt Reporting Advisers*:
- ☐ Submit an initial report to the SEC.
- ☐ Submit a report to one or more *state securities authorities*.
- ☐ Submit an *annual updating amendment* to your report for your fiscal year ended _____.
- ☐ Submit an other-than-annual amendment to your report.
- ☐ Submit a final report.

Item 1   Identifying Information

Responses to this Item tell us who you are, where you are doing business, and how we can contact you.

A. Your full legal name (if you are a sole proprietor, your last, first, and middle names):

_____

B. Name under which you primarily conduct your advisory business, if different from Item 1.A.

_____

List on Section 1.B. of Schedule D any additional names under which you conduct your advisory business.

C. If this filing is reporting a change in your legal name (Item 1.A.) or primary business name (Item 1.B.), enter the new name and specify whether the name change is of ☐ your legal name or ☐ your primary business name:

_____

D. (1) If you are registered with the SEC as an investment adviser, your SEC file number: 801-_____

(2) If you report to the SEC as an *exempt reporting adviser*, your SEC file number: 802-_____

E. If you have a number ("*CRD* Number") assigned by the *FINRA 's CRD* system or by the IARD system, your *CRD* number: _____

If your firm does not have a CRD number, skip this Item 1.E. Do not provide the CRD number of one of your officers, employees, or affiliates.

F. *Principal Office and Place of Business*

   (1) Address (do not use a P.O. Box):

   _____
   (number and street)

   _____
   (city)   (state/country)   (zip+4/postal code)

   If this address is a private residence, check this box: ☐

   List on Section 1.F. of Schedule D any office, other than your principal office and place of business, at which you conduct investment advisory business. If you are applying for registration, or are registered, with one or more state securities authorities, you must list all of your offices in the state or states to which you are applying for registration or with whom you are registered. If you are applying for SEC registration, if you are registered only with the SEC, or if you are reporting to the SEC as an exempt reporting adviser, list the largest five offices in terms of numbers of employees.

   (2) Days of week that you normally conduct business at your *principal office and place of business*:

   ☐ Monday - Friday   ☐ Other: _____

   Normal business hours at this location: _____

   (3) Telephone number at this location: _____
   (area code)   (telephone number)

   (4) Facsimile number at this location: _____
   (area code)   (facsimile number)

G. Mailing address, if different from your *principal office and place of business* address:

   _____
   (number and street)

   _____
   (city)   (state/country)   (zip+4/postal code)

   If this address is a private residence, check this box: ☐

H. If you are a sole proprietor, state your full residence address, if different from your *principal office and place of business* address in Item 1.F.:

   _____
   (number and street)

   _____
   (city)   (state/country)   (zip+4/postal code)

SEC Form ADV

I. Do you have one or more websites?   Yes ☐   No ☐

If "yes," list all website addresses on Section 1.I. of Schedule D. If a website address serves as a portal through which to access other information you have published on the web, you may list the portal without listing addresses for all of the other information. Some advisers may need to list more than one portal address. Do not provide individual electronic mail (e-mail) addresses in response to this Item.

J. Provide the name and contact information of your Chief Compliance Officer: If you are an *exempt reporting adviser*, you must provide the contact information for your Chief Compliance Officer, if you have one. If not, you must complete Item 1.K. below.

_____
(name)

_____
(other titles, if any)

_____   _____
(area code)   (telephone number)   (area code)   (facsimile number)

_____
(number and street)

_____   _____
(city)   (state/country)   (zip+4/postal code)

_____
(electronic mail (e-mail) address, if Chief Compliance Officer has one)

K. Additional Regulatory Contact Person: If a person other than the Chief Compliance Officer is authorized to receive information and respond to questions about this Form ADV, you may provide that information here.

_____
(name)

_____
(titles)

_____   _____
(area code)   (telephone number)   (area code)   (facsimile number)

_____
(number and street)

_____   _____
(city)   (state/country)   (zip+4/postal code)

_____
(electronic mail (e-mail) address, if contact person has one)

L. Do you maintain some or all of the books and records you are required to keep under Section 204 of the Advisers Act, or similar state law, somewhere other than your *principal office and place of business*?

Yes ☐   No ☐

If "yes," complete Section 1.L. of Schedule D.

M. Are you registered with a *foreign financial regulatory authority*? Yes ☐ No ☐

Answer "no" if you are not registered with a foreign financial regulatory authority, even if you have an affiliate that is registered with a foreign financial regulatory authority. If "yes," complete Section 1.M. of Schedule D.

N. Are you a public reporting company under Sections 12 or 15(d) of the Securities Exchange Act of 1934?

Yes ☐   No ☐

If "yes," provide your CIK number (Central Index Key number that the SEC assigns to each public reporting company): _____

O. Did you have $1 billion or more in assets on the last day of your most recent fiscal year?

Yes ☐   No ☐

P. Provide your *Legal Entity Identifier* if you have one: _____

A *legal entity identifier* is a unique number that companies use to identify each other in the financial marketplace. In the first half of 2011, the *legal entity identifier* standard was still in development. You may not have a *legal entity identifier*.

Item 2

SEC Registration

Responses to this Item help us (and you) determine whether you are eligible to register with the SEC. Complete this Item 2.A. only if you are applying for SEC registration or submitting an *annual updating amendment* to your SEC registration.

A. To register (or remain registered) with the SEC, you must check **at least one** of the Items 2.A.(1) through 2.A.(12), below. If you are submitting an *annual updating amendment* to your SEC registration and you are no longer eligible to register with the SEC, check Item 2.A.(13). Part 1A Instruction 2 provides information to help you determine whether you may affirmatively respond to each of these items.

You (the adviser):

☐ (1) are a **large advisory firm** that either:

(a) has regulatory assets under management of $100 million (in U.S. dollars) or more, or

(b) has regulatory assets under management of $90 million (in U.S. dollars) or more at the time of filing its most recent *annual updating amendment* and is registered with the SEC;

☐ (2) are a **mid-sized advisory firm** that has regulatory assets under management of $25 million (in U.S. dollars) or more but less than $100 million (in U.S. dollars) and you are either:

(a) not required to be registered as an adviser with the *state securities authority* of the state where you maintain your *principal office and place of business*, or

SEC Form ADV

(b) not subject to examination by the *state securities authority* of the state where you maintain your *principal office and place of business*;

    *Click **HERE** for a list of states in which an investment adviser, if registered, would not be subject to examination by the state securities authority.*

☐ (3) have your *principal office and place of business* in **Wyoming** (which does not regulate advisers);

☐ (4) have your *principal office and place of business* **outside the United States**;

☐ (5) **are an investment adviser (or sub-adviser) to an investment company** registered under the Investment Company Act of 1940;

☐ (6) **are an investment adviser to a company which has elected to be a business development company** pursuant to section 54 of the Investment Company Act of 1940 and has not withdrawn the election, and you have at least $25 million of regulatory assets under management;

☐ (7) **are a pension consultant** with respect to assets of plans having an aggregate value of at least $200,000,000 that qualifies for the exemption in rule 203A-2(a);

☐ (8) **are a related adviser** under rule 203A-2(b) that *controls, is controlled* by, or is under common *control* with, an investment adviser that is registered with the SEC, and your *principal office and place of business* is the same as the registered adviser;

    If you check this box, complete Section 2.A.(8) of Schedule D.

☐ (9) **are a newly formed adviser** relying on rule 203A-2(c) because you expect to be eligible for SEC registration within 120 days;

    If you check this box, complete Section 2.A.(9) of Schedule D.

☐ (10) **are a multi-state adviser** that is required to register in 15 or more states and is relying on rule 203A-2(d);

    If you check this box, complete Section 2.A.(10) of Schedule D.

☐ (11) are an **Internet adviser** relying on rule 203A-2(e);

☐ (12) **have received an SEC order** exempting you from the prohibition against registration with the SEC;

    If you check this box, complete Section 2.A.(12) of Schedule D.

☐ (13) are **no longer eligible** to remain registered with the SEC.

SEC Reporting by *Exempt Reporting Advisers*

B. Complete this Item 2.B. only if you are reporting to the SEC as an *exempt reporting adviser*. Check all that apply. You:

☐ (1) qualify for the exemption from registration as an adviser solely to one or more venture capital funds;

FORM ADV Part 1A Page 6 of 19	Your Name_____ Date_____	CRD Number_____ SEC 801- or 802 Number_____

     ☐ (2) qualify for the exemption from registration because you act solely as an adviser to *private funds* and have assets under management in the United States of less than $150 million;

     ☐ (3) act solely as an adviser to *private funds* but you are no longer eligible to check box 2.B.(2) because you have assets under management in the United States of $150 million or more.

If you check box (2) or (3), complete Section 2.B. of Schedule D.

State Securities Authority Notice Filings and State Reporting by *Exempt Reporting Advisers*

  C. Under state laws, SEC-registered advisers may be required to provide to *state securities authorities* a copy of the Form ADV and any amendments they file with the SEC. These are called *notice filings*. In addition, *exempt reporting advisers* may be required to provide *state securities authorities* with a copy of reports and any amendments they file with the SEC. If this is an initial application or report, check the box(es) next to the state(s) that you would like to receive notice of this and all subsequent filings or reports you submit to the SEC. If this is an amendment to direct your *notice filings* or reports to additional state(s), check the box(es) next to the state(s) that you would like to receive notice of this and all subsequent filings or reports you submit to the SEC. If this is an amendment to your registration to stop your *notice filings* or reports from going to state(s) that currently receive them, uncheck the box(es) next to those state(s).

☐ AL	☐ CT	☐ HI	☐ KY	☐ MN	☐ NH	☐ OH	☐ SC	☐ VI
☐ AK	☐ DE	☐ ID	☐ LA	☐ MS	☐ NJ	☐ OK	☐ SD	☐ VA
☐ AZ	☐ DC	☐ IL	☐ ME	☐ MO	☐ NM	☐ OR	☐ TN	☐ WA
☐ AR	☐ FL	☐ IN	☐ MD	☐ MT	☐ NY	☐ PA	☐ TX	☐ WV
☐ CA	☐ GA	☐ IA	☐ MA	☐ NE	☐ NC	☐ PR	☐ UT	☐ WI
☐ CO	☐ GU	☐ KS	☐ MI	☐ NV	☐ ND	☐ RI	☐ VT	

If you are amending your registration to stop your notice filings or reports from going to a state that currently receives them and you do not want to pay that state's notice filing or report filing fee for the coming year, your amendment must be filed before the end of the year (December 31).

Item 3   Form of Organization

  A. How are you organized?

     ☐ Corporation   ☐ Sole Proprietorship   ☐ Limited Liability Partnership (LLP)
     ☐ Partnership   ☐ Limited Liability Company (LLC) ☐ Limited Partnership (LP)
     ☐ Other (specify):_____

If you are changing your response to this Item, see Part 1A Instruction 4.

  B. In what month does your fiscal year end each year? _____

  C. Under the laws of what state or country are you organized? _____

If you are a partnership, provide the name of the state or country under whose laws your partnership was formed. If you are a sole proprietor, provide the name of the state or country where you reside.

If you are changing your response to this Item, see Part 1A Instruction 4.

SEC Form ADV

Item 4   Successions

A. Are you, at the time of this filing, succeeding to the business of a registered investment adviser?

☐ Yes   ☐ No

If "yes," complete Item 4.B. and Section 4 of Schedule D.

B. Date of Succession: _____

                                  (mm/dd/yyyy)

If you have already reported this succession on a previous Form ADV filing, do not report the succession again. Instead, check "No." See Part 1A Instruction 4.

Item 5   Information About Your Advisory Business

Responses to this Item help us understand your business, assist us in preparing for on-site examinations, and provide us with data we use when making regulatory policy. Part 1A Instruction 5.a. provides additional guidance to newly formed advisers for completing this Item 5.

Employees

If you are organized as a sole proprietorship, include yourself as an employee in your responses to Item 5.A and Items 5.B.(1), (2), (3), (4), and (5). If an employee performs more than one function, you should count that employee in each of your responses to Items 5.B.(1), (2), (3), (4) and (5).

A. Approximately how many *employees* do you have? Include full- and part-time *employees* but do not include any clerical workers.

                             _____

B.

     (1) Approximately how many of the *employees* reported in 5.A. perform investment advisory functions (including research)?

                             _____

     (2) Approximately how many of the *employees* reported in 5.A. are registered representatives of a broker-dealer?

                             _____

     (3) Approximately how many of the *employees* reported in 5.A. are registered with one or more *state securities authorities* as *investment adviser representatives*?

                             _____

     (4) Approximately how many of the *employees* reported in 5.A. are registered with one or more *state securities authorities* as *investment adviser representatives* for an investment adviser other than you?

                             _____

     (5) Approximately how many of the *employees* reported in 5.A. are licensed agents of an insurance company or agency?

                             _____

FORM ADV Part 1A Page 8 of 19	Your Name_____ Date_____	CRD Number_____ SEC 801- or 802 Number_____

(6) Approximately how many firms or other *persons* solicit advisory *clients* on your behalf?
_____

In your response to Item 5.B.(6), do not count any of your employees and count a firm only once – do not count each of the firm's employees that solicit on your behalf.

Clients

In your responses to Items 5.C. and 5.D. do not include as "clients" the investors in a private fund you advise, unless you have a separate advisory relationship with those investors.

C. (1) To approximately how many *clients* did you provide investment advisory services during your most recently completed fiscal year?

☐0   ☐1-10   ☐11-25   ☐26-100

If more than 100, how many? _____   (round to the nearest 100)

(2) Approximately what percentage of your *clients* are non-*United States persons?* _____%

D. *For purposes of this Item 5.D., the category "individuals" includes trusts, estates, and 401(k) plans and IRAs of individuals and their family members, but does not include businesses organized as sole proprietorships*
The category "business development companies" consists of companies that have made an election pursuant to section 54 of the Investment Company Act of 1940. Unless you provide advisory services pursuant to an investment advisory contract to an investment company registered under the Investment Company Act of 1940, check "None" in response to Item 5.D.(1)(d) and do not check any of the boxes in response to Item 5.D.(2)(d).

(1) What types of *clients* do you have? Indicate the approximate percentage that each type of *client* comprises of your total number of *clients*. If a *client* fits into more than one category, check all that apply.

	None	Up to 10%	11-25%	26-50%	51-75%	76-99%	100%
(a) Individuals (other than high net worth individuals)	☐	☐	☐	☐	☐	☐	☐
(b) *High net worth individuals*	☐	☐	☐	☐	☐	☐	☐
(c) Banking or thrift institutions	☐	☐	☐	☐	☐	☐	☐
(d) Investment companies	☐	☐	☐	☐	☐	☐	☐
(e) Business development companies	☐	☐	☐	☐	☐	☐	☐
(f) Pooled investment vehicles (other than investment companies)	☐	☐	☐	☐	☐	☐	☐
(g) Pension and profit sharing plans (but not the plan participants)	☐	☐	☐	☐	☐	☐	☐
(h) Charitable organizations	☐	☐	☐	☐	☐	☐	☐
(i) Corporations or other businesses not listed above	☐	☐	☐	☐	☐	☐	☐
(j) State or municipal *government entities*	☐	☐	☐	☐	☐	☐	☐
(k) Other investment advisers	☐	☐	☐	☐	☐	☐	☐
(l) Insurance companies	☐	☐	☐	☐	☐	☐	☐

SEC Form ADV

(m) Other: _____ ☐ ☐ ☐ ☐ ☐ ☐ ☐

(2) Indicate the approximate amount of your regulatory assets under management (reported in Item 5.F. below) attributable to each of the following type of *client*. If a *client* fits into more than one category, check all that apply.

	None	Up to 25%	Up to 50%	Up to 75%	>75%
(a) Individuals (other than high net worth individuals)	☐	☐	☐	☐	☐
(b) *High net worth individuals*	☐	☐	☐	☐	☐
(c) Banking or thrift institutions	☐	☐	☐	☐	☐
(d) Investment companies	☐	☐	☐	☐	☐
(e) Business development companies	☐	☐	☐	☐	☐
(f) Pooled investment vehicles (other than investment companies)	☐	☐	☐	☐	☐
(g) Pension and profit sharing plans (but not the plan participants)	☐	☐	☐	☐	☐
(h) Charitable organizations	☐	☐	☐	☐	☐
(i) Corporations or other businesses not listed above	☐	☐	☐	☐	☐
(j) State or municipal *government entities*	☐	☐	☐	☐	☐
(k) Other investment advisers	☐	☐	☐	☐	☐
(l) Insurance companies	☐	☐	☐	☐	☐
(m) Other: _____	☐	☐	☐	☐	☐

Compensation Arrangements

E. You are compensated for your investment advisory services by (check all that apply):

☐ (1) A percentage of assets under your management
☐ (2) Hourly charges
☐ (3) Subscription fees (for a newsletter or periodical)
☐ (4) Fixed fees (other than subscription fees)
☐ (5) Commissions
☐ (6) *Performance-based fees*
☐ (7) Other (specify): _____

Regulatory Assets Under Management

F. (1) Do you provide continuous and regular supervisory or management services to securities portfolios?   ☐ Yes   ☐ No

(2) If yes, what is the amount of your regulatory assets under management and total number of accounts?

	U.S. Dollar Amount	Total Number of Accounts
Discretionary:	(a) $_____.00	(d) _____

296

FORM ADV Part 1A Page 10 of 19	Your Name_____ Date_____	CRD Number_____ SEC 801- or 802 Number_____

Non-Discretionary: (b) $_____.00   (e) _____

Total: (c) $_____.00   (f) _____

Part 1A Instruction 5.b. explains how to calculate your regulatory assets under management. You must follow these instructions carefully when completing this Item.

Advisory Activities

G. What type(s) of advisory services do you provide? Check all that apply.

- ☐ (1) Financial planning services
- ☐ (2) Portfolio management for individuals and/or small businesses
- ☐ (3) Portfolio management for investment companies (as well as "business development companies" that have made an election pursuant to section 54 of the Investment Company Act of 1940)
- ☐ (4) Portfolio management for pooled investment vehicles (other than investment companies)
- ☐ (5) Portfolio management for businesses (other than small businesses) or institutional *clients* (other than registered investment companies and other pooled investment vehicles)
- ☐ (6) Pension consulting services
- ☐ (7) Selection of other advisers (including *private fund* managers)
- ☐ (8) Publication of periodicals or newsletters
- ☐ (9) Security ratings or pricing services
- ☐ (10) Market timing services
- ☐ (11) Educational seminars/workshops
- ☐ (12) Other (specify): _____

Do not check Item 5.G.(3) unless you provide advisory services pursuant to an investment advisory contract to an investment company registered under the Investment Company Act of 1940, including as a subadviser. If you check Item 5.G.(3), report the 811 or 814 number of the investment company or investment companies to which you provide advice in Section 5.G. of Schedule D.

H. If you provide financial planning services, to how many *clients* did you provide these services during your last fiscal year?

☐ 0 ☐ 1-10 ☐ 11-25 ☐ 26-50 ☐ 51-100 ☐ 101-250 ☐ 251 – 500
☐ More than 500   If more than 500, how many? _____   (round to the nearest 500)

In your responses to this Item 5.H., do not include as "clients" the investors in a private fund you advise, unless you have a separate advisory relationship with those investors.

I. If you participate in a *wrap fee program*, do you (check all that apply):

- ☐ (1) *sponsor* the *wrap fee program*?
- ☐ (2) act as a portfolio manager for the *wrap fee program*?

If you are a portfolio manager for a wrap fee program, list the names of the programs and their sponsors in Section 5.I.(2) of Schedule D.

If your involvement in a wrap fee program is limited to recommending wrap fee programs to your clients, or you advise a mutual fund that is offered through a wrap fee program, do not check either Item 5.I.(1) or 5.I(2).

SEC FORM ADV

J.   In response to Item 4.B. of Part 2A of Form ADV, do you indicate that you provide investment advice only with respect to limited types of investments?   ☐ Yes   ☐ No

Item 6   Other Business Activities

In this Item, we request information about your firm's other business activities.

A.   You are actively engaged in business as a (check all that apply):

☐   (1) broker-dealer (registered or unregistered)
☐   (2) registered representative of a broker-dealer
☐   (3) commodity pool operator or commodity trading advisor (whether registered or exempt from registration)
☐   (4) futures commission merchant
☐   (5) real estate broker, dealer, or agent
☐   (6) insurance broker or agent
☐   (7) bank (including a separately identifiable department or division of a bank)
☐   (8) trust company
☐   (9) registered municipal advisor
☐   (10) registered security-based swap dealer
☐   (11) major security-based swap participant
☐   (12) accountant or accounting firm
☐   (13) lawyer or law firm
☐   (14) other financial product salesperson (specify): _____

If you engage in other business using a name that is different from the names reported in Items 1.A. or 1.B, complete Section 6.A. of Schedule D.

B.   (1) Are you actively engaged in any other business not listed in Item 6.A. (other than giving investment advice)?   ☐ Yes   ☐ No

(2) If yes, is this other business your primary business?   ☐ Yes   ☐ No

If "yes," describe this other business on Section 6.B.(2) of Schedule D, and if you engage in this business under a different name, provide that name.

(3) Do you sell products or provide services other than investment advice to your advisory *clients*?   ☐ Yes   ☐ No

If "yes," describe this other business on Section 6.B.(3) of Schedule D, and if you engage in this business under a different name, provide that name.

Item 7   Financial Industry Affiliations and *Private Fund* Reporting

In this Item, we request information about your financial industry affiliations and activities. This information identifies areas in which conflicts of interest may occur between you and your *clients.*

A.   This part of Item 7 requires you to provide information about you and your *related persons*, including foreign affiliates. Your *related persons* are all of your *advisory affiliates* and any *person* that is under common *control* with you.

You have a *related person* that is a (check all that apply):

☐   (1) broker-dealer, municipal securities dealer, or government securities broker or dealer (registered

FORM ADV Part 1A Page 12 of 19	Your Name_____ Date_____	CRD Number_____ SEC 801- or 802 Number_____

    or unregistered)
- ☐ (2) other investment adviser (including financial planners)
- ☐ (3) registered municipal advisor
- ☐ (4) registered security-based swap dealer
- ☐ (5) major security-based swap participant
- ☐ (6) commodity pool operator or commodity trading advisor (whether registered or exempt from registration)
- ☐ (7) futures commission merchant
- ☐ (8) banking or thrift institution
- ☐ (9) trust company
- ☐ (10) accountant or accounting firm
- ☐ (11) lawyer or law firm
- ☐ (12) insurance company or agency
- ☐ (13) pension consultant
- ☐ (14) real estate broker or dealer
- ☐ (15) sponsor or syndicator of limited partnerships (or equivalent), excluding pooled investment vehicles
- ☐ (16) sponsor, general partner, managing member (or equivalent) of pooled investment vehicles

For each related person, including foreign affiliates that may not be registered or required to be registered in the United States, complete Section 7.A. of Schedule D.

You do not need to complete Section 7.A. of Schedule D for any related person if: (1) you have no business dealings with the related person in connection with advisory services you provide to your clients; (2) you do not conduct shared operations with the related person; (3) you do not refer clients or business to the related person, and the related person does not refer prospective clients or business to you; (4) you do not share supervised persons or premises with the related person; and (5) you have no reason to believe that your relationship with the related person otherwise creates a conflict of interest with your clients.

You must complete Section 7.A of Schedule D for each related person acting as qualified custodian in connection with advisory services you provide to your clients (other than any mutual fund transfer agent pursuant to rule 206(4)-2(b)(1)), regardless of whether you have determined the related person to be operationally independent under rule 206(4)-2 of the Advisers Act.

B. Are you an adviser to any *private fund*? ☐ Yes   ☐ No

If "yes," then for each private fund that you advise, you must complete a Section 7.B.(1) of Schedule D, except in certain circumstances described in the next sentence and in Instruction 6 of the Instructions to Part 1A. If another adviser reports this information with respect to any such private fund in Section 7.B.(1) of Schedule D of its Form ADV (e.g., if you are a subadviser), do not complete Section 7.B.(1) of Schedule D with respect to that private fund. You must, instead, complete Section 7.B.(2) of Schedule D.

In either case, if you seek to preserve the anonymity of a private fund client by maintaining its identity in your books and records in numerical or alphabetical code, or similar designation, pursuant to rule 204-2(d), you may identify the private fund in Section 7.B.(1) or 7.B.(2) of Schedule D using the same code or designation in place of the fund's name.

Item 8   Participation or Interest in *Client* Transactions

In this Item, we request information about your participation and interest in your *clients'* transactions. This information identifies additional areas in which conflicts of interest may occur between you and your *clients*.

SEC FORM ADV

Like Item 7, Item 8 requires you to provide information about you and your *related persons*, including foreign affiliates.

Proprietary Interest in *Client* Transactions

A. Do you or any *related person*:   <u>Yes</u>   <u>No</u>

   (1) buy securities for yourself from advisory *clients*, or sell securities you own to advisory *clients* (principal transactions)?   ☐   ☐

   (2) buy or sell for yourself securities (other than shares of mutual funds) that you also recommend to advisory *clients*?   ☐   ☐

   (3) recommend securities (or other investment products) to advisory *clients* in which you or any *related person* has some other proprietary (ownership) interest (other than those mentioned in Items 8.A.(1) or (2))?   ☐   ☐

Sales Interest in *Client* Transactions

B. Do you or any *related person*:   <u>Yes</u>   <u>No</u>

   (1) as a broker-dealer or registered representative of a broker-dealer, execute securities trades for brokerage customers in which advisory *client* securities are sold to or bought from the brokerage customer (agency cross transactions)?   ☐   ☐

   (2) recommend purchase of securities to advisory *clients* for which you or any *related person* serves as underwriter, general or managing partner, or purchaser representative?   ☐   ☐

   (3) recommend purchase or sale of securities to advisory *clients* for which you or any *related person* has any other sales interest (other than the receipt of sales commissions as a broker or registered representative of a broker-dealer)?   ☐   ☐

Investment or Brokerage Discretion

C. Do you or any *related person* have *discretionary authority* to determine the: <u>Yes</u>   <u>No</u>

   (1) securities to be bought or sold for a *client's* account?   ☐   ☐

   (2) amount of securities to be bought or sold for a *client's* account?   ☐   ☐

   (3) broker or dealer to be used for a purchase or sale of securities for a *client's* account?   ☐   ☐

   (4) commission rates to be paid to a broker or dealer for a *client's* securities transactions?   ☐   ☐

                                                                 <u>Yes</u> <u>No</u>

D. If you answer "yes" to C.(3) above, are any of the brokers or dealers *related persons*?   ☐   ☐

E. Do you or any *related person* recommend brokers or dealers to *clients*?   ☐   ☐

300

FORM ADV Part 1A Page 14 of 19	Your Name_____ Date_____	CRD Number_____ SEC 801- or 802 Number_____

F. If you answer "yes" to E above, are any of the brokers or dealers *related persons*? ☐ ☐

G. (1) Do you or any *related person* receive research or other products or services other than execution from a broker-dealer or a third party ("soft dollar benefits") in connection with *client* securities transactions? ☐ ☐

    (2) If "yes" to G.(1) above, are all the "soft dollar benefits" you or any *related persons* receive eligible "research or brokerage services" under section 28(e) of the Securities Exchange Act of 1934? ☐ ☐

H. Do you or any *related person*, directly or indirectly, compensate any *person* for *client* referrals? ☐ ☐

I. Do you or any *related person*, directly or indirectly, receive compensation from any *person* for *client* referrals? ☐ ☐

In responding to Items 8.H and 8.I., consider all cash and non-cash compensation that you or a related person gave to (in answering Item 8.H) or received from (in answering Item 8.I) any person in exchange for client referrals, including any bonus that is based, at least in part, on the number or amount of client referrals.

Item 9   Custody

In this Item, we ask you whether you or a *related person* has *custody* of *client* (other than *clients* that are investment companies registered under the Investment Company Act of 1940) assets and about your custodial practices.

A. (1) Do you have *custody* of any advisory *clients'*: **Yes** **No**

    (a) cash or bank accounts? ☐ ☐
    (b) securities? ☐ ☐

If you are registering or registered with the SEC, answer "No" to Item 9.A.(1)(a) and (b) if you have custody solely because (i) you deduct your advisory fees directly from your clients' accounts, or (ii) a related person has custody of client assets in connection with advisory services you provide to clients, but you have overcome the presumption that you are not operationally independent (pursuant to Advisers Act rule 206(4)-(2)(d)(5)) from the related person.

    (2) If you checked "yes" to Item 9.A.(1)(a) or (b), what is the approximate amount of *client* funds and securities and total number of *clients* for which you have *custody*:

    U.S. Dollar Amount   Total Number of *Clients*

    (a) $_____   (b) _____

If you are registering or registered with the SEC and you have custody solely because you deduct your advisory fees directly from your clients' accounts, do not include the amount of those assets and the number of those clients in your response to Item 9.A.(2). If your related person has custody of client assets in connection with advisory services you provide to clients, do not include the amount of those assets and the number of those clients in your response to Item 9.A.(2). Instead, include that information in your response to Item 9.B.(2).

SEC Form ADV

B. (1) In connection with advisory services you provide to *clients*, do any of your *related persons* have custody of any of your advisory *clients'*:

Yes   No

    (a) cash or bank accounts?   □   □

    (b) securities?   □   □

You are required to answer this item regardless of how you answered Item 9.A.(1)(a) or (b).

(2) If you checked "yes" to Item 9.B.(1)(a) or (b), what is the approximate amount of *client* funds and securities and total number of *clients* for which your *related persons* have custody:

U.S. Dollar Amount   Total Number of *Clients*

(a) $_____   (b) _____

C. If you or your *related persons* have custody of *client* funds or securities in connection with advisory services you provide to *clients*, check all the following that apply:

    □ (1) A qualified custodian(s) sends account statements at least quarterly to the investors in the pooled investment vehicle(s) you manage.

    □ (2) An *independent public accountant* audits annually the pooled investment vehicle(s) that you manage and the audited financial statements are distributed to the investors in the pools.

    □ (3) An *independent public accountant* conducts an annual surprise examination of *client* funds and securities.

    □ (4) An *independent public accountant* prepares an internal control report with respect to custodial services when you or your *related persons* are qualified custodians for *client* funds and securities.

If you checked Item 9.C.(2), C.(3) or C.(4), list in Section 9.C. of Schedule D the accountants that are engaged to perform the audit or examination or prepare an internal control report. (If you checked Item 9.C.(2), you do not have to list auditor information in Section 9.C. of Schedule D if you already provided this information with respect to the private funds you advise in Section 7.B.(1) of Schedule D).

D. Do you or your *related person(s)* act as qualified custodians for your *clients* in connection with advisory services you provide to *clients*?

Yes   No

    (1) you act as a qualified custodian   □   □

    (2) your *related person(s)* act as qualified custodian(s)   □   □

If you checked "yes" to Item 9.D.(2), all related persons that act as qualified custodians (other than any mutual fund transfer agent pursuant to rule 206(4)-2(b)(1)) must be identified in Section 7.A. of Schedule D, regardless of whether you have determined the related person to be operationally independent under rule 206(4)-2 of the Advisers Act.

E. If you are filing your *annual updating amendment* and you were subject to a surprise examination by an *independent public accountant* during your last fiscal year, provide the date (MM/YYYY) the examination commenced: _____

FORM ADV Part 1A Page 16 of 19	Your Name_____ Date_____	CRD Number_____ SEC 801- or 802 Number_____

F. If you or your *related persons* have *custody* of *client* funds or securities, how many *persons*, including, but not limited to, you and your *related persons*, act as qualified custodians for your *clients* in connection with advisory services you provide to *clients*? _____

Item 10 Control Persons

In this Item, we ask you to identify every *person* that, directly or indirectly, *controls* you.

If you are submitting an initial application or report, you must complete Schedule A and Schedule B. Schedule A asks for information about your direct owners and executive officers. Schedule B asks for information about your indirect owners. If this is an amendment and you are updating information you reported on either Schedule A or Schedule B (or both) that you filed with your initial application or report, you must complete Schedule C.

A. Does any *person* not named in Item 1.A. or Schedules A, B, or C, directly or indirectly, *control* your management or policies? ☐ Yes ☐ No

If yes, complete Section 10.A. of Schedule D.

B. If any *person* named in Schedules A, B, or C or in Section 10.A. of Schedule D is a public reporting company under Sections 12 or 15(d) of the Securities Exchange Act of 1934, please complete Section 10.B. of Schedule D.

Item 11 Disclosure Information

In this Item, we ask for information about your disciplinary history and the disciplinary history of all your *advisory affiliates*. We use this information to determine whether to grant your application for registration, to decide whether to revoke your registration or to place limitations on your activities as an investment adviser, and to identify potential problem areas to focus on during our on-site examinations. One event may result in "yes" answers to more than one of the questions below.

Your *advisory affiliates* are: (1) all of your current *employees* (other than *employees* performing only clerical, administrative, support or similar functions); (2) all of your officers, partners, or directors (or any *person* performing similar functions); and (3) all *persons* directly or indirectly *controlling* you or *controlled* by you. If you are a "separately identifiable department or division" (SID) of a bank, see the Glossary of Terms to determine who your *advisory affiliates* are.

If you are registered or registering with the SEC or if you are an exempt reporting adviser, you may limit your disclosure of any event listed in Item 11 to ten years following the date of the event. If you are registered or registering with a state, you must respond to the questions as posed; you may, therefore, limit your disclosure to ten years following the date of an event only in responding to Items 11.A.(1), 11.A.(2), 11.B.(1), 11.B.(2), 11.D.(4), and 11.H(1)(a). For purposes of calculating this ten-year period, the date of an event is the date the final order, judgment, or decree was entered, or the date any rights of appeal from preliminary orders, judgments, or decrees lapsed.

You must complete the appropriate Disclosure Reporting Page ("DRP") for "yes" answers to the questions in this Item 11.

	Yes	No
Do any of the events below involve you or any of your *supervised persons*?	☐	☐

SEC FORM ADV

For "yes" answers to the following questions, complete a Criminal Action DRP:

Yes   No

A. In the past ten years, have you or any *advisory affiliate*:

    (1) been convicted of or pled guilty or nolo contendere ("no contest") in a
        domestic, foreign, or military court to any *felony*?   ☐ ☐

    (2) been *charged* with any *felony*?   ☐ ☐

    If you are registered or registering with the SEC, or if you are reporting as an exempt reporting adviser,
    you may limit your response to Item 11.A.(2) to charges that are currently pending

B. In the past ten years, have you or any *advisory affiliate*:

    (1) been convicted of or pled guilty or nolo contendere ("no contest") in a domestic,
        foreign, or military court to a *misdemeanor* involving: investments or an
        investment-related business, or any fraud, false statements, or omissions,
        wrongful taking of property, bribery, perjury, forgery, counterfeiting, extortion,
        or a conspiracy to commit any of these offenses?   ☐ ☐

    (2) been *charged* with a *misdemeanor* listed in Item 11.B.(1)?   ☐ ☐

    If you are registered or registering with the SEC, or if you are reporting as an exempt reporting adviser,
    you may limit your response to Item 11.B.(2) to charges that are currently pending.

For "yes" answers to the following questions, complete a Regulatory Action DRP:

Yes   No

C. Has the SEC or the Commodity Futures Trading Commission (CFTC) ever:

    (1) *found* you or any *advisory affiliate* to have made a false statement or omission?   ☐ ☐

    (2) *found* you or any *advisory affiliate* to have been *involved* in a violation of SEC
        or CFTC regulations or statutes?   ☐ ☐

    (3) *found* you or any *advisory affiliate* to have been a cause of an *investment-related*
        business having its authorization to do business denied, suspended, revoked, or
        restricted?   ☐ ☐

    (4) entered an *order* against you or any *advisory affiliate* in connection with
        investment-related activity?   ☐ ☐

    (5) imposed a civil money penalty on you or any *advisory affiliate*, or *ordered* you
        or any *advisory affiliate* to cease and desist from any activity?   ☐ ☐

D. Has any other federal regulatory agency, any state regulatory agency, or any *foreign*
    financial regulatory authority:

    (1) ever *found* you or any *advisory affiliate* to have made a false statement or
        omission, or been dishonest, unfair, or unethical?   ☐ ☐

    (2) ever *found* you or any *advisory affiliate* to have been *involved* in a violation of
        investment-related regulations or statutes?   ☐ ☐

A GUIDE TO CAPITAL MARKETS

	Yes	No

(3) ever *found* you or any *advisory affiliate* to have been a cause of an *investment-related* business having its authorization to do business denied, suspended, revoked, or restricted? ☐ ☐

(4) in the past ten years, entered an *order* against you or any *advisory affiliate* in connection with an *investment-related* activity? ☐ ☐

(5) ever denied, suspended, or revoked your or any *advisory affiliate's* registration or license, or otherwise prevented you or any *advisory affiliate*, by *order*, from associating with an *investment-related* business or restricted your or any *advisory affiliate's* activity? ☐ ☐

E. Has any *self-regulatory organization* or commodities exchange ever:

(1) *found* you or any *advisory affiliate* to have made a false statement or omission? ☐ ☐

(2) *found* you or any *advisory affiliate* to have been *involved* in a violation of its rules (other than a violation designated as a *"minor rule violation"* under a plan approved by the SEC)? ☐ ☐

(3) *found* you or any *advisory affiliate* to have been the cause of an *investment-related* business having its authorization to do business denied, suspended, revoked, or restricted? ☐ ☐

(4) disciplined you or any *advisory affiliate* by expelling or suspending you or the *advisory affiliate* from membership, barring or suspending you or the *advisory affiliate* from association with other members, or otherwise restricting your or the *advisory affiliate's* activities? ☐ ☐

F. Has an authorization to act as an attorney, accountant, or federal contractor granted to you or any *advisory affiliate* ever been revoked or suspended? ☐ ☐

G. Are you or any *advisory affiliate* now the subject of any regulatory *proceeding* that could result in a "yes" answer to any part of Item 11.C., 11.D., or 11.E.? ☐ ☐

For "yes" answers to the following questions, complete a Civil Judicial Action DRP:

	Yes	No

H. (1) Has any domestic or foreign court:

(a) in the past ten years, *enjoined* you or any *advisory affiliate* in connection with any *investment-related* activity? ☐ ☐

(b) ever *found* that you or any *advisory affiliate* were *involved* in a violation of *investment-related* statutes or regulations? ☐ ☐

(c) ever dismissed, pursuant to a settlement agreement, an *investment-related* civil action brought against you or any *advisory affiliate* by a state or *foreign financial regulatory authority*? ☐ ☐

SEC Form ADV

(2) Are you or any *advisory affiliate* now the subject of any civil *proceeding* that could result in a "yes" answer to any part of Item 11.H(1)? ☐ ☐

Item 12 Small Businesses

The SEC is required by the Regulatory Flexibility Act to consider the effect of its regulations on small entities. In order to do this, we need to determine whether you meet the definition of "small business" or "small organization" under rule 0-7.

Answer this Item 12 only if you are registered or registering with the SEC <u>and</u> you indicated in response to Item 5.F.(2)(c) that you have regulatory assets under management of less than $25 million. You are not required to answer this Item 12 if you are filing for initial registration as a state adviser, amending a current state registration, or switching from SEC to state registration.

For purposes of this Item 12 only:

- Total Assets refers to the total assets of a firm, rather than the assets managed on behalf of *clients*. In determining your or another *person's* total assets, you may use the total assets shown on a current balance sheet (but use total assets reported on a consolidated balance sheet with subsidiaries included, if that amount is larger).

- *Control* means the power to direct or cause the direction of the management or policies of a *person*, whether through ownership of securities, by contract, or otherwise. Any *person* that directly or indirectly has the right to vote 25 percent or more of the voting securities, or is entitled to 25 percent or more of the profits, of another *person* is presumed to *control* the other *person*.

	<u>Yes</u>	<u>No</u>
A. Did you have total assets of $5 million or more on the last day of your most recent fiscal year?	☐	☐

If "yes," you do not need to answer Items 12.B. and 12.C.

B. Do you:

(1) *control* another investment adviser that had regulatory assets under management (calculated in response to Item 5.F.(2)(c) of Form ADV) $25 million or more on the last day of its most recent fiscal year? ☐ ☐

(2) *control* another *person* (other than a natural person) that had total assets of $5 million or more on the last day of its most recent fiscal year? ☐ ☐

C. Are you:

(1) *controlled* by or under common *control* with another investment adviser that had regulatory assets under management (calculated in response to Item 5.F.(2)(c) of Form ADV) of $25 million or more on the last day of its most recent fiscal year? ☐ ☐

(2) *controlled* by or under common *control* with another *person* (other than a natural person) that had total assets of $5 million or more on the last day of its most recent fiscal year? ☐ ☐

306

FORM ADV	Your Name_____	SEC File No._____
Schedule A	Date_____	CRD No._____

Direct Owners and Executive Officers

1. Complete Schedule A only if you are submitting an initial application or report. Schedule A asks for information about your direct owners and executive officers. Use Schedule C to amend this information.

2. Direct Owners and Executive Officers. List below the names of:

   (a) each Chief Executive Officer, Chief Financial Officer, Chief Operations Officer, Chief Legal Officer, Chief Compliance Officer (Chief Compliance Officer is required if you are registered or applying for registration and cannot be more than one individual), director and any other individuals with similar status or functions;

   (b) if you are organized as a corporation, each shareholder that is a direct owner of 5% or more of a class of your voting securities, unless you are a public reporting company (a company subject to Section 12 or 15(d) of the Exchange Act);

   Direct owners include any person that owns, beneficially owns, has the right to vote, or has the power to sell or direct the sale of, 5% or more of a class of your voting securities. For purposes of this Schedule, a person beneficially owns any securities: (i) owned by his/her child, stepchild, grandchild, parent, stepparent, grandparent, spouse, sibling, mother-in-law, father-in-law, son-in-law, daughter-in-law, brother-in-law, or sister-in-law, sharing the same residence; or (ii) that he/she has the right to acquire, within 60 days, through the exercise of any option, warrant, or right to purchase the security.

   (c) if you are organized as a partnership, all general partners and those limited and special partners that have the right to receive upon dissolution, or have contributed, 5% or more of your capital;

   (d) in the case of a trust that directly owns 5% or more of a class of your voting securities, or that has the right to receive upon dissolution, or has contributed, 5% or more of your capital, the trust and each trustee; and

   (e) if you are organized as a limited liability company ("LLC"), (i) those members that have the right to receive upon dissolution, or have contributed, 5% or more of your capital, and (ii) if managed by elected managers, all elected managers.

3. Do you have any indirect owners to be reported on Schedule B? ☐ Yes ☐ No

4. In the DE/FE/I column below, enter "DE" if the owner is a domestic entity, "FE" if the owner is an entity incorporated or domiciled in a foreign country, or "I" if the owner or executive officer is an individual.

5. Complete the Title or Status column by entering board/management titles; status as partner, trustee, sole proprietor, elected manager, shareholder, or member; and for shareholders or members, the class of securities owned (if more than one is issued).

6. Ownership codes are: NA - less than 5%   B - 10% but less than 25%   D - 50% but less than 75%
                         A - 5% but less than 10%   C - 25% but less than 50%   E - 75% or more

7. (a) In the Control Person column, enter "Yes" if the person has control as defined in the Glossary of Terms to Form ADV, and enter "No" if the person does not have control. Note that under this definition, most executive officers and all 25% owners, general partners, elected managers, and trustees are control persons.
   (b) In the PR column, enter "PR" if the owner is a public reporting company under Sections 12 or 15(d) of the Exchange Act.
   (c) Complete each column.

FULL LEGAL NAME (Individuals: Last Name, First Name, Middle Name)	DE/FE/I	Title or Status	Date Title or Status Acquired MM YYYY	Ownership Code	Control Person PR	CRD No. If None: S.S. No. and Date of Birth, IRS Tax No. or Employer ID No.

SEC FORM ADV

FORM ADV Schedule B	Your Name_____ Date_____	SEC File No._____ CRD No._____

Indirect Owners

1. Complete Schedule B only if you are submitting an initial application or report. Schedule B asks for information about your indirect owners; you must first complete Schedule A, which asks for information about your direct owners. Use Schedule C to amend this information.

2. Indirect Owners. With respect to each owner listed on Schedule A (except individual owners), list below:

   (a) in the case of an owner that is a corporation, each of its shareholders that beneficially owns, has the right to vote, or has the power to sell or direct the sale of, 25% or more of a class of a voting security of that corporation;

   For purposes of this Schedule, a *person* beneficially owns any securities: (i) owned by his/her child, stepchild, grandchild, parent, stepparent, grandparent, spouse, sibling, mother-in-law, father-in-law, son-in-law, daughter-in-law, brother-in-law, or sister-in-law, sharing the same residence; or (ii) that he/she has the right to acquire, within 60 days, through the exercise of any option, warrant, or right to purchase the security.

   (b) in the case of an owner that is a partnership, all general partners and those limited and special partners that have the right to receive upon dissolution, or have contributed, 25% or more of the partnership's capital;

   (c) in the case of an owner that is a trust, the trust and each trustee; and

   (d) in the case of an owner that is a limited liability company ("LLC"), (i) those members that have the right to receive upon dissolution, or have contributed, 25% or more of the LLC's capital, and (ii) if managed by elected managers, all elected managers.

3. Continue up the chain of ownership listing all 25% owners at each level. Once a public reporting company (a company subject to Sections 12 or 15(d) of the Exchange Act) is reached, no further ownership information need be given.

4. In the DE/FE/I column below, enter "DE" if the owner is a domestic entity, "FE" if the owner is an entity incorporated or domiciled in a foreign country, or "I" if the owner is an individual.

5. Complete the Status column by entering the owner's status as partner, trustee, elected manager, shareholder, or member; and for shareholders or members, the class of securities owned (if more than one is issued).

6. Ownership codes are: C - 25% but less than 50%   D - 50% but less than 75%   E - 75% or more   F - Other (general partner, trustee, or elected manager)

7. (a) In the *Control Person* column, enter "Yes" if the *person* has *control* as defined in the Glossary of Terms to Form ADV, and enter "No" if the *person* does not have *control*. Note that under this definition, most executive officers and all 25% owners, general partners, elected managers, and trustees are *control persons*.
   (b) In the PR column, enter "PR" if the owner is a public reporting company under Sections 12 or 15(d) of the Exchange Act.
   (c) Complete each column.

FULL LEGAL NAME (Individuals: Last Name, First Name, Middle Name)	DE/FE/I	Entity in Which Interest is Owned	Status	Date Status Acquired MM YYYY	Ownership Code	Control Person PR	CRD No. If None: S.S. No. and Date of Birth, IRS Tax No. or Employer ID No.

308

A GUIDE TO CAPITAL MARKETS

| FORM ADV
Schedule C | Your Name_____
Date_____ | SEC File No._____
CRD No._____ |

Amendments to Schedules A and B

1. Use Schedule C only to amend information requested on either Schedule A or Schedule B. Refer to Schedule A and Schedule B for specific instructions for completing this Schedule C. Complete each column.

2. In the Type of Amendment column, indicate "A" (addition), "D" (deletion), or "C" (change in information about the same *person*).

3. Ownership codes are:

NA - less than 5%	C - 25% but less than 50%	G - Other (general partner, trustee, or
A - 5% but less than 10%	D - 50% but less than 75%	elected member)
B - 10% but less than 25%	E - 75% or more	

4. List below all changes to Schedule A (Direct Owners and Executive Officers):

FULL LEGAL NAME (Individuals: Last Name, First Name, Middle Name)	DE/FE/I	Type of Amendment	Title or Status	Date Title or Status Acquired MM/YYYY	Ownership Code	Control Person		CRD No. If None: S.S. No. and Date of Birth, IRS Tax No. or Employer ID No.
							PR	

5. List below all changes to Schedule B (Indirect Owners):

FULL LEGAL NAME (Individuals: Last Name, First Name, Middle Name)	DE/FE/I	Type of Amendment	Title or Status	Date Title or Status Acquired MM/YYYY	Ownership Code	Control Person		CRD No. If None: S.S. No. and Date of Birth, IRS Tax No. or Employer ID No.
							PR	

309

SEC Form ADV

<table>
<tr><td>FORM ADV
Schedule D
Page 1 of 13</td><td>Your Name _____
Date _____</td><td>CRD Number _____
SEC 801- or 802 Number _____</td></tr>
</table>

Certain items in Part 1A of Form ADV require additional information on Schedule D. Use this Schedule D to report details for items listed below. Report only new information or changes/updates to previously submitted information. Do not repeat previously submitted information.

This is an ☐ INITIAL or ☐ AMENDED Schedule D

SECTION 1.B.   Other Business Names

List your other business names and the jurisdictions in which you use them. You must complete a separate Schedule D Section 1.B. for each business name.

Check only one box: ☐ Add   ☐ Delete   ☐ Amend

Name _____   Jurisdictions _____

SECTION 1.F.   Other Offices

Complete the following information for each office, other than your *principal office and place of business*, at which you conduct investment advisory business. You must complete a separate Schedule D Section 1.F. for each location. If you are applying for SEC registration, if you are registered only with the SEC, or if you are an *exempt reporting adviser*, list only the largest five offices (in terms of numbers of *employees*).

Check only one box: ☐ Add   ☐ Delete

_____
(number and street)

_____
(city)   (state/country)   (zip+4/postal code)

If this address is a private residence, check this box: ☐

_____
(area code)   (telephone number)   (area code)   (facsimile number)

SECTION 1.I. Website Addresses

List your website addresses. You must complete a separate Schedule D Section 1.I. for each website address.

Check only one box: ☐ Add   ☐ Delete

Website Address: _____

SECTION 1.L.   Location of Books and Records

Complete the following information for each location at which you keep your books and records, other than your *principal office and place of business*. You must complete a separate Schedule D Section 1.L. for each location.

Check only one box: ☐ Add   ☐ Delete   ☐ Amend

Name of entity where books and records are kept: _____

_____
(number and street)

_____
(city)   (state/country)   (zip+4/postal code)
If this address is a private residence, check this box: ☐

_____
(area code)   (telephone number)   (area code)   (facsimile number)

This is (check one):   ☐ one of your branch offices or affiliates.
                       ☐ a third-party unaffiliated recordkeeper.
                       ☐ other.
Briefly describe the books and records kept at this location. _____

FORM ADV Schedule D Page 2 of 13	Your Name_____ Date_____	*CRD* Number_____ SEC 801- or 802 Number_____

Certain items in Part 1A of Form ADV require additional information on Schedule D. Use this Schedule D to report details for items listed below. Report only new information or changes/updates to previously submitted information. Do not repeat previously submitted information.

This is an ☐ INITIAL or ☐ AMENDED Schedule D

SECTION 1.M.   Registration with *Foreign Financial Regulatory Authorities*

List the name and country, in English, of each *foreign financial regulatory authority* with which you are registered. You must complete a separate Schedule D Section 1.M. for each *foreign financial regulatory authority* with whom you are registered.

Check only one box: ☐ Add   ☐ Delete

Name of *Foreign Financial Regulatory Authority* _____
Name of Country _____

SECTION 2.A.(8) Related Adviser

If you are relying on the exemption in rule 203A-2(b) from the prohibition on registration because you *control,* are *controlled* by, or are under common *control* with an investment adviser that is registered with the SEC and your *principal office and place of business* is the same as that of the registered adviser, provide the following information:

Name of Registered Investment Adviser _____
CRD Number of Registered Investment Adviser _____
SEC Number of Registered Investment Adviser 801-_____

SECTION 2.A.(9) Newly Formed Adviser

If you are relying on rule 203A-2(c), the newly formed adviser exemption from the prohibition on registration, you are required to make certain representations about your eligibility for SEC registration. By checking the appropriate boxes, you will be deemed to have made the required representations. You must make both of these representations:

☐ I am not registered or required to be registered with the SEC or a *state securities authority* and I have a reasonable expectation that I will be eligible to register with the SEC within 120 days after the date my registration with the SEC becomes effective.

☐ I undertake to withdraw from SEC registration if, on the 120th day after my registration with the SEC becomes effective, I would be prohibited by Section 203A(a) of the Advisers Act from registering with the SEC.

SECTION 2.A.(10) Multi-State Adviser

If you are relying on rule 203A-2(d), the multi-state adviser exemption from the prohibition on registration, you are required to make certain representations about your eligibility for SEC registration. By checking the appropriate boxes, you will be deemed to have made the required representations.

If you are applying for registration as an investment adviser with the SEC, you must make both of these representations:

☐ I have reviewed the applicable state and federal laws and have concluded that I am required by the laws of 15 or more states to register as an investment adviser with the *state securities authorities* in those states.

☐ I undertake to withdraw from SEC registration if I file an amendment to this registration indicating that I would be required by the laws of fewer than 15 states to register as an investment adviser with the *state securities authorities* of those states.

If you are submitting your *annual updating amendment,* you must make this representation:

☐ Within 90 days prior to the date of filing this amendment, I have reviewed the applicable state and federal laws and have concluded that I am required by the laws of at least 15 states to register as an investment adviser with the *state securities authorities* in those states.

311

SEC FORM ADV

| **FORM ADV**
Schedule D
Page 3 of 13 | Your Name_____
Date_____ | *CRD* Number_____
SEC 801- or 802 Number_____ |

Certain items in Part 1A of Form ADV require additional information on Schedule D. Use this Schedule D to report details for items listed below. Report only new information or changes/updates to previously submitted information. Do not repeat previously submitted information.

This is an ☐ INITIAL or ☐ AMENDED Schedule D

SECTION 2.A.(12) SEC Exemptive *Order*

If you are relying upon an SEC *order* exempting you from the prohibition on registration, provide the following information:

Application Number: 803-_____   Date of *order*: _____
                                                              (mm/dd/yyyy)

SECTION 2.B. *Private Fund* Assets

If you check Item 2.B.(2) or (3), what is the amount of the *private fund* assets that you manage? _____.

NOTE: "*Private fund* assets" has the same meaning here as it has under rule 203(m)-1. If you are an investment adviser with its *principal office and place of business* outside of the United States only include *private fund* assets that you manage at a place of business in the United States.

SECTION 4   Successions

Complete the following information if you are succeeding to the business of a currently registered investment adviser. If you acquired more than one firm in the succession you are reporting on this Form ADV, you must complete a separate Schedule D Section 4 for each acquired firm. See Part 1A Instruction 4.

Name of Acquired Firm _____

Acquired Firm's SEC File No. (if any) 801-_____   Acquired Firm's *CRD* Number (if any) _____

SECTION 5.G.(3) Advisers to Registered Investment Companies and Business Development Companies

If you check Item 5.G (3), what is the SEC file number (811 or 814 number) of each of the registered investment companies and business development companies to which you act as an adviser pursuant to an advisory contract? You must complete a separate Schedule D Section 5.G.(3) for each registered investment company and business development company to which you act as an adviser.

Check only one box: ☐ Add   ☐ Delete

SEC File Number 811- or 814-_____

SECTION 5.I.(2) *Wrap Fee Programs*

If you are a portfolio manager for one or more *wrap fee programs*, list the name of each program and its *sponsor*. You must complete a separate Schedule D Section 5.I.(2) for each *wrap fee program* for which you are a portfolio manager.

Check only one box: ☐ Add   ☐ Delete   ☐ Amend

Name of *Wrap Fee Program* _____

Name of *Sponsor* _____

312

| **FORM ADV**
Schedule D
Page 4 of 13 | Your Name_____
Date_____ | CRD Number_____
SEC 801- or 802 Number_____ |

Certain items in Part 1A of Form ADV require additional information on Schedule D. Use this Schedule D to report details for items listed below. Report only new information or changes/updates to previously submitted information. Do not repeat previously submitted information.

This is an ☐ INITIAL or ☐ AMENDED Schedule D

SECTION 6.A.   Names of Your Other Businesses

If you are actively engaged in other business using a different name, provide that name and the other line(s) of business.

☐ Add   ☐ Delete   ☐ Amend

Other Business Name: _____

Other line(s) of business in which you engage using this name: (check all that apply)

- ☐ (1) broker-dealer (registered or unregistered)
- ☐ (2) registered representative of a broker-dealer
- ☐ (3) commodity pool operator or commodity trading advisor (whether registered or exempt from registration)
- ☐ (4) futures commission merchant
- ☐ (5) real estate broker, dealer, or agent
- ☐ (6) insurance broker or agent
- ☐ (7) bank (including a separately identifiable department or division of a bank)
- ☐ (8) trust company
- ☐ (9) registered municipal advisor
- ☐ (10) registered security-based swap dealer
- ☐ (11) major security-based swap participant
- ☐ (12) accountant or accounting firm
- ☐ (13) lawyer or law firm
- ☐ (14) other financial product salesperson (specify): _____

SECTION 6.B.(2) Description of Primary Business

Describe your primary business (not your investment advisory business):

_____
_____
_____

If you engage in that business under a different name, provide that name:

_____
_____
_____

SECTION 6.B.(3) Description of Other Products and Services

Describe other products or services you sell to your client. You may omit products and services that you listed in Section 6.B.2. above.

_____
_____
_____

If you engage in that business under a different name, provide that name:

_____
_____
_____

SECTION 7.A.   Financial Industry Affiliations

Complete a separate Schedule D Section 7.A. for each *related person* listed in Item 7.A.

Check only one box: ☐ Add   ☐ Delete   ☐ Amend

313

SEC FORM ADV

<table>
<tr><td>FORM ADV
Schedule D
Page 5 of 13</td><td>Your Name_____
Date_____</td><td>CRD Number_____
SEC 801- or 802 Number_____</td></tr>
</table>

Certain items in Part 1A of Form ADV require additional information on Schedule D. Use this Schedule D to report details for items listed below. Report only new information or changes/updates to previously submitted information. Do not repeat previously submitted information.

This is an ☐ INITIAL or ☐ AMENDED Schedule D

1. Legal Name of *Related Person*: _____

2. Primary Business Name of *Related Person*: _____

3. *Related Person*'s SEC File Number (if any) (*e.g.*, 801-, 8-, 866-, 802-) _____

4. *Related Person's CRD* Number (if any): _____

5. *Related Person* is: (check all that apply)

    ☐ (a) broker-dealer, municipal securities dealer, or government securities broker or dealer
    ☐ (b) other investment adviser (including financial planners)
    ☐ (c) registered municipal advisor
    ☐ (d) registered security-based swap dealer
    ☐ (e) major security-based swap participant
    ☐ (f) commodity pool operator or commodity trading advisor (whether registered or exempt from registration)
    ☐ (g) futures commission merchant
    ☐ (h) banking or thrift institution
    ☐ (i) trust company
    ☐ (j) accountant or accounting firm
    ☐ (k) lawyer or law firm
    ☐ (l) insurance company or agency
    ☐ (m) pension consultant
    ☐ (n) real estate broker or dealer
    ☐ (o) sponsor or syndicator of limited partnerships (or equivalent), excluding pooled investment vehicles
    ☐ (p) sponsor, general partner, managing member (or equivalent) of pooled investment vehicles

6. Do you *control* or are you *controlled* by the *related person*?   ☐ Yes ☐ No

7. Are you and the *related person* under common *control*?   ☐ Yes ☐ No

8. (a) Does the *related person* act as a qualified custodian for your *clients* in connection with advisory services you provide to *clients*?   ☐ Yes ☐ No

    (b) If you are registering or registered with the SEC and you have answered "yes" to question 8.(a) above, have you overcome the presumption that you are not operationally independent (pursuant to rule 206(4)-(2)(d)(5)) from the *related person* and thus are not required to obtain a surprise examination for your *clients'* funds or securities that are maintained at the *related person*?   ☐ Yes ☐ No

    (c) If you have answered "yes" to question 8.(a) above, provide the location of the *related person*'s office responsible for *custody* of your *clients'* assets:

    _____
    (number and street)

    _____
    (city) (state/country) (zip+4/postal code)

9. (a) If the *related person* is an investment adviser, is it exempt from registration?   ☐ Yes ☐ No

    (b) If the answer is yes, under what exemption? _____

10. (a) Is the *related person* registered with a *foreign financial regulatory authority*?   ☐ Yes ☐ No

    (b) If the answer is yes, list the name and country, in English, of each *foreign financial regulatory authority* with which the *related person* is registered. _____

11. Do you and the *related person* share any *supervised persons*?   ☐ Yes ☐ No

FORM ADV Schedule D Page 6 of 13	Your Name_____ Date_____	*CRD* Number_____ SEC 801- or 802 Number_____

Certain items in Part 1A of Form ADV require additional information on Schedule D. Use this Schedule D to report details for items listed below. Report only new information or changes/updates to previously submitted information. Do not repeat previously submitted information.

This is an ☐ INITIAL or ☐ AMENDED Schedule D

12. Do you and the *related person* share the same physical location?   ☐ Yes   ☐ No

---

SECTION 7.B.(1) *Private Fund* Reporting

Check only one box: ☐ Add   ☐ Delete   ☐ Amend

A. PRIVATE FUND

Information About the *Private Fund*

1. (a) Name of the *private fund*: _____

    (b) *Private fund* identification number: _____

2. Under the laws of what state or country is the *private fund* organized: _____

3. Name(s) of General Partner, Manager, Trustee, or Directors (or persons serving in a similar capacity):

    Check only one box: ☐ Add   ☐ Delete   ☐ Amend

    _____

4. The *private fund* (check all that apply; you must check at least one):

    ☐ (1) qualifies for the exclusion from the definition of investment company under section 3(c)(1) of the Investment Company Act of 1940

    ☐ (2) qualifies for the exclusion from the definition of investment company under section 3(c)(7) of the Investment Company Act of 1940

5. List the name and country, in English, of each *foreign financial regulatory authority* with which the *private fund* is registered.

    Check only one box: ☐ Add   ☐ Delete   ☐ Amend

    English Name of *Foreign Financial Regulatory Authority* _____   Name of Country _____

6. (a) Is this a "master fund" in a master-feeder arrangement?   ☐ Yes   ☐ No

    (b) If yes, what is the name and *private fund* identification number (if any) of the feeder funds investing in this *private fund*?

    Check only one box: ☐ Add   ☐ Delete   ☐ Amend

    _____   _____

    (c) Is this a "feeder fund" in a master-feeder arrangement?   ☐ Yes   ☐ No

    (d) If yes, what is the name and *private fund* identification number (if any) of the master fund in which this *private fund* invests?

    Check only one box: ☐ Add   ☐ Delete   ☐ Amend

    _____   _____

NOTE: You must complete question 6 for each master-feeder arrangement regardless of whether you are filing a single Schedule D, Section 7.B.(1) for the master-feeder arrangement or reporting on the funds separately.

SEC Form ADV

<table>
<tr><td>FORM ADV
Schedule D
Page 7 of 13</td><td>Your Name_____
Date_____</td><td>CRD Number_____
SEC 801- or 802 Number_____</td></tr>
</table>

Certain items in Part 1A of Form ADV require additional information on Schedule D. Use this Schedule D to report details for items listed below. Report only new information or changes/updates to previously submitted information. Do not repeat previously submitted information.

This is an ☐ INITIAL or ☐ AMENDED Schedule D

7. If you are filing a single Schedule D, Section 7.B.(1) for a master-feeder arrangement according to the instructions to this Section 7.B.(1), for each of the feeder funds answer the following questions:

   Check only one box: ☐ Add ☐ Delete ☐ Amend

   (a) Name of the *private fund*: _____

   (b) *Private fund* identification number: _____

   (c) Under the laws of what state or country is the *private fund* organized: _____

   (d) Name(s) of General Partner, Manager, Trustee, or Directors (or persons serving in a similar capacity):

      Check only one box: ☐ Add ☐ Delete ☐ Amend

      _____

   (e) The *private fund* (check all that apply; you must check at least one):

      ☐ (1) qualifies for the exclusion from the definition of investment company under section 3(c)(1) of the Investment Company Act of 1940

      ☐ (2) qualifies for the exclusion from the definition of investment company under section 3(c)(7) of the Investment Company Act of 1940

   (f) List the name and country, in English, of each *foreign financial regulatory authority* with which the *private fund* is registered.

      Check only one box: ☐ Add ☐ Delete ☐ Amend

      English Name of *Foreign Financial Regulatory Authority* _____   Name of Country _____

   NOTE: For purposes of questions 6 and 7, in a master-feeder arrangement, one or more funds ("feeder funds") invest all or substantially all of their assets in a single fund ("master fund"). A fund would also be a "feeder fund" investing in a "master fund" for purposes of this question if it issued multiple classes (or series) of shares or interests, and each class (or series) invests substantially all of its assets in a single master fund.

8. (a) Is this *private fund* a "fund of funds"? ☐ Yes ☐ No

   (b) If yes, does the *private fund* invest in funds managed by you or by a *related person*? ☐ Yes ☐ No

   NOTE: For purposes of this question only, answer "yes" if the fund invests 10 percent or more of its total assets in other pooled investment vehicles, whether or not they are also *private funds*, or registered investment companies.

9. During your last fiscal year, did the *private fund* invest in securities issued by investment companies registered under the Investment Company Act of 1940 (other than "money market funds," to the extent provided in Instruction 6.e.)? ☐ Yes ☐ No

10. What type of fund is the *private fund*?

    ☐ hedge fund ☐ liquidity fund ☐ private equity fund ☐ real estate fund ☐ securitized asset fund ☐ venture capital fund

    ☐ Other *private fund*: _____

    NOTE: For funds of funds, refer to the funds in which the *private fund* invests. For definitions of these fund types, please see Instruction 6 of the Instructions to Part 1A.

11. Current gross asset value of the *private fund*: $_____

316

A GUIDE TO CAPITAL MARKETS

<table>
<tr><td>FORM ADV
Schedule D
Page 8 of 13</td><td>Your Name_____
Date_____</td><td>CRD Number_____
SEC 801- or 802 Number_____</td></tr>
</table>

Certain items in Part 1A of Form ADV require additional information on Schedule D. Use this Schedule D to report details for items listed below. Report only new information or changes/updates to previously submitted information. Do not repeat previously submitted information.

This is an ☐ INITIAL or ☐ AMENDED Schedule D

Ownership

12. Minimum investment commitment required of an investor in the *private fund*: $_____

    NOTE: Report the amount routinely required of investors who are not your *related persons* (even if different from the amount set forth in the organizational documents of the fund).

13. Approximate number of the *private fund's* beneficial owners: ____

14. What is the approximate percentage of the *private fund* beneficially owned by you and your *related persons*:

    ____ %

15. What is the approximate percentage of the *private fund* beneficially owned (in the aggregate) by funds of funds:

    ____ %

16. What is the approximate percentage of the *private fund* beneficially owned by *non-United States persons*:

    ____ %

Your Advisory Services

17. (a) Are you a subadviser to this *private fund*? ☐ Yes ☐ No

    (b) If the answer to question 17(a) is "yes," provide the name and SEC file number, if any, of the adviser of the *private fund*. If the answer to question 17(a) is "no," leave this question blank. _____

18. (a) Do any other investment advisers advise the *private fund*? ☐ Yes ☐ No

    (b) If the answer to question 18(a) is "yes," provide the name and SEC file number, if any, of the other advisers to the *private fund*. If the answer to question 18(a) is "no," leave this question blank.

        Check only one box: ☐ Add ☐ Delete ☐ Amend

        _____ _____

19. Are your *clients* solicited to invest in the *private fund*? ☐ Yes ☐ No

20. Approximately what percentage of your *clients* has invested in the *private fund*? ____ %

Private Offering

21. Does the *private fund* rely on an exemption from registration of its securities under Regulation D of the Securities Act of 1933?
    ☐ Yes ☐ No

22. If yes, provide the *private fund's* Form D file number (if any):

    Check only one box: ☐ Add ☐ Delete ☐ Amend

    021-_____

317

SEC FORM ADV

<table>
<tr><td>FORM ADV
Schedule D
Page 9 of 13</td><td>Your Name_____
Date_____</td><td>CRD Number_____
SEC 801- or 802 Number_____</td></tr>
</table>

Certain items in Part 1A of Form ADV require additional information on Schedule D. Use this Schedule D to report details for items listed below. Report only new information or changes/updates to previously submitted information. Do not repeat previously submitted information.

This is an ☐ INITIAL or ☐ AMENDED Schedule D

B. SERVICE PROVIDERS

☐ Check this box if you are filing this Form ADV through the IARD system and want the IARD system to create a new Schedule D, Section 7.B.(1) with the same service provider information you have given here in Questions 23 - 28 for a new *private fund* for which you are required to complete Section 7.B.(1) If you check the box, the system will pre-fill those fields for you, but you will be able to manually edit the information after it is pre-filled and before you submit your filing.

Auditors

23. (a) (1) Are the *private fund's* financial statements subject to an annual audit? ☐ Yes ☐ No

      (2) Are the financial statements prepared in accordance with U.S. GAAP? ☐ Yes ☐ No

    If the answer to 23(a)(1) is "yes," respond to questions (b) through (f) below. If the *private fund* uses more than one auditing firm, you must complete questions (b) through (f) separately for each auditing firm.

    Check only one box: ☐ Add ☐ Delete ☐ Amend

    (b) Name of the auditing firm: _____

    (c) The location of the auditing firm's office responsible for the *private fund's* audit (city, state and country): _____

    (d) Is the auditing firm an *independent public accountant*? ☐ Yes ☐ No

    (e) Is the auditing firm registered with the Public Company Accounting Oversight Board? ☐ Yes ☐ No

    (f) If "yes" to (e) above, is the auditing firm subject to regular inspection by the Public Company Accounting Oversight Board in accordance with its rules? ☐ Yes ☐ No

    (g) Are the *private fund's* audited financial statements distributed to the *private fund's* investors? ☐ Yes ☐ No

    (h) Does the report prepared by the auditing firm contain an unqualified opinion? ☐ Yes ☐ No ☐ Report Not Yet Received

If you check "Report Not Yet Received," you must promptly file an amendment to your Form ADV to update your response when the report is available.

Prime Broker

24. (a) Does the *private fund* use one or more prime brokers? ☐ Yes ☐ No

    If the answer to 24(a) is "yes," respond to questions (b) through (e) below for each prime broker the *private fund* uses. If the *private fund* uses more than one prime broker, you must complete questions (b) through (e) separately for each prime broker.

    Check only one box: ☐ Add ☐ Delete ☐ Amend

    (b) Name of the prime broker: _____

    (c) If the prime broker is registered with the SEC, its registration number: 8-_____

    (d) Location of prime broker's office used principally by the *private fund* (city, state and country): _____

    (e) Does this prime broker act as custodian for some or all of the *private fund's* assets? ☐ Yes ☐ No

Custodian

25. (a) Does the *private fund* use any custodians (including the prime brokers listed above) to hold some or all of its assets? ☐ Yes ☐ No

    If the answer to 25(a) is "yes," respond to questions (b) through (f) below for each custodian the *private fund* uses. If the *private fund* uses more than one custodian, you must complete questions (b) through (f) separately for each custodian.

A Guide to Capital Markets

<table>
<tr><td>FORM ADV
Schedule D
Page 10 of 13</td><td>Your Name_____
Date_____</td><td>CRD Number_____
SEC 801- or 802 Number_____</td></tr>
</table>

Certain items in Part 1A of Form ADV require additional information on Schedule D. Use this Schedule D to report details for items listed below. Report only new information or changes/updates to previously submitted information. Do not repeat previously submitted information.

This is an ☐ INITIAL or ☐ AMENDED Schedule D

Check only one box: ☐ Add   ☐ Delete   ☐ Amend

(b) Legal name of custodian: _____

(c) Primary business name of custodian: _____

(d) The location of the custodian's office responsible for *custody* of the *private fund*'s assets (city, state and country): _____

(e) Is the custodian a *related person* of your firm?   ☐ Yes ☐ No

(f) If the custodian is a broker-dealer, provide its SEC registration number (if any) 8-_____

Administrator

26. (a) Does the *private fund* use an administrator other than your firm? ☐ Yes   ☐ No

If the answer to 26(a) is "yes," respond to questions (b) through (f) below. If the *private fund* uses more than one administrator, you must complete questions (b) through (f) separately for each administrator.

Check only one box: ☐ Add   ☐ Delete   ☐ Amend

(b) Name of administrator: _____

(c) Location of administrator (city, state and country): _____

(d) Is the administrator a *related person* of your firm? ☐ Yes   ☐ No

(e) Does the administrator prepare and send investor account statements to the *private fund*'s investors?

☐ Yes (provided to all investors)   ☐ Some (provided to some but not all investors)   ☐ No (provided to no investors)

(f) If the answer to 26(e) is "no" or "some," who sends the investor account statements to the (rest of the) *private fund*'s investors? If investor account statements are not sent to the (rest of the) private fund's investors, respond "not applicable."
_____

27. During your last fiscal year, what percentage of the *private fund*'s assets (by value) was valued by a *person*, such as an administrator, that is not your *related person*?

_____%

Include only those assets where (i) such person carried out the valuation procedure established for that asset, if any, including obtaining any relevant quotes, and (ii) the valuation used for purposes of investor subscriptions, redemptions or distributions, and fee calculations (including allocations) was the valuation determined by such person.

Marketers

28. (a) Does the *private fund* use the services of someone other than you or your *employees* for marketing purposes? ☐ Yes   ☐ No

You must answer "yes" whether the person acts as a placement agent, consultant, finder, introducer, municipal advisor or other solicitor, or similar person. If the answer to 28(a) is "yes", respond to questions (b) through (g) below for each such marketer the *private fund* uses. If the *private fund* uses more than one marketer, you must complete questions (b) through (g) separately for each marketer.

Check only one box: ☐ Add   ☐ Delete   ☐ Amend

SEC FORM ADV

<table>
<tr><td>FORM ADV
Schedule D
Page 11 of 13</td><td>Your Name_____
Date_____</td><td>CRD Number_____
SEC 801- or 802 Number_____</td></tr>
</table>

Certain items in Part 1A of Form ADV require additional information on Schedule D. Use this Schedule D to report details for items listed below. Report only new information or changes/updates to previously submitted information. Do not repeat previously submitted information.

This is an ☐ INITIAL or ☐ AMENDED Schedule D

    (b) Is the marketer a *related person* of your firm? ☐ Yes   ☐ No

    (c) Name of the marketer: _____

    (d) If the marketer is registered with the SEC, its file number (*e.g.*, 801-, 8-, or 866-): _____ and CRD Number (if any) _____

    (e) Location of the marketer's office used principally by the *private fund* (city, state and country): _____

    (f) Does the marketer market the *private fund* through one or more websites? ☐ Yes ☐ No

    (g) If the answer to 28(f) is "yes," list the website address(es): _____

SECTION 7.B.(2) *Private Fund* Reporting

(1) Name of the *private fund* _____

(2) *Private fund* identification number _____

(3) Name and SEC File number of adviser that provides information about this *private fund* in Section 7.B.(1) of Schedule D of its Form ADV filing _____, 801-_____ or 802-_____

(4) Are your *clients* solicited to invest in this *private fund*?   ☐ Yes ☐ No

    In answering this question, disregard feeder funds' investment in a master fund. For purposes of this question, in a master-feeder arrangement, one or more funds ("feeder funds") invest all or substantially all of their assets in a single fund ("master fund"). A fund would also be a "feeder fund" investing in a "master fund" for purposes of this question if it issued multiple classes (or series) of shares or interests, and each class (or series) invests substantially all of its assets in a single master fund.

SECTION 9.C. *Independent Public Accountant*

You must complete the following information for each *independent public accountant* engaged to perform a surprise examination, perform an audit of a pooled investment vehicle that you manage, or prepare an internal control report. You must complete a separate Schedule D Section 9.C. for each *independent public accountant*.

Check only one box: ☐ Add ☐ Delete ☐ Amend

(1) Name of the *independent public accountant*: _____

(2) The location of the *independent public accountant*'s office responsible for the services provided:

_____
(number and street)

<table>
<tr><td>_____</td><td>_____</td><td>_____</td></tr>
<tr><td>(city)</td><td>(state/country)</td><td>(zip+4/postal code)</td></tr>
</table>

(3) Is the *independent public accountant* registered with the Public Company Accounting Oversight Board? ☐ Yes ☐ No

(4) If yes to (3) above, is the *independent public accountant* subject to regular inspection by the Public Company Accounting Oversight Board in accordance with its rules? ☐ Yes ☐ No

(5) The *independent public accountant* is engaged to:

FORM ADV Schedule D Page 12 of 13	Your Name_____ Date_____	*CRD* Number_____ SEC 801- or 802 Number_____

Certain items in Part 1A of Form ADV require additional information on Schedule D. Use this Schedule D to report details for items listed below. Report only new information or changes/updates to previously submitted information. Do not repeat previously submitted information.

This is an ☐ INITIAL or ☐ AMENDED Schedule D

    A. ☐ audit a pooled investment vehicle
    B. ☐ perform a surprise examination of *clients'* assets
    C. ☐ prepare an internal control report

(6) Does any report prepared by the *independent public accountant* that audited the pooled investment vehicle or that examined internal controls contain an unqualified opinion?   ☐ Yes   ☐ No   ☐ Report Not Yet Received

If you check "Report Not Yet Received," you must promptly file an amendment to your Form ADV to update your response when the accountant's report is available.

SECTION 10.A.   *Control Persons*

You must complete a separate Schedule D Section 10.A. for each *control person* not named in Item 1.A. or Schedules A, B, or C that directly or indirectly *controls* your management or policies.

Check only one box: ☐ Add   ☐ Delete   ☐ Amend

(1) Firm or Organization Name
_____

(2) *CRD* Number (if any) _____   Effective Date _____   Termination Date _____
                                                 mm/dd/yyyy   mm/dd/yyyy

(3) Business Address:
_____
                                   (number and street)

_____
       (city)   (state/country)   (zip+4/postal code)
If this address is a private residence, check this box: ☐

(4) Individual Name (if applicable) (Last, First, Middle)
_____

(5) *CRD* Number (if any) _____   Effective Date _____   Termination Date _____
                                                 mm/dd/yyyy   mm/dd/yyyy

(6) Business Address:
_____
                                   (number and street)

_____
       (city)   (state/country)   (zip+4/postal code)
If this address is a private residence, check this box: ☐

(7) Briefly describe the nature of the *control*:
_____
_____
_____

SECTION 10.B.   *Control Person* Public Reporting Companies

If any person named in Schedules A, B, or C, or in Section 10 A. of Schedule D is a public reporting company under Sections 12 or 15(d) of the Securities Exchange Act of 1934 , please provide the following information (you must complete a separate Schedule D Section 10.B. for each public reporting company):

SEC Form ADV

<table>
<tr><td>FORM ADV
Schedule D
Page 13 of 13</td><td>Your Name_____
Date_____</td><td>CRD Number_____
SEC 801- or 802 Number_____</td></tr>
</table>

Certain items in Part 1A of Form ADV require additional information on Schedule D. Use this Schedule D to report details for items listed below. Report only new information or changes/updates to previously submitted information. Do not repeat previously submitted information.

This is an ☐ INITIAL or ☐ AMENDED Schedule D

(1) Full legal name of the public reporting company: _____

(2) The public reporting company's CIK number (Central Index Key number that the SEC assigns to each reporting company):

_____

Miscellaneous

You may use the space below to explain a response to an Item or to provide any other information.

_____
_____
_____
_____
_____
_____
_____

A GUIDE TO CAPITAL MARKETS

CRIMINAL DISCLOSURE REPORTING PAGE (ADV)

GENERAL INSTRUCTIONS

This Disclosure Reporting Page (DRP ADV) is an ☐ INITIAL *OR* ☐ AMENDED response used to report details for affirmative responses to Items 11.A. or 11.B. of Form ADV.

Check item(s) being responded to: ☐ 11.A(1) ☐ 11.A(2) ☐11.B(1) ☐11.B(2)

Use a separate DRP for each event or *proceeding*. The same event or *proceeding* may be reported for more than one *person* or entity using one DRP. File with a completed Execution Page.

Multiple counts of the same charge arising out of the same event(s) should be reported on the same DRP. Unrelated criminal actions, including separate cases arising out of the same event, must be reported on separate DRPs. Use this DRP to report all charges arising out of the same event. One event may result in more than one affirmative answer to the items listed above.

PART I

A. The *person(s)* or entity(ies) for whom this DRP is being filed is (are):
   ☐ You (the advisory firm)
   ☐ You and one or more of your *advisory affiliates*
   ☐ One or more of your *advisory affiliates*

   If this DRP is being filed for an *advisory affiliate*, give the full name of the *advisory affiliate* below (for individuals, Last name, First name, Middle name).

   If the *advisory affiliate* has a *CRD* number, provide that number. If not, indicate "non-registered" by checking the appropriate box.

Your Name	Your *CRD* Number

ADV DRP - *ADVISORY AFFILIATE*

CRD Number	This *advisory affiliate* is ☐a firm ☐an individual
	Registered: ☐Yes ☐No
Name (For individuals, Last, First, Middle)	

☐ This DRP should be removed from the ADV record because the *advisory affiliate(s)* is no longer associated with the adviser.

☐ This DRP should be removed from the ADV record because: (1) the event or *proceeding* occurred more than ten years ago or (2) the adviser is registered or applying for registration with the SEC and the event was resolved in the adviser's or *advisory affiliate's* favor.

☐ This DRP should be removed from the ADV record because it was filed in error, such as due to a clerical or data-entry mistake. Explain the circumstances: _____

B. If the *advisory affiliate* is registered through the IARD system or *CRD* system, has the *advisory affiliate* submitted a DRP (with Form ADV, BD or U-4) to the IARD or *CRD* for the event? If the answer is "Yes," no other information on this DRP must be provided.
   ☐ Yes   ☐ No

   NOTE: The completion of this form does not relieve the *advisory affiliate* of its obligation to update its IARD or *CRD* records.

(continued)

SEC 1707 (09-11)
File 2 of 4

323

SEC FORM ADV

CRIMINAL DISCLOSURE REPORTING PAGE (ADV)
(continuation)

PART II

1. If charge(s) were brought against an organization over which you or an *advisory affiliate* exercise(d) *control*: Enter organization name, whether or not the organization was an *investment-related* business and your or the *advisory affiliate's* position, title, or relationship.

2. Formal Charge(s) were brought in: (include name of Federal, Military, State or Foreign Court, Location of Court - City or County and State or Country, Docket/Case number).

3. Event Disclosure Detail (Use this for both organizational and individual charges.)

    A. Date First *Charged* (MM/DD/YYYY): [   ] ☐ Exact   ☐ Explanation

    If not exact, provide explanation: _____

    B. Event Disclosure Detail (include Charge(s)/Charge Description(s), and for each charge provide: (1) number of counts, (2) *felony* or *misdemeanor*, (3) plea for each charge, and (4) product type if charge is *investment-related*).

    C. Did any of the Charge(s) within the Event involve a *felony*? ☐ Yes   ☐ No

    D. Current status of the Event? ☐ Pending   ☐ On Appeal   ☐ Final

    E. Event Status Date (complete unless status is Pending) (MM/DD/YYYY): [   ]

      ☐ Exact   ☐ Explanation

    If not exact, provide explanation: _____

4. Disposition Disclosure Detail: Include for each charge (a) Disposition Type (e.g., convicted, acquitted, dismissed, pretrial, etc.), (b) Date, (c) Sentence/Penalty, (d) Duration (if sentence-suspension, probation, etc.), (e) Start Date of Penalty, (f) Penalty/Fine Amount, and (g) Date Paid.

(continued)

CRIMINAL DISCLOSURE REPORTING PAGE (ADV)
(continuation)

5. Provide a brief summary of circumstances leading to the charge(s) as well as the disposition. Include the relevant dates when the conduct which was the subject of the charge(s) occurred. (Your response must fit within the space provided.)

SEC FORM ADV

REGULATORY ACTION DISCLOSURE REPORTING PAGE (ADV)

GENERAL INSTRUCTIONS

This Disclosure Reporting Page (DRP ADV) is an ☐ INITIAL *OR* ☐ AMENDED response used to report details for affirmative responses to Items 11.C., 11.D., 11.E., 11.F. or 11.G. of Form ADV.

Check item(s) being responded to:
    ☐ 11.C(1) ☐ 11.C(2) ☐ 11.C(3) ☐ 11.C(4) ☐ 11.C(5)
    ☐ 11.D(1) ☐ 11.D(2) ☐ 11.D(3) ☐ 11.D(4) ☐ 11.D(5)
    ☐ 11.E(1) ☐ 11.E(2) ☐ 11.E(3) ☐ 11.E(4)
    ☐ 11.F.   ☐ 11.G.

Use a separate DRP for each event or *proceeding*. The same event or *proceeding* may be reported for more than one *person* or entity using one DRP. File with a completed Execution Page.

One event may result in more than one affirmative answer to Items 11.C., 11.D., 11.E., 11.F. or 11.G. Use only one DRP to report details related to the same event. If an event gives rise to actions by more than one regulator, provide details for each action on a separate DRP.

PART I

A. The *person(s)* or entity(ies) for whom this DRP is being filed is (are):
    ☐ You (the advisory firm)
    ☐ You and one or more of your *advisory affiliates*
    ☐ One or more of your *advisory affiliates*

    If this DRP is being filed for an *advisory affiliate*, give the full name of the *advisory affiliate* below (for individuals, Last name, First name, Middle name).

    If the *advisory affiliate* has a *CRD* number, provide that number. If not, indicate "non-registered" by checking the appropriate box.

Your Name	Your *CRD* Number

ADV DRP - *ADVISORY AFFILIATE*

CRD Number	This *advisory affiliate* is ☐ a firm ☐ an individual
	Registered: ☐ Yes ☐ No

Name (For individuals, Last, First, Middle)

    ☐   This DRP should be removed from the ADV record because the *advisory affiliate(s)* is no longer associated with the adviser.

    ☐   This DRP should be removed from the ADV record because: (1) the event or *proceeding* occurred more than ten years ago or (2) the adviser is registered or applying for registration with the SEC and the event was resolved in the adviser's or *advisory affiliate's* favor.

    If you are registered or registering with a *state securities authority*, you may remove a DRP for an event you reported only in response to Item 11.D(4), and only if that event occurred more than ten years ago. If you are registered or registering with the SEC, you may remove a DRP for any event listed in Item 11 that occurred more than ten years ago.

    ☐   This DRP should be removed from the ADV record because it was filed in error, such as due to a clerical or data-entry mistake. Explain the circumstances:

    _____
    _____

B. If the *advisory affiliate* is registered through the IARD system or *CRD* system, has the *advisory affiliate* submitted a DRP (with Form ADV, BD or U-4) to the IARD or *CRD* for the event? If the answer is "Yes," no other information on this DRP must be provided.
    ☐ Yes   ☐ No

    NOTE: The completion of this form does not relieve the *advisory affiliate* of its obligation to update its IARD or *CRD* records.   (continued)

REGULATORY ACTION DISCLOSURE REPORTING PAGE (ADV)
(continuation)

PART II

1. Regulatory Action initiated by:
    ☐ SEC ☐ Other Federal   ☐ State   ☐ *SRO*   ☐ Foreign

    (Full name of regulator, *foreign financial regulatory authority*, federal, state or *SRO*)

    _____

2. Principal Sanction (check appropriate item):

☐ Civil and Administrative Penalty(ies)/Fine(s)	☐ Disgorgement	☐ Restitution
☐ Bar	☐ Expulsion	☐ Revocation
☐ Cease and Desist	☐ Injunction	☐ Suspension
☐ Censure	☐ Prohibition	☐ Undertaking
☐ Denial	☐ Reprimand	☐ Other _____

    Other Sanctions:

    _____

3. Date Initiated (MM/DD/YYYY): [_____]   ☐ Exact   ☐ Explanation

    If not exact, provide explanation: _____

4. Docket/Case Number:

    _____

5. *Advisory Affiliate* Employing Firm when activity occurred which led to the regulatory action (if applicable):

    _____

6. Principal Product Type (check appropriate item):

☐ Annuity(ies) - Fixed	☐ Derivative(s)	☐ Investment Contract(s)
☐ Annuity(ies) - Variable	☐ Direct Investment(s) - DPP & LP Interest(s)	☐ Money Market Fund(s)
☐ CD(s)	☐ Equity - OTC	☐ Mutual Fund(s)
☐ Commodity Option(s)	☐ Equity Listed (Common & Preferred Stock)	☐ No Product
☐ Debt - Asset Backed	☐ Futures - Commodity	☐ Options
☐ Debt - Corporate	☐ Futures - Financial	☐ Penny Stock(s)
☐ Debt - Government	☐ Index Option(s)	☐ Unit Investment Trust(s)
☐ Debt - Municipal	☐ Insurance	☐ Other _____

    Other Product Types:

    _____

(continued)

SEC FORM ADV

REGULATORY ACTION DISCLOSURE REPORTING PAGE (ADV)
(continuation)

7. Describe the allegations related to this regulatory action (your response must fit within the space provided):

_____
_____
_____
_____
_____
_____

8. Current status? ☐ Pending ☐ On Appeal ☐ Final

9. If on appeal, regulatory action appealed to (SEC, *SRO*, Federal or State Court) and Date Appeal Filed:

_____
_____

If Final or On Appeal, complete all items below. For Pending Actions, complete Item 13 only.

10. How was matter resolved (check appropriate item):

☐ Acceptance, Waiver & Consent (AWC)   ☐ Dismissed   ☐ Vacated
☐ Consent   ☐ *Order*   ☐ Withdrawn
☐ Decision   ☐ Settled   ☐ Other _____
☐ Decision & *Order* of Offer of Settlement   ☐ Stipulation and Consent

11. Resolution Date (MM/DD/YYYY): [_____]   ☐ Exact   ☐ Explanation

If not exact, provide explanation: _____

12. Resolution Detail:

   A. Were any of the following Sanctions *Ordered* (check all appropriate items)?

   ☐ Monetary/Fine   ☐ Revocation/Expulsion/Denial   ☐ Disgorgement/Restitution

   Amount: $ [_____] ☐ Censure ☐ Cease and Desist/Injunction ☐ Bar ☐ Suspension

   B. Other Sanctions *Ordered*:

_____
_____
_____

Sanction detail: if suspended, *enjoined* or barred, provide duration including start date and capacities affected (General Securities Principal, Financial Operations Principal, etc.). If requalification by exam/retraining was a condition of the sanction, provide length of time given to requalify/retrain, type of exam required and whether condition has been satisfied. If disposition resulted in a fine, penalty, restitution, disgorgement or monetary compensation, provide total amount, portion levied against you or an *advisory affiliate*, date paid and if any portion of penalty was waived:

_____
_____
_____
_____

(continued)

REGULATORY ACTION DISCLOSURE REPORTING PAGE (ADV)
(continuation)

13. Provide a brief summary of details related to the action status and (or) disposition and include relevant terms, conditions and dates (your response must fit within the space provided).

SEC FORM ADV

CIVIL JUDICIAL ACTION DISCLOSURE REPORTING PAGE (ADV)

GENERAL INSTRUCTIONS

This Disclosure Reporting Page (DRP ADV) is an ☐ INITIAL *OR* ☐ AMENDED response used to report details for affirmative responses to Item 11.H. of Part 1A and Item 2.F. of Part 1B of Form ADV.

Check Part 1A item(s) being responded to: ☐ 11.H(1)(a)   ☐ 11.H(1)(b)   ☐ 11.H(1)(c)   ☐ 11.H(2)
Check Part 1B item(s) being responded to: ☐ 2.F(1)   ☐ 2.F(2)   ☐ 2.F(3)   ☐ 2.F(4)   ☐ 2.F(5)

Use a separate DRP for each event or *proceeding*. The same event or *proceeding* may be reported for more than one *person* or entity using one DRP. File with a completed Execution Page.

One event may result in more than one affirmative answer to Item 11.H. of Part 1A or Item 2.F. of Part 1B. Use only one DRP to report details related to the same event. Unrelated civil judicial actions must be reported on separate DRPs.

PART I

A. The *person(s)* or entity(ies) for whom this DRP is being filed is (are):
   ☐ You (the advisory firm)
   ☐ You and one or more of your *advisory affiliates*
   ☐ One or more of your *advisory affiliates*

If this DRP is being filed for an *advisory affiliate*, give the full name of the *advisory affiliate* below (for individuals, Last name, First name, Middle name).

If the *advisory affiliate* has a *CRD* number, provide that number. If not, indicate "non-registered" by checking the appropriate box.

Your Name	Your *CRD* Number

ADV DRP - *ADVISORY AFFILIATE*

CRD Number	This *advisory affiliate* is Registered:	☐ a firm ☐ an individual ☐ Yes ☐ No

Name (For individuals, Last, First, Middle)

☐ This DRP should be removed from the ADV record because the *advisory affiliate(s)* is no longer associated with the adviser.

☐ This DRP should be removed from the ADV record because: (1) the event or *proceeding* occurred more than ten years ago or (2) the adviser is registered or applying for registration with the SEC and the event was resolved in the adviser's or advisory affiliate's favor.

If you are registered or registering with a *state securities authority*, you may remove a DRP for an event you reported only in response to Item 11.H.(1)(a), and only if that event occurred more than ten years ago. If you are registered or registering with the SEC, you may remove a DRP for any event listed in Item 11 that occurred more than ten years ago.

☐ This DRP should be removed from the ADV record because it was filed in error, such as due to a clerical or data-entry mistake. Explain the circumstances:

_____
_____
_____

B. If the *advisory affiliate* is registered through the IARD system or *CRD* system, has the *advisory affiliate* submitted a DRP (with Form ADV, BD or U-4) to the IARD or *CRD* for the event? If the answer is "Yes," no other information on this DRP must be provided.
   ☐ Yes   ☐ No

   NOTE: The completion of this form does not relieve the *advisory affiliate* of its obligation to update its IARD or *CRD* records.

(continued)

CIVIL JUDICIAL ACTION DISCLOSURE REPORTING PAGE (ADV)
(continuation)

PART II

1. Court Action initiated by: (Name of regulator, *foreign financial regulatory authority, SRO*, commodities exchange, agency, firm, private plaintiff, etc.)

2. Principal Relief Sought (check appropriate item):

   ☐ Cease and Desist   ☐ Disgorgement   ☐ Money Damages (Private/Civil Complaint)   ☐ Restraining Order
   ☐ Civil Penalty(ies)/Fine(s)   ☐ Injunction   ☐ Restitution   ☐ Other _____

   Other Relief Sought:

3. Filing Date of Court Action (MM/DD/YYYY): [_____] ☐ Exact ☐ Explanation

   If not exact, provide explanation: _____

4. Principal Product Type (check appropriate item):

   ☐ Annuity(ies) - Fixed   ☐ Derivative(s)   ☐ Investment Contract(s)
   ☐ Annuity(ies) - Variable   ☐ Direct Investment(s) - DPP & LP Interest(s)   ☐ Money Market Fund(s)
   ☐ CD(s)   ☐ Equity - OTC   ☐ Mutual Fund(s)
   ☐ Commodity Option(s)   ☐ Equity Listed (Common & Preferred Stock)   ☐ No Product
   ☐ Debt - Asset Backed   ☐ Futures - Commodity   ☐ Options
   ☐ Debt - Corporate   ☐ Futures - Financial   ☐ Penny Stock(s)
   ☐ Debt - Government   ☐ Index Option(s)   ☐ Unit Investment Trust(s)
   ☐ Debt - Municipal   ☐ Insurance   ☐ Other _____

   Other Product Types:

5. Formal Action was brought in (include name of Federal, State or Foreign Court, Location of Court - City or County <u>and</u> State or Country, Docket/Case Number):

6. *Advisory Affiliate* Employing Firm when activity occurred which led to the civil judicial action (if applicable):

(continued)

SEC FORM ADV

CIVIL JUDICIAL ACTION DISCLOSURE REPORTING PAGE (ADV)
(continuation)

7. Describe the allegations related to this civil action (your response must fit within the space provided):

_____
_____
_____
_____
_____

8. Current status? ☐ Pending ☐ On Appeal ☐ Final

9. If on appeal, action appealed to (provide name of court) and Date Appeal Filed (MM/DD/YYYY):

_____

10. If pending, date notice/process was served (MM/DD/YYYY): [＿＿＿＿＿] ☐ Exact ☐ Explanation

If not exact, provide explanation: _____

If Final or On Appeal, complete all items below. For Pending Actions, complete Item 14 only.

11. How was matter resolved (check appropriate item):

☐ Consent   ☐ Judgment Rendered   ☐ Settled
☐ Dismissed   ☐ Opinion   ☐ Withdrawn   ☐ Other _____

12. Resolution Date (MM/DD/YYYY): [＿＿＿＿＿] ☐ Exact   ☐ Explanation

If not exact, provide explanation: _____

13. Resolution Detail:

   A. Were any of the following Sanctions Ordered or Relief Granted (check appropriate items)?

   ☐ Monetary/Fine   ☐ Revocation/Expulsion/Denial   ☐ Disgorgement/Restitution

   Amount: $ [＿＿＿＿＿]   ☐ Censure   ☐ Cease and Desist/Injunction   ☐ Bar   ☐ Suspension

   B. Other Sanctions:

   _____
   _____
   _____

(continued)

CIVIL JUDICIAL ACTION DISCLOSURE REPORTING PAGE (ADV)
(continuation)

C. Sanction detail: if suspended, *enjoined* or barred, provide duration including start date and capacities affected (General Securities Principal, Financial Operations Principal, etc.). If requalification by exam/retraining was a condition of the sanction, provide length of time given to requalify/retrain, type of exam required and whether condition has been satisfied. If disposition resulted in a fine, penalty, restitution, disgorgement or monetary compensation, provide total amount, portion levied against you or an *advisory affiliate*, date paid and if any portion of penalty was waived:

14. Provide a brief summary of circumstances related to the action(s), allegation(s), disposition(s) and/or finding(s) disclosed above (your response must fit within the space provided).

Chapter 13

Swaps and Options

In this chapter, we return to derivative securities and financial instruments. A derivative is either an exchange traded or over-the-counter (OTC) contract which derives its value by reference to something else. In Chapter 1 we looked at forward and futures contracts. Derivatives allow market participants to take positions (or hedge) in markets with less or no cash outlay. In chapter 1 we examined a first generation derivative known as a forward contract (also known as a forward delivery contract). With forwards, buyers and sellers are able to arrange contracts for future delivery, at a price agreed to at the inception of the contract, without having to come up with money (or as much money) up front. Because of credit concerns, forward markets matured into futures contracts. While the credit concerns are improved upon by exchange guarantees, the futures markets are standardized (and thus somewhat inflexible) and suffer from liquidity limitation. The solution to these imperfections presented itself in the form of **swap contracts**. Swaps are OTC derivative contracts which were designed to cure liquidity constraints in the futures markets. The first type of swap contract was an interest rate swap.

Interest Rate Swaps

To understand why swaps developed, we must go back to the late 1970s. Interest rates have been rising for several years, and expectations were that they would keep rising. A corporate treasurer in this era, believing interest rates will continue to rise, borrows fixed rate money with a maturity of 10 years on July 1, 1979. By borrowing funds at a fixed rate, the treasurer hopes to avoid future interest rate increases and thus creates a "short" interest rate exposure (see chapter 3). Three years later interest rates are falling, there are seven years remaining on the original loan, and our treasurer looks like he has walked into a trap. Unless the original loan/debt agreement has a mechanism for early payoff, the treasurer is stuck with high cost funding for seven more years.

Figure 13.1 - Original Corporate Borrowing

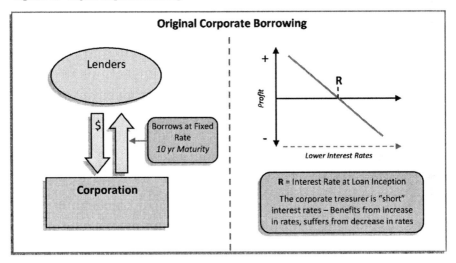

To hedge this short interest rate exposure, the treasurer has a number of ways to go "long." One choice is to purchase fixed rate bonds and hold them for all (or a portion) of the remaining life of the debt instrument that was issued by the treasurer's corporation. The problem with this approach is the purchased bonds may not perfectly hedge the debt instrument, and the treasurer will need to come up with funds to purchase the bonds (a recurring problem when hedging with cash markets).

Futures markets may do the trick, but unless futures contracts are available with seven year maturities (which they weren't), the treasurer will need to use a futures contract with a shorter life and roll it over at maturity. This can get expensive (transaction costs) and dangerous; if you have to close hedge number one at its expiration date and replace it with hedge number two, unless both transactions are done simultaneously, you run the risk the two trades won't be executed at the same price. This risk is further exacerbated by the fact that liquidity in futures markets is usually limited beyond the near term delivery months.

Interest rate swaps solve the problem. In an interest rate swap, two parties enter into an OTC contract. One party agrees to pay the other a fixed dollar amount in exchange for a dollar amount that is linked to a short-term interest rate index, usually Libor. (Libor is the London Inter-Bank Offer Rate, which is a rate of interest charged amongst banks in the London banking community. The reason this rate is used is that it is both transparent and liquid.) The arrangement between the parties would look like this:

Figure 13.2 – Interest Rate Swaps

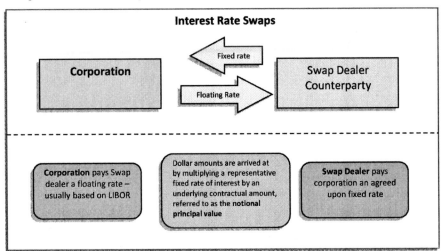

Although this contract is called an interest rate swap, there are no loans between the counterparties. Rather, the fixed dollar and floating dollar amounts are arrived at by multiplying a representative fixed rate of interest by an underlying contractual amount, referred to as the **notional principal value.** The payments are exchanged (usually a net payment is made after offsetting the amounts due), and the floating rate is reset for the next accrual period. This process continues over the lifespan of the swap. If our corporate treasurer were to use a swap, he would enter into a swap in which a fixed rate is received and a floating rate is paid semiannually (with a reset in the floating leg of the swap at each payment date). This replicates the position a hedger would have if a cash market instrument (a seven year bond) were purchased and financed with floating rate loans whose interest rates are reset at six-month intervals. Someone purchasing a seven- year bond with this type of financing would be long.

By virtue of receiving the fixed payment on the swap, the corporation would benefit (on the swap) as interest rates fell and lose if interest rates rose. Accordingly, the recipient of a fixed rate in a swap is long (and the payer of the fixed rate is short). If the corporate treasurer used a seven-year swap, the original loan would be hedged until maturity without having to roll over positions. This is a major improvement over long-term hedging strategies involving futures contracts.

Figure 13.3 – Fixed Rate Corporate Loan Hedged by an Interest Rate Swap

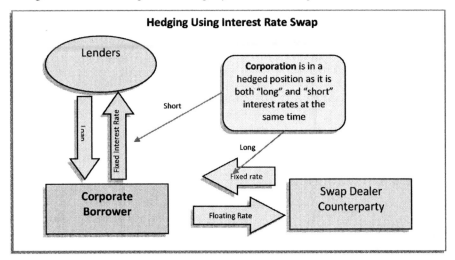

Swap dealers are middlemen in these arrangements. A dealer will reverse his position with counterparty or otherwise dispose of the risk by taking either long or short positions. The swap dealer is normally interested in earning spreads, the size of which can be increased by dealing with weaker rated counterparties on one side of the trade.

Other Types of Swaps

Swaps can be done on any number of assets, including commodities, fixed income instruments, and equities. Remember that swaps replicate positions that can be constructed in the cash markets. Thus, so called "total return swaps" are used to replicate positions in these markets. These types of swaps provide long and short equity market exposure, often at collateral levels that are often below Regulation T or U levels. Further, a user of short total return swaps may avoid squeeze risk associated with cash market short sales. A comparison of the long and short positions taken through cash markets and swap contracts appears at Figures 13.4 and 13.5.

Figure 13.4 – Long Equity Position in Cash Markets and Swap Contracts

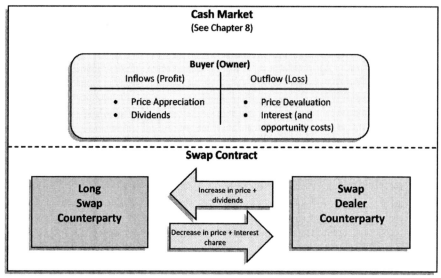

A GUIDE TO CAPITAL MARKETS

Figure 13.5 – Short Equity Position in Cash Markets and Swap Contracts

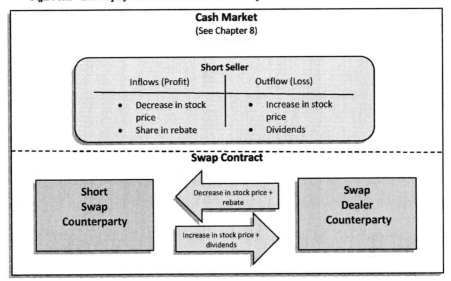

341

The last of the swaps I will discuss are **credit default swaps** (CDS). These contracts aren't really swaps. The better analogy is an insurance contract. In a CDS there are two counterparties, a protection buyer and a protection seller. The party buying the protection is really insuring against the adverse effects of a credit event, such as a bankruptcy, nonpayment, or other default by a borrower. In exchange for periodic payments (usually quarterly, but there are many variations) of an insurance type premium, the seller agrees to either buy the defaulted debt obligation at a predetermined price (physical settlement) or to pay the decline in value of the defaulted bond as determined through an industry sponsored auction mechanism (cash settlement). Cash settlement swaps are now the industry standard. The typical arrangement appears in Figure 13.6.

Figure 13.6 – A Typical Credit Default Swap

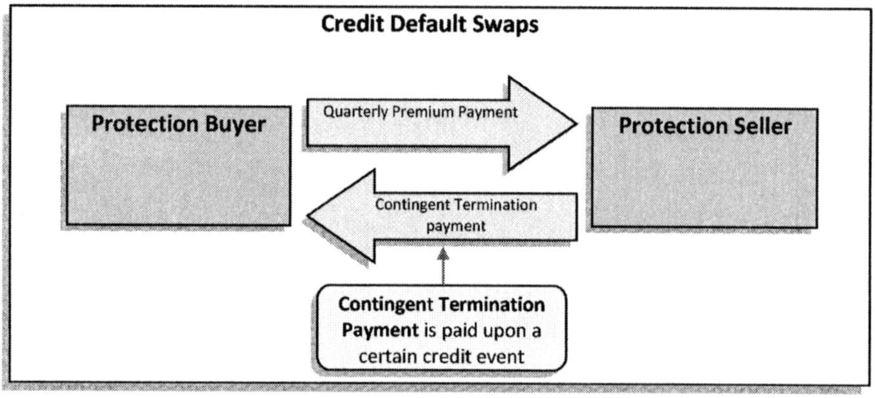

Credit Default Swaps

Protection Buyer — Quarterly Premium Payment → Protection Seller

Contingent Termination payment

Contingent Termination Payment is paid upon a certain credit event

The fundamental difference between a CDS and a total return swap is the fact that the CDS provides protection against specific credit events. The total return swap provides protection against loss of value irrespective of cause—a default, market sentiment causing credit spreads to widen, etc.

Most credit derivatives entail two sources of credit exposure: one from the reference asset (the asset on which the CDS is written) and the other from possible default by the counterparty to the transaction. What makes CDS controversial is the ability to buy insurance type protection on assets that are not owned by the CDS buyer. This allows CDS buyers to effectively take short positions in companies via the largely unregulated CDS market. CDS also provides the ability to construct short positions in markets where that had previously been impractical. A prime example of this was speculative use of CDS by multiple parties betting on a housing crash in the 2007-2008 period.

CDS may be executed on specific obligations of a single issuer (so called "single name" CDS) or on groups of reference obligations, often by altering the sequences of the defaults.

Options Contracts

Options Contracts give the holder the right (not the obligation) to either buy or sell a certain quantity of a stock, stock index, bond, bond index, commodity, currency, or futures contract ("the underlying" security or instrument) at a certain price (the strike or exercise price), up to a specified point in time (expiration date). The price is the premium. Options where the holder has an option to buy are referred to as call options. Buyers of call options have the right, but not the obligation, to buy an underlying asset at a predetermined price over the life (or at the expiration) of the option. Buyers of put options have the right, but not the obligation, to sell an underlying asset at a predetermined price over the life (or at the expiration) of the option. Sellers of call options have a corresponding obligation to sell, and put option sellers a corresponding obligation to buy, an underlying asset. Some options can be exercised any time over their life, some are exercisable only at maturity, some have hybrid features. The different types of exercise features commonly found in option contracts include:

- **American**

  — Exercisable without restriction up to the maturity date of the option.

- **European**

  — Exercisable only on the maturity date.

- **Bermudan**

  — Exercisable at multiple dates, but not any date, throughout its holding period.

- **Asian**

  — An option whose exercise price is averaged over a reference period.

- **Knock-ins**

  — An option, initially which cannot be exercised, which becomes exercisable upon the occurrence of a predetermined event.

- **Knock-out**

  — An option, initially exercisable, which terminates upon the occurrence of an event.

Positions resulting from buying and selling call and put options are summarized at Figure 13.7.

Figure 13.7 – Profile of Various Option Contracts

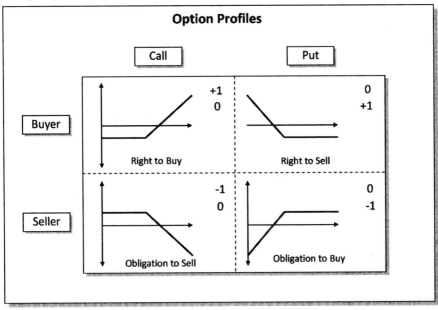

Option strategies can be directional (taking a position on price direction), based on differences in views of price volatility (without regard to price direction), some combination of both, portfolio income yield enhancement, and other reasons. A review of many popular option strategies follows.

Purchased Call Option Position

Figure 13.8 – Purchased Call Option

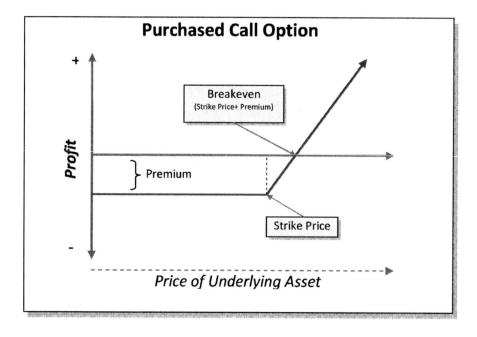

How trade is done

Purchase of a call option.

Risk / Reward

Maximum loss: limited to the premium paid.

Maximum gain: unlimited.

Breakeven point: strike price + premium.

Characteristics

Bullish directional.

Purchased Put Option Position

Figure 13.9 – Purchased Put Option

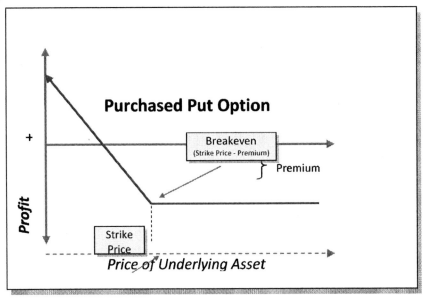

347

How trade is done

A long put is the purchase of a put option.

Risk / Reward

Maximum Loss: Limited to the net premium paid.

Maximum Gain: The difference between the exercise price and zero.

Breakeven point: strike price—premium.

Characteristics

Bearish directional.

Sold Call Option Position

Figure 13.10 – Selling Call Options

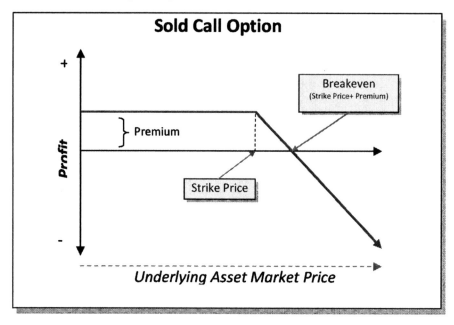

How trade is done

A sold the sale of a call option.

Risk / Reward

Maximum Loss: Unlimited as the market rises.

Maximum Gain: Limited to the premium received for selling the option.

Breakeven point: strike price—premium.

Characteristics

Bearish directional.

Sold Put Option Position

Figure 13.11 – Selling Put Options

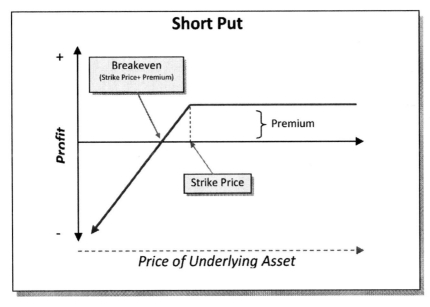

349

How trade is done

A sold put is the sale of a put option.

Risk / Reward

Maximum Loss: The difference between the exercise price and zero.

Maximum Gain: Limited to the premium received for selling the put option.

Breakeven point: strike price—premium.

Characteristics

Bullish directional.

Option Pricing

Option pricing models determine the theoretical fair value for a call or put option given certain known variables. Basically, the expected return of an option contract is a function of two variables:

- The payoff of the option at maturity date
- The probability of the option being in-the-money at maturity

Figure 13.12 – Option Pricing Probability Distribution

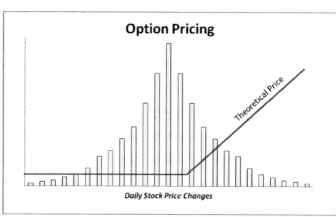

The premium consists of two components, intrinsic value and time value. Intrinsic value is the built in profit the option; for a call this exists if the market price of the underlying asset exceeds the exercise price. Because option holders have rights, and not obligations, intrinsic value will always be positive or zero, never negative. Time value represents the remaining life the option has regardless of any intrinsic value.

There are five factors that determine option premiums:

- The price of the underlying

- The strike price of the option

- The option's remaining life

- The volatility of the underlying asset

- Interest rates

These are usually input into standardized option pricing models to calculate the option premium.

Figure 13.13 – Pricing Components

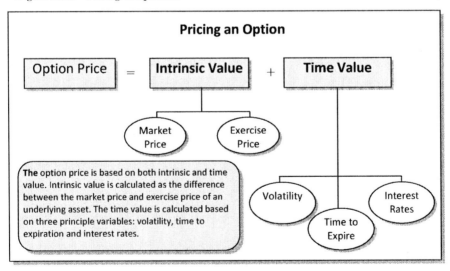

Measuring Changes in Option Prices-The "Greeks"

- **Option Delta** The delta of an option is the sensitivity of an option price relative to changes in the price of the underlying asset. It tells option traders how fast the price of the option will change as the underlying stock/ future moves.

Figure 13.14 – Option Delta

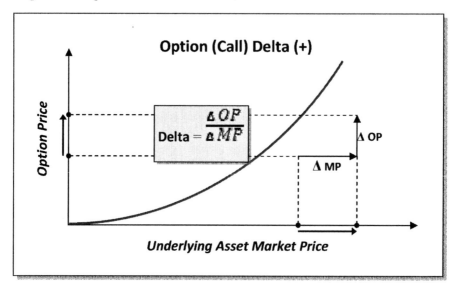

- **Option Gamma** The gamma of an option indicates
  how the delta of an option will change relative to a
  1-point move in the underlying asset. The Gamma
  shows the option delta's sensitivity to market price
  changes. Thus, Gamma measures how fast our position
  delta will change as the market price of the underlying
  asset changes.

Figure 13.15 – Option Gamma

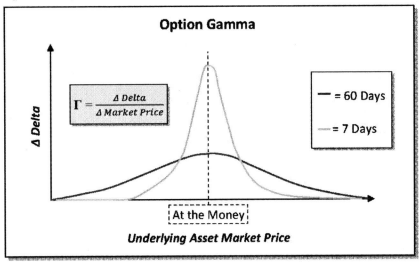

- **Option Theta** Theta measures the erosion of option value with the passage of time. An option contract has a finite life, defined by the expiration date. As the option approaches its maturity date, an option contract's expected value becomes more certain with each day. Theta is measured as each trading day passes—assuming all other inputs remain unchanged. Because of this negative impact on an option price, the Theta will always be a negative number.

Figure 13.16 – Option Theta

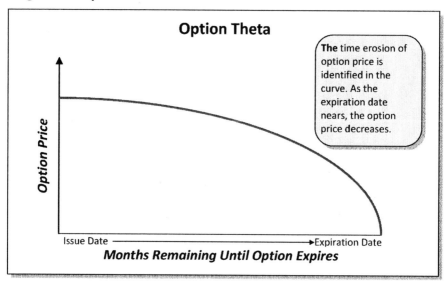

- **Option Vega** The Vega measures how the price of the option will change as the volatility of the underlying asset changes. Vega is most sensitive when the option is at-the-money and tapers off either side as the market trades above/below the strike price.

Figure 13.17 – Option Vega

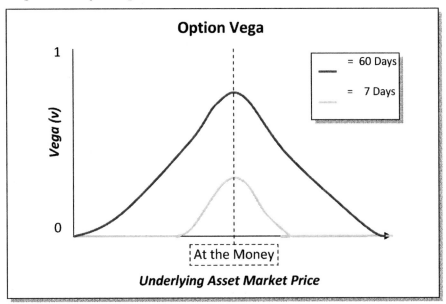

355

- **Option Rho** Rho is the change in option value that results from movements in interest rates.

Figure 13.18 – Option Rho

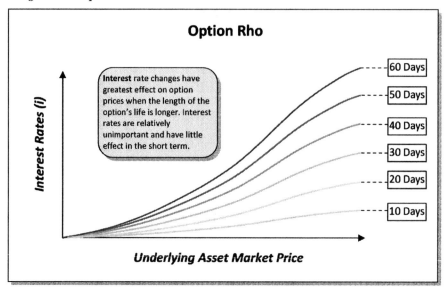

Option Rho

Interest rate changes have greatest effect on option prices when the length of the option's life is longer. Interest rates are relatively unimportant and have little effect in the short term.

Interest Rates (i)

60 Days
50 Days
40 Days
30 Days
20 Days
10 Days

Underlying Asset Market Price

Option Spreads

Options are quite attractive as a directional alternative to buying the underlying asset. The purchase requires much less money. The payment of the option premium, specifically the time value, has the effect of raising the breakeven point for a purchased option. Option selling exposes the seller to significant losses without the corresponding potential for gains. Option users therefore have two overriding objectives:

1. In the case of an option buyer, lower breakeven points. To achieve this result the option buyer may need to forgo a portion of gains they would otherwise enjoy if there is a large price movement in the underlying asset.

2. In the case of an option seller, risk reduction. To achieve this result, the option seller may need to forgo a portion of the premiums they would otherwise collect from selling the options.

356

These objectives are achieved through the use of an options strategy referred to as **spreads**. A simple spread involves buying and selling the same type of option (calls or puts) at different exercise prices to the same expiration date. A spread is a more conservative type of directional strategy.

Bullish Call Option Spreads

Components

Buy one call option with a low strike price and sell one call option with a higher strike price. Usually, the purchased option has an exercise price which is equal to today's market price (at the money), and the sold option has a higher exercise price (out of the money). The receipt of the premium from selling the out of the money option reduces the spread buyer's breakeven point.

Risk / Reward

- Maximum Loss: Limited to premium paid for the purchased option minus the premium received for the sold option.

- Maximum Gain: Limited to the difference between the two strike prices minus the net premium paid for the spread.

- Breakeven point: lower exercise price plus the net premium paid.

Characteristics

Mildly bullish directional strategy.

Figure 13.19- Bullish Call Option spread

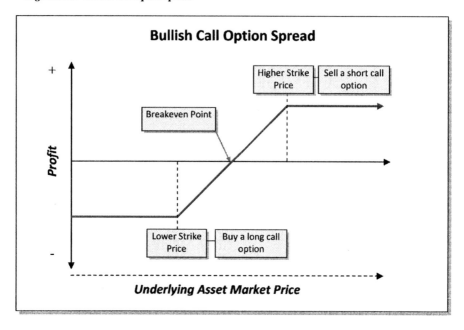

Bearish Call Option Spreads

Components

Sell one call option with a low strike price and buy one call option with a higher strike price. Usually, the sold option has an exercise price which is equal to today's market price (at the money) and the purchased option has a higher exercise price (out of the money). This is the opposite of the bullish call spread described above.

Risk / Reward

- Maximum Loss: Limited to the difference between the two strikes minus the net premium.

- Maximum Gain: Limited to the net premium received for the position.

- Breakeven point: lower exercise price plus the net premium received.

Characteristics

When to use: When you are mildly bearish on market direction. The purchase of the out of the money option protects the spread seller in the event of a large increase in the value of the underlying asset.

Figure 13.20- Bearish Call Option spread

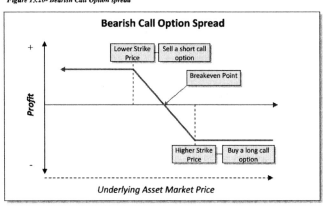

359

Bullish Put Spread

Components

Buy one put option and sell another put option with a higher strike price.

Risk / Reward

- Maximum Loss: Limited to the difference between the two strike prices minus the net premium received for the position.

- Maximum Gain: Limited to the net credit received for the spread.

Characteristics

Mildly bullish on market direction.

Figure 13.21- Bullish Put Option spread

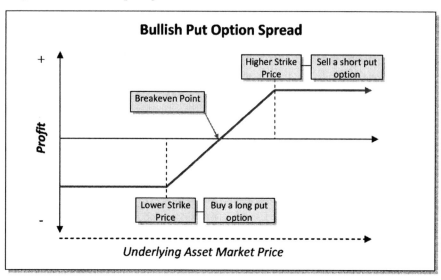

Bearish Put Spreads

Components

Sell one put option at a lower strike price and buy one put option at a higher strike price.

Risk / Reward

- Maximum Loss: Limited to the net amount paid for the spread.

- Maximum Gain: Limited to the difference between the two strike prices minus the net paid for the position.

Characteristics

Mildly bearish on market direction.

Figure 13.22- Bearish Put Option spread

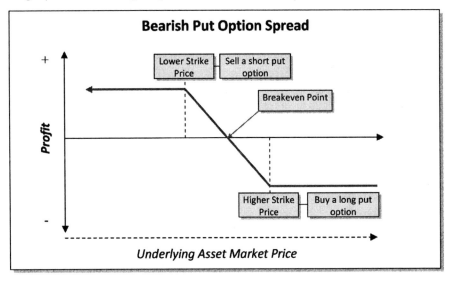

361

Volatility Strategies

Not all option strategies are based on expectations of the direction of price movements but rather the range (in either direction) that an asset can move. Two common strategies are **straddles** and **strangles.**

Long Straddles

Components

Buy one call option and buy one put option at the same strike price, usually at the money.

Risk / Reward

- Maximum Loss: Limited to the total premium paid for the call and put options.

- Maximum Gain: Unlimited (call side), limited to market price of zero (put side) as the market moves in either direction.

- There are two breakeven points for this strategy, one if the underlying price increases and one if it decreases.

Characteristics

Used when you believe there is more market volatility than is being priced (implied volatility) but are unsure of market direction.

Figure 13.23- Long Straddles

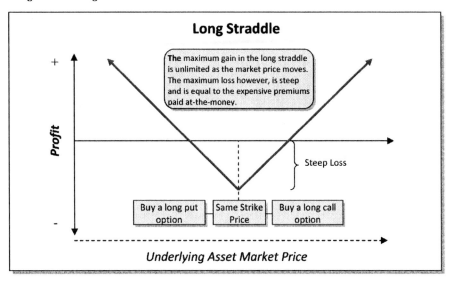

Short Straddles

Components

Sell one call option and one put option at the same strike price, usually at the money.

Risk / Reward

- Maximum Loss: Unlimited as the market moves in upper direction limited to price of zero in lower direction.

- Maximum Gain: Limited to the net premium received for selling the options.

Characteristics

Expectations of diminished volatility.

Figure 13.24- Short Straddles

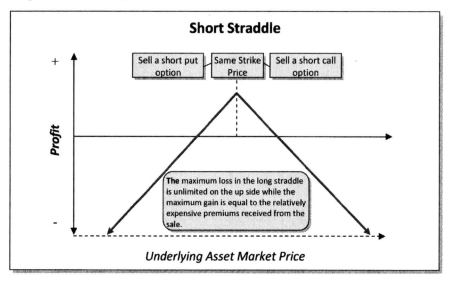

Short Straddle

Sell a short put option | Same Strike Price | Sell a short call option

The maximum loss in the long straddle is unlimited on the up side while the maximum gain is equal to the relatively expensive premiums received from the sale.

Profit

Underlying Asset Market Price

Long Strangle

Components

Buy one put option with a lower strike price and one call option at a higher strike price. Both options are usually out of the money when position is established.

Risk / Reward

- Maximum Loss: Limited to the total premium paid for the call and put options.

- Maximum Gain: Unlimited as the market moves upward, profit maximized on downside when underlying asset reaches zero.

- Like a straddle, a strangle has two breakeven points. Because the options are out of the money when purchased, there is a smaller up front outlay and a smaller potential loss.

Characteristics

- When to use: When you are bullish on volatility but are unsure of market direction.

- A long strangle is similar to a straddle except the strike prices are further apart, which lowers the cost of putting on the spread but also widens the gap needed for the market to rise/fall beyond in order to be profitable.

Figure 13.25- Long Strangles

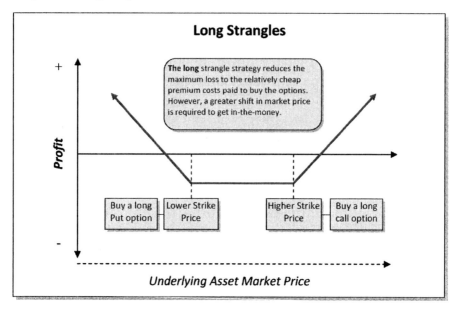

Short Strangle

Components

Sell one put option with a lower strike price and sell one call option at a higher strike price.

Risk / Reward

- Maximum Loss: Unlimited as the market moves upward, loss maximized when underlying asset reaches zero.

- Maximum Gain: Limited to the net premium received for selling the options.

Characteristics

When to use: When you are expecting diminished volatility and stable market prices.

Figure 13.26- Short Strangles

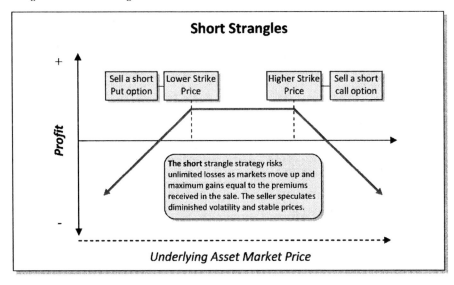

Interest Rate Option Applications

Caps, Collars, and Floors

- **Interest rate caps** are instruments that may be purchased (for a premium paid upfront) to ensure that the interest rate on a loan does not go above a certain level (the strike price).

- **Floors** pay the holder if interest rates fall below a certain level (the strike price). They are useful to **deposit holders** wanting to insure against interest rates falling.

- A **collar** is a cap and a floor combined, often in such a way as to net out to zero cost.

  - **Borrowers**: *buy* caps and *sell* floors to create a collar.

  - **Lenders**: *buy* floors and *sell* caps to create a collar.

Chapter 14

Foreign Currency Markets

The foreign exchange market is an inter-dealer, inter-broker OTC trading environment. The dealer community consists of larger bank and financial institutions, which act as liquidity providers. The geography of the market dictates many of its trading conventions; major trading centers are located in London and continental Europe (London is the world's largest foreign currency market), New York (and other US trading centers), and Tokyo (as well as other Asian trading markets). This triangular configuration allows currency to actively trade 24 hours a day, five days per week. Trading for a given week concludes at the end of business hours on Fridays.

Most dealers aim to keep their books "flat," meaning they aren't normally looking to take positions. Rather, dealers provide liquidity by making markets. Thus, they are in the market buying at a bid price and selling at a higher ask/offer price. The dealer's target profit is the difference between the bid and ask, or the spread. Dealers can make either firm or indicative quotes. In a firm quote the dealer is obligated to buy or sell without regard to having the second offsetting trade in place. This can leave the dealer with a position until a second party can be found to do the second trade. The spread therefore has to compensate the dealer for capital usage and market risk over this period. In actively traded currencies this will take seconds; therefore the spreads on actively traded currencies are quite small. If a firm quote is made in a less actively traded currency. the dealer can be left holding the position for a longer period of time, so the spread will normally be larger. The less actively traded the currency, the larger the spread. If the dealer is unwilling to take the positioning risk, an indication quote will be given. In these types of quotes the dealer is not obligated to deal unless both a buy and sell order can be executed simultaneously.

Currency markets are also defined by amount of time that passes between order and settlement. The key dates are the **transaction date,** which is the date the exchange is agreed upon and the date the rate is chosen. The **value date** refers to the date and manner in which the currencies are actually exchanged. This is normally synonymous with the **settlement date,** which is the date the currency exchange is cleared in the banking system.

The foreign exchange market is comprised of several markets corresponding with settlement conventions. The **spot market** is the market where the transaction and settlement dates are two days apart. The two-day cycle enables banking centers in different time zones to be open to facilitate the trade. Currencies of countries in the same hemisphere, like the U.S. dollar and the Canadian dollar, settle in one day.

The **forward market** is the market where the transaction date and the value date are separated by more than two days.

The **currency swap market** where currencies are exchanged and then re-exchanged on two different value dates.

The **currency futures market**, like other futures markets, are where standardized contracts trade for the future delivery of foreign currencies.

There are also active **currency options markets** where rights to currencies (or the right to enter into futures contracts) are traded.

Spot Markets

In a spot market transaction an agreement is made between two parties to exchange currencies at the outright price given by the market-maker. In an **American style quote** exchange rates using a foreign currency as the base. This is also called a **direct quote**. It expresses the price of the foreign currency by the number of U.S. dollars required to purchase the foreign currency. An example would be 1 Euro= $1.33.

International, or indirect, quotes are exchange rates using the U.S. dollar as the base. It expresses the price of foreign currency by the number of foreign currency units required to purchase one U.S. dollar. An example would be $1=79 yen.

Bid rates represent a market maker's price for buying a U.S. dollar. It indicates the amount received by buyers of foreign currencies for each U.S. dollar they have to sell.

Offer rates represent a market maker's price for selling a U.S. dollar. It indicates the amount of U.S. dollars received by sellers of foreign currencies.

Bid and offer rates fluctuate over the trading day providing momentary profit opportunities in the spot market. Bid and offer rates are quoted by market makers with the bid rate followed by the offer rate.

Forward Markets

The forward market is where the transaction date to the exchange of currencies is separated from the value date by more than two days. The forward market is used to cover foreign currency denominated transactions in an attempt to minimize foreign exchange rate risk in the future without the need to currently tie up cash or borrowing capacity. Accordingly, foreign currencies are just another market in which triangular pricing relationships exist. You may recall that forward prices are determined by adjusting spot prices for carrying costs. Carrying costs for foreign currency is the difference in interest rates (usually AA rates as these are the rates at which highly rated dealer institutions can access the markets) in the two countries. This interest rate relationship is referred to as **interest rate parity**. Thus spot values of currencies (as with everything else) are determined by supply and demand dynamics; once spot values are settled by markets, forward exchange rates reset based on interest rate differentials.

Illustration of Foreign Currency Market Relationships

Like all of the markets we have looked at, one will either become long or short by doing business in a foreign country. Let's assume that a U.S. corporation (U.S. Co.) purchases supplies and inventory in Germany. The German supplier (SupCo) provides 30-day payment terms to U.S. Co. The purchase is for 10,000,000 Euro and is payable 30 days hence. At the date of the transaction, 1Euro = 1.33 US$. As a result of talking on this obligation, U.S. Co has established a short position in the Euro. This occurs because U.S. Co. has a liability denominated in Euros. At the spot rate of $1.33 per Euro, the 10,000,000 Euro liability would cost $13,333,333 to extinguish. If the Euro devalues over the 30 day open terms period, the liability would be extinguished for less; if the Euro appreciates it would cost more. This position is illustrated in Figure 14.1.

Figure 14.1 – Purchasing Inventory Overseas

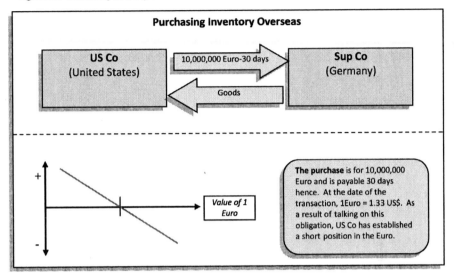

Purchasing Inventory Overseas

US Co (United States) — 10,000,000 Euro-30 days → Sup Co (Germany)

← Goods

Value of 1 Euro

The purchase is for 10,000,000 Euro and is payable 30 days hence. At the date of the transaction, 1Euro = 1.33 US$. As a result of talking on this obligation, US Co has established a short position in the Euro.

Conversely, if U.S. Co. sold goods to foreign customers, it would have a long position in the Euro.

Figure 14.2 – Selling Goods to Foreign Buyer

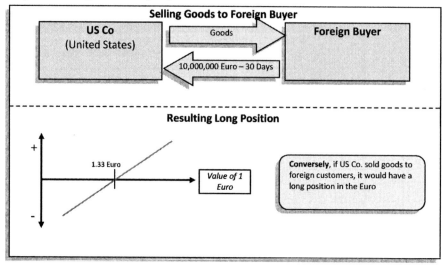

374

Hedging Foreign Currency Exposures-Spot Markets

Returning to the purchase of goods illustrated in Figure 14.1, a corporate treasurer now has a familiar menu of hedging options available. If the treasurer chooses to hedge in the spot market, Euros would be purchased creating a long position to offset the short position created by the liability. To buy the Euros, the treasurer will need to use, or more likely, borrow dollars. Once again, the use of cash/spot markets as a hedging alternative causes the acceleration of liquidity needs. To hedge the 10,000,000 Euro liability, the treasurer needs to purchase an amount of Euros, which when invested over the period beginning with the settlement up to the day the invoice is due, grows to be 10,000,000 Euros. Interest expenses (or opportunity costs) would be incurred for the dollars borrowed (used) to purchase the Euros. The entire hedging transaction is illustrated at Figure 14.3.

Figure 14.3 – Hedging a Liability Using the Spot Market

Hedging a Liability Using the Spot Market

Today — 2 Days — Settlement Day ————— Day 30

Buy Euros (Trade Transaction) → Invest for 28 Days → 10,000,000 Euro available to pay suppliers

Step 1: On transaction date...
- Buy Euros spot. Amount of Euros to be purchased is equal to $\frac{10,000,000}{1+i}$ where "i" is the effective earnings rate for 28 days

Step 2: On settlement date...
- Borrow US dollars to settle transaction

Step 3 and 4: From settlement date to day 30...
- 3) Earning interest in Euros
- 4) Pay lender of dollars

Step 5 and 6: On settlement date...
- 5) Pay supplier
- 6) Pay lender of dollars

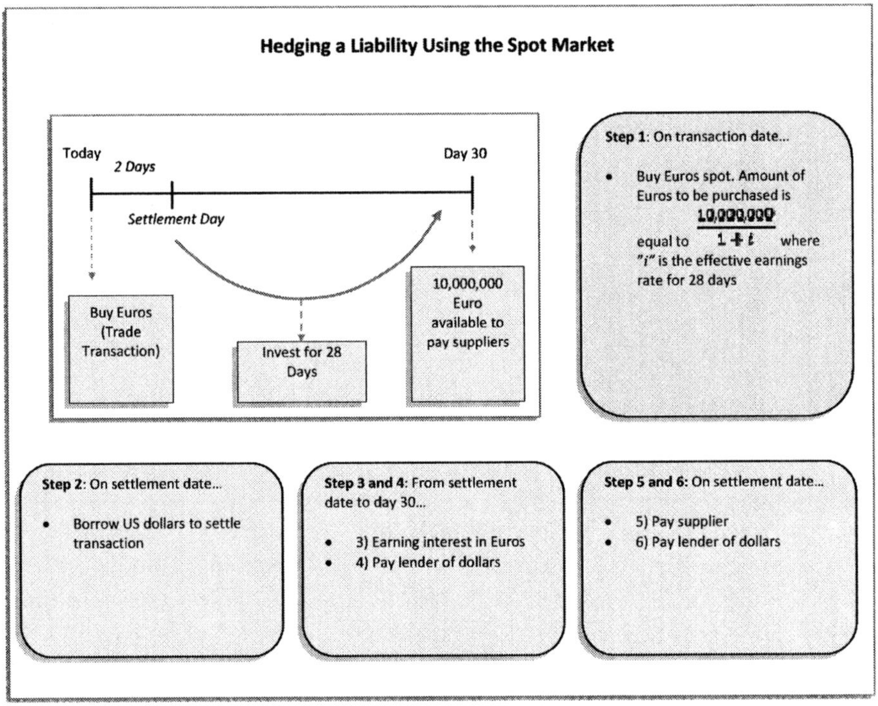

The liability will be entirely hedged using this strategy if the Euros are held through day 30. This hedging strategy does have incremental interest rate risk as the treasurer has made an investment earning interest in Euros and has a liability incurring interest in U.S. dollars.

Hedging Foreign Currency Exposures-Forward Markets

To alleviate the liquidity demands created by a spot market hedging strategy, forward markets once again present an attractive alternative. Because of the high credit quality of currency dealers, OTC forward contracts are generally more attractive to hedgers than exchange traded futures, although this has changed somewhat since the 2008 financial crisis.

Remember that forward prices are generally derived by adjusting spot/cash prices by carrying costs. The relationship is illustrated in Figure 14.4.

Figure 14.4 – Forward Pricing

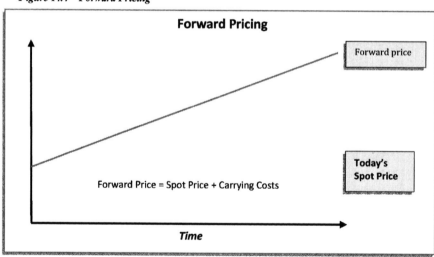

The same relationship exists with foreign currency forwards, except the item being purchased (in this case the Euro) earns interest while it is being held, and therefore reduces the carrying costs Thus, forward prices for currency forwards are derived as indicated in Figure 14.5.

Figure 14.5 – Foreign Currency Forward Pricing

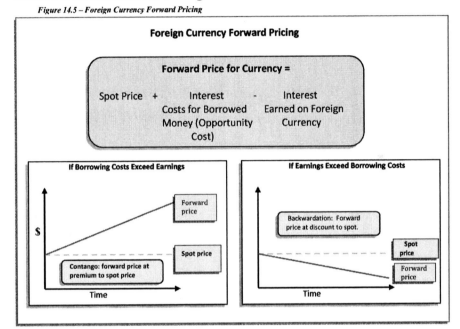

Forward prices therefore need to price to parity with the relationship illustrated at Figure 14.3, otherwise the discrepancy can be exploited through arbitrage. For example, if the forward contract were selling at too high a price, the arbitrager would buy the currency spot (a long position) and simultaneously sell forward the equivalent amount (a short position). If the net carrying costs on the spot position were less than the differential built into the forward price, an arbitrage profit would result. Because dealers would be the only parties able to arbitrage this relationship, the interest rates that need to be considered are the dealer borrowing costs, which are generally AA.

Chapter
15

Tax Consequences of Investment Decisions

For purposes of this discussion, the focus will be on the tax consequences of transactions to individual investors, as opposed to corporations such as banks or broker-dealers.

When it comes to tax planning there are two primary concepts that every investor should focus on: timing and character. Investors would prefer to pay the least amount of tax by taking advantage of lower tax rates. In addition, taking into account the time value of money, investors would like to defer paying their taxes as long as possible. Not surprisingly, the IRS has different objectives and benefits from income being taxed currently at the highest tax rates. As we will see in the following discussion, there are many rules that operate in the IRS's favor and have the result of accelerating income, deferring tax deductions, and causing income to be taxed at the highest ordinary rates (currently 35%).

From a timing perspective, taxable income from investment transactions is generally not earned until there is a realized event. This means that a stock with significant appreciation typically does not generate taxable gain until it is sold and a realized event is triggered. While this is the general rule, there are several rules that can accelerate unrealized gains, or defer realized losses.

From a character perspective there are several types of income which can receive tax-favored rates. The first type is long-term capital gain. If a capital asset, such as stock, is owned for over a year. then the sale of such property will have a reduced tax rate of 15% for taxpayers in the highest tax bracket. When a capital asset is purchased, a holding period is started; if that investment is sold less than a year after it was purchased. it will be taxed at ordinary income rates. The amount of gain on a capital transaction is usually the amount of proceeds minus the tax basis. The initial tax basis is the amount paid for the asset (including commissions in the case of stock).

Example 1 – Long-Term Capital Gain

EXAMPLE: Long-Term Capital Gain

John purchases 100 shares of ABC stock on January 18th, 2009. John sells 80 shares of ABC stock on January 17th, 2010 and the other 20 shares on February 2, 2010. The transaction on January 17th would be short term and receive ordinary income rates whereas the transaction on February 2nd would receive long-term capital gain rates because those shares were held more than a year.

The second type of favored tax rates comes from qualified dividends, which are eligible for long-term capital gains tax rates. In order to qualify, a dividend must meet several criteria. First, it must be paid by a U,S. corporation or certain specified foreign corporations. Second, the stock must be held for more than 60 days during the 121-day period that begins 60 days before the ex-dividend date.

Expenses

Expenses associated with trading or investing, such as professional fees and management fees, will be classified as either "other" expenses or as "portfolio" deductions subject to limitations. If the expenses are classified as other expenses, they will be fully deductible on Form 1040 as trade or business deductions. If the expenses are portfolio deductions, then they will only be deductible on an individual taxpayer's tax return to the extent they are above 2% of the individual's adjusted gross income and would be nondeductible for purposes of the Alternative Minimum Tax (AMT).

The classification of these expenses is dependent upon whether the taxpayer is classified as a "trader" or an "investor."[1] In order to qualify as a trader and receive the more advantageous deductions, the taxpayer must be able to prove that he is in the active business of daily trading. There is no bright line, and the determination is heavily dependent on the facts. When the U.S. Tax Court has addressed this issue, it has considered factors such as number of days the taxpayer traded, the number of trades per day, and average holding period.

Investment interest expenses are also subject to limitations. In general, this limitation only allows investors to deduct investment interest expense to the extent they have net

---

[1]The term "investor" is used frequently throughout this discussion to address all taxpayers. Where there is different treatment for "traders" it will be noted.

investment income. Net investment income is the excess of investment income over investment expenses. Investment income includes interest, dividends, and short-term capital gains. It generally does not include long-term capital gains or qualified dividends unless the investor elects to include these amounts in the net investment income.

If the election is made the income will not be eligible for lower capital gains rates so this decision requires analysis. Investment expenses are any allowed expenses, other than investment interest expense which are connected with the production of investment income. Investment interest expenses are typically related to margin borrowing or short sales. Any disallowed investment interest can be carried over to a succeeding tax year.

Interest expense incurred to purchase tax-exempt municipal bonds (discussed later) is disallowed.

Wash Sales

The wash sale rules were enacted to prevent investors from selling all of their depreciated stocks at the end of the year and then repurchasing the same positions immediately after selling the stocks. Without the wash sale rules, an investor could get the benefit of taxable losses on depreciated positions while deferring any potential gains by continuing to hold the appreciated positions. Essentially, with a sale and repurchase the investor is in the same economic position he was prior to the transaction except, absent the wash sale rule, he would have a deductible loss.

Under the wash sale rules a loss cannot be taken on the sale of a stock if the investor buys the same or "substantially identical" position 30 days prior or 30 days after the realized loss. Essentially, an investor cannot sell stock and repurchase it within a 61 day window and still recognize the loss currently. The loss associated with the wash sale is deferred until the time at which the investor is out of the replacement position entirely for an uninterrupted 30 days.

The loss deferral from a wash sale adjustment is made in proportion to the number of shares repurchased but not to exceed the original loss. The holding period from the first lot is "tacked" onto and continues on the replacement shares which originally triggered the wash sale

Example 2 – Wash Sales

EXAMPLE: Wash Sales

    5/15/2009 Investor purchases 20 shares of ABC stock for $50 per share.

    9/20/2009 Investor sells 10 shares of ABC stock for $40 per share ($100 loss).

    9/25/2009 Investor purchased 5 shares of ABC stock for $35 per share.

    6/30/2010 Investor sells remaining 15 shares of ABC stock for $60 per share.

Tax result of these transactions in 2009:

10 shares were sold for a loss of $100, however 5 of those shares were repurchased within 30 days so there is a wash sale of $50 on this transaction. That $50 of wash sale deferral is reflected in the basis of the 5 replacement shares of ABC stock purchased on 9/25/2009 and as such they have an adjusted tax basis of $45 per share. $50 of short-term loss is still recognized on the 9/25/2009 transaction as only half of the sold shares were repurchased.

Tax consequences of these transactions in 2010:

10 of the 15 shares sold in 2010 were purchased 5/15/2009 for $50 and generate a $100 long term capital gain. The other 5 shares were held from 5/15/2009 through 9/20/2009 and also held from 9/25/2009 through 6/30/2009 and thus the combined holding was greater than 365 days so the investor will receive long-term capital gain from this sale as well. The tax basis on the second lot is $45 and so the sale of the second lot of ABC stock generates $75 lon-term capital gain. The combined sale of these two lots will net a $175 long-term capital gain.

Straddles

Whenever a position is entered into which substantially diminishes the risk of another position, a straddle is created. This can occur by entering a short and a long position on the same security, a long security and a purchased put option, a short position and a purchased call option, as well as many other similar transactions. The straddle rules prevent investors from recognizing losses on one leg of the straddle position while deferring the gains from the appreciated leg of the straddle.

The straddle rules provide that a loss from one position can only be taken to the extent that it is in excess of the unrealized gain on the offsetting position. In addition to deferring the loss, if a long position were not held greater than a year at the time the offsetting position is entered into, then the holding period is terminated and does not start until the straddle is closed.

Example 3 - Straddles

EXAMPLE: Straddles

> *3/15/2009 Investor purchases 100 shares of ABC stock for $100.*
>
> *9/25/2009 Investor enters into a put option on ABC stock for $20.*
>
> *11/15/2009 Investor sells the put option for $10.*
>
> *At 12/31/2009 the investor's shares of ABC stock are worth $107.*
>
> *4/20/2010 the investor sells their shares of ABC stock for $120.*

Tax consequences in 2009:

The investor entered into an offsetting position when they purchased the put option on 9/25/2009 and thereby created a straddle. The loss from the sale of the put option is only allowable if it is in excess of any unrealized gain in the offsetting position. In this case ABC stock had only appreciated $7, so $3 of the loss on the sale of the put option is allowable in 2009 as short-term capital loss.

Tax consequences in 2010:

In 2010 the stock is sold creating a $20 capital gain, however because the appreciated leg of the straddle is sold it releases the $7 of deferred loss from the sale of the put option for a net of $13 capital gain. Ordinarily the stock sale would be treated as long-term capital gain; however the holding period was reset to 11/15/2009 (when the straddle was closed) so the holding period is less than one year and it is classified as short-term capital gain.

Constructive Sales

A classic constructive sale is when an investor owns an appreciated long position and enters a short position on the same stock (short against the box). The constructive sale rule treats this as an actual sale and forces the taxpayer to realize a capital gain. This gain is capitalized into the basis of the long security so when it is sold the gain will not be taxed again. The constructive sale rule only applies to gains, and there is no corresponding rule for constructive sales of loss positions.

There is an important exception to the constructive sale rules. If the short position (in a short against the box transaction) is closed within 30 days after the end of the year and the long position is held open, unhedged, for 60 days after the sale then the constructive sale rule would not be triggered.

Example 4 – Constructive Sales

EXAMPLE: Constructive Sales

An investor purchases 100 shares of ABC stock for $100 on 3/30/2008.

The investor sells short 100 shares of ABC stock for $120 on 3/15/2009.

At 12/31/2009 ABC stock is worth $130.

At the end of 2009 there is exactly the same number of long shares as there are short shares of ABC stock and the long shares of ABC have appreciated $30 while the short shares have only depreciated $10. Overall there is a $20 per share gain to be recognized in 2009. While the shares of ABC stock were purchased in 2008, the short position was entered into before the shares had reached the long term holding period and therefore the $20 per share gain is short-term capital gain. That $20 per share gain is capitalized into the individual share basis of the long positions and when the positions are sold in the future the gain will be decreased by $20 per share.

Short Sales

In addition to potentially creating straddles and constructive sales, short selling can cause other tax complexities. Short positions generally cannot qualify for long-term capital gain treatment. Similarly, the IRS does not allow for losses on short positions until they are closed, which means that for tax purposes short positions are not considered closed until the securities which were borrowed are repurchased and delivered. In other words, the transaction must settle before it is a realized event for tax purposes. In general, it takes a transaction three days to settle, which typically means that losses on short sales during the last three trading days of the tax year are deferred to the following year. Note that gains are not deferred because even though they have not been closed yet, technically the long and the short positions are both open and the gain is recognized under the constructive sale rules.

Dividend expenses on short positions are generally capitalized if the short position is held less than 45 days and not currently deductible.

Despite the general rule, if a long position were held longer than one year at the time at which the investor enters into a short position of the same stock, any loss on the short position would be reclassified to long-term. Similarly, if the taxpayer closes a short position at a gain with stock held more than a year, the gain may potentially be treated as long-term, if other requirements are satisfied.

Mark-to-Market Election for Traders

If a taxpayer qualifies as a "trader," he may make an election under section 475(f) to treat all unrealized gains and losses as taxable on a mark-to-market basis. This effectively eliminates any timing or character differences on stock trading as all securities are marked-to-market annually as ordinary income. Taxpayers making this election no longer

386

have to be concerned with the administrative burden of tracking wash sales, straddles, and constructive sales. Another advantage is that unrealized losses can be deducted currently.

The main disadvantage is that there is no longer any ability to defer unrealized gains, which are marked-to-market at the end of the year and taxed at ordinary income rates. Realized gains and losses are also treated as ordinary.

Taxation of Interest and Interest Equivalents on Debt Instruments

This section will focus on interest income (and equivalents) from the standpoint of the holder of a debt instrument, typically a bond. Interest is generally defined as payment for the use of money, although taxation to the holder may occur even without actual payment. This is sometimes referred to as "phantom income." Original Issue Discount ("OID"), discussed below, is a prime example of phantom income.

A threshold question in the tax law is whether an instrument is truly debt, as opposed to equity. This has significant tax implications to the holder as well as the issuer of the debt. If classified as equity, purported interest payments could instead be treated as dividends, and dividend treatment as opposed to interest has very different results. For example, dividends may qualify for a preferential rate if they meet certain requirements (described earlier), but are not deductible by the corporation that pays them. Conversely, taxable interest income is subject to ordinary income rates, but is deductible by the issuer.

Factors that are used in classifying debt versus equity are as follows: (1) whether there is a written unconditional promise to pay on demand or on a specified date a specific amount of money and to pay a fixed rate of interest; (2) whether there is subordination to or preference over any debt of the corporation; (3) the ratio of debt to equity of the corporation; (4)

387

whether there is convertibility into the stock of the corporation; and (5) the relationship between holdings of stock in the corporation and holdings of the debt in question.

This determination can get very complex given the proliferation of hybrid instruments that have characteristics of both debt and equity.

Original Issue Discount (OID)

Since bonds are issued at a discount largely due to changes in prevailing interest rates, the tax law generally treats that discount as equivalent to interest. OID arises upon issuance, as opposed to market discount, which arises in secondary market transactions.

OID is defined as the "stated redemption price at maturity (SRPM)" minus the issue price. SRPM equals the sum of all payments under the debt instrument other than interest, i.e. the principal amount.

OID is required to be accrued and included in the holder's income on a ratable basis based on a daily computation, even if the holder is otherwise a cash basis taxpayer. The inclusion of OID represents "phantom" income since it is taxed regardless of the fact that no cash is received. However, the holder is allowed to increase his tax basis in the debt instrument so that there is no double tax upon sale.

Market Discount

Market Discount is similar to OID conceptually but with some distinctions. First, market discount arises not upon original issuance but rather in a secondary market transaction. Note that a debt instrument may have both OID and market discount. Second, market discount is not required to be recognized currently, but rather is recognized upon sale of the debt instrument. The market discount rules do not create phantom income but result in a reclassification of capital gain to ordinary income to the extent of market discount that has accrued but has not yet been subject to tax.

Example 5 – Market Discount

Example: Market Discount

On July 1, 2004, Individual A acquires in the open market a bond of Corporation X having a stated redemption price of $10,000 and a maturity date of December 31, 2008. Assume that A pays $9,000 for the bond and the bond is a capital asset in the hands of A. On December 31, 2005, when the bond has accrued market discount of $333, A sells the bond to an unrelated third party for $9,500. Of A's total gain of $500, $333 is taxed as ordinary income. The remaining gain is capital in nature.

Interest expenses related to market discount instruments purchased with borrowed funds are subject to limits on deductibility. These rules are designed to prevent timing distortions whereby the holder can enjoy a deduction currently and defer the related income.

Premiums

Conversely, if a debt instrument pays a rate of interest that exceeds prevailing market rates, the instrument will be issued, or purchased in the secondary market, at a premium. Holders may elect to amortize the premium, which is treated as an offset to, and thus reduces, interest income from the instrument.

Municipal Bonds

Interest received on a debt instrument issued by a state or local government is generally tax-exempt. However, interest payments on so-called "private activity" municipal bonds may be taxable if the proceeds are used to fund non-governmental activities. Furthermore, interest payments from private activity bonds may be subject to the Alternative Minimum Tax even if exempt for regular tax purposes.

Tax-exempt municipal bonds generally pay lower interest rates than taxable bonds issued by private companies but are attractive considering the after-tax returns. For example, for a taxpayer in the highest (35%) tax bracket, a municipal bond yielding 4% after tax is more attractive than a taxable bond yielding 6% (3.9% after tax).

Taxation of Derivative Instruments

Options

Option contracts are subject to specific rules governing timing and character of income to both writers (sellers) and holders (buyers) of the contracts. Certain options are subject to section 1256 treatment, discussed later.

When the holder of a call option exercises his right to the option and purchases the underlying stock, the seller generally recognizes a capital gain if the total amount received is greater than his basis in the stock or a loss if the amount received is less than his basis. The premium received by the writer is not taxable up front but rather increases the amount realized on the sale of the stock to the holder.

When a call option is sold, the holder recognizes a capital gain or loss. Whether it is short-term or long-term in nature depends upon the holding period of the option. Gain is recognized when the sales price is greater than the holder's basis in the option. Loss is recognized when the holder's basis in the option is greater than the sales price.

If a call option expires, the option is deemed to have been sold on the date of expiration. The holder of a call option will recognize a capital loss equal to the basis in the option. The holding period of the option determines whether it is a long-term or short-term loss. As mentioned above, the writer does not incur taxable income on receipt of the premium. Instead, the premium is deferred until the option expires. Upon expiration, the writer of the option will realize short-term capital gain equal to the premium. The income is included in the year the option expires.

When a put option is exercised, the option holder sells the underlying stock to the option writer and has capital gain or loss. The holder reduces the amount realized on the sale by the option premium paid. A gain occurs if the amount realized, after taking into account the premium, is greater than the holder's basis. A loss occurs if the amount realized is less than the holder's basis. The writer of a put option realizes no gain or loss when he purchases the stock underlying his short put option position. His basis in the stock is reduced by the amount of the option premium he received when he originally sold the put option.

When a put option is sold, the holder recognizes a capital gain or loss, calculated by the difference between the premium paid and the amount realized from the sale of the put. Whether it is short-term or long-term in nature depends upon the holding period of the option. Gain is recognized when the sales price is greater than the holder's basis in the option. Loss is recognized when the holder's basis in the option is greater than the sales price. Sale of a put option by the holder does not generally impact the writer.

When a put option expires without being exercised or sold, the option is deemed to have been sold on the date of expiration. The holder of the option will recognize a capital loss equal to the basis in the option. The holding period of the option determines whether it is a long-term or short-term loss. As mentioned above the writer does not incur taxable income on receipt of the premium. Instead, the premium is deferred until the option expires. Upon expiration, the writer of the option will recognize short-term capital gain income equal to the premium. The income is included in the year the option expires.

The following table summarizes the tax consequences of options transactions to both the holder and writer[2]

---

[2]Derived from Internal Revenue Service Publication 550

Figure 15.1 – Tax Consequences of Put Options

PUTS		
When a put:	**If you are the holder:**	**If you are the writer:**
Is exercised	Reduce your amount realized from sale of the underlying stock by the cost of the put.	Reduce your basis in the stock you buy by the amount you received for the put.
Expires	Report the cost of the put as a capital loss on the date it expires.	Report the amount you received for the put as a short-term capital gain.
Is sold by the holder	Report the difference between the cost of the put and the amount you receive for it as a capital gain or loss.	This does not affect you. (But if you buy back the put, report the difference between the amount you pay and the amount you received for the put as a short-term capital gain or loss).

Figure 15.2 – Tax Consequences of Call Options

CALLS		
When a call:	**If you are the holder:**	**If you are the writer:**
Is exercised	Add the cost of the call to your basis in the stock purchased.	Increase your amount realized on sale of the stock by the amount you received for the call.
Expires	Report the cost of the call as a capital loss on the date it expires.	Report the amount you received for the call as a short-term capital gain.
Is sold by the holder	Report the difference between the cost of the call and the amount you receive for it as a capital gain or loss.	This does not affect you. (But if you buy back the call, report the difference between the amount you pay and the amount you received for the call as a short-term capital gain or loss).

Section 1256 Contracts

Section 1256 was enacted in 1981 to govern the taxation of regulated futures contracts ("RFCs"). RFCs are unique as they are subject to a daily mark-to-market system. As such, RFCs are subject to tax based on the unrealized gain/loss at year-end based on the constructive receipt doctrine since cash is available under margin rules set by the exchanges. As a trade-off for the mark-to-market tax treatment, sec. 1256 provides for 60% long-term capital gains treatment, and 40% short-term capital gains treatment, regardless of holding period. Section 1256 has been subsequently expanded to now also include certain foreign currency contracts, non-equity options, dealer equity options, and dealer securities futures contracts.

A futures contract must meet two requirements to qualify for RFC treatment under section 1256:

First, the contract must require that amounts to be deposited or allowed to be withdrawn follow a system of marking to market;

Second, the contract must be traded on or made subject to the rules of a qualified board or exchange ("QBOE").

A QBOE is:

a national securities exchange that is registered with the SEC;

a domestic board of trade designated as a contract market by the CFTC;

Any other exchange, board of trade, or other market which the Secretary determines has rules adequate to carry out the purposes of section 1256.

For section 1256 purposes, a "foreign currency contract" is a contract that requires delivery of, or the settlement of which depends on the value of, a foreign currency. The foreign currency must be a currency in which positions are also traded through RFCs. Generally, forward contracts on "major" currencies are marked to market under sec. 1256, but are taxed at ordinary rates. RFCs on major currencies are eligible for "pure" section 1256 treatment, i.e., marked to market and taxed as 60% long-term capital gain and 40% short-term capital gain. This disparity between currency forward and futures contracts demonstrates how virtually identical transactions from an economic perspective can be taxed in very different ways, depending on the form of the transaction.

A "non-equity option" is any listed option that is not an "equity option." An equity option is any option to buy or sell stock or an option that references a narrow-based index. An example of a non-equity option would be a listed option on the S&P 500 index.

Open section 1256 contracts are treated as if closed and unrecognized gains and losses are taken into account for tax purposes at the end of the tax year. This essentially causes each section 1256 contract held at the close of a tax year to be treated as if it had been sold for its fair market value on the last business day of that taxable year. Gain or loss recognized on the subsequent disposition of a section 1256 contract should take into consideration the amount previously recognized.

Under the 60/40 Rule, section 1256 contracts are taxed as 60% long-term and 40% short-term capital gain or loss, irrespective of the length of time the taxpayer held such positions. Taxpayers can use section 1256 losses incurred in one year to reduce income generated on such contracts in a prior tax year, up to three years.

The transfer of rights in a section 1256 contract is treated as a termination and gain or loss is taken into account. The 60/40 rule also applies to the termination of a section 1256 contract.

Equity Forward Contracts

A standard equity forward contract is generally viewed as having no tax effect until the contract is ultimately settled. If the forward contract is physically settled, the seller recognizes gain or loss at the time it delivers the stock in an amount determined by reference to its adjusted basis in the stock and the amount received in the sale. Likewise, the buyer takes a basis in the stock and realizes gain or loss upon its ultimate disposition of the shares. If instead, the forward contract is cash-settled (i.e., the "losing" party makes a cash payment), the recipient recognizes gain and the payor recognizes a commensurate loss at the time the payment is made.

Taxpayers selling capital assets under forward contracts have capital gain or loss on those sales. Taxpayers that acquire stock under a forward contract cannot include the period during which they held the forward contract in the holding period for the stock. Taxpayers holding forward contracts as capital assets recognize capital gain or loss upon the sale or assignment of the forward contract position.

Swaps

In the tax law, many swaps, e.g. total return swaps, are treated as so-called "notional principal contracts" ("NPCs"), which have a very specific and often complex tax regime. Under the tax regulations, an NPC is a financial instrument that provides for payment of amounts, with more than one payment by at least one party. It must be referenced to a specified index and a notional principal amount. Assuming a swap is treated as a NPC, the payments are divided into three categories: periodic, non-periodic, and termination payments.

Periodic payments are payments made in intervals of one year or less during the entire term of the swap contract. For the recipient, these are treated as ordinary income for both accrued and paid amounts. For the payor, these are treated as deductions.

Non-periodic payments are all other payments other than termination payments, which are defined below. Accrued and paid amounts are generally treated as ordinary income, or expense, over the life of the contract.

Termination payments are payments made prior to the maturity date of a NPC to "unwind" the swap position. Termination payments are included in taxable income only in the year payment is made and treated as capital in nature.

Mark-to-market treatment is available for certain NPCs under proposed regulations issued in 2004. The regulations have yet to be finalized, but in practice many NPCs are marked to market for tax purposes. Mark-to-market treatment eliminates much of the complexity associated with the general NPC rules described above.

Credit default swaps (CDS) are the source of some uncertainty in the tax law. Depending on how they are structured, CDS transactions may be taxable under the NPC rules, or potentially as options. The IRS issued proposed regulations in 2011 that would subject CDS transactions as NPCs.

Mutual Funds and Exchange-Traded Funds (ETFs)

Holders of mutual fund shares will receive a Form 1099 annually which will report their share of ordinary income and long-term capital gain distributions. Distributions are taxable even if reinvested in the fund. Capital losses generated within the fund do not flow through to investors on a current basis; instead they are carried forward by the fund and can be used to offset capital gains generated in future years.

ETFs generally are more tax efficient than mutual funds for their investors. One key distinction is that, unlike mutual funds, ETFs typically do not have to sell share holdings in order to fund redemptions. When mutual funds sell holdings to fund redemptions, they generate capital gains which are taxable to the holders. A typical ETF, on the other hand, is able to handle redemptions without selling off its holdings.

Alternative Investment Funds

Alternative investment funds include hedge funds, private equity funds, venture capital funds, as well as funds of funds. These vehicles can raise some unique tax considerations, depending on their strategy and structure.

Fund offerings are typically structured to accommodate three classes of investors: high net worth U.S. individuals, tax-exempt entities such as pensions and endowments, and foreign investors. This often involves creating more than one fund vehicle.

Alternative investment funds geared towards high net worth U.S. individuals are typically formed as partnerships. Funds formed as partnerships, i.e. flow-through entities, are generally not subject to a tax at the entity level, unlike corporations. Investors are subject to tax on their share of the fund's taxable income, which is reported on Schedule K-1. The pass-through nature of partnerships allows the tax benefits of the fund's investments to flow directly through to the partners of the fund. This includes flow-through of long-term capital gains, qualified dividends, foreign tax credits, and other tax attributes which are beneficial to a taxable investor.

Deductions also retain their character in the hands of the individual investors. So to the extent a fund generates items such as investment interest expense or portfolio deductions, they will be subject to potential limitations when reflected on an investor's personal tax return (Form 1040).

Even if not subject to those limitations, losses generated by a domestic fund are only deductible by the investor if the investor has tax basis in the fund. Tax basis is generally measured by the investor's tax capital account (the capital contributed to the fund, plus income allocated to the investor, less losses allocated to the investor, less any distributions made to the investor) plus any fund debt for which the investor is personally liable.

The general partner of a domestic fund structured as a partnership receives its incentive compensation in the form of an allocation (carried interest), which allows them to enjoy the same tax benefits as limited partners, to the extent the fund generates items such as long-term capital gains and qualified dividends. The current tax treatment of carried interests has been the subject of much criticism, and legislation intended to change the taxation has been proposed several times.

The effect of this change would be to treat some or all of the carried interest as ordinary income subject to the highest rate of tax, regardless of the tax character of the underlying income of the fund. This treatment would result in the carried interest being subject to tax in much the same way as the asset-based management fee.

To accommodate tax-exempt and foreign investors, a fund sponsor will often launch an offshore fund formed as a corporation in a low-tax jurisdiction such as the Cayman Islands. The offshore fund will trade "side-by-side" with the domestic fund. Investing in the offshore fund enables foreign investors to avoid filing tax returns with the Internal Revenue Service, and enables tax-exempt investors to avoid paying Unrelated Business Income Tax ("UBIT").

UBIT is a tax imposed on tax-exempt investors if they engage in certain investment activity, including margin borrowing. If they invested in a fund formed as a domestic partnership, and that fund bought and sold stocks on margin, the UBIT character would flow through to the tax-exempt investor. The tax-exempt entity would pay tax at the highest corporate tax rate (currently 35%). If the investment by the tax-exempt entity is in an offshore fund formed as a corporation, unless the fund has acquired the interest in the corporation with debt (which is rare), the corporation distributes such net income to the tax-exempt entity in the form of dividends. This dividend income does not cause any UBIT.

An offshore fund is not subject to United States taxation on its trading gains if its activities are limited to trading in stocks and securities. It may however, be subject to 30% withholding on dividends from U.S. companies. Funds that engage in other activities that rise to the level of a U.S. "trade or business" will be subject to tax on those activities. For example funds that engage in direct lending to U.S. borrowers, or that acquire U.S. real estate.

In the case of investments in domestic funds by foreign persons, the activity of the fund may have United States tax reporting consequences to the foreign investor. Due to the pass-through nature of a domestic fund, the foreign investor could have income allocated to them that, depending on tax treaty application, could be subject to United States tax withholding, or at a minimum reporting to the Internal Revenue Service.

A master-feeder structure is often utilized to accommodate all three classes of investors (U.S. taxable, tax-exempt, and foreign) while having one trading vehicle (the master fund). The domestic and offshore funds will then "feed" into the master fund. The feeders "feed" the investor capital to the master fund which, in turn, holds the investment portfolio and does all the trading.

Typically the master fund is formed as an offshore corporation which is treated as a partnership for U.S. tax purposes (by making a "check the box" election). This enables the tax character to flow through to the U.S. taxable investors, via the domestic feeder. Thus, the tax benefits of the income (e.g. long-term capital gain) are preserved in the hands of the U.S. taxable investors. However, UBIT and U.S. tax consequences for tax-exempt and foreign investors are "blocked" by the offshore feeder. Thus the master-feeder structure retains all the benefits of the basic side-by-side structure without the additional administrative complexities of running two separate portfolios.

Occasionally, U.S. taxable investors will invest in an offshore fund, but this has some potential negative consequences. Those negative consequences derive from the offshore fund's treatment as a "Passive Foreign Investment Company" (PFIC). A PFIC is a foreign corporation which has 75% of its gross income consisting of income from passive sources (e.g., dividends, interest, and capital gains) or has assets which generate passive income that are least 50% of its total assets.

If a U.S. taxable investor invests in a PFIC, unless a special election is made, then the later sale of the PFIC shares will carry an extra tax burden. This is in the form of a tax at the highest rate plus an interest charge. The elections to avoid this result are only available if the PFIC is publicly traded or if the PFIC provides adequate tax reporting to the investor on an annual basis. U.S. investors also face additional reporting requirements whenever they own an interest in an offshore fund.

Investment in offshore funds by U.S. taxable investors will also create additional U.S. tax reporting responsibilities for the offshore fund. As a result of legislation enacted in 2010, offshore funds with U.S. investors will have to report information to the U.S. Treasury Department regarding the identity of such investors. Failure to comply potentially carries severe consequences, including a withholding tax on gross proceeds from stock sales. These rules, known as the Foreign Account Tax Compliance Act of 2010 (FATCA), go into effect in 2013.

Figure 15.3 – Side by Side Structure of Alternative Hedge Funds

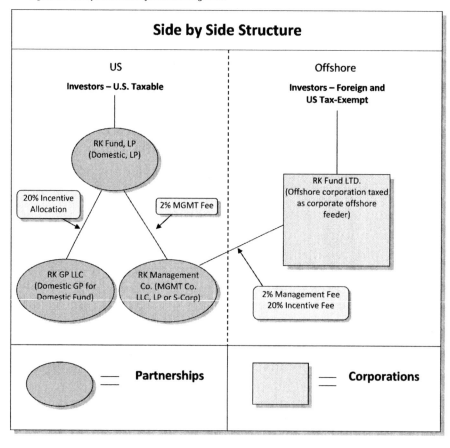

Figure 4 – Master-Feeder Structure of Alternative Hedge Funds

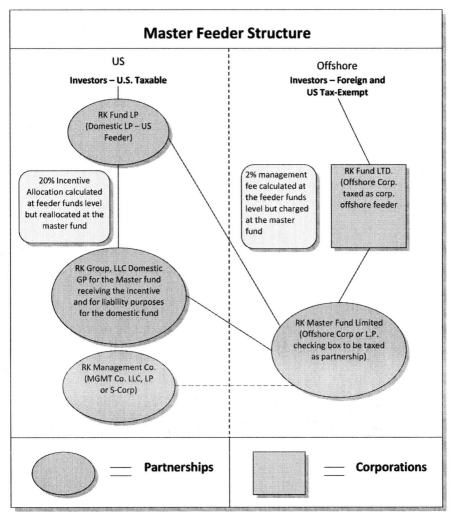

Chapter
16

Tax Issues Related to Wealth Transfers

In a letter to Jean-Baptiste Leroy dated November 13, 1789, Benjamin Franklin wrote "Our new Constitution is now established and has an appearance that promises permanency, but in this world nothing can be said to be certain, except death and taxes." This chapter focuses on how to plan for the combination of the two certainties of life—death and taxes.

Overview of Estate Planning Process

Estate planning is the process one undertakes in order to minimize the amount of taxes payable at one's death in addition to assuring that one's assets are passed smoothly and efficiently to one's intended heirs. Estate planning also encompasses making sure that a decedent's non tax desires are properly addressed at his/her demise.

At the outset of the estate planning process, the planner must help the client understand and develop his/her objectives. Each estate plan is unique and the planner must carefully listen to the client in order to truly understand the client's objectives. Oftentimes, the planner acts as a psychologist when determining the client's objectives. Some key questions to ask when assisting the client develop his objectives in no particular order are as follows:

- Do you want to minimize estate taxes and maximize the amount of assets passing to your heirs;

- Do you want to benefit any specific charities;

- Do you want your heirs to receive assets outright or in trust;

- Do you have specific tangible property, such as family heirlooms, artwork, etc., that you would like to pass to a specific person;

- Do you have any pets that you want to provide for;

- Are you (and your spouse, if applicable) United States citizens;

- Do any of your intended heirs have special needs;

- Do any of your intended heirs have alcohol or drug problems;

- Do you or one of your intended heirs have same sex partners;

- If a closely held business is part of the estate, who should inherit the business and have you developed a succession plan for the business; and

- Have you considered gifting assets during your lifetime.

In addition to determining a client's objectives, the initial phase of estate planning includes data gathering. There are many variations of checklists that can be used to gather data. The main components of the checklists request the following information:

- Name, address, telephone number, social security number, and birth date of client, partner, children, and grandchildren;

- Name, address and birth date of spouses of children and grandchildren;

- Name, address, and birth date of parents, if alive;

- Name, address and birth date of other intended beneficiaries, i.e., siblings, cousins, nephews, nieces, friends;
- Name, address and telephone number of guardian and successor guardian for minor children;
- Name, address and telephone number of Executor and successor Executor;
- Name and address of accountant, attorney, banker, investment advisor insurance agents and physicians, other advisors;
- Information regarding prior marriages, if any;
- Detailed Net Worth Statement including the following:
  - Type of ownership, i.e., joint with rights of survivorship, tenants in common, solely owned, etc.;
  - Beneficiaries of retirement assets and life insurance policies;
  - Location of real estate;
  - Insured and owner of life insurance policies;
  - Type of life insurance policy, i.e., term, whole life, universal, variable universal, etc., carrier, death benefit and annual premiums; and
  - Account numbers for all bank and securities accounts.
- Expected inheritances, if any;
- Burial wishes and list of cemetery plots;
- Current employment information;
- Current income and expenses reported by each partner;
- Expected significant cash outlays;
- Location and number of safe deposit boxes;
- Information regarding health and casualty insurance

coverage including carrier, policy number and coverage amount; and

- Information regarding disability and long term care coverage including carrier, policy number and coverage amount.

Finally, as part of the initial phase of the estate planning process, the planner should review the following existing documents:

- Current Last Will and Testaments;
- Current Powers of Attorney;
- Current Living Wills/Health Care Proxies;
- Prior gift tax returns;
- Prior three years' income tax returns;
- Pre nuptial or post nuptial agreements;
- Partnership operating agreements;
- Buy sell agreements;
- In force life insurance policy(ies) illustrations;
- Disability insurance policy(ies); and
- Casualty insurance policy(ies).

Once all the above data is gathered and documents are reviewed, the development of the estate plan can begin.

Overview of Transfer Tax System

The federal transfer tax system consists of the estate tax, the gift tax, and the generation skipping transfer tax.

Estate Tax

Estate tax is an excise tax imposed upon on the transfer of property when a person dies and it applies to estates of United States citizens, United States residents and nonresident aliens. The amount of tax is based on the fair market value of one's property owned (or deemed owned) at death plus the cumulative amount of lifetime gifts (a credit, however, is available for cumulative gift taxes paid). The estate tax rates begin at 18% and increase to 35% for 2011 and 2012. Beginning in 2013, the highest marginal estate tax rate could be as high as 55%. There are a number of deductions available to reduce the amount of one's taxable estate:

- An unlimited deduction generally exists for outright transfers (and certain transfers in trust) to a surviving spouse who is a United States citizen;

- An unlimited deduction generally exists for gifts to charitable organizations;

- Debts, estate administration expenses and funeral expenses are generally deductible; and

- A deduction generally exists for the amount of any estate, inheritance, legacy, or succession taxes paid to any State. This deduction expires on December 31, 2012.

Every United States citizen and domiciliary is generally entitled to credit in the amount of the "applicable credit" to offset estate taxes. In the marketplace, most people refer to this concept by stating the amount of assets that will pass to one's heirs free of estate taxes. During 2011 and 2012, the amount that each person can pass free of federal estate taxes is $5,000,000 (this amount is indexed for inflation beginning in 2012). In addition, during 2011 and 2012, if one spouse does not fully utilize his applicable credit at death, his/her spouse can use the unused portion subject to certain limitations. This concept is known as portability.

Some states such as New York, Connecticut, and New Jersey impose their own estate and/or inheritance tax.

Gift Tax

Gift tax is imposed upon a donor's act of making a gratuitous transfer of property during life for less than full and adequate consideration. The amount of the gift tax is based on the fair market value of the property transferred and the donor is primarily and personally liable for the gift tax due. The gift tax rates begin at 18% and increase to 35% for 2011 and 2012. Beginning in 2013, the highest marginal gift tax rate could be as high as 55%.

The gift tax is imposed on a cumulative basis (i.e., prior taxable gifts are added to current gifts to determine the applicable gift tax rate).

A taxpayer is allowed certain deductions and exclusions when computing the gift tax:

- There is generally an unlimited deduction for gifts between spouses who are United States citizens;

- There is generally an unlimited deduction for gifts to charitable organizations;

- Amounts paid directly to a medical provider on behalf of another individual and generally excluded from the computation of gift taxes;

- Amounts paid directly to an educational organization for tuition expenses of full-time or part-time students are generally excluded from the computation of gift taxes;

- Annual gifts up to $13,000, indexed annually for inflation, per donee are generally exempt from gift tax. In order to qualify for this exemption, these gifts must be gifts of "present interests" meaning the donee must have the right to the use or enjoyment of the property presently as opposed to in the future. For instance, a gift of property to a trust in which the beneficiary does not have the right to withdraw the property immediately does not qualify for this exclusion.

Every United States citizen and domiciliary generally has an applicable credit of $1,730,800 (equivalent to $5,000,000 of taxable assets) available to offset gift taxes. The $5,000,000 is indexed for inflation in 2012 and is currently reduced to $1,000,000 beginning in 2013. This is similar to the applicable credit that is available to reduce one's estate taxes. If an individual uses their applicable credit for gift tax purposes, it would reduce the amount the individual would have available for estate tax purposes.

Some states such as Connecticut impose their own gift tax.

Generation Skipping Transfer Tax

The generation skipping transfer tax (GSTT) is a tax imposed on the transfer of assets to a person two or more generations below that of the transferor. For instance, a transfer of assets from a grandfather to a grandchild would be subject to GSTT.

The GSTT rate is equal to the highest estate tax rate in effect at the time of the transfer. Consequently, for 2011 and 2012, the GSTT rate is 35%, while it could be as high as 55% in 2013. Each transferor has a GSTT exemption available during their lifetime or at death. The GSTT exemption in 2011 and 2012 is $5,000,000. For 2013, the GSTT exemption reverts back to $1,000,000 as adjusted for inflation. It is important for the reader to understand that the GSTT exemption is different than and is not unified with the estate and gift tax exemptions. As an illustration, assume grandfather gifts $5,000,000 to son in year one and then gifts $5,000,000 to grandson in year two. The gift to son in year one would be offset by grandfather's gift tax exemption so there would be no gift tax due. Since the son is only one generation below the grandfather, the gift to the son is not subject to GSTT. The gift to grandson in year two would be subject to both gift tax and GSTT. Since grandfather has already fully utilized his gift tax exemption, he would pay gift tax on the $5,000,000 gift to grandson. However, he can utilize his GSTT exemption so no GSTT would be due on the gift to grandchild.

Below is a chart that summarizes the highest marginal tax rate and the applicable exclusion/exemption for the estate, gift and generation skipping transfer tax for 2011-2013 based on existing law.

Figure 16.1—Marginal Tax Rate

	Gift Tax Annual Exclusion	Gift, Estate, GST Applicable Exclusion/ Exemption	Gift, Estate, GST Top Marginal Tax Rate
2011	$13,000	$5,000,000	35%
2012	$13,000[a]	$5,000,000[a]	35%
2013	$13,000[a]	$1,000,000/ $1,400,000[b] for GST	55%

[a]Could be higher based on inflation adjustment.
[b]Approximate based on projected inflation adjustment.

At a minimum, one's estate plan should consist of having the following documents prepared:

- Last Will and Testament—a written document which leaves the estate of the person who signed the will to named persons or entities (beneficiaries, legatees, devisees) including portions or percentages of the estate, specific gifts, creation of trusts for management and future distribution of all or a portion of the estate (a testamentary trust).[1]

- Power of attorney—a written document signed by a person giving another person the power to act in conducting the signer's business, including signing papers, checks, title documents, contracts, handling bank ac-

---

[1]Law.com

counts and other activities in the name of the person granting the power.[2]

- Living Will/Health Care Proxy—a document authorized by statutes in all states in which a person

- appoints someone as his/her proxy or representative to make decisions on maintaining extraordinary life support if the person becomes to ill.[3]

In order to take advantage of the estate tax applicable credit and the unlimited marital deduction, many individuals include the following two trusts in their Last Will and Testaments.

Credit Shelter/Unified Credit/Bypass Trust

During this discussion, we will refer to this trust as the Credit Shelter trust although it is commonly referred to as a unified credit trust as well as a bypass trust.

This trust is designed so that a decedent utilizes his "applicable credit" (see above discussion in the *Estate Taxes* section). The credit shelter trust could have various provisions, but in general, the Trust's income is distributed to the surviving spouse at least annually and the remaining principal at the surviving spouse's death is distributed to the decedent's heirs (most likely children) either outright or in further trust. The Trust could also have provisions similar to the examples provided below in the QTIP trust discussion. The amount that would pass to the credit shelter trust is generally the amount that can pass free of estate tax; for example, $5,000,000 in 2011. However, careful planning and drafting must be done when determining the amount that should pass to the credit shelter amount. For instance, assume a decedent's entire estate was $5,000,000 and the taxpayer's spouse had no assets in his/her name. If the

---

[2]Law.com

[3]Law.com

decedent died in 2011 and the decedent's Will directed that the credit shelter trust be funded with the remaining amount that could be passed free of estate tax, the decedent's spouse would receive no assets outright and would have as his/her only source of income the amounts that could be distributed from the credit shelter trust.

There are two points that should be highlighted with regard to the credit shelter trust:

1) The credit shelter trust could have the same provisions as the QTIP trust. If the provisions are the same, the main difference between the two trusts would be that the assets in the credit shelter trust would not be included in the surviving spouse's estate while the assets in the QTIP trust would.

2) A trust does not have to be employed to utilize a decedent's applicable exclusion. Bequeathing assets to anyone other than one's spouse or a charity would utilize a decedent's applicable exclusion for estate tax purposes.

The following is a general example of a credit shelter trust:

Figure 16.2 – Credit Shelter Trust

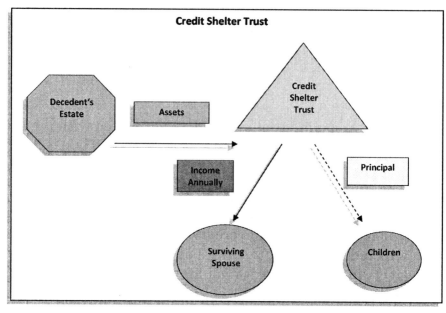

Many states, such as New York and New Jersey, have their own "applicable credit" amount. Therefore, if one tries to maximize the amount that can pass free from federal estate tax, they may create a state estate tax.

Qualified Terminable Interest Property/Marital Deduction Trust

During this discussion, we will refer to this trust as the QTIP trust. As stated above in the **Estate Tax** section, an estate is generally allowed an unlimited deduction for outright transfers (and certain transfers in trust) to a surviving spouse who is a United States citizen. This is generally referred to as an estate tax marital deduction.

If there is an outright transfer to the surviving spouse, those transferred assets will be subject to estate tax upon the death of the surviving spouse, to the extent not consumed during the surviving spouse's lifetime. However, when a bequest is placed in trust for a spouse, as opposed to an outright bequest, the transfer will qualify for the marital deduction only if certain conditions are met. These conditions are imposed because Congress wanted to assure that the assets transferred to the spouse would ultimately be subject to estate tax, assuming they were not consumed during the surviving spouse's lifetime.

One trust that meets these conditions is a qualified terminable interest property trust (QTIP trust). The QTIP trust is a trust where the surviving spouse has an income interest for life but the power to control the disposition of the trust assets at the death of the surviving spouse is set forth in the trust instrument, set up under the transferring spouse's Will. The assets of this trust are included in the estate of the surviving spouse by statute and a disposition of the surviving spouse's income interest during life would subject the remainder to gift tax. In order to qualify as a QTIP trust, the property must pass from the decedent, the surviving spouse must be entitled to all the income from the trust (payable at least annually), no other beneficiary may have any rights in the trust during the surviving spouse's life and an election to have the trust qualify as a QTIP must be made on the estate tax return.

The QTIP trust could (but is not required to under the law) have various other distributions provisions. For example:

- The trustee could be required to distribute a certain percentage of the fair market value of the trust each year to the surviving spouse;

- The trustee could be authorized to distribute a certain percentage of the fair market value of the trust each year to the surviving spouse;

- The surviving spouse could be allowed to request a certain percentage of the fair market value of the trust be distributed on a yearly basis; and

- Distributions of principal could be subject to an ascertainable standard relating to health, maintenance, education, or support.

The following is a general example of a QTIP Trust;

Figure 16.3 – QTIP Trust

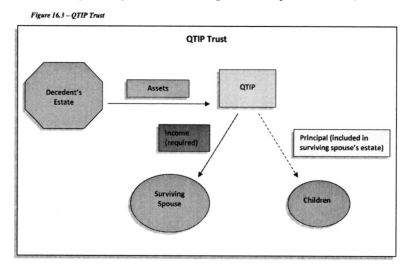

By combining a credit shelter trust with a QTIP trust, one effectively defers estate taxes, if any, to the death of the surviving spouse.

There are many estate planning techniques available to reduce one's potential estate taxes. Following is a brief discussion of some of these techniques.

Intra-Family Loans

An intra-family loan is, as its name implies, a loan between family members. In a typical intra-family loan, a senior family member loans cash to a junior family member in exchange for a note. The interest on the note could equal the applicable federal rate (AFR). The junior family member could reinvest the loan proceeds into a high yielding or potentially highly appreciated asset. If the junior family member earns more than the AFR, the senior family member effectively has given a tax-free gift to the junior family member equal to the spread between the AFR and the amount the junior family member earns on the loan proceeds. If there is no real expectation of repayment, the Internal Revenue Service would argue that a gift of the entire principal amount occurred on the date of the loan. Below is an illustration of the intra-family loan between a senior family member and a junior family member.

Figure 16.4 – Intra-family Loan

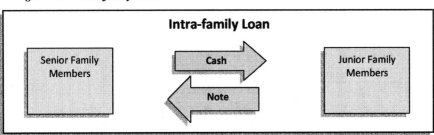

417

For example, assume a junior family member borrows $1,000,000.00 from a senior family member under the condition that 1.9% interest (the August, 2011 annual mid-term AFR) is paid annually and principal is re-paid at the end of nine years. At the end of nine years, after repayment of the loan, the junior family member would have $1,095,938.00.

Self-Canceling Installment Notes (SCIN)

An installment note is a promissory note issued in conjunction with the sale of property where at least one payment is to be made after the close of the taxable year in which the sale occurs. The SCIN is an installment note that contains a provision which states that the balance of any of the borrower's payments, due at the lender's date of death, are automatically canceled. However, the borrower must pay a premium for this feature. This premium can be in the form of a higher interest rate or a higher principal balance. A SCIN is not a device that is mentioned in any statutes or regulations; instead, its taxation is covered by interpretation of statutes by the courts, the IRS, and taxpayers. One advantage to the SCIN is that the borrower is not required to pay the balance of any payments due at the lender's death to the lender's successor. Also, the lender can exclude the unpaid balance on the note from his/her estate upon death. The benefits of a SCIN would not be realized if the lender lives to the end of the period over which installment payments are made by the borrower. As with intra-family loans, a major disadvantage of a SCIN is that the underlying loan could be construed by the IRS as a gift instead of a loan if the IRS finds the lender does not expect re-payment or the borrower does not expect to re-pay the loan.

Example: Father (F), age 50, sells business to Son (S) for $10,000,000.00 in exchange for a five-year, interest-only SCIN. Interest is payable annually at a rate of 1.9% (the August, 2011 mid-term AFR). It is assumed that the discount rate is 2.2% and that the mortality risk premium, paid by S, is $354,704.19. Therefore, the total sales price for the business is $10,354,704.19 ($10,000,000.00 + $354,704.19). S makes an initial down payment of $1,000,000.00, which reduces the principal amount of the SCIN to $9,354,704.19. On the last day of year one, S makes an interest-only payment to F of $177,739.38. F dies on the first day of year two. On the date of F's death, the principal amount owed ($9,354,704.19) is canceled; therefore, S is not required to make any remaining payments toward the principal amount. In essence, S received the $10,000,000.00 business from F in exchange for $1,177,739.38 ($1,000,000.00 down payment plus the $177,739.38 interest payment).

Grantor Retained Annuity Trust (GRAT)

A GRAT is an irrevocable trust into which a person can place cash, stocks, mutual funds, real estate, or other property. The grantor creates the trust and retains the right to annual, semiannual, quarterly, or monthly payments of a fixed amount (i.e., an annuity) for a fixed period of years. If the GRAT is structured so that the retained annuity's actuarial value is almost equal to the value of the property transferred, there is little gift tax consequence.

At the end of the trust term, the asset(s) will pass to a named beneficiary or that beneficiary's trust. In essence, the grantor is making a current gift of the right to trust assets to the beneficiary or beneficiary's trust at a specified date in the future. If the grantor survives the trust term, significant tax savings may be realized with a GRAT. The advantages of the GRAT are not recognized if the grantor fails to survive to the end of the trust term.

The annuity returned by the grantor is based on the published IRS interest rate, called the Section 7520 rate (7520 rate), which changes monthly. If the asset(s) in the trust produces a rate of return that exceeds the 7520 rate, then the beneficiary of the GRAT will receive, in effect, the difference between the rate of return and the 7520 rate at little or no gift tax cost.

Figure 16.5 – Grantor Retained Annuity Trust

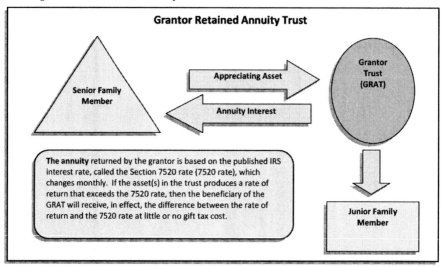

A GRAT is most effective for highly appreciating assets. Therefore, the greater the rate of return on the assets, the greater the amount that will pass to the beneficiary transfer-tax free. A GRAT is also most effective when interest rates are low because the appreciation above the 7520 rate passes to the beneficiary transfer-tax free.

Example: Father (F), age 50, transfers $10 million to a GRAT, retaining the right to receive an annual annuity of 21.33925% a year for five years, remainder to his child (C). Based on a 2.2% interest rate (the 7520 rate for August, 2011), the present value of F's annuity interest is $9,999,999.34. Thus, the gift tax value of the trust's remainder interest is $0.66. If the property contributed to the GRAT appreciates at an average annual rate of 10% over the five-year period, the value of the property available for the remainder beneficiaries (after paying the annuity amounts to F will be $3,077,274.00. Thus, in this case, $3,077,274.00 would be transferred to C, but only $0.66 was subject to gift tax on the date of contribution. In essence, $3,077,273.00 of value would pass to C free of gift tax.

Family Limited Partnerships/Family Limited Liability Companies

A family limited partnership (FLP) is a limited liability entity created under state law. Ownership in an FLP is typically members of the same family. The family members contribute property in exchange for an ownership interest in the capital and profits of the FLP at the time an FLP is formed. One or more family members either, directly or indirectly, will purchase the general partner's interest(s). The general partner is given management responsibility; however s/he also assumes personal liability for debts and other liabilities that are not satisfied from the assets of the FLP. Limited partners, who have a more passive role in the partnership, do not manage or control the assets and their personal liability is generally limited to the amount of capital they contribute to the partnership.

As an alternative to a limited partnership structure, a family may use a limited liability company (LLC), which will produce similar tax results as a limited partnership. One of the main differences between a FLP and a family LLC (FLLC) is that the FLLC provides liability protection for all owners, whereas the general partner of a limited partnership does not have unlimited liability protection.

FLPs/FLLCs can provide non-tax benefits such as creditor protection, protection from failed marriages, ease of managing assets, and facilitation of gifting programs. A typical FLP or FLLC is structured as follows:

Figure 16.6 - Family Limited Partnerships/Family Limited Liability Companies

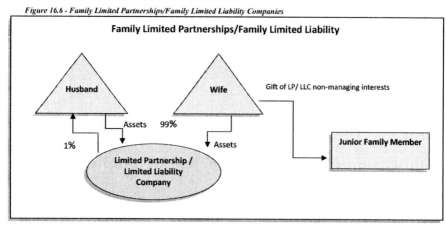

Aside from the non-tax benefits, a FLP/FLLC provides transfer tax benefits due to the illiquid and minority nature of the ownership interests transferred to the junior family members.

To illustrate the lesser value of limited partnership interests, let's say a hypothetical limited partnership owned $500,000 of Google stock and $500,000 of Apple stock, and a third party had a choice of buying $250,000 worth of Google stock and $250,000 worth of Apple stock from a stockbroker or a one-half interest in the limited partnership. In this example, the one-half interest in the partnership would be valued at less than the $500,000 worth of stock because the one-half interest is a non-controlling interest in the partnership and there would generally be restrictions on the transferability of this interest. Therefore, the third party who purchased the limited partnership interest would pay less for the 50% partnership interest than he would had he purchased the Google and Apple stock outright. This analysis helps explain why a gift of the limited partnership interest is valued at an amount less than the corresponding percentage of the value of the partnership's underlying assets.

Example: Husband (H) and Wife (W) own real estate valued at $10 million. H and W decide to contribute the real estate and other assets to a limited liability company (LLC). In exchange, H receives a 1% managing member interest and W receives a 99% non-managing member interest. The LLC's operating agreement contains restrictions on the transferability of the LLC interests. W subsequently decides to gift her 99% interest to their three children (33% to each child). On the date of the gifts, the underlying partnership assets are worth $15 million. Due to various factors, including the restrictions on transferability and the lack of management rights, a valuation expert determines that a willing buyer would pay a willing seller only $3,465,000 for a 33% non-managing member interest in the LLC (the valuation expert assigned a 30% discount to the underlying asset values). Consequently, W is able to transfer 99% of the partnership (with an underlying asset value of $14,850,000) at a gift tax value of only $10,395,000. Assuming H and W are in the 35% marginal gift tax bracket (and ignoring the gift tax annual exclusion), the gift tax savings associated with this transaction equals $1,559,250 [($14,850,000 − $10,395,000)* 35%].

Sales to Intentionally Defective Irrevocable Trusts (IDIT)

A sale to an IDIT is similar to a GRAT. Specifically, the grantor makes an initial gift to the IDIT which has typically been approximately 10% of the value of the assets involved in the transaction. The grantor then sells an asset to the trust in exchange for a promissory note. The promissory note generally requires annual interest payments with a balloon payment due at the end of the note's term. The interest rate is based on the published IRS interest rate, which changes monthly, called the applicable federal rate (AFR). Similar to a GRAT, if the trust assets produce a rate of return that exceeds the AFR rate, the beneficiary of the IDIT will receive the excess. Also like a GRAT, an IDIT is most effective when using highly appreciating assets and when interest rates are low because the appreciation above the interest rate on the note passes to the beneficiary. Unlike a GRAT, an IDIT is also effective for generation-skipping transfer tax purposes.

The grantor is treated as the owner of the trust for federal income tax purposes and pays income taxes on the income earned by the trust, as s/he does in the GRAT technique. Since the trust is a grantor trust, no income tax results from the sale of the asset to the trust because the grantor is deemed to have sold the asset to himself/herself. The payment of income taxes by the grantor is not considered a gift to the trust; and, the assets in the trust will not be included in the taxable estate of the grantor, provided the grantor survives the note term.

The following is a hypothetical illustration of an IDIT transaction. As the illustration shows, the grantor sells an asset to the IDIT in exchange for a note. The IDIT would then make installment payments to the grantor during the term of the note. Once the installment note is paid in full, any leftover income and principal that remains in the IDIT flows to the beneficiary, and the asset that the grantor sold to the trust is removed from his/ her estate.

Figure 16.7 - Sales to Intentionally Defective Irrevocable Trusts **(IDIT)**

Sales to Intentionally Defective Irrevocable Trusts (IDIT)

Initial Gift

Sale of Asset

Grantor

Note

Intentionally Defective Irrevocable Trust (IDIT)

Beneficiary

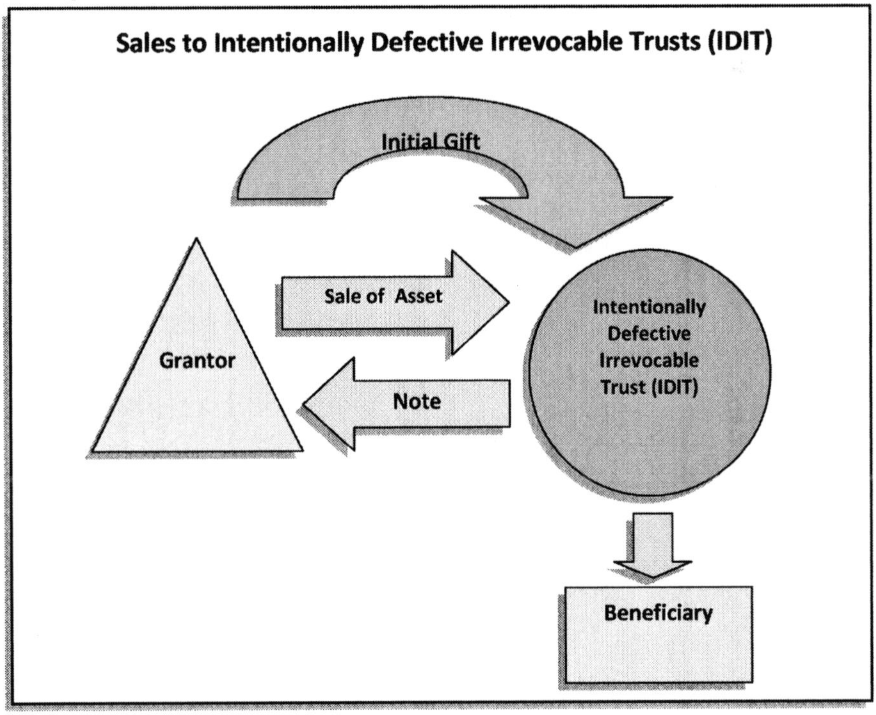

Example: Father (F), age 50, gifts $1 million cash to an IDIT. In addition, F sells 25% of his business to the IDIT in exchange for a five-year, interest-only $10,000,000 Note. Interest is payable annually at a rate of 1.9% (the August, 2011 mid-term AFR). It is assumed that the business and initial cash gift appreciates 10% annually and that the initial cash gift does not create a gift tax liability. At the end of five years, the IDIT has a remaining balance of $6,555,641. Thus, in this case, $6,555,641 would be transferred to the remainder beneficiaries of the IDIT at no gift tax cost (although F has used $1,000,000 of his gift and estate tax applicable exclusion).

Qualified Personal Residence Trusts

A personal residence, either a primary residence or a vacation home, can be transferred to a beneficiary through the use of a qualified personal residence trust (QPRT). A QPRT is another type of irrevocable trust. The transfer of the residence to the QPRT is a gift. The value of the gift equals the difference between the fair market value of the residence and the present value of the interest retained by the grantor. The value of the retained interest is based upon the 7520 rate, the grantor's age, and the term of the QPRT. As long as the grantor lives to the end of the trust term, the residence and its related appreciation would escape further transfer taxes. Even after transferring the personal residence to the QPRT, the grantor can still live in the residence during the trust term and can continue to deduct the mortgage interest and real estate tax paid on the property. At the end of the trust term, the grantor could rent, for fair market value, the residence from the trust or the beneficiary. If a personal residence is expected to significantly appreciate after the trust is created, a QPRT would work particularly well because the appreciation would escape estate and gift taxation and the residence would pass to the beneficiary. However, if the grantor fails to live to the end of the QPRT term, the value of the residence will be included in his/her gross estate. The following illustration depicts how a typical QPRT would work between senior and junior family members.

Figure 16.8 - Qualified Personal Residence Trusts

Qualified Personal Residence Trusts

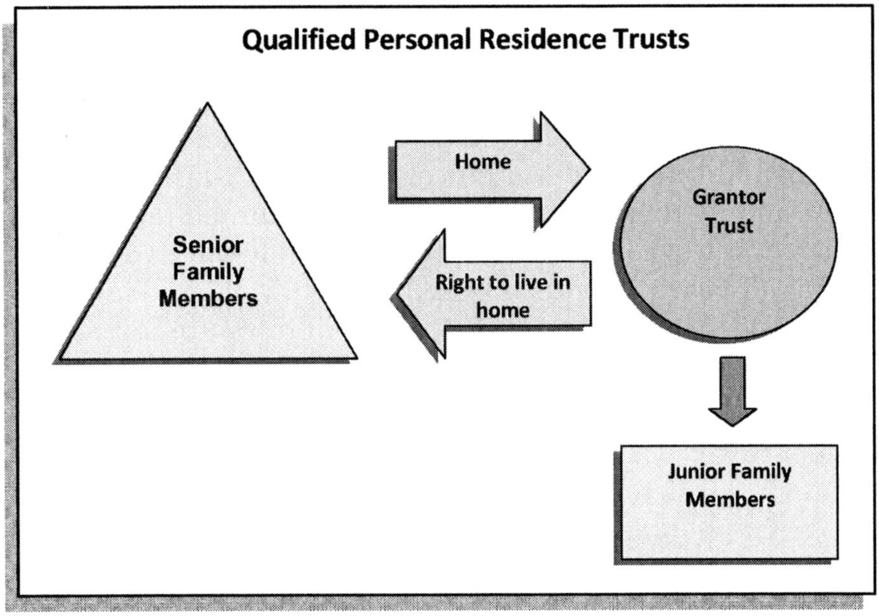

Example: F, age 50, transfers his home, valued at $5 million, into a QPRT retaining the right to live in the home for fifteen years. The home will pass to his children at the end of the fifteen-year term. Based on a 2.2% valuation interest rate (the 7520 rate for August, 2011), the present value of F's "income" interest is $1,830,650. The value of the remainder interest, and the taxable gift, is $3,169,350. After the fifteen-year period ends, the house plus all of the appreciation passes to F's children free of any additional federal gift or estate tax consequences. Assuming the home appreciates at an annual tax rate of 5% and the combined estate tax rate at the end of the fifteen-year period is 50%, $3,612,646 would have been transferred to F's children free of gift or estate taxes.

Life Insurance Planning

Life insurance is a contract under which, for a premium, the insurer agrees to pay the insured a defined amount at death. As an estate planning tool, life insurance could provide cash for the payment of federal and state estate and inheritance taxes, debts, administrative costs, and other estate expenses. Life insurance can be used to provide income for family expenses and to pay for college expenses, mortgage balances, or other large expenses. It can also be used to fund a charitable gift or to supplement an individual's retirement program.

The major advantages of life insurance are that the proceeds 1) create cash that is needed at death, 2) avoid probate, and 3) are received by the beneficiaries generally income tax free. The major disadvantages of life insurance are that 1) people in poor health either cannot obtain a policy or must pay more for the policy and 2) the different types of policies are difficult to understand, evaluate and compare. Life insurance proceeds are exempt from federal estate tax if the insured has no incidents of ownership in the policy. In order to ensure that the proceeds are exempt from estate taxation, an irrevocable trust could be created to own the policy and distribute the proceeds. An existing life insurance policy that is transferred to a trust will not be removed from a person's estate until three years after the date of transfer, and the transfer would be subject to gift tax. For new policies, the proceeds could escape estate taxation by having the trust directly purchase the policy.

Irrevocable Life Insurance Trusts

An irrevocable life insurance trust (ILIT) is created either by transferring one or more life insurance policies to an irrevocable trust or by creating an irrevocable trust and permitting the trustee of the irrevocable trust to purchase one or more life insurance policies. These policies generally insure the life of the grantor and, in some situations, the grantor's spouse.

The two primary objectives of an ILIT are 1) to ensure that the proceeds of the policy will not be subject to federal or state death taxes at the death of the insured and/or his/her spouse and 2) to provide financial security for the beneficiaries of the trust. The insured is never the owner of the policy; instead, the trustee owns the policy and would receive the proceeds of the policy. Therefore, the insurance proceeds are removed from the insured's estate and do not cause additional death taxes at the death of the insured.

In a typical irrevocable life insurance trust plan, the insured would make annual gifts to the trust, which would pay the policy premiums. In order to be excluded from gift tax under the annual exclusion, those gifts must qualify as present interest gifts. Therefore, the trust will often provide what is called a Crummey withdrawal power to the beneficiaries in order to make those annual gifts present interest gifts. The name Crummey comes from the name of a party to a lawsuit, *Crummey v. Comm.*, 397 F.2d 82 (9th Cir. 1968).

Each time a contribution is made to the trust, the Crummey

withdrawal power gives the beneficiary a temporary, but unconditional, right to demand a withdrawal of a specified amount from the trust. If the beneficiary does not exercise his/her demand right to withdraw an amount within the specified period, the annual transfer (gift) for that year remains in the trust to be managed by the trustee, and could be used to pay the insurance premiums. Alternatively, if the beneficiary does demand a withdrawal, then the trustee must deliver the funds to the beneficiary.

Gift and Estate Tax Returns

Federal gift tax returns (Form 709, entitled "U.S. Gift and Generation-Skipping Tax Return") generally must be filed with the IRS by April 15th of the year after the gift was made. Any extension of time granted for filing a taxpayer's calendar-year federal income tax return also extends the time to file that taxpayer's federal gift tax return. If a taxpayer does not request an extension of time for filing his/her federal income tax return, that taxpayer must file Form 8892 ("Payment of Gift/GST Tax and/or Application for Extension of Time to File Form 709") with the IRS to request a six-month extension to file the gift tax return. An extension of time to file a gift tax return does extend the time to pay the applicable gift taxes due.

As for federal estate tax returns (Form 706, entitled "U.S. Estate Tax Return"), they must be filed with the IRS within nine months after the date of the decedent's death. A six-month extension to file Form 706 may be obtained by filing Form 4768 ("Application for Extension of Time to File a Return and/or Pay U.S. Estate (and Generation-Skipping Transfer) Taxes"). As with gift tax extensions, an extension to file an estate tax return does not extend the time to pay the applicable estate tax; however, in certain circumstances, the federal estate tax may be paid in installments. One such circumstance is if the decedent held an interest in a closely held business with a value that exceeds 35% of his/her

430

adjusted gross estate, then the executor of the decedent's estate may elect to pay part or all of the estate tax owed in two or more (not exceeding ten) equal installments. The payments would begin on or before a date selected by the executor, which is not more than five years after the date the return was to be filed with the IRS, and interest would be charged throughout the period.

Charity

Charitable planning can be accomplished during one's lifetime or at death through one's will by using on or more of the techniques discussed below.

Outright Charitable Giving

This is directly contributing property to a charitable organization, a simple act that can be accomplished in numerous ways. However, there are some rules that go along with charitable contributions. To avoid paying the gift tax, and to receive a charitable deduction for income tax purposes, the organization must be a *qualified* charity. The IRS along with various other organizations publishes annual lists of charities that are qualified.

Charitable gifts can be deducted from an individual's Federal Adjusted Gross Income (AGI) for income tax purposes in the year the contribution is made. The amount deductible for cash contributions to public charities is limited to 50% of the taxpayer's AGI. Contributions of capital gain property, i.e., any capital asset the sale of which at its fair market value at the time of contribution would have resulted in gain which would have been long-term capital gain, to public charities is limited to 30% of the taxpayer's AGI unless a special election is made. The amount deductible for contributions to private foundations is lower than those to public charities (30% for cash contribution, 20% for appreciated capital gain property contributions). If a person contributes appreciated property

431

they have held for one year or less, he can only deduct up to his tax basis in the property as opposed to fair market value of the property. Any excess amount contributed can be carried forward and used for up to five years.

For charitable giving of tangible personal property, if it is unrelated to the charitable purpose of the organization to which it is donated, the deduction is limited to the taxpayer's adjusted tax basis (the property's fair market value reduced by the total amount of the gain that would have been long-term capital gain if sold). For tangible personal property that is related to the charitable purpose of the organization and will be used in a way related to the organization's charitable purpose, the deduction can be up to the fair market value (FMV) of the property.

Charitable giving of tangible property examples:

Example 1—Taxpayer donates a painting in which they have a tax basis of $10,000 and a FMV of $20,000 to a charity that plans to sell the painting. The charitable deduction is limited to the $10,000 basis. The taxpayer may want to consider the tax implications of selling the painting first and recognizing gain, then donating the cash received.

Example 2—Taxpayer donates a sculpture in which they have a tax basis of $10,000 and a FMV of $20,000 to a charity that displays art, and the charity displays the sculpture. The charitable deduction is the FMV of $20,000 at the date of contribution.

Charitable Giving through Philanthropic Vehicles

Instead of giving directly to a charity, one can accomplish their charitable planning objectives through one or more of the following.

Private Foundation

A private foundation is a tax-exempt charitable organization created by a donor. It gives the donor significant control over the assets of the foundation and its charitable giving. Private foundations generally distribute funds to charitable organizations that perform a charitable activity, rather than engage in them directly. As noted above, the AGI limits on gifts made to private foundations are lower than those made directly to charity (30% for cash contributions and 20% for appreciated capital gain property contributions such as marketable securities).

Private foundations have the most stringent rules and regulations among the three philanthropic vehicles mentioned in this part of the chapter. These rules allow private foundations to pay a reasonable salary to the officers running the foundationl however, there are strict rules on transactions between a private foundation and a disqualified person (one who contributes or manages the foundation). Private foundations may be required to pay a 1% or 2% excise tax on net investment income. Private foundations must distribute 5% of its assets annually for charitable purposes. Private foundations are required to file Form 990-PF (Return of Private Foundation or Section 4947(a)(1) Nonexempt Charitable Trust Treated as a Private Foundation). Private foundations are subject to attorney general oversight and may be required to file certain forms with the applicable states. Private foundations can continue for an indefinite length of time.

Donor Advised Funds

A donor advised fund is a charitable giving vehicle where the donor makes an irrevocable contribution of assets to a charity, community foundation, brokerage firm, or other financial institution. This contribution is deductible up to 50% of the donor's AGI. The donor then advises the organization of their choices in the distribution to charitable organizations, and the organization attempts to carry out the donor's choices. Unlike private foundations, donor advised funds have no minimum distribution requirement, and much lower administrative expenses. Technically, a donor advised fund has an indefinite life; however, while private foundations may continue to be run by successors indefinitely, some donor advised funds place a limit on successions, with the fund eventually going into a general pool at the organization.

Supporting Organizations

A supporting organization is an organization created by a donor to support another qualified charitable organization. It is classified as a public charity and is not subject to the lower AGI limits of private foundations. Startup costs can be significant for a supporting organization; however it is exempt from some of the administrative burdens of a private foundation.

Split Interest Charitable Giving

Rather than outright charitable giving, it is possible to create a split interest, giving to charity while the donor or donor's beneficiary maintains a present or future interest in the property. This type of giving is best for when a donor wants to provide a benefit to both charitable and non-charitable beneficiaries and is generally accomplished with the creation of a charitable trust. If the gift benefits the donor (or beneficiary) for a period of time with the remainder left to charity, the trust is called a *charitable remainder trust*. If the gift benefits the charity for a period of time, with the remainder left to the donor (or beneficiary), the trust is called a *charitable lead trust*.

Charitable Trusts

Charitable Remainder Annuity Trust

A charitable remainder annuity trust (CRAT) is an irrevocable trust that provides fixed annual payments to a beneficiary with the remainder left to charity upon the death of the beneficiary or after a chosen number of years. The donor will generally transfer cash or securities to the CRAT, and the donor (or beneficiary) receives a fixed dollar amount each year for the remainder of their life or specified number of years (not more than 20). No additional contributions are allowed after the initial transfer of assets into the CRAT. The remainder is then left to charity and must be actuarially at least 10% of the initial fair market value of assets transferred into the trust to qualify as a CRAT. For federal income tax purposes, the donor can deduct the present value of the remainder left to the charity. A CRAT requires distribution of at least 5% of assets annually, but not more than 50%.

Figure 16.9 – Charitable Remainder Annuity Trust

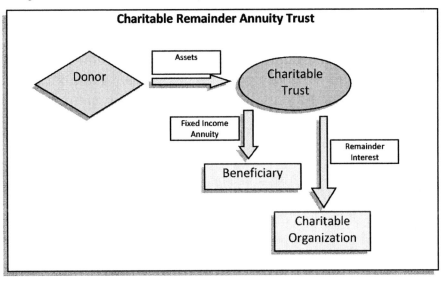

Example: P (Parent) transfers $10 million into a CRAT for a term of 15 years. The terms of the CRAT require an annual payout of 7.109% to P's children, with the remainder to pass to charity. Based on a 2.8% valuation interest rate (the 7520 rate for June, 2011),[4] the present value of the remainder interest, and therefore the charitable deduction available to P, is $1,389,224. The present value of the annuity is $8,610,776. After the 15-year period, P's children have received a total of $10,663,500 exclusive of earnings. The remainder then passes to P's appointed charity. Assuming the value of the trust increases at an annual tax rate of 10%, $19,185,424 **would** be transferred to the charity.

Charitable Remainder Unitrust

A charitable remainder unitrust (CRUT) is similar to a CRAT in that it is an irrevocable trust, where the remainder is left to a charity. Unlike a CRAT, the annual payments from a CRUT are based on a fixed percentage of assets of the trust valued annually. The donor creates this trust by transferring assets into the trust. The donor or beneficiary receives annual payments for life, or a specified number of years, based upon a fixed percentage of the value of the trust's assets. This kind of trust requires an annual valuation of the assets to determine the amount of payments. Subsequent additions of property to a CRUT are permitted. The donor can deduct, for federal income tax purposes, the present value of the remainder left to charity. The rules regarding distributions (not less than 5%, not more than 50%), length of time (life or period not exceeding 20 years), and the 10% remainder rule are the same as for a CRAT.

One type of CRUT is the net income with makeup CRUT or

---

[4]Note that for a charitable remainder trust, a higher valuation interest rate is advantageous to the taxpayer, however for a charitable lead trust the opposite is true.

NIMCRUT. This pays to the beneficiary the lesser of the specified percentage or actual income of the trust. If the payment is less than the specified percentage there is a "makeup" that requires the trust to pay the difference once the trust has sufficient income. This can be used as an alternative to a retirement plan, as assets can grow tax-free over a period of time.

Figure 16.10 – Charitable Remainder Unitrust

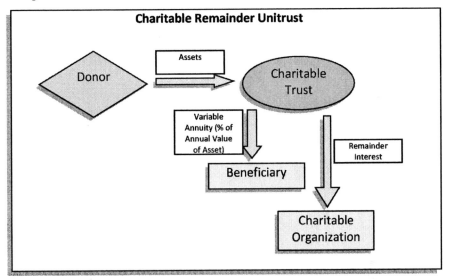

Charitable Lead Annuity Trust

A charitable lead annuity trust (CLAT) is an irrevocable trust in which a charity receives fixed annual payments from the trust for a specified number of years with the remainder left to the donor's beneficiary. A CLAT can be established as a grantor CLAT or a non-grantor CLAT. Creation of a grantor CLAT allows the donor to deduct the value of the income interest, generally a large amount. However, the donor is taxed each year on the income of the trust, even though the donor does not immediately receive that income. There is no minimum distribution of assets in a CLAT, and there is no restriction on the term of a CLAT.

Figure 16.11 – Charitable Lead Annuity Trust

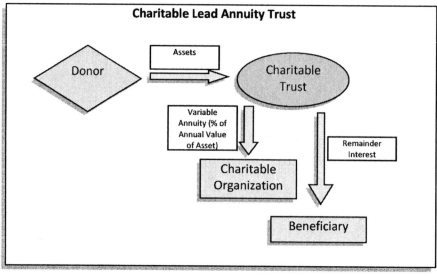

Example: P (Parent) transfers $10 million into a CLAT for a term of 15 years. The annual payout percentage to charity is 7.9%, with the remainder to pass to P's children. Based on a 2.2% valuation interest rate (the 7520 rate for August, 2011), the present value of the annuity, and therefore the charitable deduction available to P, is the full $10,000,000. The charity receives $790,000 annually for 15 years for a total of $11,850,000 (exclusive of earnings). After the 15- year period ends, the remainder passes to P's children. Assuming the value of the trust increases at an annual tax rate of 10%, a total of $16,672,221 passes to P's children.

Charitable Lead Unitrust

A charitable lead unitrust (CLUT) is similar to a CLAT except that the payments to charity are a fixed percentage of the value of the assets determined annually, not a fixed amount. The remainder then passes to a beneficiary. Otherwise, it shares the same rules as a CLAT and can also be set up at death through a will.

Figure 16.12 – Charitable Lead Unitrust

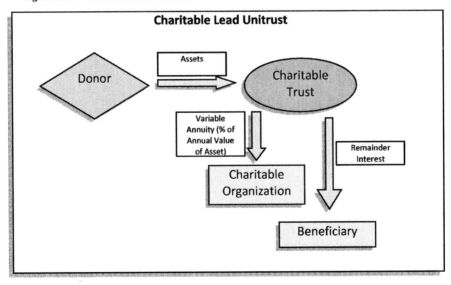

Giving to Minors

The next part of this chapter focuses on the transfer of property to minors.

Uniform Gifts/Transfers to Minors Act (UGMA/UTMA)

The Uniform Transfer to Minors Act has been adopted by most states and superseded the Uniform Gifts to Minors Act. Under the UTMA property may be gifted to minors by transferring it to a custodian. Contributions to an UGMA/UTMA account are considered gifts and subject to the annual gift tax exclusion ($13,000 for 2011). The minor must be allowed to take possession upon reaching the age of majority (either 18 or 21, depending upon the state). Income in a custodial account can be subject to the "Kiddie tax" rules if the child is (a) under age 18, or (b) is 18, or 19–23 if a full time student and; (1) his earned income doesn't exceed half of his support; (2) if either parent is alive; (3) the child doesn't file a joint tax return; (4) and the child's earned income is more than $1,900 for 2011. If the custodian dies before the minor reaches the age of majority, the amount is included in the custodian's estate.

2503(c) Trust

A 2503(c) trust, also called a Minor's Trust, is a trust established for the benefit of a minor. This trust is named after Section 2503(c) of the Internal Revenue Code, which creates the rules regarding this trust. The requirements for this type of trust are as follows:

- The property of the trust or the income of the trust can be expended for the benefit of the minor before they reach the age of 21 and

- To the extent that assets remain when the minor reaches 21 they must pass to the donee

- If the donee dies before reaching this age it is payable to donee's estate or whoever donee appoints

Gifts made to a 2503(c) trust are irrevocable, and the grantor cannot receive any income from the assets of the trust. The gifts are subject to the annual gift tax exclusion ($13,000 for 2011). A 2503(c) trust is taxed at regular trust rates. Further, the trust is treated as an asset of the minor beneficiary. The trust does not actually need to distribute all assets upon the minor reaching 21, but the minor must be informed that he or she now has a right to request its total distribution.

2503(b) Trust

A 2503(b) trust, or Mandatory Income Trust, is a simple trust that is established for the benefit of a minor and requires that income is distributed to a minor annually. This distribution can be made to a custodial account. One important difference between a 2503(b) trust and a 2503(c) trust is that the age of distribution can be set after 21 in a 2503(b) trust. In addition, unless the trust contains Crummey provisions (discussed below), only the income interest is eligible for the gift tax annual exclusion. This can be a useful tool in providing income for a minor if the donor is concerned about the minor's sense of financial responsibility.

Crummey Rights

Crummey rights were named after the first taxpayer who succeeded in using the strategy to take advantage of the annual gift tax exclusion. These rights give the beneficiary of a trust a right to withdraw contributions from a trust for a limited period—usually 30, 60, or 90 days immediately after it is contributed. By giving the beneficiary the right to withdraw immediately and notice of this right, it is considered a gift of a present interest and subject to the annual gift tax exclusion. An ordinary trust can be set up with Crummey rights with the benefit of no required annual distribution.

Further, this kind of trust can be established for the benefit of multiple beneficiaries.

Protecting Yourself or Your Business

Buy-Sell Agreement

A buy-sell agreement is an agreement on how ownership stakes in a business will be sold and bought by co-owners upon the occasion of certain triggering events. Buy-sell agreements are an important tool in protecting closelyheld businesses and heirs in the event of the death or disability of one owner. However, death and disability are not the only event that could trigger a buy-sell agreement. Other triggering events include divorce, retirement, bankruptcy, or desire to sell to a third party.

Buy-sell agreement example:

An agreement between three owners states that upon the retirement of one partner, the retiree must offer to sell his stake in the company to the other two owners for X amount of dollars. In this way, the two remaining owners are protected from the retired partner selling his interest in the business to a third party who may have a different vision for the business.

If the triggering event for a buyout is death, one common way to be certain there will be enough cash on hand for the buyout is to use a life insurance policy on an owner to provide that cash.

Index